A WORLD BANK COUNTRY STUDY

Slovak Republic

*A Strategy for Growth
and European Integration*

*The World Bank
Washington, D.C.*

Copyright © 1998
The International Bank for Reconstruction
and Development/THE WORLD BANK
1818 H Street, N.W.
Washington, D.C. 20433, U.S.A.

World Bank Country Studies are among the many reports originally prepared for internal use as part of the continuing analysis by the Bank of the economic and related conditions of its developing member countries and of its dialogues with the governments. Some of the reports are published in this series with the least possible delay for the use of governments and the academic, business and financial, and development communities. The typescript of this paper therefore has not been prepared in accordance with the procedures appropriate to formal printed texts, and the World Bank accepts no responsibility for errors. Some sources cited in this paper may be informal documents that are not readily available.

The findings, interpretations, and conclusions expressed in this paper are entirely those of the author(s) and should not be attributed in any manner to the World Bank, to its affiliated organizations, or to members of its Board of Executive Directors or the countries they represent. The World Bank does not guarantee the accuracy of the data included in this publication and accepts no responsibility for any consequence of their use. The boundaries, colors, denominations, and other information shown on any map in this volume do not imply on the part of the World Bank Group any judgment on the legal status of any territory or the endorsement or acceptance of such boundaries.

ISSN: 0253-2123

Library of Congress Cataloging-in-Publication Data

Slovak Republic : a strategy for growth and European integration.
      p.   cm. — (A World Bank country study)
  "Based on the findings of missions that visited the Slovak
Republic in December, 1996, and January, 1997"—P.
  Includes bibliographical references.
  ISBN 0-8213-4211-8
  1. Slovakia—Economic conditions.   2. Slovakia—Economic policy.
I. World Bank. II. Series.
HC270.3.S55 1998
338.94373—dc21
                                              98-15112
                                                CIP

CONTENTS

Map IBRD 27947

Figures

Tables

Boxes

ABSTRACT

This Country Study is based on the findings of missions that visited the Slovak Republic in December 1996, and January 1997. The report analyzes the main economic developments of the past few years and the challenges faced by the country in its EU accession quest, including the ability to take on the obligations of membership, which implies full compliance with the *acquis communautaire*--the set of rules and regulations applicable to all Member States.

The teams that traveled to the Slovak Republic were led by Roberto Rocha (task manager) and included Robert E. Anderson (enterprise sector), Emily Andrews (social sectors), Stanislas Balcerac (capital markets), Tito Boeri (labor markets), Bruce Courtney (macroeconomics), Marinela Dado (enterprise sector and bank performance), Simeon Djankov (enterprise sector), Martin Herman (agricultural sector), Bernard Hoekman (foreign trade), Christian Kirchner (legal framework for enterprises and capital markets), Philipe Lefevre (legal framework for banking operations), Albert Martinez (financial sector), Katarina Mathernova (general legal framework), Witold Orlowski (agricultural sector and macroeconomics), Helmut Schreiber (environment), Patrick Wiese (pensions), and Juan Zalduendo (macroeconomics). Burcak Inel contributed to the capital markets section. Sandeep Mahajan provided research assistance. The report was processed by Andrea Toth.

The Acting Director of the Department was Hans Apitz, the Lead Economist was Luca Barbone, and the Division Chief was Michel Noël. Alan Winters and Nemat Shafik were the peer reviewers.

CURRENCY AND EQUIVALENT UNITS

Currency Unit = Koruny

	1992	1993	1994	1995	1996
US$1 =	28.3	30.8	32.1	29.7	30.7

ACRONYMS AND ABBREVIATIONS

ALMP	Active labor market policies
BAT	Best available techniques
BATNEEC	Best available technology not entailing excessive costs
BOD	Biological oxygen demand
BOE	Bratislava Options Exchange
BSE	Bratislava Stock Exchange
CAP	Common Agricultural Policy
CAR	Capital adequacy ratio
CEE	Central and Eastern Europe
CEFTA	Central European Free Trade Agreement
CET	Common External Tariff
CIS	Commonwealth of Independent States
CMEA	Council for Mutual Economic Assistance
CO_2	Carbon dioxide
CPI	Consumer price index
CSOB	Foreign Trade Bank
EBRD	European Bank for Reconstruction and Development
EC	European Commission
ECU	European currency unit
EF	Environmental Fund
EU	European Union
FAO	Food and Agriculture Organization of the United Nations
FDI	Foreign direct investment
FGDs	Flue gas desulphurization units
GATS	General Agreement on Trade in Services
GDP	Gross domestic product
GNFS	Goods and non-factor services
IAS	International accounting standards
ICOR	Incremental capital-output ratio
IEF	Index of Economic Freedom
IFC	International Finance Corporation
ILO	International Labor Organization
IMF	International Monetary Fund
IPPC	Integrated pollution prevention and control
IRB	Investicna Rozvojova Banka
KB	Konsolidacna Banka
LFS	Labor Force Survey

Acronyms and abbreviations (cont'd)

LR	Listing Requirements
LTU	Long-term unemployment
MFN	Most-favored nation
MOE	Ministry of Environment
MOF	Ministry of Finance
MOL	Ministry of Labor and Social Affairs
MWth	Megawatt hours thermal
NBS	National Bank of Slovakia
NFA	Net foreign assets
NLO	National Labor Office
NO_x	Nitrogen oxide
NPF	National Property Fund
OECD	Organization for Economic Cooperation and Development
PAYG	Pay-as-you-go
PES	Public Employment Service
PM	Particulate matter
PPI	Producer price index
PPP	Purchasing power parity
PSE	Producer subsidy equivalent
PUJ	Publicly useful jobs
RCA	Revealed comparative advantage
REF	Revolving Environmental Fund
SEF	State Environmental Fund
SFMR	State Fund for Market Regulation
SGB	Slovak Guarantee Bank
SIC	Social Insurance Company
SITC	Standard international trade classification
SLF	Slovak Land Fund
SLPF	State Land Protection Fund
SLSP	Slovenska Sporitel'na
SO_2	Sulphur oxide
SOB	State-owned bank
SOE	State-owned enterprise
SPJ	Socially purposeful jobs
SRO	Self-regulatory organization
SSFAA	State Support Fund for Agriculture and Agroindustries
TR	Turnover ratio
UCITS	Undertakings for collective investment in Ttansferable securities
VAT	Value added tax
VUB	Vseobecna Uverova Banka
WTO	World Trade Organization

Fiscal Year
January 1 - December 31

EXECUTIVE SUMMARY

An Overview of Macroeconomic Performance After Independence

The Slovak Republic has registered one of the best macroeconomic performances in Central Europe since its independence from the Czechoslovak Federation in 1993. Inflation has declined steadily to around 6 percent p.a., and is currently one of the lowest among transition economies. Real GDP has grown by more than 6 percent p.a. on average, one of the best growth performances in the region. The recovery has been driven by the private sector, which increased its participation in GDP to around 80 percent, and has been accompanied by a reduction in the rate of unemployment--from a peak of 14 percent in 1994 to around 12 percent more recently. The ratio of gross fixed investment to GDP has been maintained above 30 percent--the highest in Central and Eastern Europe--raising prospects of further capital accumulation and growth.

The success in reducing inflation to one-digit levels was due to the stabilization package implemented at the time of independence, which included a fixed exchange rate, a very strict fiscal policy, and moderate wage increases. The extent of fiscal support to the exchange rate anchor is revealed by the 12 percent improvement in the General Government budget between 1992 and 1995. This impressive fiscal adjustment was achieved primarily through expenditure cuts, leading to a sharp decline in the ratio of expenditures to GDP--from 58 to 47 percent between 1992 and 1995. This contraction in expenditures more than offset the loss of transfers from the Czechoslovak Federation--7 percent of GDP--and resulted in a small fiscal surplus of 0.1 percent of GDP in 1995.

The fiscal contraction did not prevent the economy from recovering, as it was more than offset by a significant growth of exports and fixed investment. Exports in US dollars grew by 25 percent p.a. in 1994 and 1995, driving GDP growth in those two years. The strong export performance was due to the very competitive levels of the exchange rate at the time of independence, the strong output activity in foreign markets, and initial progress at enterprise restructuring. Fixed investment replaced exports as the main source of GDP growth in 1996, increasing its share in GDP to an impressive 36 percent.

The main question faced by Slovak policy-makers is whether this impressive growth performance can be sustained. The report argues that the answer to this question is positive, provided that the Government is able to meet two conditions. The first is the elimination of the severe external imbalances that emerged in 1996. The second is the completion of the structural reforms initiated in the early 1990s. More specifically, the challenge faced by the Slovak Republic is to reverse the recent deterioration in the current account, which shifted from a surplus of 2 percent of GDP in 1995 to a deficit of 11 percent of GDP in 1996, while continuing the process of enterprise restructuring and strengthening the Slovak Republic's financial system. The central argument of the Country Study is that restoring current account sustainability would imply reducing the ratio of investment to GDP, but the adverse impact of such a reduction on the Slovak Republic's growth performance could be offset by the efficiency gains that would result from further progress in structural reform.

The dramatic deterioration of the current account was due to a slowdown in the growth of exports combined with a buoyant, 25 percent increase in imports. The export slowdown was partly due to cyclical factors (slower output growth in the EU) and partly to structural factors (decline in exports to the Czech Republic, reflecting the disruption of traditional commercial links). The large imports were partly due to one-time factors, such as imports of military equipment and very large imports of small cars (triggered by a temporary and pre-announced reduction in tariffs). However, these factors are not sufficient to explain the large imports and the large external deficit.

In examining other factors, it is natural to investigate the situation in the public finances, as large external imbalances are frequently associated with fiscal imbalances. However, the strong growth in domestic demand and imports during 1996 were not related to strong fiscal pressures--the fiscal deterioration was mild (1.5 percent of GDP), compared with the current account deterioration (more than 13 percent of GDP). Instead, the external imbalance seems to have been associated primarily with an investment expansion. That could suggest that the external imbalance was not so severe after all, as it was being accompanied by a build-up of future output, exports, and debt repayment capacity. Moreover, the Slovak Republic's external debt to GDP ratios do not look excessive by international comparison, providing some headroom for modernizing imports.

There are, however, a number of other indicators suggesting that the current account deficit is indeed cause for concern, despite having been due primarily to an investment expansion. First, current account deficits of more than 10 percent of GDP can hardly be sustained for a long period, as they would soon result in debt to GDP ratios of above 100 percent, even if all investments were of high return and the Slovak Republic were able to maintain very high growth rates. Second, the persistence of large enterprise losses (8.8 percent of GDP in 1996) and the incomplete restructuring of the banking sector provides an indication that corporate governance is not yet consolidated, and that some inefficient enterprises could have borrowed and invested. Third, more than 80 percent of investment has taken place outside the manufacturing sector, and may not help to develop debt repayment capacity. Fourth, the investment expansion may have been partly due to the privatization rules introduced in 1996, which allowed new owners to offset payments to the National Property Fund (the privatization agency) by investing in the purchased enterprise.

In addition to these microeconomic indications that many investments may not have been optimal, there is also strong evidence that investment and imports were excessively stimulated by a liberal monetary and credit policy during 1995 and the first half of 1996--money and credit grew well in excess of the growth of nominal GDP during this period. Finally, the real appreciation that resulted from the use of the exchange rate as a nominal anchor may have also contributed to the current account deterioration during this period.

The clearest indication that private agents had changed their perceptions about the sustainability of the external situation happened in May 1997, when the Slovak crown was subject to a series of speculative attacks, following similar events in other countries with large external deficits, and revealing clearly the need for policy corrections. In response to these adverse developments, the National Bank of Slovakia tightened further monetary policy (a policy initiated in mid-1996), and the Government instituted a 7 percent import surcharge. These measures have generated some improvements in the current account (the deficit should decline to around 7.5 percent of GDP in 1997) and have deflected the speculative attacks, although at the cost of very high real interest rates (around 20 percent p.a. for Government securities) and the introduction of a distortionary trade policy instrument. Moreover, the efforts to generate further improvements in the external accounts have been undermined by the expansionary fiscal policy followed thus far in 1997--despite the introduction of the import surcharge, fiscal policy has shifted to a deficit of more than 4 percent of GDP, partly on account of large investment projects, but also due to low revenues from corporate income and social security taxes.

The report suggests that sustaining growth will require some reduction in investment levels, in order to release the excessive pressures on the current account and avoid financing problems, while making an effort to offset the reduction in investment levels by completing structural reforms and increasing investment efficiency. This strategy is within the reach of Slovak policy-makers. In the macroeconomic area, it requires the central bank's adherence to the tighter monetary policy targets that have been pursued since mid-1996, but also reversing the expansionary fiscal policy adopted in 1997. Although, fiscal policy was not a major cause of the current account deterioration in 1996, it is now making the recent improvement excessively dependent on a restrictive monetary policy and high interest rates and hindering the permanent adjustment which is needed in the external accounts. Reversing the fiscal expansion in 1997 will require, inter alia, a smoother implementation of the ambitious public investment program, containing the growth of real wages in the public sector, avoiding excessive increases in pension benefits, and strengthening tax compliance.

In addition to a return to fiscal discipline, the Government should also avoid the policies that could have led to artificially high levels of investment or to excessive foreign borrowings by enterprises. These would include abstaining from making excessively generous concessions in future privatizations (such as the cancellation of payments in exchange for additional investment), abstaining from making special temporary tariff concessions in the purchase of small cars or any other investment/consumption item, and ensuring that foreign creditors are not extending credits to enterprises on the expectation of guarantees by the National Property Fund or the Government.

In the structural area, there is a variety of issues to be addressed, two of which merit special attention, namely, the persistence of loss-making activities at the level of enterprises, and the large volume of classified loans held by the major banks. Whereas the Slovak Republic has a group of very efficient and profitable enterprises, capable of generating a high ratio of profits to GDP (14 percent in 1996), it also has a relatively large group of inefficient enterprises, as indicated by gross losses of 8.8 percent of GDP in 1996. The weak financial situation of this group of enterprises is reflected in the balance sheet of major banks (most of which remain State-owned), as indicated by the large stock of classified loans held by these banks--18 percent of GDP, of which more than 5 percent of GDP in unpaid interests. These figures suggest that there is still a significant drainage of scarce resources by inefficient firms, and lingering problems in financial intermediation. They also suggest that, removing these structural bottlenecks, and solving other institutional and regulatory problems, could yield significant efficiency gains, and allow the Slovak Republic to maintain growth performance with somewhat lower investment ratios and a sustainable current account.

The Slovak Republic faces the dual challenge of sustaining the impressive growth performance achieved after independence, while preparing the economy for EU accession. The report stresses that these two objectives are closely intertwined, as the measures required to eliminate large macroeconomic imbalances, increase microeconomic efficiency, and sustain growth, would coincide to a large extent with the economic requirements for EU accession. Although the Slovak Republic has already made substantial progress in transforming its economy and approximating its legal framework to EU legislation, the reform agenda has not been fully implemented yet. The report aims at contributing to the Slovak Republic's efforts to meet the dual challenges successfully, by identifying the problems that remain in several sectors of the economy, and providing recommendations for further gains in efficiency.

This Country Study is structured as follows. Chapter I reviews the Slovak Republic's macroeconomic performance after independence and sets the stage for the rest of the report. This is followed by a chapter on trade performance and trade policies in the light of increasing integration with the EU. Chapters III and IV cover the enterprise and financial sectors, respectively, and identify the measures that would reduce loss-making activities and improve financial intermediation. The next chapter examines the performance of the agriculture sector after independence, and identifies the measures required to increase productivity in the sector. Chapter VI analyzes the current situation in the labor market, and assesses the effectiveness of labor market policies and social programs. Chapter VII assesses the recent improvements in the environment, after 40 years of neglect under the former economic regime, and examines the policies and investments that would enable the Slovak Republic to meet EU standards. Finally, the last chapter summarizes the main findings and recommendations of the report, and proposes a framework for sustained growth that would allow the Slovak Republic to converge to the EU's income levels in a reasonable period of time. The main findings of Chapters II through VIII are summarized below.

Trade Developments and Trade Policy

Chapter II examines the Slovak Republic's recent trade performance and makes an evaluation of current trade policies vis-à-vis the EU. The chapter points out that the Slovak Republic is an open economy, with total exports and imports of goods accounting together for more than 100 percent of GDP, and that there has been a reorientation of trade since independence, away from traditional CMEA markets and towards the EU. The chapter also notes that the structure of exports has been changing, and the number of new products exported provides an indication of the underlying dynamism of exports. However, the chapter also notes that these goods are not yet contributing significantly to total exports, and that the share of the more sophisticated EU markets in total exports is still lower than the other Visegrad countries. The report notes that greater opening to foreign direct investment and partnerships with foreign firms may contribute to faster absorption of modern technology and greater access to new markets.

As to trade policies, the report highlights that the Slovak Republic's import regime is already liberal, as indicated by an average nominal tariff of 8 percent in 1996. The effective tariff burden (measured by the ratio of tariff revenues to imports) is even lower, around 3 percent, reflecting the various preferential trading arrangements. The commitments undertaken under the Europe Agreements stipulate further liberalization of industrial imports from the EU, including the reduction in tariffs and the complete elimination of remaining quota restrictions by the year 2002. The impact of this additional liberalization on imports and on fiscal revenues is likely to be moderate, as protection is already low. Use of other trade restrictions is limited, with non-automatic import licensing being applied to only one significant product-- coal. Finally, customs administration is close to being harmonized with EU rules and procedures. However, it must be noted that the Slovak Republic has recently deviated from the open trade policies followed after independence--as mentioned before, in May 1997 the Government introduced a 7 percent import surcharge affecting 80 percent of all imports. The surcharge represents a deviation from the Europe Agreements, and will have to be removed in the near future, implying the need for offsetting policy corrections, particularly in the fiscal area.

The chapter highlights that the Europe Agreement and accession agenda will largely determine the shape of the Slovak Republic's trade policy in the next few years. However, the report also stresses that the Government still faces some policy options during the pre-accession period. These include the transition towards the EU's common external tariff, the implementation of instruments to restrict unfair trade, and the liberalization of trade in services. With respect to the transition path towards adoption of the EU's common external tariff, the report stresses that raising tariffs to EU levels before accession would be economically harmful, by reducing competition from imports and raising prices for consumers. As a result, the best option is to maintain an independent tariff policy until accession, and limit any changes in tariffs to reducing those that are now significantly above the EU's most-favored-nation (MFN) level. With respect to instruments of contingent protection, the report points out that anti-dumping laws have been an inefficient and costly instrument in most countries, that upon accession an anti-dumping law will become redundant, as these instruments will be applied by the European Commission, and that the Slovak Republic will benefit from following a less intrusive policy. The report finally recommends that liberalization in the services area should be extended on an MFN basis, without discriminating against non-EU firms.

Progress in Enterprise Privatization and Restructuring

Chapter III examines the progress that has been achieved at enterprise privatization and restructuring, and also assesses the progress achieved in approximating the legal framework for enterprises with EU legislation. The chapter starts by pointing out that the Slovak Republic has achieved significant progress at privatization, as all small enterprises and more than 50 percent of the original equity portfolio of medium and large enterprises have already been handed to the private sector through two different privatization waves. The combination of privatization and the entry of new private enterprises have increased the share of the private sector in GDP to more than 75 percent. Enterprise governance is also tending to improve, because of the increasing concentration of enterprise ownership. Such a consolidation of ownership is being driven by two factors. First, the second wave has focused on standard sales, as opposed to the coupon privatization employed in the first wave. Second, there has been trading of shares of enterprises and investment funds employed in the first wave, as well as the reconfiguration of these funds into holding companies. These trends have resulted in a larger number of voting shares held by fewer individuals or institutions, instead of the more fragmented ownership structure that followed the first wave of privatization.

The chapter examines progress at enterprise restructuring, and notes the significant progress achieved between the 1993-95 period, as indicated by a 6 percent of GDP reduction in enterprise losses--from 11.5 percent of GDP in 1993 to 5.6 percent of GDP in 1995. Such a reduction can be attributed not only to privatization, but to the initial environment in which enterprises operated. In the macroeconomic area, enterprises faced a situation of fiscal discipline, open trade, a competitive exchange rate, and moderate wage pressures, which created an overall environment of financial discipline and enabled an early export-based recovery. Financial discipline was further strengthened by an overall decline in real bank credits to troubled enterprises. However, the chapter also stresses that the restructuring task is unfinished, as indicated by the increase in enterprise losses to 8.8 percent of GDP in 1996, half of which are in manufacturing. These numbers suggest that the drainage of scarce resources by inefficient enterprises may still be substantial, and that further efforts at restructuring (involving liquidation in many cases) may yield significant efficiency gains to the Slovak economy.

The report recommends that the Government remove the legal and institutional obstacles to further improvements in governance and further progress at enterprise restructuring. More specifically, the government needs to: (i) complete the privatization of the bulk of enterprises that remain in State ownership; (ii) refrain from interfering in the operations of the so-called "essential" or "strategic" enterprises; (iii) adopt more competitive and transparent privatization methods that will encourage the best possible owners (including foreigners) to purchase Slovak enterprises; (iv) refrain from limiting or restricting the transfer of ownership of those enterprises already privatized to new investors, both domestic and foreign, that are likely to have a better strategy for restructuring these enterprises; (v) improve the legal framework, in particular, minority shareholder protection, the bankruptcy system, and accounting standards; and (vi) repeal the 1995 Price Law which opens room for interference in the price system.

This chapter also argues that the above recommendations are superior to any attempt by the Government to manage the restructuring of these enterprises directly. In this regard, the report stresses that the recently enacted Enterprise Revitalization Act, whose objective is to encourage further enterprise restructuring, may fail to accomplish such a desirable goal, because it may involve excessive political interference in a process that should be conducted exclusively by enterprises and their creditors (especially the banks, as the main creditors). Whereas it would be desirable to elaborate a strategy to facilitate the joint restructuring of enterprises and banks loaded with bad loans, the report suggests that this strategy should involve as little direct interference from the Government as possible, and should not harm the development of a legal framework supportive of a market economy. The report stresses that a more effective approach would involve improving the bankruptcy framework, and strengthening the banks' conditions to recognize their losses and work out their bad loans with debtors.

Progress in Financial Sector Reform

Chapter IV examines the progress achieved in reforming the banking sector, developing the capital market, and approximating the regulatory framework for banks and capital market institutions to EU legislation. The chapter starts by examining the structure of the banking sector and noting the significant number of new entries into the sector since 1990, mainly private sector banks with foreign participation. As a result of the new entries, by end-1996 the 25 new private banks accounted for 43 percent of the assets in the banking system, and the 5 remaining State-owned banks accounted for the remaining 57 percent, a marked change in shares relative to the years prior to independence. The Slovak financial system is relatively deep, as indicated by a ratio of broad money to GDP of 70 percent. To enhance confidence in the new banks and improve competition in the retail market (still largely dominated by the State Savings Bank), a deposit guarantee scheme was established in mid-1996, although the impact of this measure cannot be assessed yet, since the State will continue to insure citizens' deposits in the major State banks until the end of 1997.

Despite these positive developments, the report stresses that there is much that the Government can do to deepen reform in the banking sector. For one, the major State banks continue to suffer from a weak financial condition, as indicated by the large stock of classified claims (principal and interest) at mid-1997--Sk117 billion, the equivalent of 21 percent of total balance sheet claims and 18 percent of GDP. The large residual core of loss-makers in the Slovak Republic (as indicated by gross losses of 8.8 percent of GDP in 1996) and the large stock of the banks' classified claims, provide clear evidence of an unfinished restructuring program, and lingering problems in the process of financial intermediation. Also, the report stresses that the banks' lack of assertiveness in handling problem debtors is revealed not only by the large losses and the large stock of classified loans, but also by the very low number of completed bankruptcy and liquidation cases.

The chapter recommends that the Government deepen the reform of the banking sector along three main directions. First, the privatization of State banks should be completed. That includes the privatization of banks still under majority State ownership and the sales of minority shares in the banks that have been partly privatized. Privatization should involve the participation of strategic investors and should exclude large bank debtors. The best approach would be to engage an investment bank and charge this institution with the task of identifying potential buyers, and examining the restructuring that has to take place in order to enable successful privatization. Second, legal, institutional, and taxation issues will have to be addressed, to increase the ability of banks to play a more active role in enterprise restructuring. In particular, deduction of loan loss provisions from the taxable base of banks would enable banks to build provisions faster, and create more room for the restructuring of enterprises. Third, the regulatory and supervisory framework should be further upgraded. In this regard, the chapter provides a detailed analysis of the extent of approximation of the regulatory framework to EU legislation, and the steps that must be taken to achieve full conformity with EU directives in this area.

The chapter ends with an analysis of the performance of capital markets in the Slovak Republic. In particular, the chapter notes that as of end-1996 there were 970 equities and 91 bonds registered with the Bratislava Stock Exchange (BSE). Most of these securities are also registered in the parallel RMS market, which deals mostly with small retail investors and operates as an off-exchange market. The number of registered shares is more than 20 times that of other transition economies, partly the result of the privatization method used by the former Czechoslovak Federation. In sum, the market is fragmented, illiquid, and overburdened with a large number of registered shares that do not fit the profile of a publicly-traded company. The bond market is also plagued by structural deficiencies, resulting in low turnover and a predominance of short maturities. The report stresses that the lack of an independent regulatory and supervisory body aggravates these problems, as it leads to a weak enforcement of regulations, and opens room for politically-driven interventions. Failure to address these issues will hinder the future development of the capital market, and deprive enterprises from a potentially important source of investment finance.

In this framework, the report suggests policy recommendations in three major areas: (i) increasing market transparency by, inter alia, reducing the number of publicly traded firms and implementing strict information disclosure requirements for those firms that remain registered; (ii) developing a strong and independent regulatory and supervisory body; and (iii) introducing targeted legal and regulatory changes aimed at supporting capital market development. That includes introducing adequate protection for minority shareholders, enhancing market transparency and liquidity through the integration of the operations of the BSE and RMS markets, ensuring better quality of disclosed information, and removing regulatory and taxation barriers, as these hinder the development of capital markets and are not consistent with EU accession requirements. As to the insurance sector, the report suggests that much remains to be done to harmonize the Slovak legislation with EU regulations and to prepare it for cross-border competition and future EU integration.

The Agriculture Sector in Transition

Chapter V reviews recent developments in the Slovak Republic's agricultural sector and evaluates alternative policies that could serve to strengthen the sector's competitiveness prior to EU accession. Primary agriculture and food processing represent in the Slovak Republic a relatively small share of total GDP (8.5 percent) and employment (9 percent). There was a sharp deterioration in the agriculture terms of trade, following the price liberalization in the early 1990s, and this shift in relative prices contributed to a 30 percent decline in agricultural output in the early stages of the transition. However, output stabilized in 1995 and even registered a small increase in real terms during 1996. Important for this recovery has been the legal transformation of ownership through the re-establishment of individual rights to land and non-land assets. The deterioration in the terms of trade also induced the Government to introduce minimum price regulations for some commodities in an attempt to soften the impact of the transition. The report stresses, however, that the aggregate level of support to Slovak farmers has declined by more than 50 percent in real terms since 1989, making the producer subsidy equivalent about half as generous as the support extended to EU farmers. While privatization of the food processing industry has been completed, a number of related input industries still have a large share of Government involvement, particularly in fuel production, farm chemicals, and farm equipment.

Despite these transformation efforts and the recent output recovery, the report highlights that more needs to be done to increase productivity of primary agriculture and agroindustry, which remain significantly below the respective EU averages. Any significant increase in the efficiency of primary agriculture will depend on further transformation of cooperatives into profit-oriented farms, and more efforts by new owners to adjust to domestic and foreign competition. Land ownership remains fragmented in cooperatives, although land use is less fragmented, as cooperatives retain about 70 percent of farm land in large contiguous plots and most owners lease land to cooperatives. However, leasing has not eliminated all the problems resulting from fragmented ownership, since most lease contracts have a one-year termination clause and this insecurity of tenure undermines long-term investment plans. There are other obstacles to the development of a land market, such as the exclusion of foreigners from land purchases.

Similarly, many problems in the agroindustry sector linger unsolved, because of fragmented ownership, weak management and the lack of capital.

In this context, it is necessary to consolidate land ownership, resist pressure of various interest groups for protection against foreign competition, refrain from excessive government intervention, and continue to strengthen the business environment. Ownership consolidation is one of the most critical improvements required, as it would allow the more effective exploration of economies of scale, the activation of the land market, and acceptance of land as collateral. The report proposes to give active members of cooperatives more options to buy out land owners. Another possibility is to restructure Government subsidies to support ownership consolidation as a policy objective. Agroindustries are particularly vulnerable to foreign competition and ways to facilitate productivity growth should be considered. For example, the report stresses that large investments are needed to improve logistics in food distribution and to overcome an excessive market fragmentation at the wholesale and retail levels. The chapter also suggests that minimum prices should be gradually reduced and de-linked from production costs. The report recommends that income support payments to disadvantaged areas be gradually modified from a per hectare basis to targeted support programs, such as capital grants for development of rural infrastructure. Access to rural credit should be improved using market-based instruments, such as a warehouse receipt system, and the development of mortgage finance. The report also recognizes that new instruments might need to be introduced to comply with the EU's Common Agricultural Policy (CAP). However, since the CAP is likely to evolve prior to accession taking place, the Government should postpone for the time being the implementation of related policies.

Labor Market and Social Policies

Chapter VI examines the current situation in the labor market, analyzes the status of labor policies and social programs, and identifies the progress in meeting EU accession requirements in the social areas. The chapter starts by reviewing labor market developments since independence, and notes the improvement in labor market conditions after three years of strong economic growth, as indicated by the decline in the rate of unemployment, from 14 percent in 1993 to around 12 percent in 1996. Despite the decline in unemployment, however, the problem of long-term unemployment has worsened further--the share of the unemployed out of work for more than one year increased from about 40 percent in 1994 to more than 50 percent in the first three quarters of 1996. The persistence of substantial regional differences in unemployment rates is also worrisome--unemployment rates ranged from 4 to 24 percent, and vacancies reported to the labor exchanges continue to be concentrated in low unemployment regions, revealing the low degree of labor mobility.

A considerable effort is being made to adjust the regulatory framework to EU accession requirements. The effort has included the introduction of regulations on collective redundancies providing for advanced notification of planned dismissals, the introduction of a guarantee fund to pay employees in case of employer insolvency, and a law on occupational safety. In addition, provisions on health and safety in the workplace, equal employment opportunity, working time, and consultation of employees in Community-scale undertakings, are contained in the draft Labor Code, which the Slovak authorities hope to have approved by Parliament in 1998.

While recognizing the effort at approximation with the EU, the chapter recommends that the Slovaks avoid introducing measures that are not really required for EU accession, and that could prove detrimental to the creation of jobs. For example, there are no proposals to exempt small employers from some of the more rigid restrictions contained in the labor code, such as the obligation to reinstate workers who have been unfairly dismissed. Such exemptions are usually granted in EU countries. As small and medium-sized firms represent the engine of employment growth, it would be highly undesirable to hinder their expansion. The report also points to the need to increase the scope for decentralized bargaining (also the current trend in the EU), in order to ensure a greater adjustment of real wages to productivity and local conditions. Another impediment to a successful labor market lies in the resistance of employers to high payroll taxes, which in the Slovak Republic amount to 50 percent of gross wages, whereas the average contribution rate for the EU countries is 36 percent.

The chapter reviews the status of unemployment benefits and recommends greater coordination between unemployment insurance and social assistance, in order to restrict the possibility of multiple recipiency of benefits and the resulting work disincentives. The chapter also recommends stricter enforcement of job search and availability-to-work tests for individuals receiving social assistance, in order to enhance incentives to work. The chapter indicates the very large size of the Slovak Republic's active labor market programs (participants amounted to almost 5 percent of the labor force in 1995), noting that programs of this size are only found in Sweden, and that some of these programs (e.g. employment subsidies) have not proven to be effective.

The social chapter proceeds to evaluate the performance of Slovak social insurance programs. It notes that if the Government avoids excessive increases in pension benefits and tax evasion does not occur, pension fund deficits should not occur in the next few years. However, the report also notes that contribution rates are excessively high--27 percent of gross wages--with adverse effects on the labor market. In addition, these high contribution rates are not enough to make the system sustainable in the long-run. By the end of the next decade the pension system will run deficits, and these deficits are projected to increase to 6 percent of GDP by 2050. The chapter recommends a reform package that would allow the Slovak Republic to restore long-run balance and reduce contribution rates by 6.5 percent points, in line with the European average. The recommendations include the elimination of early retirement, the phase-out of partial disability pensions, the switch from wage indexation to a Swiss formula (comprising wages and prices with equal weights), and the gradual increase in retirement age to 65 for both men and women, in line with those of Western Europe.

The chapter also provides a number of recommendations that would improve the cost-effectiveness of social insurance and assistance programs. The recommendations include the transfer of initial responsibility for sick leave from social insurance to the employer, and the introduction of more stringent medical conditions for the granting of sick leave. In the case of maternity benefits, the chapter recommends a reduction of the six month period of paid maternity leave for small firms, as the costs of hiring and training replacement employees are relatively higher for these firms. The chapter ends with an evaluation of social assistance programs, noting that the bulk of payments are directed towards families with children, and that the focus of reform should rest in this area. The chapter suggests that child benefits be targeted to the lowest quartile of the income distribution, in order to reduce expenditures while providing a floor of protection. Other recommendations to improve cost-effectiveness and reduce work disincentives include means-testing of allowances for one-earner families, and greater coordination of the various programs to eliminate multiple recipiency of benefits.

Environment and EU Accession

Chapter VII reviews the progress already achieved in improving the environment, examines the implications of EU accession for environmental policy, and presents preliminary estimates of the investments required for compliance with EU requirements in this area. The chapters starts by noting that the amount of pollutants emitted into the air has been substantially reduced since the late 1980s. The resulting improvement in air quality has been due both to the initial contraction of economic activity and to emission reduction measures. Ambient air quality has also improved in the Slovak Republic since the start of the transition. In addition, 86 percent of waste water is currently discharged to treatment plants, 87 percent of which have biological treatment, and about half of all the households were linked to sewer systems. Produced waste has decreased by close to 30 percent between 1992 and 1995, enabling a reduction in the number of landfill sites.

Notwithstanding these positive developments, much more remains to be done. The improvement in air quality has been very modest since 1995, revealing the difficulties of achieving additional progress in the environment in the context of a growing economy. In fact, the main challenge facing the Slovak environmental authorities is to ensure additional improvements in environmental quality in a scenario of continued economic recovery. Also, the Slovak Republic and other transforming countries are now observing a shift in pollution sources. Heavy industry, which used to be the major cause of pollution, is retrenching and is being overtaken by traffic and chemical waste from a large number of small and medium-sized enterprises. These new sources are far more difficult to control and supervise.

Complying with EU environmental legislation is a challenge faced by all CEE countries, and The Slovak Republic is no exception. The report points out that compliance involves not only legal harmonization issues, but also a strategy that will enable the Slovak Republic to meet EU standards as rapidly and as cost-effectively as feasible. Although there has been significant progress in legal harmonization, there are some areas, such as the Integrated Pollution Prevention and Control directive, where Slovakian law still needs to be modified. This directive represents a shift from a focus on emissions, which involves reliance on end-of-pipe controls, to one on waste minimization, for which clean technologies and good management are usually critical. The country's basic water infrastructure falls short of what would be required by EU directives, since the quality of drinking water often does not meet EU standards. This is not a matter of microbiological contamination which might pose a serious threat to health. Rather, the problem is linked to the presence of minerals and pollutants, either because of the quality of the water source used, or because of the contamination that arises during distribution as a result of neglected infrastructure maintenance. Thus, investments will be required to improve raw water quality, upgrade treatment facilities, and replace parts of the water distribution system. Meeting the directive on urban waste water treatment will require sewer systems with at least secondary treatment of sewage for most villages, towns, and cities with a population equivalent of 2,000 or more.

Preliminary estimates suggest that total investments would amount to around US$5-6 billion, including US$2.5 billion of investments in water, US$1.5-2.5 billion of investments in air quality, and US$0.9 billion of investments in waste management. This would imply annual investments of around US$300 million distributed over a period of 20 years, or approximately 1.5 percent of GDP. These amounts are significantly above the ones prevailing in CEE countries, indicating the need for developing least-cost strategies. Financing environmental projects through Environmental Funds (EF) is suggested by the report. However, these funds are only effective if the environmental problems are simultaneously tackled at the policy level and strong efforts are undertaken to strengthen environmental regulations and enforcement. Although the Slovak Republic has undertaken considerable efforts to set environmental priorities, the report stresses that more work is needed in this area.

A Framework for Growth and EU Accession

Chapter VIII reviews the main recommendations of the report, and proposes a framework for growth and EU accession centered in the completion of structural reforms and the achievement of efficiency gains. The chapter starts by arguing that the very high investment ratios have also been increasingly accompanied by current account deficits financed in a disproportionate amount by increased indebtedness.

While a transition economy should be expected to register external deficits as its capital stock is modernized and past repressed consumption loosens, these deficits should remain at sustainable levels. The chapters reiterates that the Slovak Republic faces the challenge of maintaining its growth performance, while correcting its external imbalances, and that meeting this challenge successfully will require more efforts at structural reforms. The chapter also reiterates that the challenges of sustained growth and EU accession are intertwined, as the measures required to increase efficiency coincide to a large extent with the EU accession requirements.

In this context, the chapter reiterates that a credible strategy for sustained growth and EU accession would involve a reduction in investment levels to around 30 percent of GDP, roughly the same levels as in the years that followed independence, and offsetting the growth impact of such a reduction by measures aimed at increasing efficiency. The chapter reviews the major recommendations of the report that would enable both the macroeconomic adjustment and the microeconomic improvements in efficiency. It also argues that, if these strategies are followed, the Slovak Republic would be able to reduce the current account deficit to around 4 percent of GDP, while maintaining an initial growth rate of 5.5 percent a year. If approximately half of this deficit is financed by non-debt flows (FDI and portfolio investment), then the ratios of external debt to GDP and to exports would be stabilized or even decline gradually over time. If the structural transformation is also completed and the Slovak Republic is able to increase the efficiency of its economy to levels at least as high as the EU's, it would converge to 75 percent of the EU's average per capita income in less than 30 years.

The failure to complete structural reforms implies that efficiency gains do not materialize, and that the same investment ratios produce less output growth. The report presents growth simulations showing that the failure to proceed with structural transformation would result in a longer period for convergence for the same investment ratios--approximately 13 more years, for a total of 41 years. The chapter also argues that failure to proceed with the reforms would probably result in a lower investment ratio in the steady-state, mainly because of a more pessimistic evaluation of the business environment in which the private sector operates, and a deterioration in the EU accession prospects. The main implication of these developments would be a further lengthening of the period of convergence to over 46 years, and would result by the mid-2020s in a level of per capita income which is 20 percent lower than the level in the reform scenario. This alternative scenario was elaborated on the assumption that policy-makers do not address Slovak microeconomic inefficiencies, but do adopt the macroeconomic measures necessary to reduce the external imbalances. If these measures are not adopted, the Slovak Republic could face balance of payment problems that could prove more disruptive to long-run growth and EU accession prospects.

CHAPTER I: ECONOMIC PERFORMANCE AFTER INDEPENDENCE

Introduction

The Slovak Republic has registered one of the best macroeconomic performances in Central Europe, in sharp contrast to the economic collapse predicted by many observers at the time of independence in January 1993. Inflation declined to around 6 percent p.a., and is currently lower than most other transition economies. Real GDP has grown by more than 6 percent p.a. since 1993--one of the best growth performances in the region. The ratio of fixed investment to GDP has been maintained at very high levels-- around 30 percent in the first half of the 1990s and 36 percent in 1996 (the highest in the region)--raising prospects of rapid capital accumulation and growth.

One of the central questions faced by Slovak policy-makers is whether the good growth performance registered after independence can be sustained. The examination of Slovak economic and social indicators suggests that the answer to this question is positive, provided that the Government is able to meet two conditions. The first is the elimination of the severe external imbalances that emerged in 1996. The second is the completion of the structural reforms initiated in the early 1990s. Success in addressing these two challenges would allow the Slovak Republic to sustain high growth rates and converge to the EU average levels of per capita income in a reasonable period of time.

In the macroeconomic area, the central issue to be addressed is the recent deterioration in the external accounts--the current account shifted from a surplus of 2 percent of GDP in 1995 to a deficit of 11 percent of GDP in 1996. Preliminary data for 1997 indicate a deficit still excessively large (8-9 percent of GDP). This sharp deterioration in the current account was not accompanied by an increase in the levels of foreign direct investment (which remained under 1 percent of GDP, the lowest in the region), implying a substantial recourse to foreign borrowings. Although the Slovak external debt still looks manageable by international comparison (gross and net debts are approximately 50 and 20 percent of GDP), and the country enjoys an investment grade credit rating, deficits of these orders of magnitude cannot be sustained for many years.

In the structural area, there is a variety of issues to be addressed, two of which merit special attention: the persistence of loss-making activities at the level of enterprises, and the high level of classified loans held by major banks. Despite the significant progress achieved in reducing gross enterprise losses (by more than 6 percent of GDP since independence), the Slovak economy remains affected by a relatively large core of inefficient enterprises, as indicated by losses of 8.8 percent of GDP in 1996. The large stock of classified loans (18 percent of GDP) held by major banks, most of which remain State-owned, reveals the banks' lack of assertiveness towards problem debtors and weaknesses in the process of financial intermediation.

Slovak policy-makers must address these macroeconomic and structural problems while preparing the Slovak economy for EU accession, a process initiated in 1993 with the signing of the Europe Agreements. Eliminating the structural problems inherited from the previous regime and strengthening the regulatory and institutional framework would allow the Slovak Republic to generate substantial efficiency gains and ultimately to maintain a good growth performance with a lower ratio of fixed investment to GDP and a sustainable current account deficit. That would enable the Slovak Republic to approach the period of EU accession with a demonstrated capacity to face the competitive pressures of a common internal market and to reap the potential benefits of full EU membership.

This chapter makes an evaluation of the Slovak Republic's macroeconomic performance after independence and sets the stage for the rest of the report. The second section describes the progress achieved in reducing inflation and promoting the recovery of output and employment after independence in 1993. The third section examines the external imbalances which emerged in 1996, whereas the fourth section assesses the initial policy response to these imbalances. The fifth and final section analyzes the dual challenges of sustained growth and EU accession, and provide a guide to the analysis contained in the other chapters of the report.

Stabilization and Growth

Success in Reducing Inflation

The Slovak Republic has achieved an impressive success in reducing inflation, after a temporary increase in 1993 (Table 1.1). The increase in the first year of independence was due primarily to the introduction of the VAT and a 10 percent devaluation of the Slovak koruna. However, the continued use of the exchange rate as a nominal anchor, combined with a very strict fiscal policy and moderate wage increases, quickly reversed this increase and placed inflation on a firm downward path.[1] The decrease in the average VAT rate in 1996 contributed to the slowdown in prices, and since that year CPI inflation has been around 6 percent p.a., the lowest among CEE countries (Table 1.1).

Table 1.1
Inflation and GDP Growth in Selected CEE Countries, 1992-97

Country	1992	1993	1994	1995	1996	1997
	Inflation (average CPI (percent per annum)					
Czech Republic	11.1	20.8	10.1	9.1	8.8	10.0
Hungary	23.0	22.5	18.8	28.2	23.6	18.0
Poland	43.0	35.3	32.2	27.8	19.9	14.8
Slovak Republic	10.0	23.2	13.4	9.9	5.8	6.2
Slovenia	201.3	32.3	19.8	12.6	8.8	9.0
	GDP Growth (percent per annum)					
Czech Republic	-6.6	-0.7	2.6	5.1	4.1	0.5
Hungary	-3.1	-0.6	3.0	1.5	1.3	4.0
Poland	2.6	3.8	5.2	7.0	6.1	6.0
Slovak Republic	-6.5	-3.9	5.0	7.0	6.9	5.5
Slovenia	-5.4	2.8	5.3	3.9	3.1	3.5

Source: National sources and World Bank staff estimates.

The strong fiscal support to the exchange rate-based stabilization program is revealed by the 12 percent of GDP improvement in the General Government budget between 1992 and 1995 (Table 1.2). This impressive fiscal adjustment--achieved primarily through expenditure cuts--more than offset the loss of transfers from the Czechoslovak federation (7 percent of GDP) and resulted in a small fiscal surplus in 1995. More specifically, from 1992 to 1995, General Government expenditures declined from around 58 percent of GDP to 48 percent of GDP, mainly due to reduction in consumption expenditures (6 percent of GDP), investment expenditures (2 percent of GDP), subsidies to enterprises (1.5 percent of GDP), and ill-targeted social expenditures.

---

[1] After the 10 percent devaluation in 1993, the Slovak crown continued to be pegged to a basket of five foreign currencies. In mid-1994, the currency basket was redefined to consist only of the German Mark and the US dollar with weights, of 60 and 40 percent respectively.

Despite this impressive fiscal adjustment, it must be noted that public finances continue to be very complex. In addition to the State budget, which accounts for more than half of total General Government expenditures, there are four Social Security Funds (the Health, Sickness, Employment, and Pension Funds) accounting for 35 percent of total expenditures; eleven extra-budgetary funds accounting for 5 percent of total expenditures; and local governments accounting for 6 percent of the total. Finally, special investment projects financed outside the State budget have increased their size from negligible levels in 1992, to 2.3 of total expenditures or 1.2 percent of GDP in 1996. In addition to the institutional complexity, the tax burden remains very heavy by comparison with countries with similar per capita incomes, and some tax rates are excessively high. In particular, the payroll tax rate amounts to 50 percent of gross wages, being significantly higher than the OECD and EU averages.

Strong Output Recovery

The contraction of Government expenditures did not prevent the economy from recovering, as the fiscal slack was more than offset by a significant growth of exports and investment. As shown in Table 1.2, the Slovak Republic initiated its recovery in 1994, due primarily to a strong growth of exports, and maintained a very good growth performance in 1995 and 1996, due primarily to increases in aggregate domestic demand.[2] Fixed investment was a major source of GDP growth in those two years, particularly in 1996 when it grew by 33 percent, increasing its share in GDP to an impressive 36 percent. Private consumption grew less than GDP in the first stages of the recovery (1994-95), in line with the moderate increase in wage income observed during this period, but grew slightly more than GDP in 1996, the year when wages grew slightly more than productivity (Table 1.2).

The Slovak Republic's recovery started somewhat late relative to other CEE countries (Table 1.1), possibly because of the residual effects of a stabilization program implemented in 1991 under the Czechoslovak federation, and the disruptions caused by independence in 1993. However, its recent growth performance has been superior to that of other CEE countries, except for Poland. The recovery has been driven by the private sector, which through the privatization process and the entry of new enterprises, was able to increase its share in GDP to more than 75 percent, and has also been accompanied by a reduction in the unemployment rate--from around 14 percent at end-1994 to around 12 percent at end-1996 (Table 1.2).

The Emergence of External Imbalances

The Slovak Republic's initial success in combining output recovery with a surplus in the current account was due to an impressive export performance in the period immediately after independence. However, by end-1995, exports started to falter and GDP growth started being driven by the strong expansion in domestic demand. Whereas other CEE countries also experienced a slowdown in exports during 1996, the decline in export growth to only 3 percent during 1996, combined with a buoyant, 24 percent increase in imports (both measured in US dollars), resulted in a much larger current account deficit in the case of the Slovak Republic--more than 11 percent of GDP in 1996, compared to 8.5 percent of GDP for the Czech Republic and to moderate deficits for the other CEE countries (Table 1.3).

---

[2] Exports also contributed significantly to GDP growth during 1995, although there is conflicting information about the extent of the contribution, as indicated by the large differences between balance of payments and national accounts data (Table 1.2).

Table 1.2
Key Economic Indicators, 1992-96

	1992	1993	1994	1995	1996	1997
I. REAL SECTOR						
Nominal GDP (US$ million)	11,757	11,996	13,746	17,336	18,963	19,217
Nominal GDP per Capita (US$)	2,216	2,253	2,571	3,232	3,529	3,562
rowth Rates (percent):						
DP	-6.5	-3.9	5.0	7.0	6.9	5.5
Total Consumption	-1.7	-1.6	-4.4	3.9	12.1	4.5
Private Consumption	-6.4	-1.4	-0.5	3.8	7.2	5.5
Gross Investment	-14.6	-7.3	-8.4	27.4	42.8	-3.1
Fixed Investment	-4.5	-4.1	-5.5	6.2	33.3	-0.4
Exports of GNFS	47.4	-0.2	13.7	3.9	-1.6	5.8
Shares of GDP (percent)						
Total Consumption	75.1	78.2	71.7	69.2	73.1	71.7
Private Consumption	49.5	53.2	50.4	49.0	49.0	48.7
Gross Investment	28.1	27.3	23.1	28.5	38.2	35.1
Fixed Investment	32.9	32.7	29.4	29.2	36.6	34.5
Exports of GNFS	70.3	61.7	65.1	63.2	57.5	57.5
Private Sector Share in GDP (percent)	32.4	39.0	58.2	62.6	76.8	80.0
Unemployment Rate (end-year, percent)	10.4	14.4	14.8	13.1	12.8	13.0
Real Unit Labor Costs-Industry (PPI, 1993=100)	86.4	100,0	97.3	96.0	103.3	n.a.
Basket Real Exchange Rate (PPIs, 1993=100) [1/]	90.2	100.0	103.5	110.0	117.1	n.a.
II. FISCAL ACCOUNTS [2/]						
Government Balance (percent of GDP)	-11.9	-7.0	-1.3	0.2	-1.4	-4.5
Government Revenues (percent of GDP)	46.1	44.3	46.5	47.1	46.9	41.5
Government Expenditures (percent of GDP)	58.0	51.4	47.8	46.9	48.4	46.0
III. EXTERNAL ACCOUNTS						
Growth of Exports of Goods in US$ (percent per annum))		-16.4	22.8	28.2	2.9	2.0
Growth of Imports of Goods in US$ (percent per annum))		-11.8	4.0	32.8	24.2	-1.0
Current Account Balance (percent of GDP)	0.4	-5.0	4.8	2.3	-11.1	-7.5
Foreign Direct Investment (percent of GDP)	0.9	1.1	1.2	0.8	0.7	0.8
Gross External Debt (percent of GDP)	25.4	30.0	34.9	33.6	41.2	55.8
Net External Debt (percent of GDP)	17.7	18.5	13.3	5.3	9.8	21.4
Share of Banks and Enterprises in Gross Debt (percent)				65.3	78.3	81.7
Share of Short-Term Debt in Gross Debt (percent)				30.2	38.5	45.8

n.a.: not available
1/ Real exchange rate with official basket of 60 percent DM and 40 percent US dollar.
2/ Fiscal indicators for 1997 estimated from below the line flows in January through November.
Source: Slovak Republic Central Statistical Office, Ministry of Finance, National Bank of Slovakia and World Bank staff estimates.

The export slowdown occurred across all destinations, but the decline was particularly impressive in the case of exports to the Czech Republic (Table 1.4). The slowdown in exports to the EU was partly cyclical (slower output growth in the EU), whereas the decline in exports to the Czech Republic was more structural, reflecting the disruption of traditional commercial links between enterprises in the two countries after independence. Export performance in the first nine months of 1997 confirms this picture. As shown in Table 1.4, there has been some recovery in exports, but this recovery is due primarily to larger exports to the EU, because exports to the Czech Republic have remained stagnant.[3] These trends suggest that future export performance may continue to depend on further penetration on the more sophisticated markets of the EU.

---

[3] There is a large difference between growth rates quoted in US dollars (2 percent) and German Marks (18 percent) in 1997 due to exchange rate fluctuations. Adjusting for cross exchange rate changes, the increase was around 10 percent in the first nine months of 1997, compared to 5 percent in 1996. Adjusting for foreign inflation yields real growth rates of around 7 and 2 percent in 1997 and 1996, respectively.

Table 1.3
External Accounts of Selected CEE Countries

Country	Export Growth 1993-1995 (percent per annum)	Export Growth 1996 (percent per annum)	Current Account 1996 (percent of GDP)	FDI 1996 (percent of GDP)	Gross External Debt 1996 (percent of GDP)	Net External Debt 1996 (percent of GDP)
Czech Republic	28.1	1.1	-8.6	2.7	39.8	7.6
Hungary	25.8	4.8	-3.9	4.1	63.7	41.2
Poland	30.0	6.7	-1.0	2.1	30.3	16.8
Slovak Republic	**25.5**	**2.9**	**-11.1**	**0.5**	**41.2**	**10.4**
Slovenia	17.1	0.1	0.3	1.0	22.9	0.6

Source: World Bank staff estimates.

Table 1.4
Export and Import Growth and Major Trading Partners

	1995	1996	1997 (Jan-Sept.)	1995	1996	1997 (Jan-Sept.)
		Exports			Imports	
Growth Rate in US$ (percent per annum)	28	3	2	33	24	-1
Growth Rate in DM (percent per annum)	14	7	18	18	30	14
Shares in Total (percent)						
EU	37	41	45	35	38	39
Czech Republic	35	31	27	28	25	23
Russia	4	3	3	16	18	16

Source: Slovak Republic authorities.

The rapid growth of imports was partly due to one-time factors, such as imports of military equipment from Russia, received in payment for accumulated debts, and very large imports of small cars, resulting from a temporary elimination of tariffs on these cars during 1996. The impact of the above factors on the trade account amounted to nearly 3 percent of GDP during 1996 (more than 1 percent of GDP in military equipment, and approximately 2 percent of GDP in above average imports of small cars). However, that still leaves large imports and a large trade deficit of approximately 8 percent of GDP to be explained by other factors.

In examining other factors, it is natural to start by investigating the situation of the public finances in 1996, as large external imbalances are frequently associated with large imbalances in the public sector. However, the strong growth in domestic demand and imports in 1996 were not related to strong fiscal pressures. The General Government budget shifted from a small surplus to a deficit during 1996, but the fiscal shift was very moderate by comparison with the current account shift--only 1.6 percent of GDP between 1995 and 1996, compared with a shift of 13 percent of GDP in the current account (Table 1.2). Therefore, the Slovak Republic does not seem to have experienced a problem of "twin deficits" during 1996. Instead, the large imports and the current account shift seem to have been associated primarily with an expansion of fixed investment (Table 1.2).

The fact that the expansion of domestic demand was centered in a rapid growth of investment, and the fact that 30 percent of imports consisted of purchases of capital goods (consumer goods amounted to only 20 percent), would perhaps give the impression that the external imbalance was not so severe after all, as it was being accompanied by a build-up of future debt repayment capacity. Moreover, the Slovak Republic's external debt to GDP ratios do not look excessively high by international comparison (although they are higher than most other Visegrad countries, as shown in Table 1.3), and the current account deficit in 1996 was mostly financed by borrowings by domestic banks and enterprises from private creditors (Table 1.2). These additional facts could reinforce the impression that the current account deficit was a strict private sector affair, and that the external borrowings were "optimal" (i.e., reflecting well-informed private decisions unaffected by distorted incentives), with no obvious implications for the conduct of macroeconomic policies.

There are, however, a number of other indicators suggesting that the external borrowings were far from "optimal", and that the current account deficit is indeed a cause for concern. First, it must be noted that even if all borrowings were associated with investments of high return, and the Slovak Republic were able to sustain very high growth rates (around 7 percent p.a.), deficits of this order of magnitude could hardly be sustained for a long period, as they would result in debt to GDP ratios above 100 percent in less than 10 years.

Second, there are no guarantees that all the external borrowings were associated with high return investments in sectors producing traded goods. For one, the investment data includes a significant share of the small cars imported in 1996, assets which hardly contribute to the build-up of debt repayment capacity. Also, the persistence of large enterprise losses (Chapter III) provides an indication that corporate governance is not yet consolidated, and that some inefficient enterprises may have obtained access to foreign borrowings, either directly or through the banks. Investment decisions may also have been distorted by the privatization rules, which allowed new owners to offset payments to the National Property Fund by investing in the enterprise (Chapter III). Furthermore, the share of manufacturing in total fixed investment was only 17 percent in 1996 (Appendix Table 2.5), suggesting that sectors producing non-traded goods accounted for a large share of investment. Although efficiency gains in services may very well increase the productivity of sectors producing traded goods, its impact on future debt-repayment capacity is more indirect and possibly more limited.

Third, the trends in the maturity composition of foreign borrowings do not fit the paradigm of an economy borrowing abroad to finance investment. Instead of lengthening the average debt maturity (matching an increased level of investment relative to GDP), there was a significant increase in the share of short-term debt in total debt--from 30 percent in 1995 to 46 percent in 1997. The increase in the share of short-term debt probably involved intensive recourse to short-term trade financing and tended to increase the Slovak Republic's vulnerability to changes in the perception of foreign creditors.

Fourth, the sharp investment expansion was to a good extent stimulated by a liberal monetary policy during 1995 and the first half of 1996. As shown in Figure 1.1, the growth of broad money and bank credits started accelerating in mid-1995, well in excess of inflation or the growth rate of nominal GDP during the same period (which was around 15 percent p.a.).[4] Although an increase in the real demand for financial assets was expected, as a result of lower inflation and growing output, the expansion of broad money probably exceeded the increase in demand by some margin. The increase in domestic spending generated by this excess probably spilled over into the current account without producing an impact on inflation because of the exchange rate anchor and the openness of the Slovak economy.

Finally, the real appreciation that resulted from the use of the exchange rate as a nominal anchor (Table 1.2) may have also contributed to the increase in imports and the slowdown of exports, particularly in the case of very price-sensitive exports, such as those conducted through processing arrangements

---

[4] The expansion of broad money was fueled by a strong expansion in base money resulting from the NBS's decision to stop sterilizing increases in net foreign assets.

(Chapter II). However, it is unclear the extent to which the real appreciation has affected the current account, given the very competitive levels of the Slovak crown at the time of independence--the exchange rate was then fixed at a level 3.4 times higher than the PPP exchange rate, compared to a factor of 2.8 for the Czech Republic, 2.2 for Poland, and 2 for Hungary in that year.

Figure 1.1
Growth of Money and Credit, 1994-97

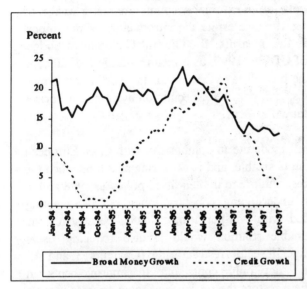

Source: National Bank of Slovakia.

Figure 1.2
Recent Evolution of Interest Rates

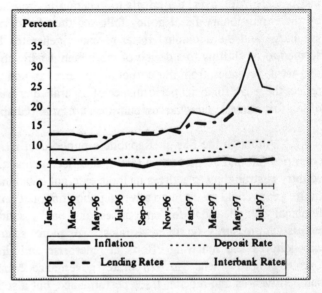

Source: National Bank of Slovakia.

The clearest indication that private agents had changed their perceptions about the sustainability of the external situation occurred in May 1997, when the Slovak crown was subject to a series of speculative attacks. The currency attacks in the Slovak Republic followed similar events in other countries experiencing large current account deficits, such as the Czech Republic and a number of East Asian countries, forcing the National Bank of Slovakia to intervene in the foreign exchange market and revealing clearly the need for policy corrections.

The Policy Response

The recognition that the shift in the current account had been excessive, partly due to a relaxation of monetary policy, led the National Bank of Slovakia (NBS) to tighten monetary policy in mid-1996, primarily through increases in reserve requirements. Further measures were adopted in early 1997, including regulatory changes designed to curb the growth of foreign exchange credits. These measures resulted in a significant deceleration of money and credit expansion (Figure 1.1), and caused an upward pressure on interest rates (Figure 1.2), but failed to produce an immediate impact on the current account in the first four months of 1997--the annualized deficit was around 11 percent of GDP. In May 1997, the situation was aggravated by the emergence of a speculative attack on the Slovak crown, forcing NBS to tighten monetary policy further, and causing additional pressures on interest rates (Figures 1.1 and 1.2).

The tightening of monetary policy seemed to be finally producing an effect on the external accounts in mid-1997, with the halving of average monthly current account deficits--from US$210 million to US$110 million. In addition, in late July the Government introduced a 7 percent import surcharge, designed to curb imports further while generating additional fiscal revenues. These measures, combined with some recovery of exports (Table 1.4), should result in a reduction in the current account deficit, from 11 percent of GDP in 1996 to about 7.5 percent of GDP in 1997.

The maintenance of a very tight monetary policy and the announcement of the import surcharge seem also to have deflected the speculative attacks, allowing the NBS to hold the Slovak crown at the same levels relative to the currency basket. However, this success in maintaining the exchange parity has been achieved at the cost of very high real interest rates and the introduction of a distortionary trade policy instrument. Moreover, the efforts to generate improvements in the external accounts are being weakened by the expansionary fiscal policy followed thus far during 1997. Despite the introduction of the import surcharge and the additional fiscal revenues generated by this measure, the General Government budget seemed to be shifting to a deficit of more than 4 percent of GDP in 1997, as a result of large investments, and weak revenues from the corporate income tax and the payroll tax. The weak tax performance may reflect the weak financial performance of several enterprises, and, possibly, speculation by some enterprises of tax forgiveness under the revitalization program (Chapter 3).

Although the Slovak Republic's public debt is still moderate in comparison with most European countries (around 30 percent of GDP), this fiscal expansion is sizable, and is occurring at a time when the country is struggling to address its large external imbalances. Failure to tighten fiscal policy in 1998 and in future years could result in an adverse policy mix, not only undermining monetary policy, but also creating financial complications for enterprises and banks saddled with non-performing loans, because of the excessive pressures on interest rates. A more sustainable solution would involve reducing fiscal expenditures and renewing efforts at enterprise and financial sector restructuring (Chapters 3 and 4). Greater improvements in corporate governance would not only contribute to improvements in competitiveness and a better trade performance, but also help restore the revenues of the corporate income tax, further strengthening the fiscal situation in the long run.

The Challenges of Sustained Growth and EU Accession

The Slovak Republic is facing the challenge of maintaining the impressive growth performance achieved after independence, while reducing the current account deficit to levels that can be sustained in the long-run. The Slovak Republic is also facing the challenge of accession into the European Union (EU), and being able to share the benefits of full participation in a very large common market. As argued below, these two challenges are to a large extent intertwined, as the Slovak Republic's efforts to meet the first will greatly contribute to meeting the second, and vice-versa.

The Challenge of Sustaining High Growth

The Slovak Republic's per capita income is currently equal to the average of the other Visegrad countries--approximately US$7,300 on a PPP basis in 1996. The Slovak Republic and the other Visegrad countries face the challenge of sustaining growth and converging to the average EU levels of per capita income (around US$19,000 on a PPP basis in 1996) in the next decades. Like the other Visegrad countries, the Slovak Republic has some of the key factors required for the maintenance of a good growth performance and convergence to EU income levels--good educational standards and a skilled labor force. In addition, the Slovak Republic holds a potential advantage over the other Visegrad countries--its levels of fixed investment have generally been much higher, and reached an impressive 36 percent of GDP in 1996, compared to 33 percent for the Czech Republic and roughly 20 percent for Poland and Hungary.

While these high investment ratios are a potential advantage, they have been accompanied by current account deficits which cannot be sustained, even under the high growth rates registered after independence.   Therefore, the Slovak Republic faces the task of closing the imbalance while sustaining growth, either by increasing domestic savings, or by reducing somewhat the levels of fixed investment, but compensating such a reduction by an increase in efficiency.   Although there is evidence that savings ratios can increase endogenously through the growth process,[5] the magnitude of the external imbalance is such as to make this option unfeasible or excessively risky--it would require several years of large external imbalances in the expectation of an eventual increase in domestic savings.   This suggests that Slovak policy-makers should focus their efforts in increasing the efficiency of the economy, in order to allow the Slovak Republic to sustain high growth with investment levels that, although lower than the current ones, would remain high by comparison with other CEE countries and most other emerging economies.

The reduction of fixed investment from the 1996 peak should not prove a daunting task.   The investment ratio should naturally decline as a result of the completion of some exceptionally large infrastructure projects, such as the construction of the Mochovce nuclear power plant, and the modernization and expansion in the steel and petrochemical sectors.   A further reduction of investment to more sustainable levels would require spreading the ambitious public investment program over a longer period, maintaining monetary control and eliminating policy distortions, such as the possibility to offset obligations to the National Property Fund by additional investment.   At the same time, there is scope for further gains in efficiency that would allow the country to sustain high growth rates with lower investment levels.   The scope for these efficiency gains is examined throughout this report, and would materialize to the extent that the Government adopts the policies required to eliminate loss-making activities in industry and agriculture, improve financial sector intermediation, and remove distortions in labor markets.

The Challenge of EU Accession

The Slovak Republic formally presented its membership application to the EU in June 1995 at the Cannes European Council.   Prior to this application, the Slovak Republic and the EU signed in October 1993 an association agreement (the Europe Agreement) which became effective in February 1995.   This agreement is the legal basis for relations between the Slovak Republic and the EU.   Its aim is to provide a framework for political dialogue, to render a basis for Community technical and financial assistance that will serve to support the Slovak Republic's integration into the EU, and to promote the expansion of trade and economic relations between the parties.

The institutional framework of the Agreement includes meetings at a ministerial level (through the establishment of the Association Council), at a senior officials level (through the Association Committee), and at a technical level (through nine sub-committees).   These meetings provide a mechanism for the implementation, management, and monitoring of all areas of the relationship.   The Europe Agreement also provides for the approximation of legislation in a number of priority areas.   In particular, it contains specific obligations relating to the approximation of competition, industrial and intellectual property, and public procurement legislation.

The trade provisions, which went into effect under the interim Europe Agreement signed with Czechoslovakia in March 1992, provide for the establishment of a free trade area in industrial products during a maximum of ten years.   For most industrial products the parties have agreed to phase out trade barriers in an asymmetrical manner; full liberalization of exports from the Slovak Republic as of January 1995, and progressive liberalization of Slovak imports from the EU.   For those products not affected by

---

[5] Schmidt-Hebel, K., L. Serven, and A. Solimano (1994), "Savings, Investment and Growth in Developing Countries: An Overview," Policy Research Working Paper No. 1382, The World Bank, Washington DC.

special provisions, free trade is expected to materialize by the year 2002. A different time schedule for the elimination of trade barriers applies, however, to some sensitive products. For example, restrictions to EU imports of steel products from the Slovak Republic applied until January 1, 1996, and similar restrictions apply to EU imports of textile products until January of 1998. For agricultural and agro-industrial products mutual concessions have been established, involving reduced tariffs and/or increased quotas.

At the Copenhagen summit of 1993, the heads of the Governments of the European Union stated that the associated countries of Central Europe could become members of the EU, as soon as they were able to assume the obligations of membership. These membership obligations were defined at the same occasion and include: (i) the stability of institutions guaranteeing democracy, the rule of law, human rights, and respect for the protection of minorities; (ii) the existence of a functioning market economy, as well as the capacity to cope with the competitive pressures of market forces within the union; and (iii) the ability to take the obligations of membership, including adherence to the aims of political, economic, and monetary union.

Important elements in defining a functioning market economy are macroeconomic stability, a substantial degree of liberalization (e.g., in prices, trade and foreign exchange), a large private sector share in the economy, a reasonably developed financial sector, an adequate institutional infrastructure, and the existence and implementation of a legal framework ensuring, *inter alia*, respect for property rights, free market entry and exit, and a level playing field for all participants. The capacity to cope with competitive pressures within the Union assumes, *inter alia*, appropriate levels of physical capital, adequate levels of investment in human capital, high degree of trade integration with the Union ahead of enlargement, a diversified industrial base, and the capacity to adapt to a rapidly changing global economy. The latter requires good corporate governance and access to investment finance, skills and technology. Finally, the ability to take the obligations of membership assumes full compliance with the *acquis communautaire*--the body of EC legislation.

The Commission's White Paper (1995) identifies the key measures in each sector of the internal market legislation and suggests a sequence in which approximation of legislation should be tackled. It highlights those measures which need priority attention within each sector, the so-called Stage One measures. While the White Paper is not a legally binding document, it provides guidance for legislative approximation. The Slovak government has put in place a National Approximation Program which aims to support the country's legal approximation to EC legislation.

Meeting the Dual Challenges

The Slovak Republic has already made significant progress in meeting several of the conditions established at Copenhagen. Since 1989, there has been substantial progress in creating a functioning market economy, as indicated by the sharp increase in the share of the private sector in GDP (to nearly 80 percent in 1996), the liberalization of prices and wages, the establishment of an open trade regime (the average tariff is lower than 8 percent), the fairly open foreign exchange regime (full current account convertibility and progressive opening of the capital account), and the opening of the financial sector to foreign institutions and joint ventures (currently accounting for nearly half of the total bank equity). There has also been an effort to harmonize the legal and regulatory framework with that of the EU, and further harmonization steps are planned for future years.

Despite this significant progress, further work is needed in several areas. In the macroeconomic area, policy-makers must address the external imbalance while also abandoning the use of distortionary trade policy instruments. This would allow the Slovak Republic to approach the accession period without excessive foreign borrowing requirements and in compliance with the Association Agreements. In the institutional and regulatory areas, more progress is also needed, particularly in the area of enterprise and bank reforms, as the persistence of loss-making enterprises and financially weak State banks would indicate problems in the functioning of the economy and inability to cope with the competitive pressures of a common market. Also, there has to be further progress not only in harmonizing the regulatory framework to the EU, but also in enforcing rules and regulations. Solving these problems early in the pre-accession period would allow the Slovak Republic to create the conditions for sustained growth in future years and at the same time comply with the requirements of EU accession .

It must be stressed that the achievement of sustained economic growth is not only an objective in itself, but would also prove a decisive factor determining the ability of the country to obtain a positive assessment by the EU. Admission to the EU should not create difficulties or instability for the Slovak Republic and the Member States. Macroeconomic imbalances and/or weak growth performance would raise justified doubts about Slovak capacity to cope with the pressure of accession. It is always easier to adjust to a new competitive situation when the economy is growing rapidly. Therefore, the Slovak Republic should tackle the structural bottlenecks early in the pre-accession period and concurrently adjust the regulatory framework to the EU.

The Objective and Structure of the Country Study

The objective of this Study is to contribute to the Slovak Republic's ongoing efforts to increase the efficiency of its economy and prepare the ground for integration with the EU. It provides an assessment of progress in several sectors and identifies the main reforms which are needed to successfully complete the transformation initiated in the early 1990s. The report is structured as follows: the second chapter deals with foreign trade and trade policies. It analyzes the trade performance in the period after independence, assesses the current status of trade policies, and identifies the main policy issues and options faced by the Government during the pre-accession period.

The third chapter deals with enterprise reform. It assesses the progress achieved at enterprise privatization and restructuring, and makes an evaluation of progress in harmonizing the legal framework for enterprises to EU legislation. The fourth chapter addresses the closely related theme of financial sector reform. It examines the changes in the financial sector resulting from the entry of foreign banks and joint ventures, and the banks' progress in dealing with bad loans and troubled debtors. It also contains a detailed analysis of legal approximation in the banking area. Finally, it also provides a preliminary analysis of the performance and legal structure of the Slovak Republic's capital market.

The fifth chapter addresses the agriculture sector. It examines the changes in land ownership, and the reorganization of the sector resulting from these changes. It also examines the sector's response to the sharp deterioration in the terms of trade in the early 1990s, and verifies the sector's productivity in comparison with the average productivity in the EU. It goes on to examine Government policies in the agriculture sector and identifies the policy agenda for the pre-accession period.

The sixth chapter deals with the labor market and social policies. It starts with a section analyzing labor market developments and labor policies. This section also identifies the reforms required to increase flexibility in the labor market in order to facilitate further restructuring, while also complying with EU accession requirements. The second section examines social insurance policies, with focus on the pension system but also covering sickness insurance. This section identifies the measures required to restore long-run equilibrium to the Slovak pension system, while enabling some reduction in the high payroll tax rates.

The chapter ends with a section covering the basic social programs, and identifies the measures required to increase the cost-effectiveness of these programs.

The seventh chapter covers the environment. It examines the extent of improvements in the quality of the environment in the first half of the 1990s, the extent of legal approximation with EU legislation, the investments required to improve further the quality of the environment, and the mechanisms for financing these investments. Finally, the eighth chapter summarizes the major findings and the recommendations of the report, in the context of a proposed macroeconomic framework for high growth under a sustainable current account. This includes an assessment of Slovak growth potential under different policy scenarios, stressing the need to complete economic transformation in order to achieve convergence with EU income levels in a reasonable period of time.

CHAPTER II: FOREIGN TRADE AND TRADE POLICY

Introduction

The Slovak Republic is an open economy, with total exports and imports of goods accounting together for more than 100 percent of GDP. In the period following independence, the country achieved an impressive export performance as indicated by exports in US dollars, growing at an annual rate of 26 percent p.a. between 1993 and 1995. This export performance allowed the Slovak Republic to shift from a current account deficit of 5 percent of GDP in 1993, to surpluses of 5 and 2 percent of GDP in 1994 and 1995 respectively, while maintaining a relatively liberal trade regime.

During 1996 the external situation changed substantially, however, with the shift of the current account to a deficit of 11 percent of GDP. The abrupt shift of the current account reflected a sharp slowdown in export growth and buoyant imports--export growth slowed to 3 percent, while imports continued to increase by 24 percent. These developments justify a more detailed analysis of the Slovak Republic's trade performance after independence, as that may provide some insights on the sources and the magnitude of the underlying external imbalance, as well as inputs for the design of a strategy to deal with such an imbalance.

Slovak policy-makers have to address the imbalances in the trade and current accounts while also preparing the economy for EU accession. The implementation of the Europe Agreement will involve some further reduction in tariffs until 2001, when trade with the EU is expected be fully liberalized. Although The Slovak Republic already runs a liberal trade regime, it is important to assess how much additional import pressure is implied by the implementation of the Europe Agreement. This assessment is even more important given the recent recourse by the Slovak authorities to an import surcharge aimed at addressing both fiscal and external disequilibria. EU accession also raises a number of other questions for trade policy, such as the optimal timing for adopting the EU's common external tariff. More specifically, the question is whether it would make sense for the Slovak Republic to adopt the common external tariff already during the pre-accession period.

This chapter seeks to contribute to an assessment of these issues. The second section starts with an overview of trade developments since 1993. This is followed by a more detailed analysis of the composition of exports and imports, as well as other related indicators of trade performance. The third section examines the current status of Slovak trade policies, and assesses the remaining gaps between Slovak and the EU's policies in this area. The fourth and final section identifies the major trade issues to be addressed in the pre-accession period, and makes some policy recommendations. The chapter does not contain an analysis of current account sustainability, as this requires the use of a macroeconomic model. However, it provides an analysis of some key trade issues that are used as inputs for the analysis of sustainability which is developed in chapter VIII.

Trade Performance Since Independence

The former Czechoslovakia was very dependent on the former CMEA system, as indicated by a share of 63 percent of the former CMEA in total exports in 1990 (Table 2.1). This dependence on the former CMEA was particularly strong in the case of the Slovak Republic, which still directed more than 60 percent of its exports to former CMEA countries at the time of its independence in 1993. Since then, exports have been significantly redirected, as shown by a decrease in 10 percentage points in the former CMEA's share of total exports and a 12 percentage point increase in Western Europe's share between

1993 and 1996 (Table 2.1). The declining share of the former CMEA has been essentially due to decreasing trade with the Czech Republic. The increase in Western Europe's share in total exports was larger than the increase achieved by the other Visegrad countries, although Western Europe's share remains comparatively lower due to its low initial base. On the import side the trends are similar.

Table 2.1
Exports of the Slovak Republic and Other Visegrad Countries, 1990-96

Country	Exports/ GDP 1996 (percent)	Export Growth 1993-95 (percent per annum)	Export Growth 1996 (percent per annum)	Export Growth 1993-96 (percent per annum)	Ex-CMEA Share [1] (percent)			Western European Share (percent)		
					1990	1993	1996	1990	1993	1996
Czechoslovakia	n.a.	n.a.	n.a.	n.a.	63.0n .a.	n.a.	n.a.	42.8	n.a.	n.a.
Czech Republic	42.0	28.1	1.1	18.3		35.0	30.3	n.a.	50.8	59.8
Slovak Republic	46.6	25.5	2.9	17.5	n.a.	60.6	50.1	n.a.	30.3	42.5
Hungary	30.9	25.8	4.8	18.4	33.1	26.0	20.3	47.4	60.1	65.8
Poland	18.1	30.0	6.7	21.6	23.9	12.5	21.2	60.5	71.1	68.7

n.a.: not available.
Note: Data for 1996 are preliminary.
1/ Excludes the German Democratic Republic.
Sources: National Sources; IMF Direction of Trade Statistics.

Such a reorientation of trade took place initially in a situation of rapidly growing exports, as shown by average growth rates of 26 percent in the period following independence. However, at the end of 1995 exports started slowing down, having grown by only 3 percent during 1996 (Table 2.1). Such a slowdown in exports was also experienced by other Visegrad countries, but in the case of the Slovak Republic it combined with a robust 24 percent growth of imports to generate a sharp 11 percent of GDP shift in the trade account--from a deficit of 1 percent of GDP in 1995 to a deficit of 12 percent of GDP in 1996 (the shift in the current account was larger, having amounted to 12 percent of GDP). The other Visegrad countries have also experienced a deterioration in the trade account linked to the export slowdown (except for Hungary, which was undergoing a stabilization program), but their trade and current account deficits are not nearly as large as the Slovak Republic's (Chapter I).

Table 2.2
Direction of Trade, 1995-97

	Exports			Imports			Balance		
	1995	1996	1997 (Jan-Sept)	1995	1996	1997 (Jan-Sept)	1995	1996	1997 (Jan-Sept)
TOTAL (US$ billion)	8.6	8.8	6.6	8.8	10.9	7.8	-0.2	-2.1	-1.2
TOTAL (DM billion)	12.3	13.2	11.4	12.6	16.4	13.4	-0.3	-3.2	-2.0
Growth rate (percent per annum)									
Current US$	28	3	2	33	24	-1			
Current DM	13	7	18	18	30	14			
Of which:									
EU (US$ billion)	3.2	3.6	3.0	3.1	4.1	3.1	0.1	-0.4	-0.1
Share of Total (percent)	37	41	45	35	38	39			
Czech Republic (US$ billion)	3.0	2.7	1.8	2.5	2.7	1.8	0.5	0.0	-0.0
Share of Total (percent)	35	31	27	28	25	23			
Russia (US$ billion)	0.3	0.3	0.2	1.5	1.9	1.2	-1.1	-1.6	-1.0
Share of Total (percent)	4	3	3	16	18	16			

Source: Slovak authorities.

The shifts in the trade and current accounts in 1996 reflected partly one-time factors operating on the side of imports, and cyclical factors operating on the side of exports. One-time factors included a surge in imports of small cars resulting from the temporary abolition of tariffs and VAT on these imports (while concurrently announcing the re-imposition of tariffs in January 1997), and the receipt of aircraft from Russia as a settlement on outstanding debt. These two factors accounted for nearly 3 percentage points of the deterioration in the trade balance in 1996. In addition, the completion of the Mochovce nuclear power plant and the restructuring of large segments of industry (e.g. steel) had an important impact on import volumes during 1996. On the side of exports, performance was negatively affected by capacity constraints faced by several important Slovak exporters during 1996. Finally, the slowdown of GDP growth in Germany and other major EU countries (from 2.5 percent in 1995 to 1 percent in 1996), may also help explain the slowdown of exports to EU markets, from 37 percent growth in 1995 to 13 percent in 1996 (Table 2.2).

Although these factors account for part of the trade account deterioration, the trade deficit has also been due to factors of longer duration, operating on both the exports and imports side. The Slovak Republic is experiencing a decline in the volume of trade with the Czech Republic which seems structural rather than cyclical. Some Slovak firms are now exporting directly to buyers in third countries instead of via traditional Czech intermediaries, and some Czech firms are diversifying away from Slovak suppliers of components. The decline in exports to the Czech Republic was particularly impressive during 1996 (10 percent drop over 1995) having resulted in the elimination of the 3 percent of GDP trade surplus achieved in 1995 (Table 2.2). Finally, the trade deficit has also been due to the impact of a very strong domestic demand, reflected on an overall high growth of imports. Note, however, that the increased imports from Russia reflect not only increased volumes of oil imports resulting from the expansion of domestic demand, but also higher average prices, due to the expiration of some older contracts at more favorable prices.

As mentioned in Chapter I, the recognition that the shift in the trade and current accounts had been excessive and abrupt, led the NBS to tighten monetary policy in mid-1996, in an attempt to reduce the deficits from the side of imports. To further support this policy, a 7 percent import surcharge was imposed in July 1997. While export growth resumed somewhat in the first three quarters of 1997, and import growth has declined (Table 2.2), the trade deficit remains large (about 8 percent of GDP). Moreover, the sustainability of the recent improvement in the external balance is partly questionable, since the import surcharge is being phased out in 1998 to enable the Slovak Republic to comply fully with its trade agreements.

The trade developments in the first three quarters of 1997 suggest that sustained improvements in the external accounts will continue to depend on NBS's efforts to restrain an excessive growth of domestic demand and imports, and on the ability of Slovak firms to compensate for losses in traditional markets by increasing their penetration of other markets, particularly Western European ones, in which they still hold a relatively modest share. Although it is difficult to predict the extent to which Slovak firms will be able to access new markets in the EU and in the rest of the world, an assessment can be made by examining changes in the composition of exports and imports, as well as other related trade indicators. Changes in the composition of exports may reveal ongoing efforts by enterprises to break into new markets, whereas the composition of imports may reveal the extent to which exports may expand in the future (e.g., through the acquisition of modern equipment and increased capacity to export).

Composition of Exports

The Slovak Republic has traditionally exported manufactured goods, especially iron and steel products, chemicals, transport equipment and textiles and apparel. Demand for many of these commodities is price sensitive, making export growth vulnerable to the ability of Slovak firms to maintain their competitiveness by controlling their input costs, including real wages. A useful measure of export specialization is the share of a commodity in a country's total exports relative to the average share of that product in world trade. This is called the Revealed Comparative Advantage index (RCA) of a country in a commodity. As shown in Table 2.3, iron and steel have the highest RCA among export items. Iron and steel are also the most important commodities exported, accounting for 16 percent of total exports in 1995. Of the top ten export items, only 3 categories have RCAs below one, suggesting that these are products in which the Slovak Republic does not have an export specialization.[6] However, in some cases the country may develop skills in the elaboration of non-traditional products, and eventually become an exporter of these products. One example is road vehicles, whose RCA has increased very rapidly, rising from 0.51 to 0.92 in three years. Indeed, this is one of the most dynamic sectors in Slovak Republic, with exports having grown by 80 percent between 1993-95.[7]

Table 2.3
Composition of Exports, 1993 and 1995

Category	Share in Total (percent)		Growth (percent)	RCA	RCA
	1993	1995	1993-95	1993	1995
0 Food	5.0	3.6	19.4	0.69	0.52
1 Beverages	0.8	0.6	17.0	0.78	0.62
2 Crude Materials	5.4	5.4	41.3	1.21	1.09
3 Fuels	4.3	4.4	41.7	0.49	0.51
4 Oils and Fats	0.1	0.1	37.8	0.34	0.29
5 Chemicals	12.2	12.1	40.4	1.37	1.27
Of which:					
58 Plastic Materials	4.0	4.1	43.5	1.84	1.71
51 Organic Chemicals	3.3	3.4	42.4	1.13	1.05
6 Manufactures	36.6	38.5	44.5	2.34	2.39
Of which:					
67 Iron/Steel	14.1	16.2	51.0	4.75	5.21
65 Textiles	4.8	4.4	35.6	1.59	1.61
64 Paper, Paperboard	3.1	4.0	61.2	1.73	2.04
66 Non-Metallic Mineral Manufactures	4.4	4.0	33.6	1.98	1.86
7 Machinery and Transport Equipment	18.8	21.3	49.9	2.34	2.39
Of which:					
73 Transport Equipment	6.4	9.2	69.4	0.51	0.92
72 Electrical Machinery	6.1	6.1	40.7	0.64	0.48
71 Non-Electric Machinery	6.3	6.0	37.2		
8 Miscellaneous Manufactures	15.6	12.8	27.8	1.12	1.01
Of which:					
84 Clothing	6.3	5.4	30.1	1.61	1.5
9 Other	1.0	1.1	48.5	0.36	0.45

Source: UN COMTRADE.

There was a slight increase in the share of the top five 2-digit Standard International Trade Classification (SITC) groups--from 39 to 43 percent of all exports between 1993 and 1995 (Table 2.3). That might suggest less export diversification and more vulnerability to fluctuations in foreign demand.

---

[6] The RCA is a useful summary measure of trade specialization which eliminates scale effects. However, deviations of this index from unity not always indicates comparative advantage, as export specialization might vary significantly over time. In addition, the index does not control for schemes that might temporarily and artificially favor the exports of a particular sector. See Bowen, H. (1983), "On the theoretical interpretation of indices of trade intensity and revealed comparative advantage," Weltwirtschaftliches Archiv, vol. 119, No. 3.

[7] Data for 1996 were not yet available from COMTRADE at the time of writing.

However, Slovak export concentration ratios do not look high by international comparison, and seem to have declined somewhat relative to the 1980s (Table 2.4). Further information on changes in the structure of exports can be obtained by computing simple correlation coefficients between RCAs for commodities in different years. High correlation coefficients indicate little change in RCAs and in the composition of exports. As shown in Table 2.5, the correlation coefficients are generally lower in the case of the Slovak Republic, whether they are computed at the 2-digit or the 4-digit level.[8] This provides evidence of more changes in the product mix and greater export diversification in the case of the Slovak Republic. However, the exports of some of these product groups are still small in volume, also suggesting that this potential has not yet fully materialized.[9]

Table 2.4

Export Concentration, Selected Countries, 1980-95

Country	Share of Top 5 Two-Digit SITC Items in Total Exports				Share of Top 10 Four-Digit SITC Items in Total Exports
	1980	1985	1990	1995	1995
Argentina	52.0	60.9	45.4	41.5	43.0
Brazil	49.1	42.1	40.6	36.9	34.6
Chile	77.8	81.1	75.3	71.5	68.6
Mexico	77.4	78.0	67.9	66.0	45.0
Korea, Republic of	56.5	61.7	59.6	67.0	47.5
Thailand	61.0	53.1	49.8	55.0	40.7
India	49.3	52.2	51.4	53.3	43.9
Turkey	69.5	56.1	65.3	64.1	42.8
Hungary	43.4	43.7	39.4	39.0	n.a.
Poland	51.1	50.0	39.8	38.9	35.6
Czechoslovakia	42.3	48.3	45.9	n.a.	n.a.
Czech Republic	n.a.	n.a.	n.a.	42.1	19.3
Slovak Republic	n.a.	n.a.	n.a.	42.9	28.3
Unweighted average	57.2	57.0	52.8	51.5	37.4

na: not available
Source: UN COMTRADE database.

Table 2.5

Change in the Composition of Exports, 1990-95

Period	Partner	Hungary	Poland	Slovak Republic	Czech Republic
	Correlation coefficients of RCAs (2-digit level: 63 and 99 categories for the world and EU)				
1993-95	World	.90	.96	.77	.91
	EU-12	.96	.91	.71	.95
	Correlation coefficients of RCAs in the EU market (4-digit level: 1,238 categories)				
1993-95	EU-12	.89	.80	.68	.58

Source of raw data: EU COMEXT and UN COMTRADE.

In addition to export growth rates and changes in the structure of exports, two other important indicators of adjustment can be inferred from the available trade statistics. The first is the change in the

---

[8] RCAs are calculated for total exports to the world and exports to the EU. The latter measure is defined as the EU's imports of a commodity from the Slovak Republic divided by total imports from the Slovak Republic relative to total imports by the EU of that commodity divided by total EU imports.

[9] RCAs are greater than one for: iron and steel, fertilizer, rubber manufactures, furniture and bedding, prefabricated buildings, non-primary plastics, footwear, cork and wood, paper, non-metallic mineral products, primary plastics, textiles, paper pulp, wooden manufactures, live animals, clothing, leather goods, cereals, metalworking machinery, tobacco products, pharmaceuticals, nonferrous metals, and organic chemicals. However, the exports of some of these products are still relatively small in volume.

unit value of exports, and the second is the number of new Slovak products that are exported. Increases in unit values provide valuable information about export performance, as they could indicate that the quality of products has been increasing, or that the need to discount goods to overcome reputation problems has been declining. The evolution of unit values supports the conclusion that Slovak firms have succeeded in upgrading quality--unit values were calculated at the 6-digit level for 1993 and 1995, and of the 94 product categories accounting for two-thirds of total exports to the EU in 1995, only 9 items accounting for 4 percent of total exports did not register an increase in unit values.

The number of new products exported also provides an indication of the underlying dynamism of exports. This indicator was obtained by calculating the number of items where exports were negligible or zero in 1993, and over ECU 500,000 in 1995. In 1995, the Slovak Republic exported 2,337 6-digit commodity items to the EU. Out of this total, 640 items or 27 percent were new on the basis of the above criterion. However, they account for only 5.7 percent of total exports in value terms. Of the 6-digit items accounting for 50 percent of total exports to the EU, only two are "new". Thus, although there is clearly a trend towards developing new product lines, these goods are not yet contributing significantly to total exports. These findings are consistent with the evidence presented earlier, namely, of underlying efforts to diversify exports and improve quality not yet translated into a significant increase in the volume of these exports.

Composition of Imports

According to national statistics, during 1996 the EU accounted for 35 percent of total imports, CEFTA for around 30 percent, and CIS countries for around 22 percent (mostly fuels and coal). The share in 1995 was 35 percent, though it increases to around 50 percent if EU and UN statistics are used.[10] Imports of capital goods and intermediate goods accounted for the bulk of total imports--30 and 47 percent, respectively (Table 2.6). The high ratio of imports to GDP (57 percent in 1996) implies that purchases of imported machinery amounted to 17 percent of GDP, or nearly half of fixed investment during 1996.

Large imports of capital goods accounting for a significant share of investment usually reflect industrial upgrading and improvements in product quality, which eventually translate into larger exports (or larger domestic production of import substitutes). This may also be the case in the Slovak Republic, although this result must be qualified by the relatively low share of manufacturing in total investment--16.7 percent of total investment, or 6 percent of GDP in 1996. This suggests that a significant share of imported machinery may not be employed in the production of traded goods, but rather in the services sector. Improvements in the efficiency of the services sector may very well improve the productivity of the sectors producing traded goods, but its impact on future exports and the production of import substitutes is more indirect and uncertain.

---

[10] The difference may be due to the fact that some Slovak exports and imports are routed through the Czech Republic. Note that the EU share remains lower in the case of the Slovak Republic, even if the EU statistics are more accurate than the national sources.

Table 2.6

Structure of Imports in the Visegrad Countries, 1990-96

		Structure of Imports by Major Groups (percent)			EU Share in Total Imports (percent)		
		1990	1995	1996	1990	1995	1996
Poland	consumer	37	34				
	intermediate	51	46	n.a.	59	70	n.a.
	capital	12	20				
Hungary	consumer	42	39				
	intermediate	42	31	n.a.	52	57	n.a.
	capital	16	30				
Czechoslovakia	consumer	24	n.a.				
	intermediate	60	n.a.	n.a.	46	n.a.	n.a.
	capital	16	n.a.				
Czech Republic	consumer	n.a.	20				
	intermediate	n.a.	47	n.a.	n.a.	68	n.a.
	capital	n.a.	33				
Slovak Republic	consumer	n.a.	21	23			
	intermediate	n.a.	51	47	n.a	35/50	37/n.a.
	capital	n.a.	28	30			

n.a.: not available.
Note: Shares for the Slovak Republic are for total imports; for the other countries are for imports from the EU.
Source: EU COMEXT, IMF Direction of Trade Statistics, National Sources.

Absorption of Technology and Market Penetration

The foregoing analysis suggests that Slovak enterprises have been making efforts to improve quality and diversify the export base, but also that these efforts have not yet translated into a significant increase in the exports of non-traditional products. The reason for this apparent delay in export response may be just due to natural lags, implying that larger exports of these products will eventually materialize. It may also reflect other factors, such as some loss in competitiveness deriving from real appreciation, remaining gaps in quality, and problems in establishing tighter commercial links with Western markets (in many cases, trade relations with the West were conducted by trade departments or companies located in Prague).

There are two main avenues through which enterprises in transforming economies can accelerate absorption of technology and acquire greater penetration in new markets. The first is through sub-contracting and processing arrangements, and the second is through equity participation by foreign companies, either in the form of joint ventures or foreign direct investment. It is useful to examine the extent to which Slovak enterprises have resorted to these two methods, as this may also shed some light on the prospects for future export performance.

Sub-contracting and processing. The establishment of links with foreign buyers and suppliers can materialize through sub-contracting and processing operations. Sub-contracting arrangements usually do not involve equity participation in Slovak firms by EU or other foreign partners. These partner firms provide intermediate inputs and equipment to Slovak enterprises, as well as a variety of services ranging from design, production and management techniques, to distribution and marketing. Sub-contracting is a traditional avenue for the transfer of "soft" technologies--suppliers of equipment or components often provide information on the technologies used by other (Western) firms they supply, and provide some technical assistance and training as well.

EU customs statistics on inward and outward processing trade provide information on the importance of sub-contracting. This is a customs regime under which EU-based enterprises ship components abroad for processing, and re-import the processed commodities free of duty. The share of CEE countries' exports to the EU under outward processing regimes increased from 10 percent in 1993 to 17 percent in 1995. Similarly, exports from the EU for processing abroad grew from 7 to 12 percent of total EU exports. However, the share of Slovak exports to the EU under this regime fell from 13 to 10 percent during the same period (Table 2.7).

Sub-contracting arrangements are very price sensitive and may have been affected by the real appreciation that occurred since independence. At the same time, the decline in the relative importance of processing trade between 1993-95 may not reflect a deterioration in the competitiveness of Slovak firms in all cases. For some enterprises, sub-contracting was regarded as a temporary strategy that allowed existing production capacity to be used and provided opportunities to establish contacts in export markets and upgrade management and quality systems. The EU customs data on outward processing provides some support for this possibility. Sub-sectors such as tools, vehicles, and furniture experienced a large reduction in the share of outward processing in total exports to the EU, but the total exports of these products grew significantly during the same period (Table 2.7).

Table 2.7
Slovak Republic's Use of the EU Outward Processing Customs Regime, 1993-95

	CN code	Share in Total Slovak Exports to EU		Growth Rate of Exports	Share in Total EU Exports to Slovak Republic	
		1993	1995	(1995/93)	1993	1995
Total		13.5	10.05	50.0	11.66	8.52
Meat, Vegetables	0	0.00	0.04	-1.1	0.16	0.00
Animal Products	1	5.58	0.00	62.9	0.02	0.04
Beverages, Fuels	2	0.00	0.02	18.6	0.02	0.05
Chemicals	3	0.17	1.19	60.8	2.21	1.02
Rubber, Leather	4	1.28	3.69	52.0	18.51	11.47
Textiles	5	0.69	0.66	47.5	66.17	59.23
Clothing, Footwear	6	54.00	50.68	31.2	35.30	28.75
Iron, Steel	7	0.22	0.49	43.3	1.74	2.75
Tools, Machinery	8	12.24	5.79	95.9	5.26	4.7
Instruments, Toys	9	13.12	6.11	40.5	6.58	4.55
Hides	41	0.94	42.58	47.0	41.99	39.22
Knitted Clothing	61	63.62	60.63	27.7	65.93	66.78
Other Clothing	62	71.16	76.83	26.5	42.77	50.98
Footwear	64	32.41	5.30	71.6	25.33	5.52
Non-Electric Machinery	84	3.33	8.07	50.5	4.02	2.67
Electric Machinery	85	13.91	11.29	113.7	11.85	12.80
Railway Equipment	86	0.27	5.88	144.3	0.05	8.05
Vehicles	87	34.15	1.5	159.3	0.71	0.47
Instruments	90	11.75	13.35	53.0	1.06	1.40
Furniture	94	11.82	5.96	35.6	0.72	1.96
Toys	95	52.03	20.85	37.7	25.28	15.79

Source: EU COMEXT.

Foreign direct investment. Although sub-contracting arrangements and imports of capital goods may be an important avenue of technological upgrading, foreign direct investment (either through joint ventures or majority equity participation) is likely to generate greater transfers of know-how to partner firms in CEE countries, as well as greater penetration in new export markets. Foreign direct investment (FDI) inflows to the Slovak Republic have generally been smaller as a share of GDP than in other Visegrad countries, and a relatively low share of the total went to manufacturing (Table 2.8). Noteworthy is the virtual absence of FDI in the machinery and engineering sectors, activities where great potential would appear to exist. Encouraging greater inflows of FDI could greatly strengthen Slovak external accounts, not only by opening new markets for Slovak companies, but also by increasing the flows of non-debt finance.

Table 2.8
Foreign Direct Investment in the Visegrad Countries

FDI	Poland	Hungary	Czech Republic	Slovak Republic
Cumulative 1992-1996 (US$ billion)	4.7	10.7	5.7	0.7
1996 (US$ billion)	2.14	1.79	0.87	0.15
1996 (percent of GDP)	1.5	4.1	1.7	0.8
Manufacturing Share, 1990-1995 (percent)	38	44	56	41

Sources: National Sources for US$ amounts; EBRD, Transition Report, 1996, for manufacturing shares.

Summary of Trade Indicators

As mentioned before, the Slovak Republic ran a large current account deficit during 1996, as a result of slow exports and buoyant imports. The magnitude of the deficit (10 percent of GDP), and the fact that it has been primarily financed by debt flows, suggests that some corrections are called for. However, a number of other indicators suggest that the underlying imbalance may not be so severe. For one, one-time factors accounted for 3 percent of GDP, reducing the underlying deficit to around 7 percent of GDP. Adjustment for cyclical factors, such as the recovery of output growth in Western Europe, would result in a smaller deficit. However, it is not clear the extent to which the recovery of EU markets will have an impact on Slovak exports. That will depend, among other factors, on the ability of Slovak enterprises to upgrade quality and penetrate markets in which they still hold a small share, relative to the other Visegrad countries.

There are some indications that Slovak enterprises have been making greater efforts to change the product mix and diversify than its counterparts in the other Visegrad countries. There is also some indication that the large volume of imports may be building future export capacity. These indicators would justify some optimism about future export performance. At the same time, there are other indicators suggesting that Slovak firms may be developing a handicap relative to their counterparts in other Visegrad countries, due to their lower progress in establishing closer links with Western firms. The possibility of a strong and sustained export recovery covering a wider range of products could be enhanced if the Slovak Republic were able to attract larger volumes of foreign capital and engage in closer partnerships with Western firms. In addition to reducing the flows of debt finance, that would also allow the Slovak Republic to speed the absorption of technology, and acquire greater access to the more sophisticated Western markets.

Trade Policy and Administration

The Slovak Republic's import regime is liberal, with much of its trade occurring under preferential trading arrangements, most importantly the customs union with the Czech Republic, the Association Agreement with the EU, the Central European Free Trade Area (CEFTA), and bilateral free trade agreements. These agreements cover over 80 percent of exports and 70 percent of imports. Indeed, the only major trading partners without a free trade agreement are Russia and the Ukraine, which provide some

20 percent of total imports (mostly fuels and natural resources that enter into the country free of duty). The applied Most-Favored Nation (MFN) tariffs are bound under the WTO.[11]

Tariffs

Tariffs on industrial products are generally very low, with an average (unweighted) statutory nominal tariff of about 8 percent (including agricultural items which often have significantly higher tariffs than manufactures) in 1996. The effective tariff burden is lower, reflecting the various preferential trading arrangements--total tariff revenue in 1996 was equivalent to only 3 percent of the total value of imports, of which about one third was generated by a temporary import surcharge on certain consumer goods. The surcharge was introduced in 1995 at the rate of 10 percent, and lowered to 7.5 percent in July 1996. As of late 1996, the surcharge applied to only 20 percent of all imports. Effective tariff rates were further reduced in January 1997, with the elimination of the import surcharge and the implementation of tariff reduction commitments embodied in the Europe Agreement with the EU and the WTO.[12]

The progress in removing trade restrictions was interrupted in May 1997, however, when the Government introduced an import deposit scheme, in response to the large trade deficit and a similar policy introduced by the Czech Republic, the Slovak Republic's main trading partner. This scheme had the effect of raising the effective tariff level by imposing additional transactions costs on importers and was vehemently opposed by the European Union.[13] In late July the Slovak authorities eliminated this controversial deposit scheme, while concurrently announcing the re-imposition of an import surcharge. The new surcharge was introduced at a rate of 7 percent, but should have a stronger impact on imports than the previous surcharge, as it applies over a larger base--over 80 percent of Slovak imports.

In order to meet its commitments under the Europe Agreement, the Slovak Republic will have to eliminate all tariffs on industrial imports from the EU by 2001. Tariffs on some 75 percent of all tariff lines are already at zero for imports originating in the EU, with the remainder currently taxed at 60 percent of the MFN rate (except for automobiles, which are taxed at a lower rate). These tariff lines cover, inter alia, certain chemicals, plastics, glass and paper products, as well as textiles and clothing. Duties on these items are to be reduced to 40 percent of the MFN rate in January 1999, and eliminated in January 2001. Duties on automobiles are currently 40 percent of the MFN rate and will drop to 20 percent of the MFN rate in January 1999, before being eliminated. Therefore, the implementation of the Europe Agreement implies some further trade opening, but its impact on imports and the output of most branches of industry

---

[11] See WTO (1996), "Trade Policy Review--Slovak Republic", Geneva: WTO, for a comprehensive description of Slovak Republic's trade policy.

[12] In January 1997, the Slovak Republic eliminated tariffs on goods imported from the EU listed in Annexes IV and V of the Europe Agreement, therefore reaching the halfway stage in reducing tariffs on goods listed in Annexes VI and VII (certain chemical products, plastics, textiles and clothing, types of glass and paper products, and automobiles). However, the re-imposition of an import surcharge in July 1997 is a setback for what otherwise represents a relatively open economy.

[13] Under the import deposit scheme, importers were required to deposit 20 percent of the value of imports in a non-interest bearing account for a six-month period. The import deposit scheme acts as a tariff on trade. The magnitude of the tariff equivalent of these deposit schemes is difficult to determine, as it depends on the terms on which importers can obtain credit. For large firms that are able to borrow at market rates or self-finance the deposit, the tariff equivalent would be at least in the 1 to 2 percent range; for small and medium sized companies it is likely to be higher.

should be moderate because the level of tariff protection is also moderate. The fiscal impact of these tariff reductions would also be moderate for the same reasons.

Full compliance with the Europe Agreement and other trade agreements will also require the eventual elimination of the new import surcharge. The elimination of the surcharge will have a significant impact on the budget--a 7 percent surcharge applied on 80 percent of imports has the potential to generate revenues of nearly 1.5 percent of GDP in the second half of 1997 and twice as much if applied for the whole year. This indicates the need for fiscal corrections in other areas of the budget during 1998 and in future years, in order to enable the elimination of the surcharge without generating fiscal imbalances.

Accession to the EU will also imply the adoption of the common external tariff of the EU by Slovak Republic. A comparison of the Slovak and EU MFN tariff rates suggests that adoption of the common external tariff should not give rise to any major difficulties. As shown in Table 2.9, the unweighted average tariff of the Slovak Republic is 8 percent, as compared to 6 percent for the EU (for all items). If the tariff schedules are compared on a line-by-line basis, Slovak tariffs are higher than those of the EU for 50 percent of all commodities. The average difference between tariff rates in the cases where the Slovak Republic has duties above EU levels is only 4 percentage points. A similar difference exists in the cases where Slovak rates are below EU rates (Table 2.9).[14]

Table 2.9
Comparison of MFN Tariffs, the Slovak Republic and the EU

	Slovak Republic	European Union
Total Number of Items (8 digit HS)	10,484	9,721
Unweighted Average of MFN Tariff, All Items	8.0%	5.9%
Unweighted Average of 8,620 Matched Items [1/]	5.8%	6.0%
Unweighted Average of All Slovak Tariffs > EU Tariffs (4,332 items)	8.0%	3.8%
Unweighted Average of All Slovak Tariffs < EU Tariffs (4,228 items)	3.9%	7.7%

1/ 1,002 items could not be matched.
Source: World Bank staff estimate based on national sources.

The industries that tend to have tariffs exceeding EU tariffs include wood products, pulp and paper, glass and cement, machinery and equipment, transport equipment, and furniture, toys, and lamps. The tariff differential for these categories ranges from 1.5 to 4.7 percentage points (Table 2.10.). Reducing the tariffs on these items would help increase competition, enhance productivity, and lower prices for consumers (note also that some of these sectors are major export industries--e.g., pulp and paper, glass, and transport equipment). The fiscal impact of further tariff reductions would be moderate. Import duties generated only 1.7 percent of GDP in revenues in 1996, out of which one third was generated by the old import surcharge, and much of the remainder generated by MFN tariffs on imports from outside the EU. Therefore, moving MFN duties down to EU levels would result in a revenue loss of the order of 0.3 percent of GDP.

---

[14] This comparison was limited to 8,620 items (out of a total of 10,500 items) that could be matched in the two tariff schedules.

Table 2.10
Sectoral Comparison of MFN Tariffs, the Slovak Republic and the EU

Product	Slovak Tariff	EU Tariff	Difference
Animals, Animal Products	2.5	8.6	6.2
Vegetable Products	4.8	6.5	1.8
Animal and Vegetable Oil	8.7	8.3	-0.4
Beverages, Tobacco	9.4	20.1	10.6
Minerals and Fuels	1.8	0.9	-0.9
Chemical Products	4.6	4.3	-0.3
Plastics	5.6	6.0	0.5
Leather and Hides	2.4	3.2	0.7
Wood Products, Excluding Furniture	4.2	2.7	-1.5
Pulp and Paper	8.7	5.1	-3.6
Textiles and Clothing	7.9	9.6	1.7
Footwear and Headgear	9.4	8.8	-0.6
Glass and Cement	9.2	4.5	-4.7
Jewelry, Precious Metals	2.4	1.3	-1.1
Base Metals and Products	4.8	4.0	-0.8
Machinery and Equipment	5.3	3.1	-2.2
Transport Equipment	8.0	5.4	-2.6
Precision Instruments	4.2	3.7	-0.4
Arms	3.2	3.5	0.2
Furniture, Toys, Miscellaneous Manufactures	7.2	4.3	-2.9
Art works, Antiques	1.4	0.0	-1.4
All Products (8,620 items)	5.8	6.0	0.2

Source: National tariff schedules.

Non-tariff Policies

Non-automatic import licensing is applied to only one significant product--coal. Recently this was complemented by a quota on non-alcoholic beverages from the Czech Republic, and the possibility of imposing quantitative restrictions on imports of additional food products is being considered. Non-automatic export licensing is used to monitor and control the export of narcotics, poisons, arms, as well as a limited number of "sensitive" goods (coal, meat, dairy products, wood, certain minerals). Licenses are allocated on a first-come, first-serve basis until the quantity limit specified in the relevant Ministerial decree has been reached. Such export restrictions, if binding, are an implicit subsidy to domestic industries and may raise their level of effective protection. A new decree requiring fewer export license requirements is under preparation that will reduce the coverage of export license requirements. Under the Europe Agreement, all such restrictions are to be eliminated by 2002. There are also export restrictions imposed by bilateral trade arrangements, mostly pertaining to apparel and products that have been subjected to the threat of anti-dumping or safeguard actions. However, quotas for the 20 items affected by such restrictions in the EU market were not binding in 1996--utilization rates ranged from a low of zero percent to a high of 78 percent (the average was 31 percent).

Customs administration is close to being harmonized with EU rules and procedures. The EU Single Administrative Document is used (the EUR-1 and EUR-2 forms). A new Customs law modeled on the EU was adopted in July 1996, and regulations are implemented according to EU procedures. Rules of origin are basically harmonized across the EU and CEFTA. Since January 1997, diagonal cumulation across all countries operating under free trade agreements has been allowed.

As in the case of many countries that have experienced significant increases in imports over a relatively short period of time, some sectors have pressed for the imposition of higher levels of protection. These are mostly sectors that are negatively affected by competition from imports, such as agriculture and food processing, and has included trade with the Czech Republic, which is duty free. Partly in response to such pressures, the Government has been developing anti-dumping, countervailing duty and safeguards legislation, in line with its rights and obligations under the WTO.

Policy Issues in the Transition to EU Accession

EU membership implies free trade with other Member States and the transfer of trade policy to the EU. Free intra-EU trade consists not only of the elimination of tariffs and contingent measures of protection such as anti-dumping, but also of quantitative restrictions and other equivalent measures. As noted above, the existing Customs law and the implementation of regulations are already harmonized with EU law and procedures to a significant extent. Under the Europe Agreement, elimination of tariffs on trade with the EU is to be achieved by January 1, 2001, and quantitative restrictions are to be eliminated by 2002. Thus, full implementation of the Europe Agreement will result in the elimination of trade barriers before accession negotiations are likely to be completed.

The Europe Agreement will largely determine the shape of Slovak trade policy in the next few years. However, the Government still faces some policy options during the pre-accession period. These include: (i) the transition path towards adoption of the EU's Common External Tariff (CET); (ii) the utility of applying instruments of contingent protection, such as anti-dumping mechanisms; and (iii) the decision of whether liberalization in the services area should be extended on a MFN basis.[15] The Government must face these trade issues while also reducing the trade imbalances that emerged in 1996, and ensure that the Slovak Republic approaches the period of accession with a sustainable situation in its external accounts.

Approaching the Common External Tariff

The main policy issue during the pre-accession period is whether to start moving towards the CET before accession, or whether to maintain the tariffs on goods imported from outside the EU until accession. There would be economic justification for adopting the CET immediately, if it implied a lower average rate of protection with less dispersion. The comparison of MFN tariffs applied by the EU and the Slovak Republic suggests that the two tariff structures are generally similar, but in a number of instances adoption of the EU's CET would increase protection. Examples include beverages and tobacco (20 percent versus 9 percent), textiles and clothing (9.6 percent vs. 7.9 percent), food items, and certain types of electronic equipment. These averages hide a significant degree of dispersion, as there are 1,300 items at the 8-digit level where EU tariffs are 5 to 20 percentage points higher than in Slovak Republic. Raising tariffs to EU levels before accession would be economically harmful by reducing competition from imports and raising prices for consumers. The fact that the Slovak Republic has bound its tariffs in the WTO further bolsters this argument, as any increase in bound rates as part of a strategy to gradually converge to the CET may give rise to compensation claims in the WTO. This is less likely to occur in the accession context, as a result of the WTO rules in this connection (Art. XXIV GATT).

The best option with regard to tariffs would be to maintain an independent tariff policy until accession, and limit any changes in tariffs to reducing those that are now significantly above the EU's MFN level. As noted earlier, there are almost 1,000 items where Slovak MFN rates are above those of the EU. Although in many cases the free trade agreements that the Slovak Republic has signed implies that traders pay lower duty rates, consideration should be given to the possible trade diversion that may be induced by higher tariffs. This suggests it would be beneficial to reduce tariffs on these items to the EU level.

---

[15] For a discussion of trade policies for acceding countries see Messerlin, P. (1996), "The MFN and Preferential Trade Policies of the Central and East European Countries: Singapore and Geneva are on the Shortest Road to Brussels," unpublished manuscript.

Other Trade Policy Instruments

The Government is developing legislation and mechanisms that will enable Slovak industries to petition for protection against imports in a variety of circumstances. These include action against both "unfair" imports that injure domestic industries (goods that are being sold in the Slovak Republic at prices below those charged by exporters in their home market; and goods that have been subsidized), and against "fair" imports (cases where the domestic industry cannot compete against foreign industries that are not dumping and have not been subsidized). In terms of dealing with pressures for protection, experience with "unfair-trade" laws (in particular anti-dumping laws) around the world strongly suggests that it is an inefficient and costly instrument. Anti-dumping mechanisms frequently make no economic sense--they impute anti-competitive behavior to exporters for practices that are usually fully compatible with domestic competition law. Moreover, the administrative resource requirements for application of a WTO-consistent anti-dumping regime are significant. It is preferable to rely on a mechanism that allows imports to be restricted in instances where they are seriously injuring domestic producers, without having to impute "unfair" behavior on foreign exporters. Such a "safeguard" mechanism is under development in the Slovak Republic, and should be sufficient to deal with pressures for protection. It should also be noted that upon EU accession an antidumping law will become redundant, as these instruments will be applied by the European Commission.[16]

Under the Europe Agreement the quantitative restrictions implied by existing import and export licensing must be eliminated. From both an economic and administrative efficiency point of view, it is advisable that this abolition be pursued on an accelerated basis and that it is applied on an MFN basis. Maintenance of such measures against countries with which no free trade agreements have been signed may otherwise give rise to costly trade diversion.

Extending Liberalization of Services on an MFN Basis

One of the greatest challenges confronting the Government during the transition to EU accession is to ensure that trade policy is conducive to growth in trade. Liberalizing the access to service markets more generally than foreseen under the Europe Agreement is of particular importance in this connection. Care must be taken that a situation does not emerge that favors EU-based entities over other service providers. Without action to expand multilateral commitments in the area of services, there is a danger that this may occur. For example, currently the Slovak Republic has made specific liberalization commitments for only about 50 percent of its service sector under the WTO's General Agreement on Trade in Services (GATS). Of these commitments, only one half imply a full commitment to the national treatment principle for all possible ways of contesting the market. Therefore, in the majority of services there is no commitment in the GATS for free access to markets. However, such a commitment will be implied vis-à-vis European firms in the context of the Slovak Republic's accession. Extending this to third parties by expanding the coverage of GATS commitments, would help to create an environment that is more conducive to foreign investment and economic growth.

Addressing the External Imbalance before Accession

The implementation of the Europe Agreement will imply the elimination of the surcharge and further reduction in tariffs until the year 2001, when trade with the EU is expected to be fully liberalized.

---

[16] A detailed enumeration of the arguments against the implementation of anti-dumping procedures can be found in J. Michael Finger (ed.) 1993, *Antidumping*, Ann Arbor: University of Michigan Press.

If the Government decides to lower tariffs on imports from non-EU countries, in the cases where these tariffs are higher than the EU's CET, there would be additional pressures on imports, although these pressures would be moderate, because the reduction in tariffs would be very small in most cases.

The Slovak Republic faces the task of reducing large external imbalances registered in 1996 and in 1997 while eliminating the new import surcharge and lowering import tariffs in order to comply fully with the Europe Agreement. Trade protection, be it the import deposit scheme (introduced in May 1997 and later eliminated), the new import surcharge (introduced in July 1997), or other policies to restrict imports, are not adequate instruments to deal with trade imbalances, because they represent a violation of trade arrangements and also because they tend to protect inefficient producers, thus hindering needed enterprise restructuring.

Success in reducing trade imbalances while also removing trade distortions will depend on, *inter alia*, fiscal corrections in other areas of the budget, NBS's success in meeting its new monetary targets, the ability of enterprises to offset the loss of traditional export markets by gaining access to the more sophisticated markets of the EU, and the ability to attract larger inflows of non-debt finance.

As argued above, success in establishing closer links with Western firms through larger FDI would contribute to greater penetration of Slovak exports in the EU and other markets and also reduce reliance on debt finance. Limited flows of foreign direct investment seem to result from the exclusion of foreign companies and individuals from the privatization process, and a general perception that foreign capital is not welcome, rather than formal obstacles to the entry of foreign capital in the Company Law or other pieces of legislation. For this reason, the Government may envisage measures to encourage greater inflows of FDI during the pre-accession period. As mentioned in Chapter III, this could be achieved by allowing greater participation of foreign firms in the privatization of remaining State assets, and encouraging greater participation in the enterprises that have already been privatized, especially those privatized in the second wave.

CHAPTER III: ENTERPRISE REFORM IN THE CONTEXT OF EU ACCESSION

Introduction

One of the most important tasks in the transition to a market economy is the restructuring of former state-owned enterprises. This restructuring can be thought of as the transition from a highly distorted economy with many large loss-making enterprises, to a market economy in which most enterprises are profitable. Improvements in enterprise efficiency and profitability set the foundations for sustained economic growth and an increase in living standards. Restructuring will also be a precondition for accession to the European Union, as it is necessary to ensure that Slovak enterprises can compete with EU enterprises without the need for Government subsidies.

Progress at restructuring proceeds faster when corporate governance is improved by privatization, and the enterprise is subject to a hard budget constraint by the Government and its creditors. The Slovak Republic has achieved significant progress in privatizing and improving governance, with the near completion of the second wave of privatization and the consolidation of ownership that has taken place. The initial environment in which enterprises operated also encouraged restructuring. In the macroeconomic area, enterprises faced a situation of fiscal discipline, open trade, a competitive exchange rate, and moderate wage pressures, which created an overall environment of financial discipline and enabled an early export-based recovery. Financial discipline was further strengthened by an overall decline in real bank credits, particularly to troubled enterprises. The combination of these factors allowed the Slovak Republic to generate positive net enterprise profits in the early stages of the transition (a period when most transitional economies recorded net losses), and to improve financial performance further, as indicated by a reduction of 6 percent of GDP in gross losses between 1993 and 1995.

While there was an overall improvement in financial performance after independence, the figures also reveal the existence of a hard core of loss-makers, as indicated by gross losses of 5.6 percent of GDP in 1995. More worrisome, the progress in reducing loss-making activities seems to have been interrupted in 1996, as suggested by preliminary estimates of gross losses of 8.8 percent of GDP during that year. The reasons for such an apparent deterioration in financial performance are not entirely clear. The slowdown in export growth and the growth of wages above productivity probably contributed to this outcome. Bank lending also resumed strongly in 1996, although it cannot be determined whether this increased lending involved a relaxation of financial discipline, i.e., whether some of this lending was directed towards loss-makers.

Whereas the recent increase in gross losses merits a more detailed analysis of its causes, the Government may already start removing the legal and institutional obstacles to further enterprise restructuring, both at the level of enterprises themselves and at the level of banks. This chapter and the next chapter (which addresses the financial sector) identify the improvements in the institutional and regulatory environment that would encourage enterprises and banks to continue restructuring. The two chapters also argue that this strategy is superior than any attempt by the Government to manage the restructuring of these enterprises directly.

The current chapter is structured as follows. The second section makes an assessment of the progress that has already been achieved at privatization. The third section examines the progress that has been achieved at restructuring and eliminating loss-making activities over time and in comparison with other CEE countries. The fourth section provides an analysis of the legal and institutional framework. It examines the degree of approximation with EU legislation, and the improvements in the regulatory framework that would facilitate further restructuring.

Progress in Privatization

An Overview of the Current Status of Privatization

The Slovak Republic implemented its privatization program in two major waves, and has used both coupon privatization in which assets are essentially given away to citizens, and standard methods in which assets are sold directly to investors. As shown in Table 3.1, estimates of privatization in Central and Eastern Europe indicate that the Slovak Republic had achieved a progress at privatization comparable to countries seen as leading reformers by end-1995. During 1996, the Slovak Republic carried out a rapid sale of most of its remaining manufacturing enterprises. As a result, today most enterprises are in private hands, and the share of GDP generated by the private sector has increased to more than 70 percent.

Despite these positive developments, several large enterprises remain in State hands. These are primarily public utilities, armaments, and energy companies, although there are also enterprises in other sectors, such as agro-industry. In addition, the state still has equity participation in other enterprises, with and without controlling interests. If firms not scheduled for privatization are included, such as essential enterprises, then state ownership still accounts for approximately 50 percent of the original equity of medium and large enterprises in State hands at the start of transformation process (see Table 3.2), suggesting a significant scope for further privatization. At the same time, there has been a strong bias towards domestic ownership in the privatization of State assets (Figure 3.1), suggesting the scope for greater participation of foreign capital in the Slovak Republic, not only in the enterprises awaiting privatization, but also in those that have already been privatized. Failure to attract more foreign capital could lead to a slower absorption of modern technology and more restricted access to foreign markets, with adverse medium-run effects on enterprise restructuring and profitability.

Table 3.1
Extent of Privatization in CEE Countries (end 1995)
(percentage of enterprises and of output)

	EBRD (Rank)	OECD (All Enterprises)	World Bank (Large Manufacturing Enterprises)	
			(Enterprises)	(Output)
Bulgaria	2	15	8	7
Czech Republic	4	87	89	93
Hungary	4	82	67	65
Poland	3	55	57	59
Romania	3	20	15	12
Slovak Republic	3	74	79	83
Slovenia	3	54	41	41

Sources: EBRD: *Infrastructure and Savings* (1996).
OECD: *Trends and Policies in Privatization* (1996).
World Bank staff estimates for large manufacturing enterprises.

The First Wave of Privatization

The Government's privatization program has been subject to several changes since its start in 1991 (see Box 3.1). The privatization program divided enterprises in two broad groups according to size, and was implemented in two parallel tracks. About 10,000 small shops and establishments were privatized in 1991-94 using various methods, whereas the privatization program for medium and large enterprises was further divided into two waves.[17] In an innovative mass privatization program, enterprises were sold to those citizens who obtained coupons from the Government (a nominal fee was charged). Citizens could use the coupons to bid for shares in the enterprises in both the Slovak Republic and the Czech Republic. About 2.6 million Slovak citizens or almost three-quarters of the eligible population bid for equity in the 487 enterprises offered in the first coupon wave.

Table 3.2
Privatization of Medium and Large Enterprises
(Book Value of Equity, end-1996)

	Book Value of Equity (Sk billion)	Percent of the Total
Voucher Privatization	80	18
Standard Methods	146	33
"Essential Enterprises" not Scheduled for Privatization	100	23
Left to be Privatized	110	25
Total	436	100

Source: National sources.

Figure 3.1
Sources of Revenue from Privatization
(cumulative, end-1995)

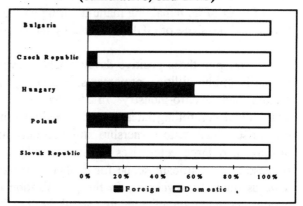

Source: National sources.

Individual coupon holders were allowed to turn over the management of their coupons to investment privatization funds. The funds (165 in the Slovak Republic) were formed spontaneously by individual entrepreneurs, enterprises, and financial institutions. A key restriction was that a fund could not hold more than 20 percent of the shares in any company. The funds emerged as key players in the privatization process. Encouraged by aggressive advertising, over two-thirds of coupon holders entrusted their coupons to funds. The twenty largest funds controlled more than 50 percent of the coupons. The coupon scheme privatized 47 percent of the equity of enterprises that were earmarked for privatization during the first wave, while standard methods privatized 24 percent. The balance remained in the hands of the National Property Fund (NPF).

The Second Wave of Privatization

After the division of Czechoslovakia, Slovak policy makers raised several concerns about coupon privatization, primarily on the grounds that it did not generate strong corporate governance, and announced that the second wave of privatization would rely more on standard methods. A vote by Parliament of no confidence resulted in the emergence of an interim Government which announced its intent to return to coupon methods for the second wave of privatization. However, this government did not succeed in carrying out its plans since later that year it was replaced by the newly elected Meciar Government which

---

[17] The rapid privatization of small retail shops and other establishments was pursued through the direct sale to domestic legal and natural persons. This privatization of small enterprises totaled approximately 12 billion Slovak crowns (i.e., US$ 400 million) and was finalized by April of 1994.

canceled the second coupon privatization and announced the sale of Sk230 billion of equity through standard methods.

Box 3.1 Chronology of Privatization	
Mid 1991 - Mid 1992	Transformation of enterprises into joint stock companies and preparation of privatization projects.
July 1991 - April 1992	Registration for coupon books by individuals.
February - April 1992	"Zero round": Transfer of coupon points by individuals to the investment funds.
May - December 1992	Five bidding rounds of coupon privatization.
May 1993	Distribution of shares of coupon privatization to successful bidders.
Early 1993	Preparation of second wave of privatization and shift in privatization strategy.
March - September 1994	Interim coalition government in office.
September 1994	Sale of coupon books for second wave.
September 30/October 1, 1994	National elections.
December 12, 1994	Formation of new government.
December 14, 1994	Postponement of second wave of coupon privatization.
July 1995	Cancellation of second wave of coupon privatization and replacement with standard privatization methods.
January 1, 1996	Distribution of "privatization bonds" to coupon holders.
August 5, 1996	Beginning of trading of "privatization bonds".
October 22, 1996	Announcement of preliminary list of companies whose shares are to be sold in exchange for bonds.

Source: National sources.

To encourage standard methods, generous financial terms were provided to potential buyers. They could make a downpayment of around 20 percent of the sales price, with the remainder paid in installments. Often, the sales price was agreed at an amount below the book value of the enterprise. In addition, the installment payments would be reduced by the extent of future investments to be undertaken by the new owners. As mentioned above, privatization proceeded rapidly under these conditions.

The cancellation of the second wave of coupon privatization led the Government to exchange the coupon books that had already been issued for "privatization bonds" with a total value of Sk33 billion, or about 6 percent of GDP. The bonds were issued in January 1996, have a face value of Sk10,000 each, a maturity of 5 years, and bear an interest rate equal to the NBS's discount rate. Bondholders can use the bonds in the following ways: (i) hold the bonds until maturity and receive the full principal and interest; (ii) sell the bonds before maturity for a guaranteed price of 75 percent of their nominal value; (iii) purchase health and pension insurance or apartments from the municipalities; (iv) bid for shares in enterprises to be offered by the NPF; and (v) repay debts owed to the NPF arising from sales.

Companies and individuals with debts to the NPF have found it attractive to buy bonds from citizens at a discounted price and use the bonds at their face value to settle their obligations to the NPF (the bonds are accepted at their full face value). The Government has encouraged secondary trading of the privatization bonds in the RMS stock trading system, which began in August 1996. Although the Government has intervened to enforce a minimum price, many bondholders have been willing to sell at a price lower than the guaranteed minimum, rather than wait for a buyer through the RMS system at the guaranteed price. The NPF redeemed about Sk3 billion of the bonds in 1996, and expects to redeem more than Sk10 billion in 1997. To this end, the NPF has already offered to exchange bonds for shares totaling Sk8 billion in a preliminary list of 155 companies.

Essential and Strategic Enterprises

When the second coupon wave was canceled, 29 enterprises with a combined equity of over Sk100 billion were earmarked as "essential" enterprises and excluded from privatization in the near future. They included utility companies in the energy and water sectors, armaments and machinery, post and telecommunications, pharmaceuticals, agro-industry, and railways. The Government also has attempted to enact a law that would empower it to veto decisions in some 45 "strategic" enterprises with a total equity of about Sk110 billion, although some of these enterprises have already been privatized. The state veto power was to be exercised over important decisions, such as the distribution of dividends and representation on management and supervisory boards. However, the Constitutional Court declared such veto power as unconstitutional, and future attempts to impose similar limitations on property rights should be avoided. These two special categories of enterprises in which the Government intends to retain substantial control have created the impression that the Government is restricting the normal functioning of a market economy. Concurrently, however, the Government has manifested that it is considering reducing the number of enterprises in these two categories, a development which would enhance the perception of Slovak commitment to a market economy.

During 1997, the NPF intends to privatize some Sk60 billion of equity out of Sk110 billion still in state ownership, but slated for privatization (Table 3.2). This includes minority stakes remaining in NPF ownership and majority or larger stakes in some 10 well-known companies (most of which are on the "strategic" list). Furthermore, the Ministry of Privatization is preparing projects to privatize, by mid-1988, one bus company, five water and sewage companies, and some health clinics, amounting to a total of over Sk30 billion of equity.

Increasing Ownership Concentration

One of the concerns about coupon privatization in the Czech and Slovak Republics was that it would lead to widely dispersed ownership of enterprises. Critics argued that enterprises would be owned by thousands of small investors who would not have the ability or resources to bring about needed restructuring. This concern was partially dispelled by the rise of the coupon investment funds who became the primary owners of most enterprises included in the first wave of voucher privatization in the Slovak Republic. At least in some cases, these funds elected their representatives to sit on the supervisory and management boards of the enterprises and attempted to work with management to bring about restructuring.

In the last couple of years, there appears to have been additional concentration of enterprise ownership through mergers, acquisitions, and buyouts. In some cases, existing large owners, for example funds, simply traded shares with each other. In other cases, new investors purchased shares from existing owners who were often small investors who wanted cash for their shares. It is reported that many of the new investors were managers who wanted to take control of their own companies. Some of these purchases were financed by bank loans, though the amount of bank loans used for this purpose is unknown.

A complementary development has been the transformation of most investment funds into holding companies. Instead of the funds having small minority stakes in many companies, these new holding companies have restructured their investment portfolios so that they have large majority stakes in fewer companies. This transformation of investment funds into holding companies was made possible by a concentration of fund ownership parallel to the concentration of enterprise ownership. Large investors have bought the shares of the funds on the stock markets, accumulated controlling stakes, and then at a general meeting of fund shareholders approved a conversion of the fund into a holding company. The computation of the Herfindahl index (a widely used measure of ownership concentration) for more than 600 firms privatized in the first wave confirms that concentration has increased significantly--the index increased from 0.126 to 0.172 between 1993 and 1995, implying a significant increase in concentration. The trend towards increasing ownership concentration seems to have proceeded during 1996.

Advantages of Concentrated Ownership

This increasing concentration of ownership will probably benefit the economy, as it will tend to improve governance and encourage enterprise restructuring (one or two large shareholders will have greater incentive and ability to monitor the performance of managers). This conclusion is supported by an econometric study of ownership concentration in 706 firms in the Czech Republic, a country that has experienced a similar increase in ownership concentration. The evidence suggests that a firm with higher ownership concentration has higher profits and a higher valuation on the stock market.[18]

Enterprise ownership is likely to change further, particularly for the newly privatized enterprises in the second wave. The initial owners of a second wave enterprise (for example, the managers who bought the enterprise from the NPF) may sell their ownership interest or merge with another company. This should not be prohibited or discouraged, because it may result in better owners and faster restructuring. In particular, the new owners may decide to bring in foreign capital, technology, and management skills. Greater foreign participation could contribute to further restructuring and greater access to foreign markets. However, a foreign company may only be willing to invest in a Slovak company if they acquire some control in the management of that company, in order to protect its investment. It is reasonable to assume that several new Slovak owners would accept the need for greater foreign participation, and would find solutions agreeable to themselves and foreign investors.

Potential Problems with Concentrated Ownership

Although the greater concentration of ownership will on balance be favorable to the Slovak economy (because it will improve governance and encourage enterprise restructuring), it may also generate problems that will have to be monitored. For one, the new majority shareholder who controls the company may take advantage of minority shareholders by transferring company profits directly to himself and not pay reasonable dividends to all shareholders. The most common way to achieve this is to sell the company's production to a trading company owned by the majority shareholder at low transfer prices, thus shifting profits from one company to another. Weak protection of minority shareholders also makes it difficult for enterprises to sell equity to small investors in a public offering, and also discourages foreign portfolio investors such as mutual funds from investing in the shares of Slovak enterprises.[19] Corporate governance is most effective when it involves a combination of concentrated ownership and legal protection

---

[18] See Claessens, S., S. Djankov, and G. Pohl (1997), "Ownership and Corporate Governance: Evidence from the Czech Republic", The World Bank, Washington DC.

[19] Weak minority shareholder protection is probably the major reason why investment funds converted into holding companies. Initially, funds were not allowed to own more than 20 percent of the shares of any company, and this limit was later reduced to 10 percent. To escape these ownership restrictions, the funds found legal loopholes to convert into joint stock companies that did not have such restrictions.

of smaller investors.[20] Whereas ownership seems to be more concentrated in Slovak Republic, protection of minority shareholders remains deficient.

Another possible problem is that these changes in ownership may result in monopolies or oligopolies in certain industries. For example, a single investor may have become the controlling owner of most of the enterprises selling a particular product or service, and thus is in a position to raise prices and earn excessive profits. Although it is difficult to determine the extent to which greater concentration has led to monopolies, it is important to ensure that the Antimonopoly Office has the resources and legal authority to review mergers and takeovers for anti-competitive impact. This is discussed in more detail below.

A third potential problem lies less on greater concentration per se, but on the risks arising from the way enterprises were sold in the second wave of privatization. Purchases at substantial discounts and possible default on installment payments may lead to lower revenues for the National Property Fund (NPF) and could reduce its capacity to meet its financial obligations. Defaults may be particularly large if many new owners sell the enterprise's assets for cash, creating companies that are empty "shells" with only debt obligations. Although the record of payments to the NPF still seems to be high--around 80-90 percent of the scheduled payments--it is essential to monitor the performance of new owners to prevent perverse behavior and abuse. The possibility to reduce installments through investments may also distort investment decisions and reallocate capital away from more productive uses, because they create an artificial incentive to invest in enterprises included in the second wave (these annual investment commitments may amount to 1 percent of GDP).

Progress in Restructuring

During the transition to a market economy, enterprises in the Slovak Republic and other CEE countries experienced severe shocks unlike anything experienced by their counterparts in Western countries. The collapse of CMEA trade resulted in a sharp contraction of the demand for their products, and they have been forced to find new markets in Western countries with higher quality standards. Lower trade barriers meant fierce competition from imported products even in their home markets. These problems were aggravated by the related collapse of GDP and purchasing power that affected all CEE countries in the early stages of the transition.

The extent to which enterprises have coped with these shocks can be assessed by examining enterprise data for the CEE countries after 1992 (the period is dictated by data availability). The exercise can be conducted both at the aggregate level and for a sample of large manufacturing enterprises. It is useful to consider the two sets in making such an evaluation.[21] The larger set can capture not only losses generated in sectors such as agriculture, but also transfers of losses between the energy sector and other sectors, due to changes in energy prices. The smaller sample is more representative of the universe of enterprises operating in the traded goods sectors and capable of generating exports. In both cases, the analysis has to be qualified by problems of data quality and comparability, due to differences in coverage,

---

[20] See Shleifer, A., and R. Vishny (1996), "A Survey of Corporate Governance", National Bureau of Economic Research, Working Paper No. 5554.

[21] The larger sample comprises all enterprises with more than 15-25 employees. The smaller sample comprises the largest 700-1,000 enterprises in the manufacturing sector, accounting for 40-90 percent of employment in the sector. See Claessens, S., S. Djankov, and G. Pohl (1997), "Determinants of Performance of Manufacturing Firms in Seven European Transition Economies," The World Bank, Washington DC.

and accounting standards and practices across countries. These figures may not reflect with accuracy the true financial situation of enterprises in CEE countries, but they probably provide a reasonable idea about the trends in financial performance in each country.

Gross and net losses of enterprises declined significantly between 1993 and 1995 in all Visegrad countries and Slovenia, as shown in Table 3.3. The reduction in gross losses amounted to 6-7 percent of GDP in the Czech Republic, Hungary and the Slovak Republic, and to 2-3 percent of GDP in Poland and Slovenia. The reason for the smaller decline in Poland and Slovenia is probably due to the fact that enterprise losses peaked at earlier dates in these two countries due to specific shocks--Poland's GDP collapsed during a drastic stabilization program implemented in early 1990, while Slovenia's GDP contracted sharply during 1991 and 1992, as a result of independence from the former Yugoslavia.

Table 3.3
Gross and Net Enterprise Losses in Selected CEE Countries, 1992-96
(percent of GDP)

	1992	1993	1994	1995	1996
Gross Profits					
Czech Republic	n.a.	16.4	13.7	11.8	8.9
Hungary	8.1	6.7	7.3	5.3	n.a
Poland	11.6	10.3	10.0	10.2	9.1
Slovak Republic	n.a.	18.5	14.0	13.9	14.5
Slovenia	2.5	3.9	4.5	6.2	n.a
Gross Losses					
Czech Republic	n.a.	10.9	5.7	3.5	4.3
Hungary	14.2	10.1	7.2	3.1	n.a
Poland	8.6	6.2	3.9	3.5	3.8
Slovak Republic	n.a.	11.5	7.2	5.6	8.8
Slovenia	16.7	8.1	6.4	6.2	n.a
Net Profits (+ equals profit, - equals loss)					
Czech Republic	n.a.	5.5	8.0	8.3	4.6
Hungary	-6.1	-3.4	0.1	2.2	n.a
Poland	3.0	4.1	6.1	6.7	5.3
Slovak Republic	n.a.	7.0	6.8	8.3	5.7
Slovenia	-14.2	-4.2	-1.9	0.0	n.a

n.a.: not available
Note: Preliminary figures.
Sources: Statistical offices in the respective countries.

There are three aspects of the Slovak adjustment that merit attention. First, the 6 percent of GDP reduction in gross losses between 1993 and 1995 can be considered as a good result, given the contraction of traditional export markets (primarily in the Czech Republic) that took place during this period. Second, the ratio of gross and net profits to GDP in the Slovak Republic seem larger than in the other CEE countries. That reveals a segment of highly profitable enterprises, and may help explain the high investment ratio in the Slovak Republic, as internally generated funds (retained profits and depreciation) constitute a large source of investment finance in most economies. Finally, there is also evidence of a relatively large core of loss-makers in the Slovak Republic, as indicated by gross losses of 5.6 percent of GDP in 1995.

The preliminary numbers for 1996 are more worrisome, as they indicate a reversal of the declining trend in gross losses observed after independence--losses increased to 8.8 percent of GDP during that year. Approximately 50 percent of the losses were generated in manufacturing, 15 percent in agriculture, and the rest in transport, communications, and other services, excluding the energy sector, which generated profits (Appendix Table 2.10). Within the manufacturing sector, the largest losses were generated in the heavy machinery (which includes the former large arms manufacturers) and agro-industry, but many other sub-sectors also have loss-making enterprises (Table 3.4).

The reasons for such an increase in gross losses are not entirely clear. The slowdown in exports, the higher prices of imported fuel from Russia, the growth of wages above productivity, and the larger depreciation expenses (resulting from the investment expansion) probably contributed to this outcome. The increase in gross losses could also be due to asset stripping and/or the divestiture of enterprises into smaller units, some of which are profitable while others are making losses. However, the pronounced decrease in net profits--from 8.3 to 5.7 percent of GDP--indicates a marked deterioration in overall profitability in 1996, suggesting that this last factor was not a major cause of the increase in gross losses during that year.

Table 3.4
Sectoral Breakdown of Losses in Manufacturing during 1996

	Number of Companies	Losses (percent of GDP)
Total Manufacturing	1050	4.6
of which:		(percent of the total)
Food Products	172	10.7
Textiles	96	3.8
Paper and Pulp	54	4.9
Chemicals	25	4.8
Non-Metal Products	63	9.5
Metal Products	131	10.3
Heavy Machinery	122	28.0
Transport Equipment	30	9.2
Other	357	18.8

Source: National sources.

The sample of large manufacturing enterprises allows for a breakdown of financial statements and provides important complementary information to the aggregate figures. As shown in Table 3.5, between 1992 and 1995 the Slovak Republic was able to eliminate enterprises in the worst category--the so-called value subtractors, or enterprises which are not able to cover even their material costs. The share of enterprises in the two following categories (from worst to best) also decreased, resulting in a decline in the overall number of loss-makers in the sample, from 52 percent in 1992 to 44 percent in 1995. Despite these improvements, the number of large loss-making enterprises still looked comparatively high in 1995.

There is no reliable information on the share of losses generated by essential and strategic enterprises (which cannot be sent to bankruptcy or liquidation by their creditors). There is no accurate information on how these losses are financed either, although depreciation and unpaid interest are likely to account for a large share. Depreciation expenses not matched by actual resources imply the decapitalization of the enterprise and its eventual demise. Unpaid interests (estimated at 1.5-2 percent of GDP per year) automatically capitalized by banks imply an indirect form of financing that helps keep the loss-maker afloat (it is equivalent to a situation where the bank extends a new loan to allow the enterprise to pay the interests due). Bank lending to loss-makers (above and beyond the amounts implied by the recapitalization of unpaid interests) was probably very limited, given the contraction of real bank credits after 1993. However, the possibility that some loss-makers benefited from fresh bank loans during 1996 (a period where bank lending increased by 15 percent) cannot be discarded. Finally, there is no reliable information on inter-enterprise arrears and tax arrears.

The apparent slowdown of enterprise restructuring raises the question of which are the best policy options available to the Government to encourage further restructuring. This chapter and the next argue that the Government should avoid interfering directly in the restructuring process, and should envisage measures to engage more effectively the two actors that seem to have been under-utilized in the effort to restructure enterprises, namely, foreign investors and the banks. As mentioned before, the Government should consider opening more room for foreign investors to participate in future privatizations, and also encourage new owners to negotiate further foreign participation in the enterprises that have already been privatized. Greater involvement by the banks and the other creditors would require a combination of measures, including changes in the bankruptcy framework, and improvements in the financial condition of banks, as specified below and in the next chapter.

Table 3.5
Classification of Large Manufacturing Enterprises in CEE Countries, 1992-95
(percent of firms weighted by employment)

	Year	Profitable A	Cannot Cover Depreciation B	Cannot Service All Debt C	Cannot Pay All Wages D	Cannot Pay All Suppliers E	Total
Bulgaria (828 firms)	1995	45	13	17	22	4	100
	1994	43	11	29	13	4	100
	1993	22	18	23	32	5	100
	1992	28	10	31	27	4	100
Czech Republic (675 firms)	1995	75	19	6	0	0	100
	1994	71	20	6	3	0	100
	1993	63	25	10	2	0	100
	1992	60	11	15	13	1	100
Hungary (1044 firms)	1995	70	14	6	9	1	100
	1994	67	11	9	11	2	100
	1993	67	9	8	12	4	100
	1992	59	9	12	14	6	100
Poland (940 firms)	1995	37	32	16	14	2	100
	1994	41	25	12	20	2	100
	1993	40	17	12	23	8	100
	1992	37	16	17	20	10	100
Romania (1,092)	1995	24	16	9	40	11	100
	1994	23	13	11	40	14	100
	1993	24	16	8	42	10	100
	1992	30	7	9	41	12	100
Slovak Republic (905 firms)	1995	56	27	7	10	0	100
	1994	57	21	9	13	0	100
	1993	51	22	12	13	2	100
	1992	48	16	13	19	4	100
Slovenia (727 firms)	1995	64	17	9	8	2	100
	1994	67	14	13	6	0	100
	1993	67	13	15	5	0	100
	1992	65	13	17	5	0	100

Source: National sources.

Financial and Operational Restructuring of Enterprises

The persistence of relatively large losses together with a large stock of bad loans (examined in more detail in Chapter IV) raise questions as to the role that banks have played in the process of enterprise restructuring. The very low number of completed bankruptcy and liquidation cases (next section) suggests that banks and other creditors have not resorted to the legal and institutional framework as a major vehicle for enterprise restructuring in the Slovak Republic. There may have been more bank involvement through more informal channels, but there are no indications that this is happening to any significant extent either. As indicated in the rest of this chapter and in the next chapter, there have been real obstacles for a more active involvement by banks (and the other creditors) in the restructuring process, including serious deficiencies in the regulatory and institutional framework, and the weak financial condition of the banks themselves. These obstacles have greatly diminished the power of banks and other creditors, irrespective of whether workout negotiations are conducted in formal or informal settings.[22] The political environment may also have played a role, as most banks loaded with bad loans remain State banks, usually subject to more political pressures.

There seems to be scope for further progress in enterprise restructuring through a more active engagement of banks and other creditors, and this engagement should be encouraged through the removal of legal and institutional obstacles. More bank involvement would hopefully produce a successful interaction between financial and operational restructuring. If the enterprise can restructure its operations to achieve a positive operating cash flow, then the enterprise should continue in operation even though it may not be able to service all of its outstanding debts. In these cases, it could be rational for the banks to forgive (write-off) part of the debts in exchange for the enterprise agreeing to restructure its operations, paying the remaining part of the debt, and generating additional business for the bank in the future. However, if the enterprise has little chance of achieving a positive operating cash flow and eventually becoming profitable, the only alternative is liquidation, in which the enterprise ceases operating, its assets are sold to other enterprises or individuals, and the proceeds are used to pay at least some of the debts.

Table 3.5 provides an indication of how much loss reduction could happen through liquidation, and how much through operational restructuring. At end-1995 about 10 percent of all large manufacturing firms were in such difficulty that they could not pay all of their workers and suppliers (Category D). Unless their performance improves dramatically, these firms should be liquidated. Another 7 percent could in principle pay workers and suppliers, but not all the interest on outstanding debts (Category C). Still another 27 percent could in principle pay all their obligations, but were being "decapitalized" by not covering depreciation costs, and could also be failing to meet some of their obligations (Category B).[23] The firms in Categories B and C are more likely candidates for a negotiated financial restructuring, since they have a positive operating cash flow and probably brighter future prospects. The remaining 56 percent were profitable and should be capable of honoring their debt obligations (Category A).

Although it would be desirable to encourage negotiations between the banks (and other creditors) and the over-indebted enterprises, it is also important to establish transparent rules and avoid politicizing the restructuring process. It is most important to avoid direct intervention in the process, as the

---

[22] The debtor has a greater incentive to engage in informal, out-of-court negotiations, if the threat of liquidation by creditors is credible.

[23] These firms could be also defaulting on their obligations, and using the released resources to invest in new machinery.

Government's attempts to identify the "winners" could delay the demise of unviable enterprises and contaminate the banks' portfolios again. A more productive approach involves removing the bottlenecks in the bankruptcy and liquidation framework, and equipping the banks with the means to work out a larger number of loans. As argued in Chapter IV, that would involve removing the current tax disincentives for a faster build-up of provisions and preparing their privatization. Any additional financial support from the Government to the banks should only be considered under this transparent and disciplined framework.

The Legal and Regulatory Environment

Background

The Slovak Republic has made tangible progress in reforming its legal and institutional framework, to transform its economy, and to approximate its legal system with the EU's *acquis communautaire*. This effort has included the passage of enabling legislation, the establishment of working groups in each of the relevant sector ministries, and the creation of an overall coordination mechanism within the Office of Government, whose Institute for Legislative Approximation is charged with screening all legislation submitted to the National Council in regard to its compatibility with EC legislation. Despite these efforts, much remains to be done in the legal area, not only to ensure the successful completion of Slovak transformation, but also to achieve harmonization with legislation in the EU. Indeed, there are some pieces of legislation which are critical for the good functioning of a market economy, but which are still not working properly in the Slovak Republic (e.g. the bankruptcy framework). Also, the working groups in charge of legal approximation to the EU seem to be concentrating on the passage of laws and decrees without paying sufficient attention to implementation and enforcement.

This section assesses the progress that has been achieved in reforming the legal framework for enterprises, and identifies the scope for improvements in this area.[24] The section focuses on the main pieces of legislation and examines whether these laws are generally consistent with the objective of establishing a well functioning market economy. Such an assessment takes into consideration the objective of EU accession, but does not include an exhaustive and detailed analysis of legal approximation to the EU's *acquis communautaire*. This approach was adopted for two major reasons. First, because the EU does not have a complete legal and institutional system, leaving many important areas of law to the competence of the Member States (e.g., property, company, bankruptcy, civil procedures, and administrative laws). Second, because an exhaustive and detailed analysis of the progress in legal harmonization with the EU is a task that would be better performed by joint groups of Slovak and EU experts created pursuant to the Europe Agreement.

An Overview of the Current Status of the Legal Framework

The legal and institutional framework that supports the development of a market economy should meet the following objectives: (i) clearly define and protect a wide range of property rights; (ii) provide for low entry barriers into the market, including foreign investment; (iii) set up functioning enterprise governance structures; (iv) ensure low transaction costs for contractual relations; (v) ensure functioning competition, including enforcement of competitive practices through antimonopoly legislation and prohibition of unfair competition; (vi) enable the development of capital markets and banking and insurance systems with supervision and regulation in the hands of independent institutions without political

---

[24] The next chapter examines the legal framework of financial institutions.

interference; (vii) provide for bankruptcy procedures enabling efficient market exit; and (viii) enable speedy and efficient resolution of disputes and competing claims.

The current legislative and institutional framework fulfills many of these roles. Most importantly, the Commercial Code, the various amendments to the Civil Code, and specialized laws regulating the financial markets are well drafted and provide a solid foundation for efficient and low-cost economic transactions. Commercial branches of the courts have been gaining experience in resolving commercial disputes. The private bar has adapted to new economic realities and provides a wide range of advice in commercial matters. However, the legal framework still has some gaps and deficiencies. These include the treatment of minority shareholders under the company law, the absence of accounting standards for groups of affiliated companies, the lack of transparency of capital markets, inadequate bankruptcy rules and procedures, and various problems in the regulation and supervision of banks, capital markets and insurance companies. The rest of this section deals with the major issues in the company, accounting, competition, and bankruptcy laws, as well as other related pieces of legislation. The next chapter covers banking, capital markets and insurance legislation.

Company Law and Accounting Law

One of the most severe deficiencies in Slovak legislation is the lack of *protection of minority shareholders*. This problem undermines public confidence in the transformation process, hinders company access to capital markets, and discourages foreign investment. Thus, it also constrains the expansion of profitable enterprises and the development of efficient governance structures. In addition to the lack of protection for minority shareholders, Slovak company law also fails to ensure *transparency in corporate governance* and to encourage capital inflows into the companies. Indeed, many ownership and governance structures resulting from the second wave of privatization are not transparent, raising concerns that groups of inter-connected companies may engage in anti-competitive practices. As one example of non-transparency, groups of affiliated enterprises are still not required to prepare consolidated financial statements.

The Slovak authorities should consider introducing legal measures to increase the protection of minority shareholders and improve transparency in corporate governance. The EU company law directives provide only partial guidance in this area, as they aim simply at lowering the existing barriers between the markets of the Member States (Art. 54 sec. 3 lit. g). However, mechanisms to ensure greater protection of minority shareholders may be found in the national laws of EU member states. These mechanisms may include:

(i) improved information rights of shareholders (including general transparency of actions by corporate officers and directors) which are protected by clear procedural rules and court enforcement;

(ii) clearly defined civil liability of officers and directors who do not fulfill their obligations and do not act in the best interest of all shareholders, including minority shareholders (this should serve as a functional equivalent of the common law concept of "fiduciary duty");

(iii) functioning take-over rules (due to different position of Member States, the proposed EU directive on take-overs has not been adopted yet and cannot serve as an example for the Slovak Republic);

(iv) accounting rules which restrict the power of managers and majority shareholders to manipulate financial records (for example, in order to hide profits). The European Company Law Directives on Accounting and Auditing (4th, 7th and 8th directive) are intended to protect shareholders against such a manipulation; .

(v) accounting rules in the area of consolidated financial statements designed to improve information on the financial situation of holdings and groups of affiliated companies. Transformation of the 7th EU Directive on Company Law (Art. 54 sec. 3 lit. g EC) should be considered as a minimum standard;

(vi) in general, greater approximation of Slovak accounting rules to international standards, in order to increase transparency and lower costs. At the moment, large companies wishing to raise capital in international markets are compelled to keep double financial and accounting records. This imposes a financial burden on large companies, and is usually cost prohibitive for small- and medium-size enterprises;

(vii) auditing provisions which are enforced by strong civil liability rules for auditors (the 8th company law directive of the EU can only serve as a starting point, as there are no EU rules on the civil liability of auditors); and

(viii) non-legal measures designed to improve the protection to minority shareholders, such as the creation of credit rating and reporting agencies; active and well-informed mass media; and a functioning market for corporate control.

Competition Law and Price Regulation

Well drafted competition rules (also known as anti-trust laws) coupled with adequate institutional capacity to enforce these rules, are a key element of modern legal systems. The present Slovak *Act on Protection of Economic Competition*, No. 188/1994 Zb., is in line with the requirements of European law and competition policy.[25] The Act is modeled on European rules and the German cartel law. Its intent is to protect competition in the Slovak market by preventing the abuse of dominant market positions by single enterprises, groups of enterprises, or contractual ties among enterprises. It deals with monopoly abuses such as price fixing and market allocation agreements, and provides for merger control and notification.

The agency vested with implementing the law is the Slovak *Antimonopoly Office*, established in 1990 as an independent "central administrative office". The Office is autonomous under the law, although the Government exercises considerable influence by appointing the chairman. The Office has received substantial Western technical assistance and has become expert in this area of law.[26] The Office is also supposed to provide legal advice to other parts of the Government on the impact of various policies on competition (especially trade policy).

The privatization process provided an opportunity to improve the market structure for various products and services. By not allowing the Antimonopoly Office a more active role in the second privatization wave,[27] however, some non-transparent and non-competitive ownership structures may have emerged in certain industries. For this reason, the Antimonopoly Office should make an effort to determine the ownership structure among the newly privatized enterprises, and monitor the performance of these enterprises, to ensure the protection of economic competition.

Two additional areas of concern are the exclusion of "strategic enterprises" from the application of the Act on Protection of Economic Competition and the November 1995 Price Law. This law gives wide discretionary powers to the MoF to intervene in any market for products, services, works, leases, rents and

---

[25] The Act No. 188/1994 Zb. replaced the original competition rules adopted under former Czechoslovakia, No. 63/1991 Zb., as amended by No. 495/1992 Zb.

[26] In 1993 it brought a case against a cement cartel to stop it from allocating markets amongst its members.

[27] Although the Office can in principle issue opinions on the competition aspects of specific privatization proposals, during the second wave of privatization its role was marginalized, and it was pressed to issue opinions favorable to the interests of the future owners.

intangibles, and to intervene in import and export markets. The wording of the law is excessively broad and vague, including concepts such as "unusual situation of the market," "threat to the market due to an insufficient competition environment," "public interest," and "temporary imbalance of the market". Instead of the Antimonopoly Office, the MoF is vested with the implementation of the law. This law poses competition on the Slovak market and could reduce the attractiveness of greater foreign engagement on that market.

Bankruptcy Law and Enterprise Restructuring

A functioning bankruptcy procedure is essential to a modern legal system. It allows inefficient firms to exit the market, their assets to migrate to more efficient uses, and less efficient firms to restructure and become more efficient. The need for an effective exit mechanism is even stronger in transition economies like Slovak Republic, due to the misallocation of resources under the former centrally planned economies and the inefficiency of many state-owned enterprises. A functioning bankruptcy system also provides security to creditors and, as a result, makes it easier for enterprises to access bank or supplier credit.

The Slovak Republic has a bankruptcy law inherited from the former Czechoslovakia--the *Act on Bankruptcy and Settlements* (No. 328/1991 Zb)--which has undergone several major amendments. The overindebtedness of many Slovak enterprises and the bad loan problems of major banks would suggest that both creditors and debtors would make use of the bankruptcy framework as a vehicle for restructuring and debt resolution. However, the law has not been successfully implemented--out of the 4,000 cases that have been filed, about half were aimed at threatening the debtors and were subsequently withdrawn. Another 1,500 cases were filed in order to avoid filing other commercial suits and the considerably larger filing fees, and were dismissed by the courts. The remaining 500 cases were dismissed for insufficient debtors' property to cover the costs of the proceedings. As a result, there have been about 10 cases of completed bankruptcies.

There are several reasons why bankruptcy (and liquidation) procedures have not worked well in Slovak Republic. First, the legal framework contains major systemic flaws that hamper the entire procedure. Among the most significant are: (i) lack of a clear and precise definition of insolvency and overindebtedness; (ii) no obligation for debtors to file for bankruptcy if excessively indebted or not servicing debt over a long period of time; (iii) obligatory restructuring-related negotiations, without time limits, that a creditor must undertake even in instances where restructuring has no economic justification; (iv) equal status of all domestic creditors in these negotiations, regardless of the size of their claims; (v) discrimination against foreign debtors in the case of restructuring; (vi) insufficient protection for secured creditors; and (vii) courts' obligation to ascertain debtor's property, resulting in long delays in the cases where the debtor does not cooperate. In other words, the liquidation and settlement procedures are too debtor-friendly and act as disincentives for creditors to file for bankruptcy.

Second, State-owned banks have generally failed to deal more assertively with their bad loan portfolios and, where appropriate, apply for bankruptcy procedures. This attitude may persist until these banks are fully privatized (Chapter IV). Third, bankruptcy courts and judges are not sufficiently equipped and trained to handle these procedures. There are only three courts that can hear bankruptcy cases, in Bratislava, Banska Bystrica, and Kosice. These are all overloaded, and cases can linger on for a long time. Consequently, creditors often lose large portions of their claims to inflation. Fourth, the Slovak Republic lacks administrators/trustees that would be interested in pursuing bankruptcies. This is mainly due to the lack of training and poor remuneration.

Finally, there is insufficient political will to make bankruptcies a viable option, in part due to the very unfavorable public perception in the Slovak Republic. According to a 1995 survey, a majority of the general public and a significant portion of business and bank managers see bankruptcy as harmful rather than encouraging restructuring of enterprises. Evidence of the lack of political will can be found in the initial deferrals of the applicability of the law until May 1994, and on the exemptions granted to a wide range of enterprises and organizations, including so called "strategic" and "essential" enterprises, state budgetary and contributory organizations, municipalities, and the National Property Fund as a debtor.

A new amendment to the bankruptcy law is under preparation by a committee of experts. Its main aim is to simplify procedures and make reorganization and liquidation viable options for indebted enterprises and their creditors. The new draft clearly defines insolvency and overindebtedness and makes it a sanctioned obligation for overindebted enterprises to file for bankruptcy if unable to service debt. The debtor would decide whether to file for liquidation or reorganization. Unfortunately, in creditor-filed cases, the debtor would still retain the right to propose reorganization. The draft would also eliminate the mandatory nature of the negotiations/bargaining procedure for restructuring and abolish discrimination against foreign creditors. Further, it would introduce a temporary administrator to protect creditors between the time of filing and the decision of a court to start a procedure.

The new draft provides solutions to some of the problems outlined above, but may still fail to ensure efficient bankruptcy and settlement. Unfortunately, European law does not provide much guidance on bankruptcy reform--the diversity of settlement and bankruptcy laws and procedures among the Member States has so far prevented the development of EC legislation in this area. However, the Slovak Republic can look for inspiration in Member States with similar legal traditions, such as Germany, Austria, or the Netherlands. Among the measures required to make reorganization and liquidation a realistic option for creditors and debtors alike, it would be desirable to include the following changes in the law:

(i) abolish preferential treatment for claims by the state or its agencies (including taxes, labor payments and claims by the National Property Fund) vis-à-vis secured creditors in both reorganization and liquidation proceedings;

(ii) provide an option for creditors to apply for reorganization or liquidation procedures without having to prove excessive indebtedness or insolvency by means of documents (creditors may be required to post a bond prior to filing to cover the cost of the court proceedings);

(iii) apply the Act on Bankruptcy and Settlements to all business enterprises; i.e., eliminate the exemption for "strategic" and "essential" enterprises;

(iv) ensure adequate protection to creditors during bankruptcy procedures, especially against the dilution of debtors property by unauthorized transfers (including invalidating such transfers);

(v) further ensure the protection of creditors by, *inter alia*, linking their voting rights to the size of their claims;

(vi) considerably broaden the authority of administrators and liquidators to enable him/her to run the day-to-day operations of an enterprise under bankruptcy; and

(vii) simplify the asset-divestiture procedures in liquidation cases.

In addition to these legislative changes, it is further important to strengthen the *institutional structure* for carrying out reorganization and liquidation proceedings by: (i) training commercial judges that deal with bankruptcies, or instituting a separate category of judges to hear bankruptcy cases; (ii) broadening the list of administrators/trustees to include non-lawyers; (iii) restructuring the remuneration scheme for administrators/trustees to enhance financial incentives to dispose of bankruptcy cases in an efficient manner. One possible scheme would be to give administrators/trustees a percentage of the debtors' assets after their sale and to conduct a public education campaign to inform enterprises, creditors, and the general public about the nature and economic benefits of bankruptcy procedures.

Once the above changes are adopted and implemented, debtors and creditors would both have more incentives to look for out-of-court procedures. The Slovak Republic should explore *alternatives to formal court bankruptcy procedures*, for example, in cases of financial restructuring. Many industrialized nations are moving away from court procedures to some form of commercial mediation or negotiations in these cases.

The Enterprise Revitalization Act

The Slovak Parliament has recently approved an Act on the financial and operational restructuring of enterprises--the Enterprise Revitalization Act--whose objective is to encourage further enterprise restructuring, particularly in the arms industry and agro-industry sub-sectors (the largest loss-makers). Such a revitalization program expects to achieve this objective primarily by forgiving enterprises' tax liabilities and debts to banks, in exchange for the submission of a restructuring plan by enterprise management. A commission consisting of representatives from five ministries (Finance, Economy, Labor, Justice, and Public Works), the NBS, the three largest banks and the State insurance company would be empowered to screen the applicants and to judge the adequacy of the proposals.

Whereas it would be highly desirable to elaborate a strategy to facilitate the joint restructuring of enterprises and banks loaded with bad loans, this strategy should involve as little direct interference from the Government as possible, and should not harm the development of a legal framework supportive of a market economy. The revitalization program, as currently designed, may involve too much political interference in the selection of enterprises and the assessment of their restructuring plans. As a result, it may keep unviable enterprise afloat for a long period of time, lead to a waste of fiscal resources, possibly result in further contamination of banks' portfolios, and ultimately delay needed restructuring. A more effective approach would involve improving the bankruptcy framework, and strengthening the banks' conditions to recognize their losses and work out their bad loans (see Chapter IV). In addition, the Act, if implemented, may go counter to a fundamental principle of a market economy--a level playing field for all economic actors.

Summary of the Recommendations

To rejuvenate the process of enterprise restructuring, the government should: (i) complete the privatization of the few but very large and important enterprises that remain in State ownership; (ii) refrain from exercising control over the so-called "essential" or "strategic" enterprises; (iii) adopt more competitive and transparent privatization methods that will encourage the best possible owners (including foreigners) to purchase Slovak enterprises; (iv) refrain from limiting or restricting the transfer of ownership of those enterprises already privatized to new investors, both domestic and foreign, that are likely to have a better strategy for restructuring Slovak enterprises; (v) improve the legal framework, in particular, minority shareholder protection, the bankruptcy system, and accounting standards for groups of affiliated companies; (vi) repeal the 1995 Price Law; (vii) restrict to the minimum the number of enterprises eligible to participate in the Enterprise Revitalization Act, and refrain from pressing the banks to resume lending to these enterprises. Instead, the Government should strengthen the banks' capacity to get more involved in enterprise restructuring. As discussed in Chapter IV, that will involve, *inter alia*, the implementation of a privatization plan for these banks.

CHAPTER IV: THE FINANCIAL SECTOR

Introduction

Since financial sector reform began in 1990 with the break-up of the monobank system, the restructuring of the financial system has developed along three main themes. First, there has been a significant number of new entries into the banking sector, mainly private banks with foreign participation. The banking system has grown from two banks in 1990 to 24 banks and 6 branches of foreign banks at end-1996. Second, a reasonable legal and regulatory framework for banking has been established, after several changes in the Act on Banks and the Act on the NBS in the past few years, and the issuance of other pieces of legislation. Third, capital market institutions have begun to emerge. A stock market was established in 1993 and related laws and regulations have also been issued.

Despite these positive developments, there is much that the Government can do to deepen financial reform. The recommended agenda for further financial reform covers three major areas. First, the restructuring and privatization of the state owned banks should be completed. This involves issues relating to non-performing loans and solvency, as well as the method of privatization. Second, the regulatory and taxation framework for banking require further improvements and further harmonization with EU regulations. These are mainly in the areas of accounting and taxation of loan loss provisions. Third, the development of capital markets would have to be accelerated. The major areas of reform include the legal framework, prudential regulations, supervision capacity, and the development of contractual savings institutions such as pension funds and insurance companies.

This chapter has been structured to examine these three sets of issues. The second section describes the structure and performance of the banking system in recent years. It also deals with the challenge of bank restructuring and its interface with enterprise restructuring. The third section examines the progress that has been achieved in harmonizing the regulatory framework for banks with EC legislation. Finally, the fourth section deals with capital markets. It examines the current status of equity and bond markets, as well as the progress achieved in approximating the Slovak regulatory framework in these areas to the EU framework. The section also includes a brief examination of the insurance sector in Slovak Republic.

The Banking System

Structure

Over the past five years, the main structural change has been the growth in the number of commercial banks--from 1991 to 1996, 28 new banks (including branches of foreign banks) were licensed and 12 foreign banks set up representative offices. As of end-1996, there were 5 majority State-owned banks (SOBs) accounting for 57 percent of assets in the banking system, and 25 privately owned banks accounting for the remaining 43 percent. The four major banks are Vseobecna Uverova Banka (VUB), Slovenska Sporitel'na (SLSP), Konsolidacna Banka (KB), and Investicna Rozvojova Banka (IRB). The first three are SOBs, whereas the fourth is not considered as a State bank any longer, given the decline of the State share in capital to less than 35 percent.[28] Out of the 25 private banks, 19 were joint stock companies with foreign participation and 6 were branches of foreign banks (Table 4.1).

---

[28] SOBs are defined as banks with majority (i.e., greater than 50 percent) state ownership, direct or indirect.

Table 4.1
Structure of the Slovak Banking System, 1993-96

Year	State-Owned Banks		Private Sector Banks			
			Joint Stock Companies		Branches of Foreign Banks	
	Number	Share of Assets (percent)	Number	Share of Assets (percent)	Number	Share of Assets (percent)
1993	4	70.5	14	19.7	10	9.7
1994	4	66.9	15	23.4	10	9.7
1995	4	61.3	20	28.4	9	10.3
1996	5	56.9	19	33.0	6	10.1

Source: National Bank of Slovakia.

While the SOBs have the major share of the stock of banking assets, there has been a major shift in lending flows. Private sector banks accounted for 81 percent of the increase in loans during the period 1992-96, causing a sharp decline in VUB's (the largest corporate lender) share in total loans, from 78 percent in 1990 to 35 percent in 1996. In the retail market, SLSP (the State Savings Bank) continues to be the dominant institution, accounting for about 80 percent of household deposits. However, there has been greater competition in the non-household deposit market, with the private banks holding about 40 percent of this market (the equivalent of 20 percent of total deposits) at end-1996. Figure 4.1 summarizes the share of the four largest banks in total banking assets, loans, deposits, and paid-in capital.

The entry of new private banks and the partial privatization of certain SOBs have resulted in a significant increase in the private sector's share of the banking system. The new private banks (excluding IRB) now account for more than 56 percent of capital in the banking system (Figure 4.1). VUB has been partially privatized, such that 48 percent of the shares are in private hands. IRB has been privatized through both voucher sales of state shares and increases in private investor equity, lowering the share of the state to 35 percent as of end-1996. However, both SLSP and KB continue to be fully State-owned. There are two additional small SOBs--Slovenska Zarucna Banka, which provides guarantees to small enterprises, and Banka Slovakia, which was established to promote regional development but has not started operations yet.

Main Monetary and Credit Developments

The Slovak financial system is relatively large, as indicated by a ratio of broad money to GDP of 70 percent in 1996. Such a high ratio results in part from the relatively low inflation experienced during the Czechoslovak federation--as shown in Figure 4.2, the Slovak Republic entered the 1990s with lower rates of inflation and much higher ratios of broad money to GDP than Hungary and Poland. In 1991, there was a sharp increase in prices, but that increase proved to be short-lived (as a result of a strict stabilization program) and does not seem to have affected money and credit ratios. The rapid stabilization of inflation achieved after independence, combined with the increase in real interest rates on deposits (Figure 4.3) has enhanced confidence in the new currency and has promoted further resource mobilization by the banking system.

Bank deposits account for 90 percent of broad money and household deposits account for about 54 percent of total deposits. Approximately 80 percent of household deposits are still mobilized by SLSP, which also dominates the interbank market. To enhance confidence in the new banks and improve competition in the deposit market, a deposit guarantee scheme was established in mid-1996, guaranteeing the deposits of individuals up to 30 times the monthly salary in the Slovak Republic. However, the impact of this measure cannot be determined for some time, because the State will continue to insure citizens' deposits in SLSP, VUB, and IRB until the end of 1997. It is likely that SLSP's monopoly position will be eroded only gradually, as the other banks strengthen their capacity to conduct retail operations.

Figure 4.1
Concentration in the Banking System

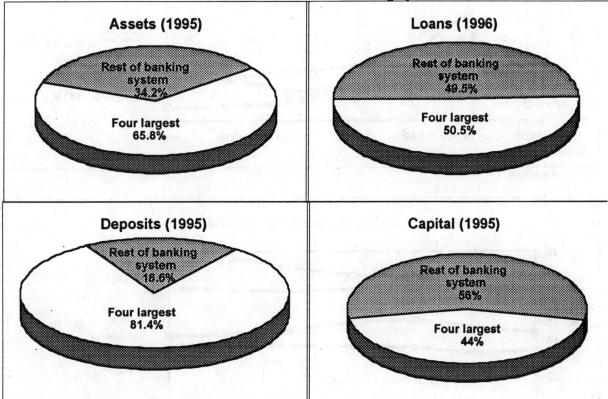

Source: National Bank of Slovakia.

The growth of money supply after independence was initially dominated by the increase in net foreign assets, implying a slow growth of credits and an initial decline in the ratio of average credit to GDP (Figure 4.2). However, banks increased lending in real terms during 1996, raising the ratio of average credit to GDP to around 60 percent. The share of private sector borrowers in total credits has increased dramatically (Table 4.2), in line with the privatization of SOEs, the decline in real lending by SOBs, and increased real lending by the new private banks. These trends suggest that the decline in real lending volumes was probably accompanied by an increase in the average quality of new lending. In particular, VUB's lending portfolio declined sharply in real terms during 1992-1995 because of the credit ceilings imposed on the large banks during this period, difficulties to mobilize resources and probably a more conservative attitude from the side of management. SLSP was subject to tighter lending constraints by NBS, and its loan portfolio has barely increased in nominal terms. However, there has been an increase in the real lending activities of VUB in 1996 (15 percent nominal increase over 1995, compared to a 6 percent inflation rate), despite its failure to meet the required capital adequacy ratio.

Figure 4.2 Inflation and Money Supply

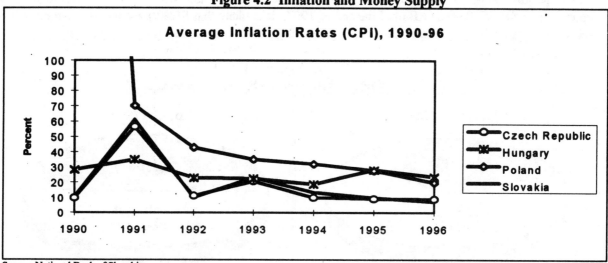

Source: National Bank of Slovakia.

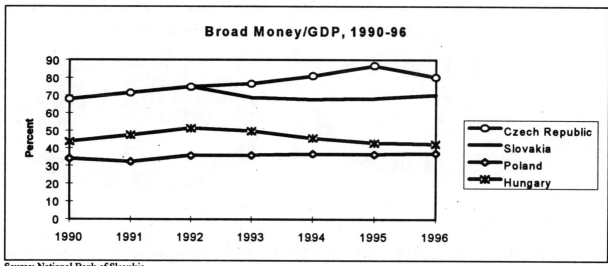

Source: National Bank of Slovakia.

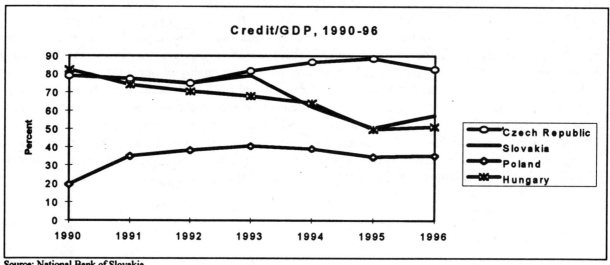

Source: National Bank of Slovakia.

Table 4.2
Breakdown of Bank Loans by Bank and Borrower Ownership, 1992-96
(percent)

Year	Banks without Foreign Participation		Banks with Foreign Participation		Branches of Foreign Banks		Total	
	Public	Private	Public	Private	Public	Private	Public	Private
1992							67.5	32.5
1993	44.2	40.9	1.7	4.8	3.1	5.2	49.0	51.0
1994	39.1	42.6	1.6	7.3	6.1	3.2	46.9	53.1
1995	28.3	50.2	1.7	10.0	3.9	6.0	33.8	66.2
1996	23.7	52.9	2.1	12.6	4.3	4.4	30.1	69.9

Note: Public and Private refer to the borrower.
Source: National Bank of Slovakia.

Average real interest rates on deposits increased gradually after 1993, and have stabilized at around 4 percent p.a.. Average real interest on credits had stabilized at around 9 percent p.a., but increased to around 13 percent p.a. in late 1997, due to the tightening of monetary policy (Figure 4.3). Real spreads have remained higher than nominal spreads due to some persistent differences in price indices.[29] Average real lending rates have become excessively high, and are probably significantly higher for second-tier enterprises. Indeed, first-tier enterprises have obtained foreign credits at very competitive terms, and can demand similar conditions from domestic banks.[30] The new private banks have clean portfolios and low operating costs and can match these conditions. This implies pressures on the State banks, which also have to extend loans at very competitive terms to their prime borrowers in order to avoid losing their business entirely, and are forced to charge much higher rates from their second-tier clients in an attempt to recapitalize themselves. This problem may only be eliminated after the full restructuring of banks facing portfolio problems.

Financial Conditions of the Major Banks

The major banks continue to suffer from a weak financial condition. In 1993, the NBS concluded that the capital adequacy ratio (CAR) of the four major banks[31] would be extremely low; if international accounting standards were adopted. Since 1995, the NBS has reviewed the financial situation of banks based on stricter loan classification and provisioning rules. The last available review indicates that the stock of classified claims (loans, securities, and unpaid interest) amounts to Sk117 billion, the equivalent of 21 percent of total balance sheet claims and 18 percent of GDP. In order to comply with prudential rules, the banking system would need to build Sk74 billion of provisions for loan losses and off-balance sheet commitments, of which only Sk35 billion has been created. Therefore, the additional provisions required would amount to Sk39 billion, the equivalent of 6 percent of GDP (Table 4.3).

[29] The difference between nominal and real spreads is due to the fact that the changes in the PPI (the deflator of lending rates) have remained lower than the changes in the CPI (the deflator of deposit rates).

[30] In early 1997, prime borrowers could expect to borrow at a nominal interest rate of around 9-10 percent p.a.-- the prime rate in US$ (8 percent p.a.) plus a reasonable spread (1-2 percent). This amounts to 3-4 percent less than the average lending rate in Sk during the same period (12-13 percent p.a.).

[31] VUB, SLSP, KB, and IRB.

Figure 4.3 Interest Rates

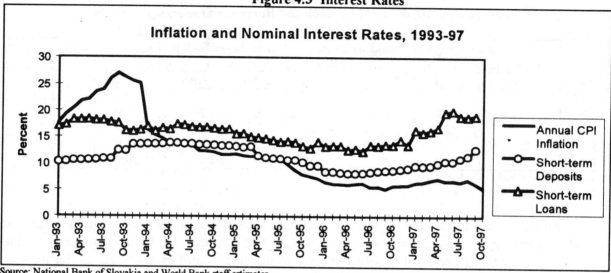

Source: National Bank of Slovakia and World Bank staff estimates.

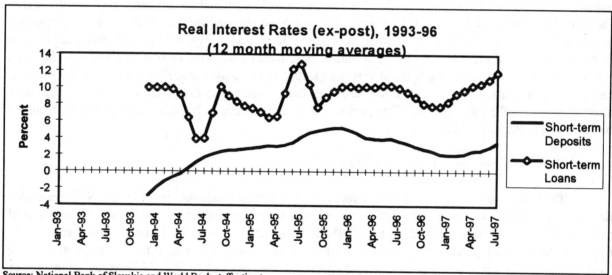

Source: National Bank of Slovakia and World Bank staff estimates.

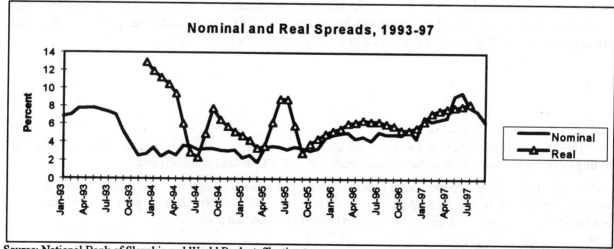

Source: National Bank of Slovakia and World Bank staff estimates.

The uncovered losses would reportedly be smaller, if reserves were used to cover part of the overall losses (related both to on-balance sheet and off-balance sheet items). However, the uncovered losses would still amount to Sk12 billion, or 2 percent of GDP (Table 4.3). Moreover, whereas these figures do reflect generally stricter criteria (international accounting standards) for loan classification and provisioning, it is more difficult to assess whether loan collateral was correctly valued in the computation of the required provisions.

It is possible that the large required provisions are due primarily to the application of stricter rules for loan classification and provisioning to the same stock of bad loans, rather than new fresh loans to bad borrowers, but the numbers still look large as a share of GDP. The size of classified claims and the required provisions are high relative to GDP, because bank claims are also very high relative to GDP-- more than 80 percent, including loans, securities and unpaid interests. Other transforming economies also face situations where classified claims amount to 20-30 percent of the total portfolio, but classified claims and provisions are smaller relative to GDP, because their real value has been eroded by high and unanticipated inflation. The Slovak Republic (and the Czech Republic) experienced a more moderate and shorter inflationary episode than most other transforming economies, and that helps explain why the size of classified claims and provisions may look high by comparison.

Table 4.3
Bank Claims and Estimated Claim Provisions as of June 30, 1997 (Sk million)

	Principal	Interest	Total Claims	Required Provisions	Created Provisions	Additional Required Provisions
Loans	517,389	39,994	557,383	71,646	34,704	36,942
Standard	365,385	1,054	366,439	-	-	-
Special Mention	68,097	6,131	74,228	3,711	-	3,711
Classified	83,907	32,809	116,716	67,935	34,704	33,231
Substandard	7,671	508	8,179	838	516	322
Doubtful	9,487	983	10,470	2,584	1,422	1,162
Loss	66,749	31,318	98,067	64,513	32,766	31,747
Contingent Liabilities	85,315	-	85,315	1,871	-	1,871
Standard	81,433	-	81,433	-	-	-
Classified	3,883	-	1,882	1,871	-	1,871
Substandard	858	-	858	110	-	110
Doubtful	895	-	895	83	-	83
Loss	2,128	-	2,128	1,677	-	1,677
Total	-	-	-	73,517	34,704	38,813
Disposable Reserves	-	-	-	-	-	26,717
Uncovered Losses	-	-	-	-	-	12,096

Source: National Bank of Slovakia.

VUB. As the main conduit for allocating resources to SOEs during the socialist era, VUB inherited most of the enterprise debts[32] at the start of transformation in 1990. In 1991, some 25 percent of its loans were transferred to the federal KB,[33] and another 9 percent of loans were exchanged for 5 year State bonds.

---

[32] The newly created IRB inherited about 20 percent of the enterprise debts.

[33] The federal Konsolidacna Banka was split with the dissolution of the Czechoslovak Federation and a separate Konsolidacna Banka was established in Slovak Republic.

Despite these initial measures, the bank has not been able to comply with prudential rules. After the introduction of stricter regulations by NBS, the CAR at end-1996 was estimated at 4.4 percent. Moreover, the bank's CAR reportedly increased during 1996 through recourse to a foreign subordinated loan, but the terms and conditions of this loan are not clear. Provisions for loan losses amounted to about 18 percent of loans at end-1996, but these were still insufficient to meet the new provisioning rules. The bank has been granted a period of regulatory forbearance to comply with prudential rules.

In addition to low capitalization, VUB suffers from other structural problems in its balance sheet. The dependence of VUB on SLSP's short-term deposits for 20 percent of its funding exposes VUB to both liquidity and interest risk. Furthermore, 36 percent of VUB's funding comes from enterprise deposits, which also tend to be short-term and relatively volatile. Only 18 percent of VUB's liabilities come from more stable household deposits. Overall, the financial position of VUB does not permit the bank to expand lending and at the same time meet prudential regulations. During the 1993-95 period, its nominal loan portfolio hardly increased, but the trend reversed in 1996 with a 15 percent increase in loans. Its share of total bank loans has gone down in the recent years, but the bank continues to have the largest exposure to enterprise debts, with 35 percent of total bank loans.

SLSP. During 1992, SLSP financed small scale privatization, and expanded from its traditional lending to households (mainly for housing) to commercial lending to small entrepreneurs. The pressure to finance small privatization combined with the lack of lending skills resulted in portfolio problems, leading NBS to impose lending constraints on SLSP. Nominal loans have remained at about the same level since 1993, and now account for less than 30 percent of assets, with the rest of the asset portfolio consisting of deposits in other banks (mainly VUB), and investments in Government and other securities. SLSP's CAR was estimated by NBS at 6.5 percent at the end of 1996, and the bank probably operates on a positive cash-flow, given its cheap deposit base. However, the efforts of other banks to penetrate the retail market will imply increasing pressures on its cash flow position and its market share.

In addition to the bad loans in its asset portfolio, SLSP has two other structural problems. First, the bank has large exposure to two State-owned banks (VUB and KB), the sum of which is equivalent to eight times SLSP's capital. Second, SLSP has significant housing and "social" loans to households at below market rates, and receives a subsidy from the MoF equivalent to the difference between the NBS discount rate and the SLSB rate for these loans. There is uncertainty as to the commitment and timing of Government subsidies, as well as the extent to which the NBS discount rate reflects the market rate.

IRB. When the Slovak IRB was established in 1992, it inherited two types of loans from the former federal Investicna Banka. The first consisted of loans to SOEs, some of which were subsequently privatized, and the second consisted of loans to cooperative building societies. The major problem with the first type of loans is their size--the loans to Mochovce, the nuclear power company, account for more than 200 percent of IRB's equity and about one-third of its total loan portfolio. Furthermore, the financial viability of Mochovce is uncertain, and IRB has relied on the Government to guarantee the financial obligations of this company. With respect to the second type of loans, there is uncertainty with regard to the Government's commitment to pay the difference between the NBS discount rate and the lower rate charged on these loans. During 1996, the MoF did not pay the difference regularly, creating liquidity problems for IRB. Furthermore, because delayed payments by MoF did not accrue interest, this reduced the already relatively low margin on these loans.

Since end-1992, IRB loans have grown by only 3 percent in nominal terms. The bank had a CAR close to zero at that time, but has subsequently increased its capital from private sources (partly from foreign investors) and benefited from the carving out of Sk1.5 billion of nonperforming loans (60 percent of equity) by NPF. The bank's estimated CAR was still very low at the end of 1996, but management claims that the CAR would increase to around 8 percent, assuming that the Mochovce loans were categorized as "standard" due to implicit guarantees by the Government. IRB's management believes that, except for the Mochovce loans, the bank can solve its problems without further Government support.

KB. Konsolidacna Banka is the repository of doubtful loans, and the financial condition of the bank depends on its success in collecting these loans. The loans transferred to KB were portions of the working capital loans originally held by VUB. Hence, KB and VUB have common clients and are likely to be similarly affected by enterprises with insufficient cash flows to pay their debts. The collateral positions of the two banks with respect to the same clients may be different, however, with VUB possibly holding the upper hand. Because the loans transferred to KB have a fixed, below market interest rate, even with a low proportion of non-performing loans KB would experience a negative operating cash flow since the bank's spreads are marginal. To date, the bank's operating deficits are financed from the collection of principal, which is possible given that KB's main liability--NBS credits--are payable only starting in 1997. KB's external auditors estimate that about 35 percent of the bank's assets need to be provisioned for losses. Given its low capital position, this means that its liabilities will only be fully paid with Government support.

Past Attempts at Financial Restructuring of the Banking and Enterprise Sectors

The first attempt at financial restructuring was made in 1991 during the Czechoslovak federation. During that year, Konsolidacna Banka was created and received permanent (without a defined maturity) working capital loans to SOEs previously held by VUB. These loans amounted to 25 percent of VUB's portfolio. The affected enterprises effectively received an interest subsidy, since the working capital loans which were transferred carried a low interest rate. The second attempt at restructuring was made in 1992, when a program was established to clean enterprises and banks prior to mass privatization. VUB was allowed to write-off 10 percent of its outstanding loans with a corresponding reduction of the enterprises' liabilities. The third attempt was made in 1993, when certain enterprise loans (mainly to arms manufacturers) were carved out of VUB and IRB, and replaced by deposit claims against KB in the case of VUB, and by NPF bonds in the case of IRB.[34] On the enterprise side, the corresponding debts were converted into equity by NPF. In addition, certain export receivables of enterprises were purchased by KB at a discount, with NPF eventually absorbing them. Finally, in 1994, the foreign trade bank (CSOB) was also bailed out through the transfer of some loans to KB.

These various past efforts to improve the financial situation of banks raise three interrelated questions. The first is whether these various programs have effectively cleaned the banks' portfolios and restored an adequate capital position. The second is whether these financial restructuring actions have been accompanied by conditions on the banks, such as the dismissal of redundant staff, the submission of a privatization plan, and a plan for working out bad loans. Third, and most important, is whether these initiatives contributed to enterprise restructuring.

The answer to the first question is probably negative, at least for VUB. As shown in the previous section, the stricter loan classification and provisioning rules introduced by NBS in 1995 have revealed the low level of capitalization of State-owned banks, including VUB (one of the main beneficiaries from these past restructuring efforts) and the uncertainties that still surround IRB's capital position. These rules have

[34] The equity of IRB was increased through a transfer by NPF directly to reserves (rather than through an increase in paid-up capital), thus maintaining private control in IRB.

also revealed the low capital position of SLSP. These banks seem to be making efforts to strengthen their capital position further from their own resources, but this has been difficult for two reasons. First, because increased competition from new banks and foreign lending has put pressure on intermediation spreads, particularly regarding first tier enterprises. Second, because the tax system creates obstacles for a faster build-up of provisions--banks have not been allowed to deduct these costs from their taxable income.

The answer to the second question--whether these financial restructuring actions have resulted in efficient and competitive banks--is very unclear. For example, VUB (the major lender among State-owned banks) has been partly privatized, but it is questionable whether this partial privatization has generated the improvement in governance and skills that the bank needs to correct its inherited deficiencies and compete effectively with the new private banks. The sharp and continuing decline in market shares of VUB and the other State banks provides indirect evidence that these banks are still not equipped to deal with increasing competition.

The answer to the third question--whether these financial restructuring actions have contributed to enterprise restructuring--can hardly be positive, as it depends partly on the answer to the first and the second questions. Indeed, bank restructuring contributes to enterprise restructuring only to the extent that it creates the conditions for banks to become independent and assertive towards their creditors, thus pressing for enterprise restructuring, either through the formal bankruptcy and liquidation framework, or through more informal channels. These conditions do not seem to have been fully met. The low capitalization of State banks acted as a disincentive to renegotiate bad loans and recognize explicitly loan losses, as these would reveal their weak financial position. The failure to implement full privatization with a strategic investor prevented a faster absorption of banking skills and opened room for continuing political pressures on the banks. In addition to these problems, the banks have also faced problems in the legal and institutional framework for bankruptcy and liquidation, preventing greater use of one of the major vehicles for enterprise restructuring in market economies (Chapter III).[35]

It is clear from the analysis of enterprise restructuring in Chapter III that these deficiencies did not prevent initial progress at enterprise restructuring in Slovak Republic. Indeed, between 1993 and 1995 gross losses were reduced by about 6 percent of GDP (Chapter III, Table 3.3). Also, during the same period the worst class of loss-makers--the value subtractors--virtually disappeared, at least within the sub-set of largest enterprises (Chapter III, Table 3.4). However, what is not clear is what was the contribution of State-owned banks to such an initial reduction in loss-making activities. To pass a fair judgment on these banks, it may be said that they probably contributed indirectly by not extending new fresh loans to bad borrowers. Although there is no detailed information on the lending practices of these banks, it is likely that they concentrated their declining resources in their prime borrowers, in order to avoid losing entirely their best clientele to the fast growing private banks. Deprived of new credits, the troubled enterprises were forced to make efforts to restructure and survive.

At the same time, there is evidence of a relatively large residual core of loss-makers in the Slovak Republic, as indicated by gross losses of non-financial enterprises of 5.6 percent of GDP in 1995, and the increase in gross losses to 8.8 percent of GDP in 1996. The large stock of the banks' classified claims--18 percent of GDP, of which 6 percent of GDP of unpaid interests--provide additional evidence of an incomplete restructuring program. There is no detailed information on the set of loss-making enterprises and the set of classified bank borrowers, but there is probably a very large intersection between the two sets. These numbers suggest that, although State banks may not have provided new fresh loans to these

---

[35] In addition to these problems, banks have also faced problems with auctioning real estate.

enterprises in the 1992-95 period, they also did not go far enough in collecting their unpaid claims and pressing these enterprises for further restructuring. The figures for 1996 are more worrisome, as they indicate a simultaneous increase in enterprise losses and in bank lending (including VUB). The possibility that some of the new lending was directed to loss-making enterprises cannot be discarded, and merits further investigation.

The banks' lack of assertiveness in handling problem loans is revealed not only by the large stock of these loans, but also by the very low number of completed bankruptcy and liquidation cases (Chapter III). It is possible that banks are engaged in enterprise restructuring through more informal channels, but there is no evidence indicating that this is occurring on any significant scale. At end-1996, KB had 167 clients under liquidation, 61 under bankruptcy proceedings, and was negotiating with 29 clients prior to a possible bankruptcy filing. These numbers look rather modest, compared with the total number (2,000) and quality of KB's clients. IRB has pursued bankruptcy proceedings against 34 of its clients, while SLSP had 25 percent of its loan portfolio reportedly under bankruptcy or liquidation proceedings at end-1996. However, there is insufficient information to assess the size of these figures relative to the universe of bad borrowers and the size of classified loans, particularly taking into account the absence of detailed information on VUB.

Recommendations for Further Reform

The reform of the financial sector has so far been based on two essential components: the entry of private banks (mainly with foreign participation) and the establishment of a stricter regulatory and supervisory framework. While there has been significant progress in these two areas, the reform strategy remains incomplete, for failing to comprise a more articulated treatment of the State banks. In the initial stages of transition, the approach adopted was actually counter-productive, as VUB and SLSP were encouraged to expand lending to some SOEs and to finance small scale privatization, leading to portfolio problems. The containment of their lending activities in more recent years, reinforced by the application of stricter prudential standards and increased competition from new private banks, has forced State banks to make efforts at restructuring, and to contain lending to troubled enterprises. However, a strategy to privatize these banks and give them the conditions to compete with the new banks is still lacking. IRB was quickly privatized, but the NPF stopped further private capital infusion to prevent a decline in State participation to 35 percent below capital. VUB was only partly privatized, and a full privatization has been blocked. Finally, the establishment of Banka Slovakia has sent a confusing signal on government policy regarding the State role in the banking system.

Further reform of the banking system should focus on three main issues. First, the privatization of SOBs and the sale of minority holdings in IRB. This will require bank-specific strategies (as outlined below), where State intervention may be needed to address some of the inherited problems and facilitate privatization. Second, legal, institutional, and taxation issues will have to be addressed, to increase the ability of banks to play a more active role in enterprise restructuring. In particular, deduction of loan loss provisions from the taxable base of banks would enable banks to build provisions faster, and create more room for the restructuring of enterprises. Third, bank supervision capacity should be further upgraded. This would involve designing new IAS accounting standards for both banks and enterprises, developing the accounting and auditing professions, and developing supervision skills based on risk assessment and analysis, rather than mechanical verification of compliance with prudential regulations.

The containment of SOB lending should continue (or be introduced in the case of VUB), in order to avoid a reemergence of bad loans in their portfolios before privatization. Note that NBS should have the legal authority to impose such a condition, as these institutions have been granted a period of regulatory forbearance, and should be subject to conditions in return for this privilege. The containment of SOB lending does not preclude the implementation of restructuring measures designed to improve operational efficiency and financial conditions. However, these measures should be designed and implemented in connection with a privatization program. Moreover, the unique characteristics of these banks, and the different ownership structure in the SOBs and IRB, strongly indicates the need to contract investment bankers or privatization advisers to develop bank-specific plans for privatization. Investment bankers could then identify possible investor markets, recommend modes of privatization (including timing), and design the restructuring measures that are necessary for privatization to succeed. Any additional financial support to SOBs (above and beyond the required changes in the tax treatment of provisions) should only proceed under these conditions, in order to enable the conclusion of a successful privatization.

VUB. In the short term, VUB would need to set up adequate loan loss provisions based on audits and NBS analysis. This would affect the computed CAR of VUB, which would not be able to meet prudential standards. VUB would have to submit a restructuring plan indicating how to improve its CAR. The main impact of provisioning would be the inability of VUB to increase is lending portfolio until the CAR requirement is met. The medium-term objective should be the privatization of VUB. Such a privatization should not be based on subordinated loans, because this alternative does not infuse needed skills nor improve governance. Instead, an investment bank should be utilized to assess the potential strategic owners of VUB. Potential buyers may require a prior restructuring of VUB, where the options may include carving-out bad loans, and reduction of redundant staff. The impact of restructuring options and privatization on the existing private shareholders would have to be assessed, since they should bear part of the restructuring cost.

SLSP. It is envisioned that SLSP would continue to play a major role in the household deposit market. To minimize the risks on its household deposits, SLSP should focus its investments on high grade tradable paper and interbank lending with prudent limits. Commercial lending to enterprises and entrepreneurs should be avoided, although consumer lending on a limited and collateralized basis could be allowed.[36] While privatizing SLSP is not recommended at this time due to its market power in the household deposit and interbank markets, as the domestic financial market nears integration with the EU market, plans for the privatization of SLSP should be elaborated.

IRB. The Mochovce loan was inherited by IRB when the bank was created in 1992, and the amount of the loan is above the single borrower's limit. In the short term, the Mochovce loan should be covered by a formal government guarantee to allow IRB to treat the loan as standard. Otherwise, the amount of provisions that may be required is beyond the absorption ability of IRB's capital. A longer term decision would have to be made on whether the loan should be moved out of IRB. In addition, the privatization of IRB should be completed with the sale of the remaining NPF shares.

KB. KB should continue focusing on its main mission--maximizing the collection of its claims on enterprises. The methods utilized include financial restructuring of its clients, initiating bankruptcy and liquidation proceedings, and enhancing collateral coverage. Because KB is not envisioned to function as a commercial bank, its banking license should be withdrawn. Based on auditor's reports, KB's assets will not be able to cover its liabilities, which means that the bank's obligations to the NBS would have to be restructured and covered by an MoF guarantee (or NBS would have to make loan loss provisions).

---

[36] The temporary lending restrictions would be imposed by NBS under its role of supervisor, as a *quid pro quo* for the temporary regulatory forbearance granted to SLSP and VUB. The objective of these restrictions would differ from the restrictions observed in 1993-95, which were primarily imposed for reasons of monetary policy, in a period when indirect instruments of monetary policy were not well-developed.

Harmonizing the Legal Framework in the Banking Sector with the EU

Background

The section of the White Paper dealing with financial services divide the measures that are to be adopted during the pre-accession period into two stages. Stage one comprises those measures which address fundamental principles and provide the overall framework for more detailed legislation. Stage two consists of measures designed to reinforce the prudential regulation, and which are more closely linked with the creation of the EU's internal market. In addition to the measures listed in the White Paper, the approximation of legislation in the financial sector also requires the pre-existence of a basic legal framework (e.g., company law, accounting law and auditing), and the development of supervisory capacity. The establishment of an adequate supervisory capacity should be actually regarded as an important prerequisite to the implementation of the technical measures listed in the White Paper.

The task of harmonization with EU directives is dealt within the following Acts and Decrees:

The National Bank of Slovakia Act, dated November 18th, 1992;
The Banking Act N° 21/1991 dated December 20th, 1991 as amended by several other Acts;
The Act on Protection of Bank Deposits N° 118 dated March 20th, 1996;
The Foreign Exchange Act N° 202 dated September 20th, 1995;
The Money Laundering Act N° 249 dated August 19th, 1994;
The Act on Accounting N° 563/1991 dated December 12, 1991;
Several Decrees issued by the National Bank of Slovakia or the Ministry of Finance.

The following sections provide an assessment of the degree of compliance of those laws and decrees to the provisions mentioned in the White Paper (Box 4.1 provides a summarized description of the Slovak regulatory framework for banking).

The Creation of a Supervisory Authority to Ensure Implementation of Bank Legislation

Banking supervision in the Slovak Republic has been entrusted to the National Bank of Slovakia (NBS). The relevant pieces of legislation seem to give NBS sufficient legal powers to fulfill that mission, as it is allowed to issue binding prudential regulations, to grant or refuse a license, to revoke the license if necessary and, more generally, to verify that credit institutions comply with the prudential regulations. However, the credibility of the NBS as banking supervisor could be enhanced by an amendment to section 37 of the NBS Act, in order to eliminate any risk of duplication of the supervision exercised by the NBS (e.g., by the MoF). Moreover, the NBS should develop its on-site inspection capacity on the basis of section 36 (3) of the NBS Act, as on-site inspections are increasingly considered as essential to an efficient supervision. Finally, the NBS should introduce strict conditions on banks which are granted temporary regulatory forbearance, including the requirement of credible restructuring and privatization plans. That would create a level-playing field in the financial system and improve the system's credibility.

Stage One Measures

The following sections assess the progress that has been achieved in implementing Stage One measures, as described in the relevant Directives:

The First Banking Directive (77/780/EEC) of December 12, 1977
The Own Funds Directive (89/299/EEC) of April 17, 1989

The Solvency Ratio Directive (89/647/EEC) of December 18, 1989
The Directive on Deposit Guarantee Schemes (94/19/EEC) of May 30, 1994
The Directive on Money Laundering (91/308/EEC) of June 10, 1991

First Banking Directive (December 1977). The provisions of this Directive can be found in the Banking Act and two NBS Decrees stipulating the terms and conditions for obtaining a license to establish and operate a bank (or a branch of a foreign bank), as well as the minimum amount of equity capital. However, the definition given to the concept of "bank" in Article 1 of the Banking Act may be broader than the definition given by the Directive. The Directive defines a credit institution as being an undertaking whose business is to receive deposits or other repayable funds from the public and to grant credits for its own account. The two underlined conditions are not taken over in Article 1 of the Banking Act. A broader definition could constitute a problem, as only credit institutions complying with the definition of the Directive can be given the "European passport".

The provisions of the Directive on professional secrecy (applied to professionals employed by the supervisory authority), as well as the exemptions to that professional secrecy for the purpose of exchange of prudential information between supervisory authorities, have not yet been fully incorporated in the Banking Act or in the NBS Act.[37]

Own Funds Directive (April 1989). The provisions of this Directive have been incorporated in NBS Decree N°1/1994 adopted pursuant to Article 15 of the Banking Act. That Decree is largely harmonized with the Directive, and needs only to be adapted in some minor points where it is still less stringent than the Directive. For instance, the obligation to deduct holdings in other banks from the own funds of the reporting bank, should be extended to their holdings in other financial institutions. This is an important measure to avoid double gearing of own funds, particularly in the absence of supervision on a consolidated basis.

Solvency Ratio Directive (December 1989). The provisions of this Directive have been incorporated in NBS Decree N°2/1994 adopted pursuant to Article 15 of the Banking Act. As for the banks' own funds, the Decree is largely harmonized with the Directive and needs only to be adapted in the areas where it is still less stringent than the Directive. For instance, the 20 percent risk weight applied to claims on institutions supported by the Central Government can only be in compliance with the Directive if these institutions are supported by the State in any circumstances (and this commitment reflected in their acts of incorporation). The Directive also requests that the solvency ratio be calculated on a consolidated basis when the credit institution is the parent undertaking of a group of undertakings.

Directive on Deposit Guarantee Schemes (May 1994). The principles contained in this Directive have been implemented in Slovak law by the Act 118 dated March 20, 1996, on the protection of bank deposits. This Act, however, is not in full conformity with the Directive, as it limits the protection to deposits by natural persons (with the exception of accounts established for the purpose of business), whereas the Directive requests the coverage of all deposits, including deposits of legal persons. According

---

[37] According to Section 41 of the NBS Act, members of the NBS Board and NBS employees must maintain confidentiality in the performance of their functions. However, for the purpose of the public interest, NBS Board members may be exempted from this obligation by the Board, and other employees may be exempted by the Governor. The potential scope of those exemptions is unclear. Moreover, this section does not foresee exceptions on professional secrecy in order to allow exchanges of confidential information with other supervisory authorities within the country or abroad, whereas this is explicitly requested by the Directive (Article 12 of the First Banking Directive as amended by Article 16 of the Second Banking Directive).

to Annex 1 of the Directive, only deposits of some large companies may be excluded. These are companies which are of such a size that are not permitted to draw up abridged balance sheets pursuant to article 11 of the Fourth Council Directive (78/660/EC) of 25 July 1978.

Moreover, according to Act 118, the obligation to participate in the scheme becomes effective when the bank accepts its first cash deposit from a natural person, whereas according to the Directive, every credit institution has to join a deposit guarantee scheme. To achieve full conformity with the directive, the Banking Act should state that participation in the deposit guarantee scheme is a condition to obtain a license. In addition, whereas the Directive imposes a minimum compensation of ECU 20,000 per depositor (this amount may be reduced to ECU15,000 during a transitional period ending on December 31, 1999), Act 118 provides for a maximum amount of compensation set at thirty average monthly salaries (sixty in the case of building saving deposits), as stated by the Statistical Office of the Slovak Republic. This represents about Sk210,000 or about ECU5,300.

With the exception of these and some other minor points, however, Act 118 is largely in conformity with the Directive. The fact that the level of coverage is lower than the minimum level requested by the Directive could be accepted temporarily, provided that this level is progressively increased in order to reach the minimum level (ECU15,000 until December 31, 1999, and ECU20,000 after that date). More important is to extend the coverage to small businesses. The objective of deposit-guarantee schemes is to reinforce the confidence of the depositors in the banking system, by providing a limited protection to depositors. Therefore, it is important that small businesses, whether legal or natural persons, be also covered by the scheme[38].

The Directive on Money Laundering (June 1991). The White Book strongly recommends the establishment of adequate rules against money laundering in Stage One, in order to avoid that their financial sectors are used to launder the product of illegal activities in general, and drug trafficking in particular. Although Act 249 passed by the National Council of the Slovak Republic as of August 19, 1994, deals with many aspects of money laundering, it is still not in full conformity with the Directive. For example, one of the basic provisions of the Directive obliges banks and other financial institutions to request the identification of all their clients on the basis of a document proving their identity.[39] Act 249 introduced a new subsection (2) in article 37 of the Banking Act requesting banks to demand proof of identity from customers for each transaction "except the receipt of deposits on transferable savings

---

[38] The Slovak authorities are aware that the Act will have to be harmonized with the Directive before EU accession. They justify the differences by the fact that the Guarantee Fund would not have sufficient resources to provide for the coverage requested by the Directive. However, whereas the Directive is flexible regarding the financing of deposit guarantee schemes, it still requests that the assets of such schemes be in proportion with their liabilities. Also, the Directive allows no flexibility in the coverage of the protection, with the exception of the cases expressly listed in its Annex 1. Regarding the risk of moral hazard resulting from a generous coverage of deposits, this concern is minimized by the relatively low minimum protection. The Directive has nevertheless taken that concern into consideration by allowing Member States to shift some of the burden to the depositor. In practice, this means that depositors may bear up to 10 per cent of the loss, for deposits whose amount is lower than the minimum coverage. Member States are also free to introduce a higher percentage of co-responsibility for deposits of higher value. Note that deposits at three banks (VUB, IRB, and SLSB) are fully guaranteed by the State until December 31, 1997.

[39] This is not only applicable to clients opening a relation with a bank, but also to occasional clients if they want to make an operation for an amount higher than ECU15 000, or even for operations of lower amounts if this operation is suspect. Moreover, the Directive requests that banks and other financial institutions keep a copy of that document for at least five years.

accounts". In addition, banks are still not requested to keep the proof of identity. Finally, Act 249 did not implement another important provision of the Directive, requiring the supervisory authorities to report any proof of money laundering, whether obtained during on-site inspections or in other circumstances.

In order to render the fight against money laundering more effective, the Slovak authorities should consider creating a specific administrative body that would be in charge of receiving the reports on suspect operations made by the banks and other financial institutions. This specific body would play the role of an interface between the reporting institutions and the police or the judicial authorities that are in charge of the prosecution of money laundering, by examining the information reported by banks and other financial institutions.

Stage Two Measures

The purpose of Stage Two measures is to improve the prudential regulation of credit institutions to international standards. Some of the key measures that have to be adopted during Stage Two contain provisions directly linked to the creation of the Internal Market (freedom of establishment, free provision of services and home country control) which may be disregarded before accession.[40] The following sections assess the progress that has been achieved in implementing Stage Two measures, as described in the relevant Directives:

The Second Banking Directive (89/646/EEC) of December 15, 1989
The Large Exposures Directive (92/121/EEC) of December 21, 1992
The Directive on the Supervision of Credit Institutions on a Consolidated Basis (92/30/EEC) of April 6, 1992
The Capital Adequacy Directive (93/6/EEC) of March 15, 1993
The Directive on the annual accounts and the consolidated accounts of credit institutions and other financial institutions (86/635/EEC) of December 8, 1986.

Second Banking Directive (December 1989). Besides the provisions directly linked to the creation of the internal market which may be disregarded in a first stage, the Directive contains also a certain number of prudential rules concerning, among other things, the minimum initial capital, shareholder control, and rules on qualified holdings in non financial companies. Most of these rules have already been implemented in the Banking Act, although there are still some differences compared to the Directive. The existing provisions should be complemented by the requirement that the own funds of a credit institution may never fall below the amount of minimum initial capital (article 10 (1) of the Directive). Moreover, Article 16 and 17 of the Banking Act should be brought into line with the provisions of Articles 11 and 12 of the Directive. In particular, the banking supervisor should have the power to take appropriate measures in cases where the influence exercised by significant shareholders of the bank is likely to operate to the detriment of the prudent management of the bank (article 11(5) of the Directive). The Banking Act should also provide a clear description of the respective powers and responsibilities of the management and supervisory boards of banks, instead of leaving that entirely to the bank's articles of incorporation, as prescribed in the Commercial Code.[41]

---

[40] This is particularly the case of most provisions of the Second Banking Directive.

[41] The Banking Act (Article 8) simply states that a bank shall have a statutory body and a supervisory board and that the powers of those two bodies must be stated in the bank's articles of incorporation. Article 8(4) specifies that the members of the statutory body and supervisory board are responsible for the performance of banking activities. The Banking Act should contain rules in order to avoid pressures from the shareholders on bank

Large Exposures Directive (December 1992). The contents of this Directive are reflected in Decree No. 3/1994 of the NBS adopted pursuant to Article 15 of the Banking Act. This Decree represents a significant effort to reduce the concentration of risks towards one single client or group of connected clients, which is one of the main causes of bank failures. However, the Decree still needs some changes in the areas where it is less stringent than the Directive.[42]

The Directive on the Supervision of Credit Institutions on a Consolidated Basis (April 1992). This Directive has not yet been reflected in Slovak law, although supervision on a consolidated basis is today considered as a basic condition for effective banking supervision. When supervision is not done on a consolidated basis, the supervisors fail to obtain a global view of all the risks faced by a bank and its group, and a bank may easily escape supervision by transferring some of its activities to a non-bank subsidiary. Note that the Directive is applicable to all banking groups, including those where the parent undertaking is not a credit institution but a financial holding. The exercise of supervision on a consolidated basis is also one of the "minimum standards" developed by the Basle Committee on Banking Supervision. According to those minimum standards, host supervisory authorities should refuse the establishment on their territory of the subsidiary of a credit institution which is not supervised on a consolidated basis by the supervisory authorities in its home country. For these two reasons, the Slovak supervisory authorities should consider adopting the principle of consolidated supervision immediately, even though this measure was initially included in Stage Two.

The Capital Adequacy Directive (March 1993). This Directive addresses the other risks (other than the credit risk covered by the Solvency Ratio Directive) to which a credit institution is exposed, in particular the market risks. This Directive has not yet been implemented, but this does not constitute a problem at the present time, as the Directive has not yet been implemented by all member States either (although it should have been implemented before January 1, 1996). In addition, this is also not a priority as long as banks' trading activities remain limited in importance.[43]

---

managers and in particular specify which body is responsible for the granting of credits. For the same reasons, the Banking Act should contain rules on the plurality of mandates in a bank and in another company.

[42] The Decree is not in conformity to the Directive in the following areas: (i) the Decree allows banks to deduct from individual credit risk exposures the amounts that are fully secured by a guarantee issued by an institution supported by the state; (ii) the Decree allows banks to deduct from the individual credit exposures the amounts that are fully secured by debt securities issued by institutions supported by the state, international development banks, banks in the Slovak Republic, and in a Zone A state. The Directive allows this only subject to certain strict conditions; (iii) The Decree allows banks to transfer the credit risk exposure against a client to a third party in case of insurance where the bank will be indemnified as the insured person; (iv) The Decree did not introduce the sub-limit of 20 percent applicable when the client or group of connected clients is the parent or a subsidiary of the credit institution; (v) the Decree states that the individual exposures that exceed 15 percent of the bank's own funds shall not exceed 800 percent of its capital. The Directive specifies a stricter limit of 10 percent for the individual exposures; (vi) The Decree has not included the three limits specified by the Directive (20, 25 and 800 percent); (vii) The Decree just requires that banks do not increase further the exposures that exceeded the limits on the day the Decree entered into force, whereas the Directive is more demanding, and requires that banks reduce those exposures within a reasonable period.

[43] The Directive imposes new capital requirements for market risks contained in the trading portfolios of the credit institutions. Those risks result from variations in interest rates and equities prices, as well as settlement and counter-party risks. The Directive also requires credit institutions to cover foreign exchange and other risks with their own funds, and to set up systems to control the interest rate risk they face on their operations. Contrary to some legal views, this Directive is not reflected in the Decree N° 2/1994 of the NBS on capital adequacy, as

It should be noted, however, that the NBS issued a Decree N°5/1994 imposing limits to the foreign exchange risks faced by banks. Although this is not the approach that has been retained by the Directive (the Directive prescribes capital requirements instead of limits), it can be considered as appropriate for the time being. The NBS Decree could be complemented by requirements to monitor and control the interest rate risks in the banks' balance sheets and in off balance sheet derivative transactions. This would also complement the existing NBS Decree N°4/1994 on the supervision of the liquidity position of banks.

The Directive on the Annual Accounts and the Consolidated Accounts of Credit Institutions and Other Financial Institutions (December 1986). This Directive is not yet reflected in Slovak law. The Act on Accounting N°563/1991, which is applicable to all natural and legal persons, is very succinct and is not in line with international standards. As regards credit institutions, it has been complemented by a specific accounting plan, but the plan is incomplete, sometimes unclear, and lacks stability as it is amended every year. Some of those gaps were to a certain extent filled in by a Provision N°3 of the NBS of March 3, 1995 "on rules for evaluating bank's claims and off-balance sheet liabilities according to the risk contained therein and of reserving funds in order to provide against those risks". However, a full implementation of that Directive should be considered as a priority, not the least because it provides the foundations for the calculation of the solvency ratio on individual and consolidated basis.

Capital Movements

The White Paper indicates the basic conditions that would allow the Slovak Republic to introduce currency convertibility and enjoy the potential benefits of full integration in European and international capital markets. These conditions include: (i) macroeconomic stability, to avoid serious balance of payments difficulties and disruptive capital outflows; (ii) appropriate monetary policy instruments, to be able to cope with the potential repercussions of capital movements on inflation and the current account, and (iii) an efficient financial system, to ensure the channeling of capital inflows into productive investment.

The White Paper also distinguishes two stages in the liberalization process. In the first stage, all current payments and all long- and medium-term capital movements (with maturity longer than one year) should be liberalized unconditionally. The second stage is related to short term (with maturity less than one year) capital movements, such as the admission of, and the trade in, money-market securities, the opening of deposit accounts abroad, and the physical export and import of money. The White Paper indicates that this second stage should only take place in the last stages of the transition, when associated economies have established track records of stability and have turned into fully fledged market economies. Note that the effective liberalization of capital movements lifts not only foreign exchange restrictions, but also all administrative regulations which imply a discrimination based on the origin or the destination of capital. Moreover, this liberalization must apply both to residents and non-residents, and exclude all implicit or explicit authorization procedure.

Foreign exchange controls in the Slovak Republic are regulated by the Foreign Exchange Act N° 202 dated as of September 20, 1995. This Act requires a foreign exchange permit for most capital operations, although it also empowers foreign exchange authorities (NBS and Ministry of Finance) to move ahead with liberalization by means of Decrees (article 41). The Act also specifies that its provisions shall apply only where an international agreement does not stipulate otherwise (article 42).

---

amended by Decree N° 10/1995. Those two Decrees implemented in reality the Solvency Ratio Directive (the confusion results from the fact that the solvency rules are called capital adequacy rules in the NBS Decree).

The Slovak Republic seems to have made progress in adopting the Stage One measures specified in the White Paper. The country introduced full current account convertibility of the koruna as of October 1, 1995, achieving Article VIII Status in the IMF for those transactions. Also, the Foreign Exchange Act specifies that direct investments in the Slovak Republic by non-residents do not require a foreign exchange permit, although they must still be reported to the NBS.[44] However, foreign investors are not permitted to acquire real estate, unless the company concerned is incorporated in the Slovak Republic as an independent legal entity (subsidiary).

Direct investment abroad by Slovak residents normally requests a foreign exchange permit issued by the NBS upon agreement with the Ministry of Finance. However, Article 3 (e) of Decree N° 5 of the NBS as of September 25, 1995 authorizes payments abroad in connection with direct investments stipulated by an international agreement to which the Slovak Republic is party, without a foreign exchange permit. This covers direct investments in all EU countries in application of article 61 of the EU Association Agreement of December 19, 1994. This exemption has been recently extended to direct investments in a member state of the OECD (Article I point 4 of Decree N° 335 of the NBS and the Ministry of Finance of December 1, 1996).

The same Decree has further liberalized capital movements in order to comply with the requirements of OECD membership. As a consequence, the following operations require no more foreign exchange permits: (i) financial credits extended by a domestic entity to a non-resident with its seat in a member state of the OECD, if those credits are intended to cover goods and services delivered by the domestic entity abroad or if they have a maturity of five or more years; (ii) financial credits accepted by a domestic entity from a non-resident if these credits have a maturity of three or more years as well as financial credits accepted from a non-resident seated in a member state of the OECD in order to cover goods or services delivered by that non-resident; (iii) acquisition of real estate in a member state of the OECD. Moreover, limits on the export and import of banknote and coins were lifted and replaced by a reporting requirement in case of export or import of banknote and coins exceeding the aggregate amount of Sk150,000.

Foreign exchange regulations should be liberalized further in order to allow all capital movements with a maturity of over one year, and fulfill entirely the Stage One measures listed in the White Paper. In this context, it has to be noted that the Slovak authorities have already taken a certain number of engagements in the context of the negotiations for OECD membership. In particular, on March 19, 1996, the Slovak Government declared that it would extend on a non-discriminatory basis to all member states of OECD, the measures of liberalization that would be taken in the context of the EU Association Agreement.

---

[44] The 1996 OECD survey concludes that there are no direct restrictions on foreign direct investment or the remittances of profits abroad, but the institutional framework for foreign direct investment in the Slovak Republic is ambivalent. One the one side, it is characterized by liberal measures, like the absence of a specific law on foreign direct investment (foreign owned companies operate in the framework of the commercial code under the same conditions as Slovak companies), the absence of a screening procedure for foreign investment, and the absence of reciprocity measures, in particular in the banking and insurance sector. On the other side, foreign investment continues to be restricted by the public sector's extensive participation in a large number of enterprises, and the exclusion from privatization of a certain number of strategic enterprises. The lower level of foreign direct investment in comparison with other CEEs seems to be due to a large extent to the fact that domestic policy-makers do not always see the benefits from opening the capital of Slovak enterprises to foreign capital. The establishment of agreements for mutual protection and support of investments and the liberalization of the capital account should therefore be complemented by efforts to establish confidence in the sense of policy direction.

It took also the engagement not to discriminate among OECD countries in case of recourse to the escape clauses of the Association Agreement.

Following that unilateral declaration, the Slovak Republic elaborated a timetable for further liberalization of the capital account. This timetable favors capital inflows ahead of outflows, long-term flows rather than short-term and direct rather that portfolio investments. The deadlines for the further steps are the following: (i) liberalization of all inflows by end-1998; (ii) liberalization of all outflows by end-1999; (iii) permission of opening of accounts abroad by Slovak residents by end-2000. Only the freeing of purchase of real estate by non-resident individuals would have to wait until after the year 2000, as restitution processes would not have been finalized before then.

In view of the considerable progress on the macroeconomic front and the reported absence of any significant pressures from short-term capital inflows, the OECD Committee on Financial Markets felt that it should be possible to move forward with the liberalization of capital movements and cross-border financial services. In particular, priority should be given to: (i) allowing foreign direct investors to acquire real estate necessary for the conduct or their business activities, even if they establish only a branch in the country; (ii) advancing the time schedule for the liberalization of foreign credits of a maturity of one year or more; (iii) advancing the time schedule for the liberalization of the purchase of foreign shares and long-term government debt securities abroad by residents and the admission of these instruments in the domestic financial market.

Capital Markets

At the end of 1996 there were 970 equities and 91 bonds registered with the Bratislava Stock Exchange (BSE).[45] Most of these securities are also registered in the parallel RMS market (or Market Registration System), which deals mostly with small retail investors and operates as an off-exchange market via a network of 150 offices across the country. Until late 1995 a third and smaller market, the Bratislava Options Exchange (BOE), was also in operation. The existence of three exchanges, coupled with the large volumes of direct trades that took place outside the official markets, led to a high degree of market fragmentation and low transparency of transactions. The Amendment to the Securities Act in 1995 aimed to improve these conditions by introducing stricter reporting requirements and banning off-exchange trades. However, the market continues to be fragmented and overburdened with a large number of registered shares that do not fit the profile of a publicly-traded company. The bond market is also plagued by structural deficiencies, resulting in low turnover and a predominance of short maturities. The lack of an independent regulatory and supervisory body aggravates these problems, as it leads to a weak enforcement of regulations, and opens room for politically-driven interventions. These factors have affect investors' confidence in capital markets and have limited its use as source of investment finance.

The Government is faced with the challenge of defining and implementing legal and institutional reforms designed to reduce fragmentation, increase transparency, and enhance the confidence of issuers and investors through reducing uncertainty and transaction costs. Meeting this challenge successfully should generate important benefits, as there is evidence that capital markets can contribute to economic growth by providing an important complementary source of investment finance, while reducing financial intermediation costs and enhancing corporate governance.[46]

---

[45] The BSE started operations in April 1993, at which time SOEs included in the first wave of privatization were registered. The SOEs included in the second wave were also registered in the BSE.

[46] Levine, R. and S. Zervos (1996), "Stock Market Development and Long-Run Growth," World Bank Economic Review, vol. 10 (May), and Holmstrom, B. and J. Tirole (1993), "Market Liquidity and Performance Monitoring." Journal of Political Economy, Vol. 4. (August).

The improvement of the regulatory and supervisory framework for capital market operations must also take into consideration the objective of EU accession and the need to achieve legal harmonization with EU legislation. However, the challenge for the Slovak Republic goes beyond such harmonization, since EU legislation was designed at a time when most Member States had already well-functioning capital markets. Therefore, efforts to improve the capital market must proceed in two parallel tracks, namely, identifying and removing the structural obstacles to market development, and approximating the legal framework to the EU. This section describes the evolution of capital markets in recent years, identifies the areas for improvement, and examines the progress achieved in legal approximation.

The Status of Equity Markets

The small options exchange was closed in late 1995, but this measure had little impact on reducing market fragmentation due to its minor share in overall trade value.[47] Although the banning of off-exchange trades--resulting from the amendments to the Securities Act--did generate some improvements, the co-existence of two markets (BSE and RMS) handling a large number of shares and lacking coordination, still reduces market transparency, limits the number of transactions per share and the achievement of a higher degree of liquidity. In addition to these problems of market organization, there are other important problems that have reduced the incentive of both savers and issuers to resort to capital markets. For one, investors have inadequate access to the information necessary for making investment decisions (e.g., detailed information on the financial position and growth prospects of a company is not readily available). Also, minority shareholders are frequently ignored by management boards and majority investors. Furthermore, regulatory and supervisory tasks are currently delegated to the MoF, creating uncertainty about the stability of the rules and opening room for political considerations. As a result of these problems, the capital market remains underutilized, despite the appearances of a very large market size.

The Slovak equity market indeed seems large relative to other CEE countries and other middle-income countries. As shown in Table 4.4, the BSE alone had 970 listed shares, a total market capitalization equivalent to 29 percent of GDP, and an annual trade value of 13.4 percent of GDP. The Slovak equity market appears much larger than those in Poland, Hungary, Slovenia, and other emerging markets, such as Turkey. The Slovak market does not look larger than the average markets in Western Europe (Table 4.4 provides the average for France, Germany, Spain, and United Kingdom), but this is expected, since these are markets of higher income countries which have been operating for a much longer period of time.

The size of the Slovak market is overestimated, however, considering that 300-400 of the companies currently registered in the BSE have never been traded, and that most other shares are barely traded. This is a problem shared by the Czech Republic, whose equity market also emerged from voucher privatization, and which also experiences a problem of excessive number of shares. Excluding the companies whose shares have not been traded at least once a year, the market capitalization in the Slovak Republic is reduced from 29 percent to 11 percent of GDP.

---

[47] The shares of BOE, RMS and BSE in overall trade were 2, 29, and 69 percent, respectively.

Table 4.4
Equity Markets in the Visegrad, Turkey and Europe--Selected Indicators (end-1996)

	Bratislava Stock Exchange			Czech Republic	Poland	Hungary	Slovenia	Turkey	Europe (average)
	Registered with LR[1/]	Registered without LR[1/]	Total Market						
Number of Companies	21	949	970	1,588	83	45	21	229	1,039
Market Capitalization / GDP (percent)	6.8	21.8	28.6	34.9	6.4	11.8	3.5	16.5	64.9
Annual Value Traded / GDP (percent)	6.5	6.9	13.4	16.3	4.2	3.7	2.1	20.2	35.9
Turnover Ratio (percent)	95.9	31.8	46.9	46.6	66.0	31.1	60.5	122.7	74.3
Shares Traded (millions of shares)	43.5	85.1	128.6	n.a	n.a	n.a	n.a	n.a	n.a
Shares Traded / Number of Companies	2.07	0.09	0.13	n.a	n.a	n.a	n.a	n.a	n.a

n.a.: not available

1/ LR stands for "Listing Requirements." There are 13 "senior" shares and 8 "junior" shares among the registered shares that need to fulfill listing requirements.

Sources: IFC Emerging Markets Factbook 1997 and Bratislava Stock Exchange 1996 - *Annual Statistics.*

The problems in the Slovak equity markets are better reflected in the turnover ratio (TR)--a usual measure of market liquidity. As shown in Table 4.4, the Slovak TR (defined as value traded divided by market capitalization) is similar to the Czech, but lower than most other CEE countries, as well as Turkey and an average of four European countries. It becomes much smaller if we distinguish between those 21 firms that need to meet listing requirements (LR), which have a TR close to 96 percent, and the much larger segment that do not need to meet these LR, which have a TR of 32 percent.[48] Other liquidity indicators show a similar picture. For example, the number of times an "average" share is traded (volume of trade in number of shares divided by the number of companies) is 2.07 times per company in the first group, and only 0.09 times per company without LR.

In sum, the Slovak equity market is non-transparent, illiquid, and perceived as unreliable, in spite of the country's good macroeconomic performance and the good technical infrastructure of the market (BSE, RMS, and Central Securities Depository provide efficient clearing, settlement and registry services). Failure to correct the organizational, regulatory and supervisory problems that are affecting its performance, and to improve market liquidity, would deprive companies of a potentially important source of finance and limit its potential contribution to long-run growth.

The Status of Bond Markets

At the end of 1996, the Slovak bond market had a market capitalization equivalent to 13.6 percent of GDP. Government securities accounted for more than 80 percent of the total, with the outstanding stocks of Government bonds (US$2.0 billion) and Treasury bills (US$200 million) amounting to over 10 percent of GDP. The average maturity of the outstanding stock of Government bonds was 2.8 years. Most Government issues remain on the books of commercial banks and are not actively traded, which is different

---

[48] Shares meeting LR are distributed in senior and junior markets. LR for the senior tier are: (i) Sk500 million in share capital; (ii) issue size of Sk100 million; (iii) three years of business history; (iv) three years to be covered by the company prospectus; and (v) quarterly financial reporting. The respective requirements for the junior market are: (i) Sk100 million; (ii) Sk100 million; (iii) one year; (iv) one year; and (v) semi-annual.

from what is observed in Western European economies, where these securities are widely traded and used for liquidity management.

Table 4.5
Bond Markets in Selected CEE Countries

	Market Capitalization (percentage of GDP)		Value Traded (percentage of GDP)		Turnover Ratio (percent)	
	1994	1996	1994	1996	1994	1996
Slovak Republic	2.8	12.6	0.2	5.0	7.0	39.7
Czech Republic	4.8	7.0	1.9	5.6	38.9	79.4
Hungary	10.0	10.8	0.7	3.2	7.4	31.4
Poland	2.5	7.6	0.5	2.3	22.2	32.5
Slovenia	2.7	1.7	1.7	0.5	63.9	26.3
France	50.0	58.3	90.3	80.4	180.7	137.9

Note: For all countries the data excludes short-term Treasury Bills. Market capitalization corresponds to outstanding stock at the end of each year. Data for Czech Republic corresponds to 1995.
Sources: ING Barings, *A Guide to Slovak Corporate Bond Issuers*, February 1997, and national sources.

The deficiencies of the bond market in the Slovak Republic are also shared by the bond markets in other CEE countries. In these countries, Government and companies have found it difficult to issue longer-term securities, and most of the outstanding stocks are held in the portfolio of commercial banks. In fact, the Slovak bond market seems slightly more developed than the markets of other CEE countries, as indicated by a higher value traded to GDP and a relatively high turnover ratio (Table 4.5). Also, during the last calendar year, the market absorbed relatively large issues of corporate and bank bonds (Table 4.6), with the longest maturity being of 5 years. However, the municipal bond market remains relatively small and issues of commercial paper continue to be very limited.

Table 4.6
Domestic Bond Issues, 1993-96 (US$ million)

	1993	1994	1995	1996
Government	100.8	253.6	1290.7	354.3
Corporate	9.1	27.0	216.8	396.6
Banking	4.6	11.1	138.7	279.7
of which: VUB	0.0	0.0	50.7	125.4
Municipal	3.0	4.0	9.0	21.6
Total	117.5	295.7	1655.1	1052.2

Source: VUB.

Recommendations for the Development of Capital Markets

The key deficiencies that the Slovak Republic needs to address can be grouped into three major areas: (i) increasing market transparency by, *inter alia*, reducing the number of publicly traded firms and implementing strict information disclosure requirements for those firms that remain registered; (ii) developing a strong and independent supervisory body; and (iii) introducing targeted legal and regulatory changes aimed at supporting capital market development.

The Slovak Republic should reduce the number of publicly traded firms since the current number of registered companies has no relationship to market size. In most capital markets, companies apply for stock exchange listing on a voluntary basis. Their choice is based on economic, financial and strategic considerations and is supported by strict listing requirements with respect to information disclosure and corporate governance. These requirements are onerous, but viewed as justified in order to gain access to new financing sources. In the Slovak Republic, however, capital markets were used for the initial ownership distribution process that took place through the voucher privatization. As a result, many medium-sized companies with limited number of shareholders are currently registered as publicly-traded companies, but in fact operate as privately-held companies. In addition, the majority of companies registered in the market during the second wave of privatization have never been traded.

This "de-listing process" should be based on a realistic assessment of the cost of management time, information disclosure requirements, and advisory fees, and how these compare to the benefits from having direct access to the capital markets. The selection criteria of companies to be de-listed should be clearly defined and mechanisms aimed at protecting the rights of minority shareholders should be developed. Among the main benefits of this rationalization of the equity market is the expected increase in liquidity and transparency.

In the area of supervision, the objective should be the transfer of supervisory tasks from the MoF to a new independent and professional agency.[49] This agency should have the expertise and resources to enforce effectively securities regulations and legislation, and must be shielded from political influence. Also, in order to increase the predictability of market transactions and boost investors' confidence, the supervisory agency should have clearly defined powers to avoid undue administrative discretion. The establishment of such an entity should be accompanied by training programs for its staff and by the provision of sufficient resources to carry out the roles required by EU Directives.

In addition, self-regulatory organizations (SROs) should be strengthened and professional associations supported, enabling an increased coordination of market developments and an enhanced dialogue between market participants and regulatory authorities. By placing greater responsibility in the hands of SROs, most of the enforcement responsibilities (e.g., with respect to security, professional conduct, and technical requirements) become more effective.

The development of capital markets is also tied to the regulatory and legal framework within which this market operates. This refers not only to the quality of existing laws and regulations but, more importantly, to the effectiveness and transparency with which they are enforced. In this respect, several additional areas for policy changes are worth addressing to support capital market development. Among them:

Ensuring adequate minority shareholder protection. It should be one of the Government's key priorities to design effective means to protect the interests of minority shareholders. While legislation passed in 1995 introduced some rules for protection of minority shareholders during takeovers or buy-

---

[49] It should be noted that over the last several years capital markets in OECD countries have witnessed rapid growth of large financial conglomerates, and that regulators in these countries are now faced with a need to modify supervision arrangements in order to cope with the realities of the marketplace. In the case of Slovak Republic, it is important to take these market trends into account when designing a supervision agency.

outs,[50] there is a need to introduce additional protection measures and also to develop enforcement capacity (the legal section of Chapter III provides some recommendations in this area).

Enhancing market transparency and liquidity. Rationalizing the operations of the BSE and RMS markets through, for example, better integration and coordination of their information disclosure and pricing procedures, would greatly contribute to reducing fragmentation and improving transparency. Creating a full-fledged repo market, as an efficient liquidity management tool, would contribute to enhancing market liquidity, at least in the bond segment of the market.

Ensuring quality of disclosed information. The disclosure of information, while onerous, enables firms to benefit from increased access to capital markets as a financing source. However, the format and quality of disclosed information needs to be monitored in order to enhance the decision-making process of investors.

Removing regulatory and taxation barriers. Restrictions for the participation of foreign institutions (public or private) in the Government debt market should be eliminated, as it not only hinders the development of capital markets but is not coherent with EU accession requirements. Introducing tax neutrality for different groups of securities would eliminate the barriers that inhibit the practice of lending securities and would improve transparency as well.

Privatizing the Central Depository for Securities. The sale of the 100 percent stake held by the Ministry of Finance to market participants (i.e., members of the BSE and banks) would help to improve and develop custody services, securities lending and trading and, therefore, would increase the attractiveness of the Slovak market for cross-border portfolio investment.

Legal Harmonization with EU Directives

As in the case of financial institutions, measures to harmonize Slovak law with EU Directives in the area of securities regulation are divided into Stage One (those addressing the overall framework and fundamental principles of capital markets) and Stage Two (those linked with developing the internal market). The task of harmonization with EU Directives is dealt with in Slovak legislation through the following Acts and their amendments:

The Securities Act No. 600/92, as amended by Acts Nos. 88/1994, 246/1994, 249/1994, 171/1995, and 554/1996;
The Stock Exchange Act No. 214/1992;
The Investment Companies and Investment Funds Act No. 248/92, as amended by Acts 600/1992, 91/1994, and 249/1994.
Stage One Measures. The first stage focuses on general principles underlying the capital markets, such as equal treatment of investors and provision of adequate information to the public. This stage includes:

Directive on Stock Exchange Listing Particulars (79/279/EEC) of March 5, 1979;
UCITS Directive (85/611/EEC) of December 20, 1985;

---

[50] The 1995 Amendment to the Securities Act mandates investors who gain control of 30 percent or more of a publicly traded company, to make a bid within 60 days for the remainder of the shares at a price no lower than the average price in the preceding six months.

Directive on Notification of Major Shareholdings (88/627/EEC) of December 12, 1988;
Directive on Public Offering Prospectus (89/298/EEC) of April 17, 1989;
Directive on Insider Dealing (89/592/EEC) of November 13, 1989.

Directive on Stock Exchange Listing Particulars (March 1979). The provisions of this Directive regulate information disclosure requirements and conditions for the admission of securities to the official listing on a stock exchange. The Slovak Securities Act, as amended, is mostly in compliance with the requirements of this Directive, since it was originally drafted with EU accession in mind. There are some areas in the regulatory scheme which have gaps, for example in the area of mutual recognition--the Directive has established a "home country rule" in order to facilitate the listing and issuance of securities, as well as activities of investment companies across Member States. This principle has not yet been incorporated into Slovak law, but it needs to be verified whether this particular requirement relates more closely to the Internal Market, and may be complied with in a later stage.

UCITS Directive (December 1985). The aim of this Directive is to coordinate laws on undertakings for collective investment in transferable securities (UCITS), i.e., units trusts or investment funds. It provides principles for the authorization of open-ended investment funds; rules for sale and repurchase of their units; obligations concerning management, investment, depositories and prospectuses; and designation of authorities responsible for authorization and supervision of these funds. This Directive is addressed only partly by the Slovak Act on Investment Companies and Investment Funds, as amended. An important area where the law falls short of EU requirements is the treatment of foreign UCITS, namely the requirement to get a special license in the Slovak Republic, even if licensed in a member State, and the subjecting of UCITS from an EU Member State to the supervisory powers of the MoF. According to the Directive, only specific issues, such as advertising and marketing are supervised by an agency from the country where UCITS are operating; the rest of their activities are supervised by the country where they are situated.

Directive on Notification of Major Shareholdings (December 1988). Provides investors with adequate information on natural and legal persons that acquire or dispose of major holdings in publicly traded companies (defined as 10, 20, 33, 50 percent, and 67 percent of a firm's total stock). This Directive is complied with by the Slovak Securities Act, which requires disclosure of ownership changes which cross the thresholds of 5, 10, 20, 30, 50, and 65 percent.

Directive on Public Offering Prospectus (April 1989). Coordinates minimum requirements for the content of prospectuses of companies that offer transferable securities to the public for the first time. The Securities Act contains no provisions for the recognition of prospectuses when securities are issued simultaneously (or within a short period of time) in more than one Member State. Such provisions will need to be added to make Slovak law comply with this Directive.

Directive on Insider Dealing (November 1989). Aims to protect investors against improper use of insider information. The Securities Act, as amended, is in compliance with this Directive, by vesting investigative powers and procedures in the MoF and making references to the penal code.

Stage Two Measures. This stage focuses on the governance and supervision of investment companies and their capital adequacy (applicable also to banks and other credit institutions). Some of the key measures that have to be adopted during this stage contain provisions directly linked to the creation of the Internal Market which may be disregarded prior to formal accession (e.g., freedom of establishment and free provision of services and home country control). These measures are described by:

Capital Adequacy Directive (93/6/EEC) of March 1993;
Investment Services Directive (93/22/EEC) of 1993; and
Directive on the Annual Accounts and the Consolidated Accounts of Credit Institutions and Other
Financial Institutions of December 1996.

Capital Adequacy Directive (March 1993). This Directive sets minimum initial capital for
investment firms determined by type of activities and operations, and varying from ECU125,000 (while
dealing only for the customer) to ECU730,000 (while dealing for both the customer as well as oneself). The
Directive also requires consolidation in the case of two or more investment firms belonging to the same
group. As mentioned in the banking section, this Directive has not yet been incorporated into Slovak law.
Its incorporation should be one of the priorities for the Government since it will serve to strengthen the
financial markets.

Investment Services Directive (1993). Requires Member States to establish competent authorities
to grant and withdraw authorizations of investment firms and supervise their activities. The principles of
home country control and single license are established in this directive. It also defines the basis for
investment firms or banks' access to regulated markets, eliminating the need for banks to establish
subsidiaries to become members of stock exchanges. The Slovak Republic does not yet conform with the
home country rule, mutual recognition or single license principles, and also lacks the independent
supervisory agency needed to enforce these principles.

*Directive on the Annual Accounts and the Consolidated Accounts of Credit Institutions and
Other Financial Institutions (December 1996).* As mentioned in the previous section, this Directive is not
yet reflected in Slovak law, although its implementation should be given great priority. Otherwise, Slovak
companies will continue to be restrained from accessing capital in foreign financial markets.

Implementation and Enforcement

The Slovak Republic has made progress in harmonizing its legal and regulatory framework to EU
Directives. However, despite this progress at formal approximation, many of the provisions in Slovak law
are not effectively enforced through the court system or are not implemented through the competent
authorities. For example, the provisions of the Securities Act, as amended, related to the Directive on
Insider Dealing have not been effectively implemented yet. Similarly, the Directive on Notification of
Major Shareholdings calls for notifying the supervisory agency when a shareholder's ownership in a
company raises above or falls below a certain limit (the initial threshold is set at 5 percent). This
obligation is routinely ignored by many enterprises and holding companies and compliance with this
provision is neither enforced by the supervisory body nor the courts. These developments reinforce the
need to introduce an independent and strong supervisory agency.

The Insurance Sector

The Slovak insurance market grew by 18 percent in 1995, to reach Sk10.5 billion in premium
income. This is equivalent to 2 percent of GDP and in line with other Visegrad countries. The non-life
sector (motor insurance; property insurance; and other non-life activities such as accidents and natural
catastrophes) accounts for the major part of this income, and has continued to grow faster than the life
sector. The growth of the latter remains limited by tax provisions (no tax deductibility for employers'
contributions), which make company-sponsored group life insurance contracts (the most common life
insurance activities in emerging markets) expensive for the sponsoring companies. As of end-1995, there
were 16 insurance companies in Slovak Republic, half of them foreign. However, the Slovak market is still

dominated by Slovenska Poistovna, which has over 1,500 employees, 34 branch offices and 87 agencies. The company is active in all main insurance activities and has retained the monopoly for third party liability (mandatory) car insurance contracts. The National Property Fund (NPF) owns over 50 percent of the company shares.

To facilitate further growth of the insurance sector in the Slovak Republic and to prepare it for cross-border competition and future EU integration, the authorities should accelerate and pursue efforts to: (i) review the legislation in line with EU regulations (Box 4.1); (ii) ensure compliance with the international standards concerning separation of life and non-life activities; (iii) create basis of an Insurance Guarantee Fund; (iv) create a more enabling tax environment for group life insurance policies; and (v) strengthen insurance supervision (which is presently delegated to the MoF, and which has limited capacity to actively monitor and enforce the existing regulations, including the minimum technical solvency levels). Among the above, the lack of a strong and independent *supervisory agency* with the resources and expertise to effectively monitor and regulate the market and enforce insurance legislation, stands out as a key challenge still to be addressed. Developing this capacity is important both in the interest of the Slovak insurance market and as a pre-condition for legislative convergence with EU insurance sector standards. At minimum, insurance supervision should regulate market entrance, strictly enforce the solvency of the operators (existing and new entrants), regulate the methods of calculation of technical reserves, supervise the insurance products offered, and systematically analyze audits and other financial information.

Box 4.1: EU Directives for the Insurance Sector

The development of the Internal Market for insurance services has taken place in phases which are roughly commensurate to the two stages of EU measures outlined in the White Paper. Stage One focuses solely on harmonizing rules for the establishment, implementation and supervision of insurance activities. It is based on the "host country" principle (i.e., an agency in the country in which an insurance operator is active is in charge of all supervision activities). Stage Two measures go considerably further and set up the Internal Market in insurance by introducing a "single passport" in insurance. Based on the trust and cooperation among supervision agencies of the Member States, market supervision has moved to the "home country" principle (i.e., insurance operators are regulated and supervised by a competent authority of the country in which they were established).

Stage One measures are based mainly on two directives (*First Non-Life Directive 73/239/EEC* and *First Life Insurance Directive 79/267/EEC*), which coordinate and harmonize the EU member states provisions in the insurance business (conditions of admissions, operation, withdrawal of authorization, rules applicable for branches on companies based outside of the EU). These Directives prescribe that life and non-life insurance should be carried out by separate legal and financial entities; and that insurance companies should have a minimum solvency ratio and participate in a guarantee fund. Operations of the insurance companies are also strictly limited to the insurance business only (i.e., no diversification or holdings). In addition, the *Council Directive 91/674/EEC* contains rules on annual accounts and consolidated accounts of insurance companies. Its principal objective is to define minimum standards for the financial information that should be made available to the public. The directive takes into account the fact that there is a considerable convergence in the field of non-life insurance. However, the differences in life insurance in the EU (i.e., premium calculation, choice of the technical interest rate, mortality tables, treatment of costs, investment rules and policies, valuation of assets, etc.) are still considerable.

Stage Two measures (*Third Council Directive 92/49/EEC* which amends *Directives 73/239/EEC* and *Directives 88/357/EEC* and *Third Council Directive 92/96/EEC* which amends *Directives 79/267/EEC* and *Directives 90/619/EEC*) introduce a single passport rule, allow insurance companies to freely sell their products throughout the EU, and abolish prior control of premiums and tariffs. Stage Two measures also recommend rules on classification, valuation and diversification of the assets representing the technical provisions, and abolish the principle of prior systematic notification and approval of tariffs, including new products. Finally, they stipulate that competent authorities must be informed about the identity of shareholders and amounts of their shareholding participation. This applies to direct and indirect shareholders (natural or legal persons).

There are also several other directives which regulate the insurance business. These are the *Directive on Legal Expenses Insurance (87/344/EEC)*; the *Directive on Credit and Surety Insurance (87/343/EEC)*; the *Directives on Motor Insurance (72/166/EEC, 84/5/EEC, 90/232/EEC)*; the *Directive on Tourist Insurance (84/641/EEC)* and the *Directive on Co-Insurance (78/473/EEC)*. There are also two transitional directives (*Directive 88/357/EEC* for non-life and *Directive 90/619/EEC* for life) which are bridging the gap between the Stage One measures, which are focused on facilitating the freedom of establishment for insurance companies, and those directives that introduce an open inter-EU insurance market.

CHAPTER V: THE AGRICULTURAL SECTOR IN TRANSITION

Introduction

The Slovak Republic is a mountainous country with a moderate agricultural potential. Primary agriculture and food processing currently account for about 7.5 percent of GDP and 8 percent of employment. Agriculture output declined by more than 30 percent in the early stages of the transition (1990-92), but stabilized after that period and recorded a modest growth in 1996. Food prices have been liberalized and generally reflect world market levels, with a few exceptions, such as milk and sugar. The legal transformation of ownership in the sector is nearly completed, leading to a reduction in the share of state companies in output to less than 5 percent. The aggregate level of support to Slovak farmers has declined by more than 50 percent in real terms since 1989, making it about half as generous as the support extended to EU farmers. Despite these transformation efforts, more needs to be done to increase productivity in agriculture in the next few years as the Slovak Republic prepares for EU accession.

This chapter is divided into four sections. The first section reviews progress in restoring private property rights in agriculture. It argues that the legal part of the process has been completed, but that it will take more time for the new owners to turn obsolete production facilities into efficient enterprises. The second section reviews the main adjustments since 1989. It argues that agriculture has adjusted to a massive change in its terms-of-trade, but that efficiency in the sector still lags substantially behind EU standards, especially in the case of agroindustries and distribution systems. The third section reviews the Government's agricultural policy. It makes the point that while the aggregate subsidy level declined by 50 percent since 1989, government support policies may be gradually turning into obstacles for further market development. The final section makes policy recommendations aimed at improving economic efficiency, and examines selected issues of EU accession.

Transformation and Privatization

The legal process of transformation of farm cooperatives and privatization of state-owned enterprises has been completed. However, any significant increase in economic efficiency in primary agriculture will depend on further transformation of cooperatives into profit-oriented farms, and more efforts by the new owners to adjust to domestic and foreign competition. The further transformation of cooperatives seems particularly important for the achievement of further efficiency gains in agriculture, as 70 percent of farm land is cultivated by cooperatives. The remaining share is cultivated by privatized state farms (20 percent), trading companies (7 percent) and household plots (3 percent).

Transformation of Cooperatives

In a complex legal process, about 98 percent of former collective farms had transformed themselves into new cooperatives by January 1993. The main purpose of this process was to restitute land and re-establish individual rights to non-land assets. Each cooperative prepared a transformation plan offering three alternatives to participants (active and retired members, and others with restitution claims): (i) becoming a member of a new cooperative; (ii) canceling membership and requesting shares of land and other assets in order to farm independently; or (iii) leasing land and other assets to the new cooperative with an option to convert shares into cash by 1999.

Restitution of land. Difficulties to identify all former land owners led the Government to extend the deadline for restitution from January 1993 to December 1995, and to introduce a concept of "presumed ownership". Despite these measures, about 35 percent of land could not be confirmed and continues to be farmed by cooperatives pending clarification of titles. Land restitution has been accompanied by an extreme fragmentation of ownership. Land records register about 9.6 million farm plots covering a land area of 2.4 million hectares. Typically, ownership of an average size plot of about 0.5 hectares is claimed by 12 to 15 co-owners. Fragmentation of ownership has made it difficult to update the land cadastre and to account properly for land titles.

Fragmentation of land ownership has not led to fragmentation of land use, as cooperatives retain about 70 percent of farm land in large contiguous plots and most owners lease land to cooperatives for the equivalent of about 0.5 to 2.5 percent of the land appraisal values for tax purposes. However, leasing has not eliminated all the problems resulting from fragmented ownership. For one, most lease contracts have a one-year termination clause and the relative insecurity of tenure undermines long-term investment plans. The excessive fragmentation of ownership also hinders the development of an active market for farm land by increasing significantly transactions costs--the acquisition of a contiguous plot of land for commercial farming requires the purchaser to settle a large number of contracts. In addition, there are other obstacles to the development of a land market, such as the exclusion of foreigners from land purchases.

Restitution of non-land assets. The most sensitive part of the transformation process has been the re-establishment of individual rights to assets contributed by farmers during collectivization and to assets accumulated by cooperatives. In this process, the net worth of a cooperative (except for land) was divided in shares allocated among the participants as follows: (i) 50 percent in proportion to contributed land; (ii) 30 percent in proportion to contributed non-land assets; and (iii) 20 percent in proportion to the years of employment in the cooperative. About half of the participants, holding on average 40 percent of the shares, decided to exit and to convert their shares into cash (most of the participants taking this option were not current members of the cooperatives). The participants had to accept a deep discount, reflecting the distressed financial situation of most cooperatives.

Preliminary results of transformation. The legal transformation of cooperatives made it possible for farmers to exit and to farm either individually, to set up a smaller cooperative or to set up a commercial farm. So far, most farmers opted to rejoin cooperatives, mainly because they have no experience with other types of organizations, their equipment is unsuitable for small-scale farming, and the risks of self-employment and the loss of cooperative benefits

Table 5.1

Size and Number of Cooperatives, 1989-95

Year/Area (ha)	1989	1993	1995
< 500	1	55	133
500 - 1,000	30	192	240
1,000 - 1,500	91	226	246
1,500 - 2,000	101	169	157
2,000 - 2,500	105	115	103
2,500 <	308	195	140
Total	636	952	1,019

Source: Ministry of Agriculture.

are perceived as too high. As shown in Table 5.1, cooperatives have become smaller and more numerous since 1989. Many cooperatives have remained much the same in the way of conducting their business, and have not been able to stop generating losses--as shown below, gross losses in agriculture amounted to 1.3 percent of GDP in 1996.

The pressure to reduce losses and increase profits are leading more cooperatives to reorganize into corporations farming on average about 1,000 ha. However, progress in this direction is still limited--by 1995 only 100 limited liability companies with an average size of 650 ha and 29 shareholding companies with average farm size of 1,270 ha were established, accounting for less than 5 percent of farm land. On the other hand, more commercial family farms are being established with a cultivated area of 20-50 ha by spinning off from cooperatives. Further reorganization and changes in ownership may be expected as a result of the likely bankruptcy of loss-making cooperatives.

Privatization of State Farms

Cultivating 20 percent of farm land, state farms have been privatized either on the basis of restitution and compensation claims or according to privatization laws. The main difference with privatization of industry has been the large number and types of restitution claims in agriculture. Restitution claims had to be resolved prior to privatization which brought delays and privatization of only two state farms by 1995.[51] Significant progress began in 1995. As of June 1997, 109 state farms valued at Sk 14.0 billion were privatized. The privatization of state farms has followed three methods similar to those applied to industry. The first method is by direct sales to selected investors for attractive prices; repayment by installments with the first installment amounting typically to 10-20 percent of the purchase price; and deduction of part of future investments from the purchase price. The second method is by public tender according to which the first installment represent 3 percent of the purchase price with the possibility of postponement by three years. The third method is by establishment of joint stock companies. In the privatization process, 28 state farms were put into liquidation and three state farms into bankruptcy.

Privatization of Agroindustries

Privatization of the food processing industry has been completed. The largest part of the food industry was privatized in the first privatization wave mainly by coupon privatization. This included 134 enterprises valued at Sk18.5 billion, or 70 percent of the total. The remaining 46 enterprises valued at Sk6.7 billion were included in the second wave and privatized mainly through direct sales. Another 19 food processing enterprises were put into the liquidation process, out of which four enterprises were already liquidated and two were put into bankruptcy. As in other sectors of the economy, direct foreign investment played a relatively minor role. Some enterprises were restituted and others were privatized through small privatization. Excluded from privatization were some forest, water management, and service enterprises.

Privatization of Input Industries and Distribution Systems

Input and equipment industries. Most of the input industry has been privatized, but the Government still holds large ownership stakes in some sub-sectors, such as fuel production (25 percent) and distribution (46 percent). The Government owns Istrochem, the main producer of farm chemicals, and has a 20 percent stake in Duslo Sala, the only producer of nitrogen fertilizer. Also, Slovak farm equipment manufacturers remain under government control, since they had specialized in arms production and are converting to civilian production. Other suppliers of inputs and services have been either privatized or liquidated. These include equipment repair shops, construction, veterinary services, seed and planting material enterprises, research stations, and veterinary medicine.

Trade and distribution. The former state-owned wholesale distribution network has been taken over by private enterprises. Privatized grain warehouses and animal feed producers control a large share of the wheat, barley and oilseed markets. A former state enterprise for distribution of fruit and vegetables auctioned its warehouses, and this market is now dominated by a large number of small and medium trade organizations and agents. Retail food outlets have been privatized/restituted mainly to small shop owners. Multinational distribution chains control less than 7 percent of turnover, but are planning major

---

[51] State farms are either: (i) old state farms in existence prior to 1948; (ii) farms confiscated from churches and aristocracy; (iii) large private farms nationalized in 1948; or (iv) former cooperatives converted into state farms prior to 1989 because of poor performance.

investments. Privatized foreign trade companies maintain control over a large share of foreign trade in agricultural and food products, mainly because of their knowledge of foreign markets.

Adjustment of the Agriculture Sector Since Independence

Price and Trade Liberalization

Price liberalization began in 1990 with the elimination of retail food subsidies, followed in 1991 by liberalization of agricultural input and output prices, the liberalization of domestic and foreign trade, and the reduction of production subsidies. The introduction of the VAT in January 1993 brought about further adjustments in relative prices. The VAT was set at 6 percent for food and 25 percent for other goods and services. The overall price liberalization and the changes in the structure of subsidies and taxes resulted in a deterioration of the agricultural terms of trade. As shown in Figure 5.1, there was a mild deterioration at the retail level, with retail food prices increasing just slightly less than average consumer prices, but a sharp deterioration at the producer level, with farm output prices increasing at much lower rates than input prices. To mitigate the severity of the price adjustment on producers, minimum guaranteed price regulations were introduced for selected surplus commodities in 1991.

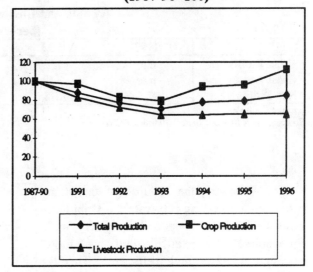

Figure 5.1
Price Adjustments 1990-1996
(1990=100)

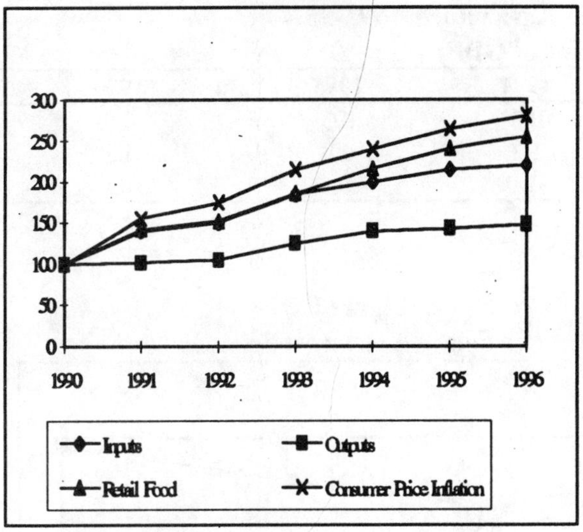

Figure 5.2
Agricultural Production
(1987-90=100)

Source: World Bank staff estimates.   Source: World Bank staff estimates.

Production and Income in Primary Agriculture

Agricultural output stabilized in 1995 at about 80 percent of pre-reform level (Figure 5.2). Crop production declined less than livestock production responding to changed relative prices, despite being affected by bad weather during some years. Cereals remain the dominant commodity group, planted on 54 percent of cultivated land, areas planted with oilseeds have nearly doubled due to strong domestic and export demand, and areas planted with sugar beet and potatoes have declined significantly, due to the lack of competitiveness with imports.

Livestock numbers declined by one-third between 1990-96. Production declines were the largest for beef (40 percent) and for dairy products (30 percent). Decline of consumption of dairy products was partly affected by consumer substitution of margarine and by import competition. Nevertheless, milk production continues to exceed domestic demand by 20-35 percent. The decline in pork and poultry production was less severe (23 and 20 percent, respectively), partly because pig and poultry production were less distorted prior to 1990.

The sharp deterioration of the agricultural terms of trade had a very adverse initial effect on farm income, especially in the case of cooperatives and state farms in mountainous areas that previously depended the most on government support. Gross losses in the agricultural sector have gradually declined from more than 3 percent of GDP before independence to 0.8 percent of GDP in 1995, but went up again in 1996 to 1.3 percent of GDP (Table 5.2). As in the case of industry, there seems to be a segment of the agriculture sector able to improve efficiency and to generate increasing profits (nearly 1 percent of GDP in 1996), whereas another segment continues to run significant losses. The improved financial conditions of the first segment allowed investment in agriculture to grow by more than 50 percent in real terms during 1996, although from a depressed base--investment in agriculture reached 1.8 percent of GDP in 1996, after falling from 1.6 to 1.2 percent of GDP between 1992 and 1995. As in the case of industry, a large share of investment is financed from internal sources, indicating that successful restructuring is key to sustained growth.

Table 5.2
Profits and Losses in Agriculture, 1992-96
(percentage of GDP)

	1992	1993	1994	1995	1996
Gross Profits	n.a.	1.2	0.3	0.3	0.9
Gross Losses	n.a.	3.0	1.3	0.8	1.3
Net Profits	-2.4	-1.8	-1.0	-0.5	-0.4

n.a.: not available
Source: Slovak Republic Central Statistical Office.

Following the collapse of the state distribution system, private distribution channels for farm inputs and equipment, and for wholesale and retail distribution of food remain fragmented and inefficient. This is reflected in high transaction costs and increasing marketing margins (Figure 5.3). Marketing margins for commodities (e.g. cereals) are at least twice as high as in other countries, when they should be lower considering the low level of value added to farm commodities by the Slovak food industry.

Figure 5.3
Selected Relative Prices

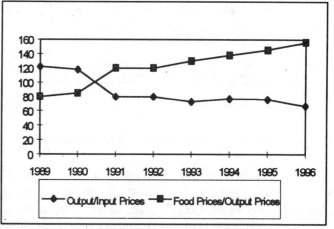

Source: Slovak Republic Central Statistical Office.

Employment and Productivity in Primary Agriculture

Employment in agriculture declined by nearly 60 percent between 1990 and 1996 (from 304,000 to 132,000), resulting in a commensurate decline in the share of agriculture employment in total employment (from 12.5 to 5.6 percent), and in the number of workers per 100 ha of agricultural land (from 13.3 to 5.4 workers).[52] Real wages and salaries also declined more steeply in agriculture than in other sectors, as indicated by the decline in the average wage from above the national average in 1990 to 80 percent of the national average in 1996. Despite the increase in productivity that resulted from this sharp decline in employment (Figure 4.5), labor productivity is still low compared to EU farmers--the gross value added per agricultural worker is about one-third of the level achieved by EU farmers (Figure 5.5). There is a wide scope for further increases in productivity, both by absorption of better technologies and by further reductions in employment. Indeed, the Slovak Republic should be capable of achieving higher productivity in agriculture than most Western European countries, because of larger farm sizes.

<table>
<tr><td>

Figure 5.4
Labor Productivity in Agriculture and Agroindustry

</td><td>

Figure 5.5
Gross Value Added per Agricultural Worker in Slovak Republic, Other Visegrad Countries, and EU Countries (ECU, 1994)

</td></tr>
<tr><td>

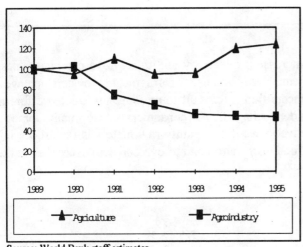

</td><td>

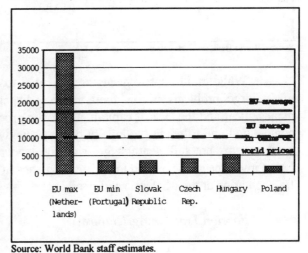

</td></tr>
<tr><td>

Source: World Bank staff estimates.

</td><td>

Source: World Bank staff estimates.

</td></tr>
</table>

Employment, Productivity and Income in Agroindustries

While production of many food items has declined substantially, employment in the agroindustrial sector has remained stable at about 53,000 workers, and wages remained about the same as the national average. Large excess capacity has been a major problem--in meat processing capacity utilization is only 30-40 percent, and in other sub-sectors (e.g., cereals) is only marginally better. There was already a large gap in productivity between Slovak and EU agroindustries in the early 1990s (Figure 5.6), which is possibly increasing due to further declines in productivity in recent years (Figure 5.4). This gap has resulted in repeated attempts of Slovak agroindustries to limit imports in order to prop up domestic production capacity.   The dairy processing industry has been most successful in this regard.

---

[52] Cooperatives are the largest employers in agriculture, with 66 percent of all farm labor, followed by state farms (19 percent), commercial farms (7 percent), and family farms (8 percent).

Agroindustries are generally struggling with large losses and debts, although some segments of the food industry remain profitable, such as breweries, flour mills, soft drinks, and bakeries.

Figure 5.6
Gross Value Added per Worker in Agroindustries
Slovak Republic, Selected Visegrad Countries and EU Countries (ECU, 1992)

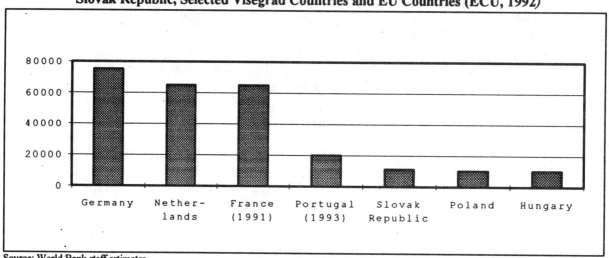

Source: World Bank staff estimates.

While rapid improvements are essential to increase productivity and to improve competitiveness, many large problems in the food industry linger unsolved because of fragmented ownership, weak management and the lack of capital. Domestic producers find it difficult to measure up to intense foreign competition and to retain the loyalty of increasingly demanding Slovak consumers. Also, many domestic producers are not sufficiently aggressive and innovative in securing quality raw materials for processing. Large investments are needed to improve logistics in food distribution and to overcome an excessive market fragmentation at the wholesale and retail levels.

Foreign Trade in Agriculture

The share of agriculture and processed food in total trade stabilized in 1995 at about 6 percent of exports and 9 percent of imports. As shown in Table 5.3, the main trading partners in agricultural products are the Czech Republic, the EU, and the FSU countries. Generally, exports have been represented by relatively low value-added products, such as cereal and flour

Table 5.3
Slovak Agricultural Trade by Region (US$ million)

Region	1993			1996		
	Imports	Exports	Balance	Imports	Exports	Balance
Czech Republic	287.7	177.7	-110.0	299.7	205.8	-93.9
EU-15	135.5	53.6	-81.9	309.1	75.9	-233.2
CIS	2.9	37.4	34.5	6.1	84.4	78.3
Other	132.1	77.5	-54.6	253.6	73.6	-180.0
Total	558.2	346.2	-212.0	868.5	439.7	-428.8

Source: Slovak Republic Central Statistical Office.

(about 30 percent of exports in 1996). Other export items include live animals, milk and dairy products. Agricultural trade between the Slovak Republic and EU more than doubled between 1993 and 1996 with a negative trade balance increasing to US$233 million, due partly to the appreciation of the Slovak currency, and to the inefficiency of Slovak agroindustries, which have been unable to compete on the domestic market with EU imports and also unable to export because of poor product quality, deficient packaging, ineffective marketing techniques and fragmented distribution systems.

Government Objectives and Support Policies in Agriculture

At the outset of the transition process, the main objective of the government in agriculture was to reduce large distortions caused by administrative prices and a maze of producer and consumer subsidies, while cushioning the impact of the adjustment on the population and on producers. In the process, Government support to agriculture was reduced by more than half between 1990 and 1996, whether measured by total budgetary transfers to agriculture (from more than 5 percent to 2 percent of GDP), or by the Producer Subsidy Equivalent (from 60 percent to 28 percent). The Slovak PSE is slightly higher than other countries, such as the Czech Republic, but lower than the EU, which has a PSE of 49 percent.[53] The impact of these adjustments was softened by various measures, such as offsetting income transfers to the population and minimum price support programs.

Despite the progress that has been already achieved more needs to be done, as the support initially intended to cushion the pain of adjustment has become entrenched and is turning into an obstacle to further adjustments. Moreover, new programs inconsistent with a pro-market reform have been either introduced (e.g., administrative price of milk coupled with a quota), or are being contemplated, with the objective of protecting producers from market uncertainties. However, some of these measures may actually increase these uncertainties and promote undesirable wait-and-see attitudes of market participants, undermining incentives for needed increases in productivity.

Agricultural Support Policy

Agricultural support is carried out by the Ministry of Agriculture either directly or through four state funds: (i) the State Fund for Market Regulation (SFMR) which is responsible for market stability and enforcement of minimum guaranteed prices for wheat, beef, and pork, and for the payment of export subsidies; (ii) the State Support Fund for Agriculture and Agroindustries (SSFAA) which supports medium- and long-term investment in agriculture; (iii) the State Land Protection Fund (SLPF) which supports measures to preserve or enhance soil fertility; and (iv) the Slovak Land Fund (SLF) which is responsible for the privatization of state farms and for the management of state lands. The funds have become independent institutions, although they continue to be chaired by the Minister of Agriculture and are financed partly by the state budget.

Budget expenditures for agriculture. Direct budget expenditures account for approximately 75 percent of total expenditures with the remaining 25 percent being provided indirectly through state funds. Total budget expenditures declined from 5.2 percent of GDP in 1991 to 2.2 percent of GDP in 1995 (Table 5.4), and declined further in 1996.

Table 5.4:
Budget Expenditures on Agriculture (Sk million)

Item	1991	1992	1993	1994	1995
Price Support	2135	1565	985	650	650
Direct Payments	8110	7466	6972	6966	7200
Income Support to Disadvantaged Areas	4752	3615	3609	3352	3318
Services	1990	2464	1789	1767	1664
Other	2423	2110	3011	931	2286
Total	14658	13605	12757	10314	11800
(in % of GDP)	5.2	4.1	3.4	2.4	2.2

Source: Ministry of Agriculture.

Support to agriculture is extended through several programs, such as price support, income support to disadvantaged areas, input subsidies and investment subsidies.

---

[53] However, it should be noted that most EU countries have a much smaller agricultural sector (1-3 percent of GDP) which results in relatively smaller distortions in the allocation of resources and budgetary cost.

Price support. The government sets minimum prices for some products (mainly wheat) at the start of the planting season for specific quantity and quality standards. These prices cover 90 percent of estimated production cost. When minimum prices are announced, producers can lock in contracts for delivery through SFMR and obtain a cash advance. Surpluses are resold on the domestic market or exported with the help of export subsidies.

Income support to disadvantaged areas. About 30 percent of agricultural support is for direct payments compensating farmers in marginal areas. These are paid on a per hectare basis according to a soil quality schedule. Although this program is preferable to production subsidies, it has been poorly monitored and beneficiaries are often paid without compliance with program criteria. A series of measures to tighten criteria and to improve monitoring by regional offices of the Ministry of Agriculture has been agreed under the 1997 budget.

Input and investment subsidies. This group of expenditures includes three major programs. First, a program of grants and rebates intended to improve efficiency of production of some commodities, but which has had a doubtful impact. Second, a program of input subsidies designed to mitigate the cost-price squeeze in agriculture. Third, a program of investment subsidies provided through capital grants to purchase farm equipment, modernize milking equipment, develop orchards, etc. Government share ranges between 30 and 40 percent of actual production cost. Rationing is needed because of limited resources and an obvious popularity of these programs. The remainder of direct budget expenditures covers mostly services such as cadastral offices, veterinary service, research institutes, and inspection.

The State Fund for Market Regulation (SFMR). SFMR is by far the largest extra-budgetary fund operating in agriculture and the main government instrument for maintaining stability in the agricultural commodities market. SFMR main activities include market intervention through processing, storage and sale; maintenance of state commodity reserves; and provision of export subsidies to eliminate

Table 5.5:
Operations of the SFMR (Sk million)

	1993	1994	1995	1996
Revenues	2150	1186	2539	3694
of which: Budget Transfers	850	650	650	650
Expenditures	1800	1933	2092	3750
(percent of GDP)	0.5	0.5	0.4	0.6
Balance	340	-747	446	-56

Source: Ministry of Finance.

surpluses on the domestic market. Total expenditures by SFMR were kept at around 0.5 percent in the first half of the 1990s but increased somewhat during 1996 (Table 5.5). Although some intervention may have been justified initially to facilitate adjustment to a market-based system, SFMR may be turning into an obstacle of market development and prevent necessary gains in efficiency. For example, SFMR's efforts to balance seasonal price variations reduces incentives by the private sector to store commodities and retards the development of market-based risk management instruments to deal with seasonal price fluctuations. Also, continued state support, particularly to primary producers, could increase resistance to reductions in minimum prices and ultimately lead to increased protection.

The State Support Fund for Agriculture and Agroindustries (SSFAA). Established in 1994, SSFAA is the main instrument of government support for investment in agriculture and agroindustries. SSFAA provides low interest loans for the purchase of farm equipment (5 percent annual rate) and for the purchase of land (1-2 percent annual rate with repayment in 50 years), as well as guarantees on development projects supported by commercial banks. SSFAA is financed from a 50 percent revenue share from privatization of state enterprises (the remaining 50 percent is retained by the NPF or the SLF), from revenues from the liquidation of State agroindustrial enterprises, contributions from the state budget, and issue of bonds. The level of its interest subsidies looks high per unit of credit, but its total outflows have remained under control, having amounted to less than 0.1 percent of GDP in recent years. To facilitate further access to credit, the government established the Slovak Guarantee Bank (SGB) in 1993. However, despite the issue of credit guarantees by SGB and the financing of working capital by Polnobanka and commercial banks, access to farm credit seems to remain restricted due to the lack of suitable collateral and the high perceived risk of default in farming.

Trade policy support measures. Indirect support to agriculture and agroindustries through foreign trade instruments has been significantly reduced since 1990, although it still remains relatively high--the weighted average tariff rate for food products is around 24 percent, compared to an overall average of 8 percent. Since January 1995, import protection is provided mainly through tariffs which are gradually phased out following WTO commitments.[54] Import quotas (e.g., beer) and voluntary restraints have been negotiated with importers of sensitive products. A 10 percent import surcharge introduced in 1993 was reduced to 7.5 percent in July 1996 and suspended in January 1997. The limited use of export subsidies is mainly to dispose of excess domestic production of commodities such as dry milk and other dairy products, beef, sugar, poultry and pork.

The use of foreign trade policy instruments is constrained by several international agreements, all intended to maintain or to enhance liberalization of trade in agricultural commodities and food. The most important ones include the customs union agreement with the Czech Republic, agreements with WTO, the Association Agreement with the EU, and agreements with CEFTA. The customs union between the Czech Republic and the Slovak Republic makes agricultural support policy for both countries nearly identical and coordination imperative in order to avoid trade disruptions.

As a member of WTO, the Slovak Republic has binding obligations on tariffs and minimum market access, limits of aggregate support, and limits on export subsidies. The Slovak Republic has agreed to reduce all tariffs from their 1994 levels on average by 36 percent over six years, while a minimum reduction in a single tariff category should be at least 15 percent. It must be noted that EU tariffs are higher for most products, except for poultry and rape seed where Slovak tariffs are higher. EU and Slovak tariffs are converging for certain products (live animals, pork meat). In the area of aggregate support to agriculture, The Slovak Republic agreed with WTO to an upper limit of Sk12 billion, including environmental measures. Actual support has reached about 60 percent of this limit. The Slovak Republic also agreed with WTO to an upper limit on export subsidies of Sk2.3 billion. Actual expenditures on export subsidies reached only 10 percent of the agreed level. In addition, the Association Agreement between the Slovak Republic and the EU contributed to some liberalization of trade in food products since 1992. Under this agreement, the EU phased out custom tariffs linked to specific Slovak EU export quotas for sensitive products such as beef and dairy products. However, both sides of the agreement preserved their own agricultural policy regimes and different protection levels.

Completing the Reform Agenda on the Way to EU Accession

Suggested Policy Adjustments

Independently of the outcome of EU accession negotiations, the Slovak agriculture and food industry needs to increase productivity on the farm and throughout the food processing and distribution system to sustain its market share in a liberalizing trade regime. The first stage of the transition process

---

[54] Following the Slovak Republic's WTO obligations, the weighted average tariff rate for basic agricultural commodities will be reduced from 8.7 to 5.6 percent by the year 2000.

has been completed by restoring private property and by eliminating major market distortions. The Government needs to consolidate ownership, resist pressure of various interest groups for special protection against foreign competition, limit its support to the provision of "public goods", refrain from excessive market intervention, and continue to create a business friendly environment.

Ownership consolidation is critical for activation of the land market and for acceptance of land as collateral. Land ownership in cooperatives remains highly fragmented and ways to facilitate consolidation should be considered. One possibility is to give active members of cooperatives more options to buy out land owners. Another possibility lies in the restructuring of Government subsidies to support ownership consolidation as a prime policy objective. A related issue is the prohibition on foreign ownership of land. These restrictions may have to be revisited as the country approaches EU accession (liberalization of purchases of real estate are part of Stage Two measures in the area of capital movements--see Chapter IV).

Agroindustries are particularly vulnerable to foreign competition and ways to facilitate efficiency and productivity growth should be considered. One important step would be to phase out the dairy quota system and export subsidies. The quota perpetuates inefficiencies in the dairy industry and helps marginal producers to remain in business. Moreover, milk in excess of domestic demand needs to be exported with subsidies. Phasing out of the dairy quota is also important as a signal to other industries not to count on protection but rather seek ways to cut costs and become more efficient. Moreover, if granted, protection would give wrong signals about the expected profitability of modernization investments.

SFMR is turning into an obstacle to market development and ways to make its interventions less frequent and more predictable should be considered. The space for private sector trade activity needs to be expanded in order to reduce trading margins and to increase efficiency. Minimum prices should be gradually reduced below the current level of 90 percent of estimated average production cost, de-linked from production cost, and reflect carrying charges. SFMR interventions should be based on clear rules and should become an exception rather than a rule. Moreover, more effective oversight of the four agricultural support funds (SFMR, SSFAA, SLPF, and SLF) would enhance the trust of the intended beneficiaries and the public. Each fund should produce an annual report with financial statements, assessment of its procedures and summary of its activities. This report should be independently audited.

Income support payments to disadvantaged areas should be gradually modified from a per hectare basis to targeted support programs. This could include capital grants for development of rural infrastructure, afforestation, rural tourism, and other non-agricultural activities especially in marginal areas. This would be consistent with EU efforts to reform its agricultural policies. Also, a growing number of small commodity-specific subsidy programs should be consolidated, simplified and possibly retargeted to land ownership consolidation.

Access to rural credit should be improved using market-based instruments and techniques. Preparation of legal amendments and new laws is underway to improve collateral law including land mortgage law. Also, a proposal to introduce a warehouse receipt system is under consideration. These legislative changes should improve liquidity and access to agricultural credit.

Pre-accession Agenda

There is still a large number of differences in legislation and technical norms between the Slovak Republic and the EU. As part of EU accession, the Slovak Republic would have to implement a large regulatory agenda to comply with EU requirements and facilitate access of Slovak farm and food products to the EU market.[55] The first part of this agenda concerns veterinary, plant health and animal nutrition. It affects a wide range of activities in the farming, production and processing of live animals, and animal and plant products. The purpose of these measures is to ensure consumer protection, public health, and animal and plant health by adopting EU regulations governing the movement of live animals, meat and meat products, fruit, vegetables, and plants.[56] The second part of this agenda concerns EU regulations on quality standards and labeling requirements. The objective of legislative approximation is to bring the Slovak Republic's whole production system to EU standards.

Besides these technical norms, several other policies might need to be implemented to comply with the EU Common Agricultural Policies which, in turn, are likely to change and evolve prior to accession taking place. It is difficult to assess, however, how much effort would be required from the Slovak side since future EU policies will probably be directed by the following principles: (i) ensuring compliance of EU support policies with WTO agreements; (ii) reducing the level of protection to domestic producers vis-à-vis foreign competition; (iii) partially replacing current price and marketing interventions by targeted income transfers; and (iv) emphasizing rural development by the provision of basic private and public services to the rural population. In this framework, it is optimal for the Slovak Republic to pursue a transparent and free trade strategy for the agricultural sector because many of the measures that are required to raise productivity, are also more consistent with the likely future EU policy requirements.[57]

---

[55] For example, it would be necessary to translate about 18,000 pages of EU agricultural legislation into Slovak, identify differences and accordingly modify Slovak legislation.

[56] For example, the upgrading of phytosanitary, veterinary, testing and other laboratories to EU standards is estimated at Sk 300 million.

[57] A package, known as the McSharry reform, was agreed by the EU in 1992 with the main objective to switch the CAP gradually from price support to income support. Some intervention prices were either lowered or eliminated (with the accompanying reduction in import tariffs), stricter quotas for intervention purchases were set aside and the program connected with compensatory payments was launched. As pressure for more reform continues, it could be expected that EU agricultural prices will gradually move closer to world levels. Also, support to EU farmers will be decoupled gradually from agricultural output or hectarage and instead linked to a number of services with specific environmental benefits.

CHAPTER VI: THE LABOR MARKET AND SOCIAL POLICY

Introduction

The overall output recovery and the rapid growth of smaller employers have resulted in considerable improvements in labor market conditions over the past two years. The implementation of active labor market programs has also helped stabilize the labor market. In the area of social insurance and social assistance there are also some favorable developments. Unlike many transition economies, the finances of off-budget social insurance programs (including pensions and short-term benefits) appear to be in balance over the next few years, and there has been an effort to reduce the cost of social assistance programs through the means-testing of family allowances. Finally, the Government is making an effort to rationalize the various social protection programs, and has also made considerable progress in harmonizing Slovak social legislation to EU legislation.

This chapter aims at contributing to the Government's efforts by assessing progress and identifying the scope for additional policy improvements in three closely linked areas: (i) the labor market; (ii) social insurance programs; and (iii) family support and assistance programs. Such an assessment is guided by three major considerations, namely, that social programs must be fiscally sustainable (whether they are financed by social contributions or by the budget), should encourage tax compliance and employment in the formal sector, and should be effective in alleviating poverty.

The chapter is structured as follows. The next section reviews the current situation in the labor market and the status of passive and active labor market programs. It examines, among other issues, whether unemployment benefits, job search assistance, and active programs may be developed further so as to promote a flexible labor market and avoid discouraging work. The third section deals with social insurance. It examines the medium and long-run finances of the pension system, and the scope for reducing contribution rates in order to encourage employment. It also examines the system of short-term benefits. The fourth section examines whether social assistance benefits are sufficiently targeted and coordinated, in order to provide effective poverty alleviation and avoid work disincentives. The final section summarizes the recommendations provided in the chapter.

The Labor Market

The Current Situation in the Labor Market

After three years of strong economic growth, the Slovak Republic is now experiencing an improvement in labor market conditions. Employment has been growing slowly but steadily since the first quarter of 1995, at an annualized rate of about 2 percent.[58] In 1996, for the first time since the start of transition, employment increases were posted not only in services, but also in industry and agriculture. The driving force behind employment growth continues to be the small business sector, although net job creation in firms with less than 25 employees slowed down somewhat in 1996, and self-employment has stabilized at about 6 percent of total employment. In earlier transition years, the labor market was also characterized by substantial reductions in labor force participation of women, but labor force participation rates have stabilized more recently (Table 6.1).

---

[58] These figures are based on Labor Force Survey (LFS) data, which offer better coverage of the small business sector than administrative data.

Table 6.1
Labor Force Participation Rates (percent)

	1989	1991	1993 [2]	1995	1996
Total	82.3	79.5	75.8	77.3	77.5
Males	83.9	83.4	82.7	82.5	81.9
Females	80.5	75.3	68.5	71.8	72.7

Notes: The participation rate is defined as the labor force including those person over the age of 15, divided by the working age population including woman aged 15 to 54 and men 15 to 59.
1/ Data for 1993 is the average of the first three quarters of the year.
Source: OECD (1996), *Labor Market and Social Policies in the Slovak Republic,* Paris.

The unemployment rate has declined sharply after the start of the recovery, reaching 11 or 13 percent in 1996, according to two different estimates (Figure 6.1). The lowest number comes from the Labor Force Survey (LFS), whereas the higher comes from the number of registered unemployed, and the difference is probably due to the tendency of women to maintain registration at labor offices, in order to qualify for social benefits, even if they no longer have any interest in finding a new job. Therefore, as in other countries, the lower survey estimate probably reflects more accurately the situation in the labor market with regard to actual unemployment.

Despite the decline in unemployment, the problem of long-term unemployment has worsened further--the share of the unemployed out of work for more than one year increased from about 40 percent in 1994 to more than 50 percent in the first three quarters of 1996 (Figure 6.2). More important, a growing proportion of the long-term unemployed (60 percent in the third quarter of 1996) has been on the job market for more than two years. Long-term unemployment continues to be more prevalent among women than men, and an alarming proportion of the long-term unemployed are in their most productive years.[59] Long-term unemployment is concentrated among unskilled and relatively uneducated workers (including those who have not completed secondary vocational education).

The persistence of substantial regional differences in unemployment rates is also a worrisome development. In December 1996, registered unemployment rates ranged from 4 percent in Bratislava to almost 24 in Rimavska Sobota. Whereas other transitional economies have experienced some convergence in regional unemployment rates,[60] in the Slovak Republic the standard deviation of regional unemployment rates has actually increased over time. Further, the regional differences in unemployment rates in the Slovak Republic, compared to European countries such as France and Spain, also appear to be substantial (Table 6.2).[61] Lastly, if expected reductions in Slovak employment take place in coal mining and armaments manufacturing, regional disparities are likely to increase further. Vacancies reported to the labor exchanges continue to be concentrated in low-unemployment regions, pointing to the need for policies to encourage labor mobility, and possibly for policies encouraging enterprises to locate in high unemployment areas.

---

[59] Unlike other countries, where the incidence of long-term unemployment typically increases with age, in the Slovak Republic the highest incidence of long-term unemployment is registered for both men and women in the 30 to 39 age group.

[60] See Boeri and Scarpetta (1996), "Regional Mismatch and the Transition to a Market Economy," *Labor Economics*, Vol. 3.

[61] While country-wide standard deviations could be affected by differences in regional population sizes, masking sub-regional differences in the larger Western European regions, the analysis suggests that in long-standing market economies, competitive forces have tended to dampen regional differences in unemployment.

Figure 6.1
Unemployment Rate, 1990-96 (percent)

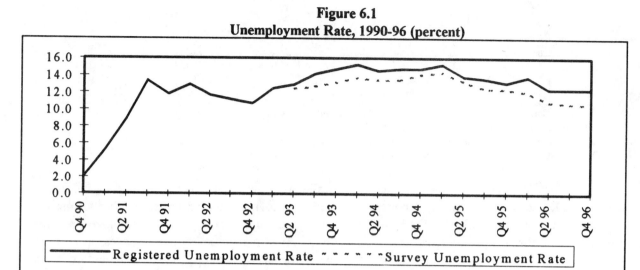

Source: Slovak Republic Central Statistical Office.

Figure 6.2
Long-term Unemployment, 1993-96 (percent of the unemployed)

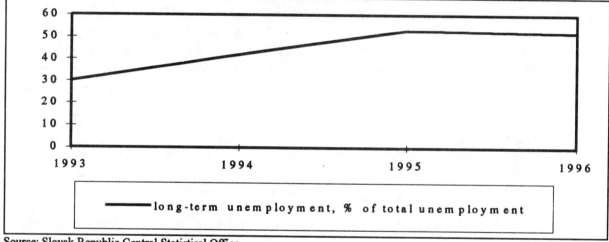

Source: Slovak Republic Central Statistical Office.

The presence of a hard core of long-term unemployed and the concentration of unemployment in regions with few employment opportunities has reduced the moderating effect of unemployment on wages. In spite of two-digit unemployment rates, there was actually an acceleration of wage growth in 1996--real wage increases in the first three quarters of 1996 over the same period of 1995 have been of the order of 6 percent, compared to about 4 percent in 1995. In addition, the real wage increases seemed to have been generalized, maintaining a relatively flat distribution of wages across sectors and regions.[62] This may have reduced incentives for worker mobility across regions, sectors and occupations, and provided negative incentives for job search, despite the presence of large regional differentials in unemployment.

---

[62] Unlike other transitional economies, the Slovak Republic has not experienced an increased dispersion of its earnings distribution. See Atkinson, A. and J. Micklewright (1994), *Economic Transformation in Eastern Europe and the Distribution of Income*, Cambridge University Press, and Rutkowski, M. (1996), *Changes in the Wage Structure During Economic Transition in CEE*, World Bank Technical Paper No. 340, Washington DC.

Table 6.2

Regional Unemployment Differentials in the Slovak Republic, France and Spain

	Year	Number of Regions	Unemployment Rate National (percent)	Standard Deviation	Coefficient of Variation	Unemployment Rate of Top Quartile (percent)	Unemployment Rate of Bottom Quartile (percent)	Top/ Bottom
Slovak Republic								
	1991	38	7	2.02	0.29	9.9	4.5	2.2
	1992	38	11.3	3.59	0.32	16.1	6.7	2.4
	1994	38	14.4	4.58	0.34	20.7	8.9	2.3
	1996	38	12.8	5.20	0.41	19.8	6.7	3.0
France								
	1983	11	8.5	1.66	0.19	11.6	7.3	1.6
	1989	11	9.5	1.78	0.19	11.6	7.4	1.6
Spain								
	1983	11	18.2	3.18	0.29	26.7	12.2	2.2
	1989	11	17.3	2.85	0.3	25.1	11.8	2.1

Source: Boeri, T., and S. Scarpetta (1996),"Regional Mismatch and the Transition to a Market Economy," *Labor Economics*, Vol. 3 and MoL.

The centralized wage setting procedures in the Slovak Republic (a tripartite scheme involving the Government, trade unions and employers) may also have contributed to the persistence of a very compressed distribution of wages by sector, region and size of firms. This is because excessive centralization may be preventing the adjustment of relative wages to differences in productivity and to local labor-market conditions, although it may also have contributed to the successful stabilization after independence. The setting procedures can apply over a large number of workers, as the Government has substantial leverage in deciding upon the extension of branch-level agreements to firms whose workers and employers are not represented in collective negotiations.[63]

Labor Market Issues and EU Accession

A considerable effort is being made to adjust the regulatory framework of the labor market to the EU accession requirements laid down in the White Paper. In particular, regulations on collective redundancies providing for advanced notification of planned dismissals, and prior consultation with workers' representatives are included in the new Employment Act passed in 1996. This legislation also paves the way for the institution of a guarantee fund to pay employees in case of employer insolvency. The plan is to allocate to this reserve one-sixth of the 3 percent contribution paid by employers to the National Labor Office. A law on occupational safety has also recently been passed by Parliament, which goes a long way towards satisfying the requirements for accession to the EU. Remaining provisions concerning health and safety in the workplace, as well as equal employment opportunity, working time, and provision of information to and consultation of employees in Community-scale undertakings, are contained in the draft Labor Code, which the Slovak authorities hope to have approved by Parliament and enacted by 1998. This is within the timetable laid out in the 1993 Association Agreement with the EU, which actually permitted some of the more stringent provisions to be adopted as late as 1999.

As the Slovak authorities work assiduously to meet the White Paper requirements, they should not lose sight of the implications of the EU accession process for the labor market, and should consequently prepare the ground for admission beyond mere legal adjustments. Indeed, the Slovak economy is likely to experience increasing competitive pressures, with the increasing economic approximation to EU markets, particularly in the case of sectors that have been lagging behind, such as the agro-industrial sector. This

---

[63] Although industry-level agreements are binding only on employers represented in collective agreements, the coverage of collective agreements is 70-80 percent, which is high by EU standards.

points to the need for further restructuring, and for a flexible environment that promotes labor mobility and allows a greater diversification of wages across industries.

In the area of the labor legislation, Government needs to focus on policies that will encourage a flexible labor market. There is a wide range of choice in these standards, which vary greatly across OECD countries. One study of EC countries suggests that the negative impact of strict employment protection standards is two-fold: countries with high standards of protection appear to have higher rates of long-term unemployment, and also higher rates of unemployment among persons age 14-24 relative to adults.[64] Both outcomes would be detrimental in the Slovak Republic, where the proportion of long-term unemployment has been growing and unemployment rates are higher among younger workers.

In attempting to approximate to the EU, the Slovak Republic should also avoid introducing measures that are not really required for accession, and that could prove detrimental to a successful adjustment. For example, there are no proposals to exempt small employers from some of the more rigid labor code provisions, even though such firms may be less able to meet current requirements. One example of regulatory rigidity is the obligation of small employers to reinstate workers who have been unfairly dismissed. Such exemptions are usually granted in the EU,[65] in recognition of the lack of an "internal labor market" in small enterprises, and of the comparative disadvantages induced by the presence of fixed (e.g. procedural) costs for small businesses.[66] The structure of employment already appears to be changing, with temporary contracts for full-time employment accounting for more than one-third of the new jobs created in the first three quarters of 1996. This may reflect reluctance on the part of some employers to deal with restrictions to hire and fire employees. As small and medium-sized firms represent the engine of employment growth, it would be highly undesirable to hinder their expansion.

Once stabilization is consolidated, and the need for a wage policy to complement the exchange rate anchor is reduced, the scope of decentralized, enterprise-level bargaining should be increased. Most EU countries are currently expanding the scope of their decentralized wage bargaining, and linking wage setting to firm performance. The extension of the coverage of collective agreements to small units should not be granted automatically. Yet in 1996, 15 out of 16 requests for extensions of branch-level agreements were granted by the Ministry, involving about 450 employers.

Another impediment to a successful labor market lies in the resistance of employers to high social insurance contributions and other types of payroll taxation. Surveys of small employers[67] suggest that excessive social security contributions represent an important impediment to the development of small enterprises (in addition to lack of credit and to severe procedural obstacles to the start-up of new businesses). Total social security contributions in the Slovak Republic amount to 50 percent of gross wages, whereas the average contribution rate for the EU countries is 36 percent (Table 6.3).

---

[64] An OECD study rates employment protection as relatively low in Denmark, Ireland, and the United Kingdom, and relatively high in Italy, Portugal and Spain. See the OECD Jobs Study (1994).

[65] To give a few examples, in Italy, firms with less than 15 employees are not compelled to reinstate workers who had been unfairly dismissed; in Germany, tighter employment security regulations apply only to firms with more than 5 or 20 (in the case of collective layoffs) employees; in France, the threshold scale for the application of employment security regulations is 11 employees.

[66] In consideration of these disparities, the new Employment Act has lifted quotas on the number of disabled employees (and associated penalties) on firms with less than 25 employees.

[67] OECD (1996), *Small Business in Transition Economies*, Working Papers, Vol. IV, Paris.

Table 6.3
Statutory Social Contributions Rates in the Slovak Republic, Europe, and the OECD
(percent of the gross wage bill)

Country	Employers	Employees	Total	Of Which: Pensions
Slovak Republic	38.0	12.0	50.0	28.5
European Union [1/]	23.6	12.9	36.5	20.6
Western Europe [2/]	22.1	11.7	33.8	19.3
OECD [3/]	16.2	8.6	24.8	13.2

1/ Unweighted average of the EU-15 excluding Denmark.
2/ The above plus unweighted average of Iceland, Norway, and Switzerland.
3/ The above plus unweighted average of Australia, Japan, Mexico, New Zealand, and the US.
Source: OECD, *The Tax and Benefit Position of Production Workers*, Paris.

There should be efforts to reduce contributions for pensions, sickness and employment insurance, as the fiscal situation permits. High taxes on labor are not only harmful to job creation, but they may also encourage widespread tax evasion. While this is currently less of a problem in the Slovak Republic than in other transition economies (perhaps in part because the proportion of employment in small firms is currently less than the proportion found in EU economies), small firms typically cannot afford the same compensation costs as larger enterprises, and are more difficult to target for audit and enforcement. Thus, if taxes are too high, fewer small firms will be established, wages will tend to be under-reported, and the size of the informal sector will tend to increase. The experience of other transitional economies suggests that in an economy undergoing rapid structural change, a vicious circle of increasingly high tax rates and a shrinking tax base could be set in motion.

Unemployment Benefits Policy

The new Employment Act approved by Parliament in December 1996 has refined the unemployment benefits system. Firstly, the link between the maximum duration of benefits and the age of applicants is phased out, to avoid unfair treatment of those who had started work early in life. Under the new regulations, and consistent with insurance principles, the maximum duration of benefits is linked to the length of the contribution period.[68] Secondly, a six-month "waiting period" is introduced before unemployment benefits are granted to school-leavers, creating greater incentives for active job search. Thirdly, "job-quitters" have become entitled to unemployment benefits (for a maximum duration three months shorter than that of workers who are unemployed as a result of dismissal), encouraging labor mobility by decreasing the risks associated with job-to-job shifts. Finally, free social insurance is to be provided only to unemployment benefit claimants.

The new Employment Act also offers a clearer definition of a "suitable" job offer that the job-seeker should accept in order to have unemployment benefits or social assistance payments continued. The definition is broadly in line with ILO conventions, and should allow a stricter and less controversial enforcement of work tests. Significantly, reference is no longer made to the presence of dependent children in the family, an excuse which seems to have been frequently used to reject job offers without losing social benefits. Moreover, only physicians appointed by labor offices, as opposed to those chosen by individuals, will be allowed to issue certificates stating the "unsuitability" of the job for health reasons.

---

[68] In detail, those with a contribution record of less than 15 years are eligible for at most 6 months of unemployment benefits, those with more than 15 but less than 25 years of contribution can draw unemployment benefits for up to 9 months, whilst those who have an employment record of over 25 years are eligible for a maximum of 12 months of benefits.

With no extended unemployment benefits offered to the long-term unemployed, the interaction between unemployment benefits and social assistance is crucial. Due to the increasing incidence of long-term unemployment, more registered unemployed receive social assistance than draw unemployment benefits (Figure 6.3). Further, a non-negligible proportion of unemployment benefit recipients also draw social assistance to top up their incomes. This means that many unemployed benefit claimants do not experience the reduction in replacement rates over time envisaged by the Employment Act. These recipients may find it disadvantageous to take up jobs at the lower end of the wage distribution and frequently fall into "unemployment traps".[69]

While "poverty traps" discourage employment in many OECD countries, the problem in the Slovak Republic is compounded by the presence of a compressed wage structure and by passive attitudes towards the state provision of income support inherited from the previous system. The incentives in the entire system of cash benefit payments need to be reconsidered to minimize work disincentives. Further, stricter enforcement of job search and availability-to-work tests for individuals receiving social assistance may greatly enhance the incentives to find a new job. This calls for greater co-ordination between social welfare centers and the labor office network, including more stringent conditions relating to the frequency with which social assistance recipients should report to labor offices.

Active Labor Market Policies

The new Employment Act merged the Public Employment Service (PES) administration, previously under the direct responsibility of the MOL, with the management of the Employment Fund by instituting a new independent administration, the National Labor Office (NLO) and its tripartite self-governing bodies. According to the Slovak authorities, this will complete the institution-building process launched by the creation of the Health, Sickness and Pension Funds, establishing self-governing and financially autonomous administrations in charge of all the substantive social programs.

There is a strong commitment on the part of the Slovak authorities to implement active labor market programs. These programs consist of socially purposeful jobs (SPJ), training programs, and publicly useful jobs (PUJ), the Slovak denomination for public works. On the average, each SPJ roughly costs 2.5 times the average unemployment benefit. Direct job creation programs like public works are even more costly from a public finance standpoint, especially considering that they are partly funded by local communities. The total annual number of unemployed entering SPJ programs significantly increased in the 1993-95 period: inflows increased from 33,500 persons in 1993 to 43 000 in 1995 (Table 6.4). The increase in inflows into PUJs was even steeper--from 15,000 persons in 1993 to 45,000 in 1995. In 1996, however, SPJs were significantly scaled down, whilst inflows to PUJs were stabilized.

---

[69] For example, an unemployed worker in a household without other earners and with two dependent children aged over 15 could have received Sk6,350 per month in 1995, compared with a gross average wage of Sk7,144. See also Lubyova and van Ours (1996), "Work Incentives and Other Effects of the Transition to Social Assistance: Evidence from the Slovak Republic," paper presented at an IHS-OECD workshop, Vienna.

Figure 6.3
Registered Unemployed, Unemployment Benefit Claimants and Social Assistance Recipients

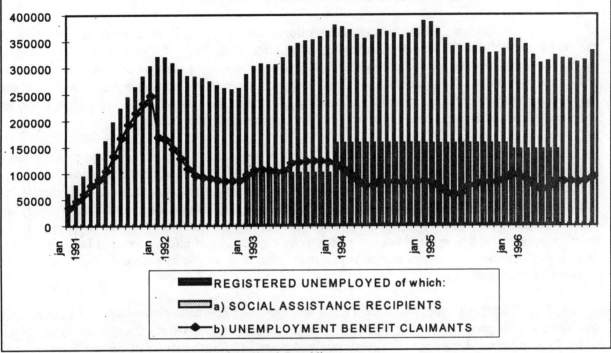

Source: Ministry of Social Affairs and Family of the Slovak Republic.

Table 6.4
Passive and Active Labor Market Policy Programs

	Expenditures as percent of GDP				Inflows as percent of the Labor Force			
	1993	1994	1995	1996[1]	1993	1994	1995	1996
1) Passive Programs (Unemployment Benefits)	0.50	0.38	0.31	0.54	7.80	5.06	5.40	4.14
2) Active Programs Of which:	0.28	0.41	0.70	0.56	2.72	2.91	4.40	2.68
a) Socially Purposeful Jobs	0.20	0.35	0.52	0.33	1.44	1.55	1.84	0.97
b) Publicly Useful Jobs	0.04	0.04	0.15	0.20	0.53	0.64	1.74	1.43
c) Training and Retraining	0.03	0.02	0.03	0.03	0.75	0.72	0.81	0.27
Subsidized Employment	0.25	0.39	0.67	0.54	1.97	2.19	3.59	2.40
Active/Passive Policies	0.56	1.08	2.27	1.04	0.35	0.57	0.81	0.65
OECD Active Policies[2]	0.91	0.90	0.92	n.a.	6.95	6.41	6.13	n.a.
Subsidized employment	0.23	0.23	0.22	n.a.	1.69	1.66	1.33	n.a.
Active/Passive	0.50	0.52	0.55	n.a.	n.a.	n.a.	n.a.	n.a.

n.a.: not available.
1/ Estimates
2/ Calculated as average of 22 countries with the available data, OECD (1996), *Employment Outlook* (July).
Source: Ministry of Social Affairs and Family of the Slovak Republic.

The new Employment Act considerably broadens the scope of wage subsidies to include support for mobility and housing costs faced by employers when hiring unemployed residents in other districts. Less strict standards in the concession of job creation grants and loans may give labor offices greater flexibility in tailoring such programs to local labor market conditions, but they may also open room for misuse, such as subsidization of jobs in ailing enterprises. Public work programs are also maintained under the new law. In most cases they represent, after all, the only job opportunity that can be realistically offered to the long-term unemployed and, hence, have lower deadweight losses than SPJs, and may also be used to enforce work-tests for social assistance beneficiaries more strictly.

Contrary to most OECD countries, more resources are allocated in the Slovak Republic to active than to passive policies (Table 6.4). Participant inflows into SPJs, PUJs, and retraining courses made up almost 4.5 percent of the labor force in 1995. Employment subsidy programs of a similar size can be found only in Sweden. The experience of OECD countries suggests that active programs work best when they are narrowly targeted on specific problem groups, rather than implemented on a wide scale, and without sufficient staff to carefully select applicants and their potential employers.

The effectiveness of such programs is not always very encouraging, as evidenced by estimates of significant "deadweight" losses--the participant in the program would have got the job even in the absence of the subsidy.[70] While further analyses could shed more light on the impact of such programs, the available evidence suggests that authorities should avoid expanding them. Also, more careful supervision of the implementation of these programs by the newly established National Labor Office is warranted. The monthly reports produced by the Ministry already offer a great deal of information, but better indications as to the effectiveness of various programs can only come from access to microdata on samples of the registered unemployed.

The vacancy coverage rate of the PES is still very low, despite improvements in macroeconomic conditions and the compulsory reporting of vacancies to the PES by employers. Greater efforts on the part of the PES to maintain relations with employers and competition with private placement agencies could contribute to enhancing the brokerage function of the PES. Also, authorities should avoid the ongoing reorganization of the NLO, involving the creation of 78 district labor offices and 8 regional offices. This will lead to larger overheads and a loss of client-orientation.

Social Insurance

The Government is preparing comprehensive reforms to social insurance programs, including old-age, disability, and survivors' pensions, as well as short-term benefits, such as sick leave and maternity leave. Starting from relatively favorable demographics and fiscal balance, the time is opportune to undertake a fundamental pension reform, as the impact of reforms in the pension area typically materializes only after a number of years. Short-term benefits also need to be reviewed, in order to avoid waste of fiscal resources and adverse effects on the labor market. Indeed, while sick leave and maternity leave benefits take up far fewer resources than pensions, employers and employees may be using sick leave as a substitute for unemployment insurance, and extensive mandatory maternity leave may discourage small and medium employers from hiring women in skilled occupations. Maternity leave is costly as new mothers must be guaranteed jobs upon their return and temporary workers must be employed in the meantime. The additional costs of hiring and training replacement workers can be substantial if company-specific skills are required.

---

[70] A recent study suggests that up to 50-70 percent of SPJs in the Slovak Republic probably involved deadweight losses. Bednarik. L., et al (1996), Evaluation of the Effectiveness of the ALMP Expenditures in the Districts of Lucenec and Rimavska Sobota" unpublished manuscript, Bratislava. A cross-country analysis is provided in Boeri, T. et al. (1996), *Lessons from Labor Market Policies in Transition Economies,* OECD, Paris.

The Current Status of Pensions

The public pension system in the Slovak Republic seems to have fewer problems than those of many other transition economies. First, the Slovak Republic is in a relatively favorable demographic position, with only 15 percent of the population age 60 and over. Second, the increase in new pensioners between 1989 and 1991 was lower than that reported by other countries in the region. Third, the ratio of pension expenditures to GDP, at 8 percent in 1996, is not exorbitant compared to other Central European countries. Fourth, the pension fund has been in balance since 1995, and should continue to accumulate some moderate surpluses during the next few years, if revenue collection performance is maintained and the Government avoids granting excessive and ad-hoc increases in benefits. Finally, the 27.5 percent contribution rate, although very high by international standards, is somewhat lower than some of its neighbors. However, the pension system in the Slovak Republic and the other countries do need reforms designed to ensure long-run viability and remove distortions in the labor market (Box 6.1 provides a description of the Slovak pension system).

Box 6.1 The Slovak Public Pension System

The Slovak pay-as-you-go (PAYG) pension system provides employment-related pensions for old-age, disability, and survivors through contributions from employers, employees, and the self-employed. It receives further funding for the unemployed and an annual assessment from the State budget for soldiers, students, and non-working parents. In addition, a small number of pensions are provided through the system that are not based on employment eligibility.

The pension system was provided off-budget financing in 1993 through the creation of the National Insurance Company. In 1995, the National Insurance Company was divided into two public service institutions--the General Health Insurance Company and the Social Insurance Company (SIC). The latter includes the pension fund and the sickness fund. Other state social support payments (non-systemic benefits) are also administered by the SIC.

Normal old-age benefits are paid to persons who have worked 25 years and who have reached age 60 for men or ages 53-57 for women, depending on the number of children they have raised. Pensions are based on the best 5 of the last 10 years of earnings. The wage base equals 100 percent of the first Sk2,500 monthly earnings, 33 percent of earnings between Sk2,500-6,000 and 10 percent of earnings between Sk6,000-10,000. The replacement rate ranges from 50 percent for a 25 year career to a maximum of 67 percent of the wage base for those with longer years of service.

Pensions adjustments are triggered every time wages increase by 5 percent or prices increase by 10 percent. The exact amount by which pensions are raised is *ad-hoc,* although they have in practice been indexed to wages. Special provisions are applicable to pensioners in particular labor categories, such as coal miners (the so-called categories 1 and 2), which lead to earlier retirement ages and more generous benefits.

Like other transforming countries, the Slovak Republic experienced a surge of new pensioners in the early stages of the transition (20 percent between 1989 and 1991), as the pension scheme was partly used as a buffer against rising unemployment. It has since then succeeded in reducing sharply the number of new pensioners, as indicated by a 40 percent decline in the number of new old age and disability pensioners since the early 1990s. It would appear that pensions no longer continue to be used as an instrument to control unemployment, even though workers within two years of retirement are still eligible for pensions in cases of workforce reduction. Despite recent efforts to curtail the number of pensions paid, 1.2 million pensioners received 1.4 million pensions in 1995 (Table 6.5). The number of pensions paid is greater than the number of pensioners as many women receive two pensions--one in their own right and one as a widow. Overall, 22 percent of the population received a pension in 1995. More worrisome, however, is the fact that very early retirement is bound to continue to exert considerable pressure on the finances of the system.

In the short run, over the next few years, projections of the PAYG system indicate that, if there is no disruption in collection performance (i.e. no increase in tax evasion) and no ad-hoc increases in benefits, pension fund deficits should not occur. However, even under these assumptions, the financial situation of the fund is not sustainable in the long-run. Based on baseline assumptions about future demographic and economic outcomes, current expenditures will exceed current revenues by the end of the next decade, and the fund's assets will be exhausted in 2018.[71] If reform measures are not taken, the pension deficit would gradually increase to 3 percent of GDP by 2024, and

Table 6.5
Expenditures of the Pension Fund, 1995

	Pensions Paid (thousands)	Expenditures (percent of GDP)	Percent of Total
TOTAL	1,381	8.1	100
Old Age	723	5.1	62.9
Disability	223	1.5	18.5
Widows	290	1.0	12.9
Partial Disability	55	0.2	2.9
Orphans	39	0.1	1.1
Old Age	17	0.0	0.8
Social	8	0.0	0.5
Spousal	19	0.0	0.3
Widowers	3	0.0	0.1
Other	0.084	0.0	0.0

Source: Ministry of Social Affairs and Family.

would end up at almost 6 percent of GDP by 2050 (Figure 6.4). If budgetary subsidies were used to balance the fund,[72] substantial cuts in government expenditures would be necessary, or the contribution rate would have to be increased to 34 percent of payroll.

One important measure taken by Government in 1996 was the passage of the private pension law which, for the first time, permits the establishment of supplemental pensions through the workplace. This legislation allows private pension plans to be established through employer-employee agreements and managed as non-profit entities by pension companies. These plans will be multi-employer plans, as regulations require a minimum coverage group of 100,000 employees. To date, only one plan has had its application approved by the Government, although three other applications are being processed.

One of the chief motivations for the establishment of these plans is the anticipated abolishment of special pensions for the so-called Category 1 and Category 2 workers (e.g., coal miners). It was envisaged that supplemental pensions provided by private plans could substitute for special provisions granted to these workers. However, while legislation abolishing these special early retirement provisions was enacted and scheduled to become effective in 1994, there have been some delays in implementation. The private pension fund law delineates investment guidelines, but the bulk of new assets will be initially deposited with the banking system, and some of the funds' resources are also expected to be placed as loans to individual plan employers (subject to a limit of 10 percent of the fund's total assets). This is expected to provide an inducement for more employers to join a plan, but needs to be carefully monitored to prevent abuse and future financial problems. More generally, the introduction of private pension funds raise the need for a good regulatory and supervisory framework in the Slovak Republic.

---

[71] These simulations use a model of the Slovak pension system developed as an extension of an earlier model used by the MOL. The current fund balance is defined as current revenues from contributions less promised benefit payments. Interest income and expenditures are not included. The base case economic scenario assumes GDP growth of 5.5 percent in 1997, gradually declining to 1.4 percent per annum in 2015. The unemployment rate in 1997 is projected to be 10.5 percent, gradually declining to an equilibrium rate of 7 percent in 2010. The overall fertility rate is assumed to increase from 1.52 to 2.05 by 2008. The long-run assumptions are generally consistent with those forecasts for established market economies.

[72] The funds received by the budget to cover entitlements for soldiers, students, and non-working parents are not considered subsidies to the fund. These expenditures are assumed to continue throughout the projection period.

Challenges for Future Pension Policies

The Government's concept paper provides the major guidelines for the new social security system: (i) benefits from social insurance should be strictly tied to economic activities performed in the past; and (ii) social insurance should continue to be compulsory and provide benefits on a PAYG basis. The document raises many unanswered questions, however, about the way in which these guidelines will be translated into actual legislative and regulatory provisions. Consequently, there is space to make informed decisions about system design.

Figure 6.4
Projected Balance of the Pension System, Base Case and Partial Reforms (percent of GDP)

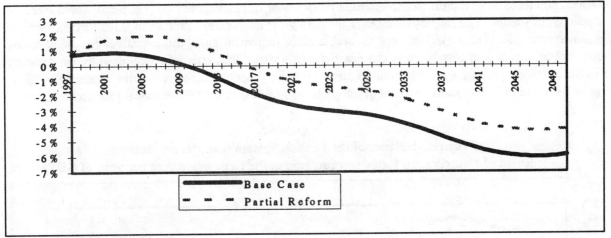

Source: World Bank staff estimates.

The proposed new social insurance legislation is scheduled to be drafted and enacted in two stages. The primary components of the first stage are likely to include: (i) lengthening the service requirement for old-age pensions from 25 to 30 years; (ii) lengthening the period included in the wage base from the best five of the last 10 years to lifetime career earnings; (iii) changing the pension earnings base to a point system; (iv) reducing the maximum income included in the base; (v) indexing for inflation on a scheduled basis; and (vi) removing social benefits from the fund. Hopefully, the already enacted legislation to remove Category 1 and Category 2 early retirement eligibility would be made effective as well. However, legislation to increase the normal retirement age will not be considered until 1998.

Actuarial simulations of one possible set of illustrative reform policies (but not specifically those proposed by Government at this time) indicate that early reforms of the PAYG system could delay the date at which the pension fund balance will turn negative. The scenario of partial reforms simulated here includes the elimination of early retirement, the phase-out of partial disability pensions, the phase-out of wives and social pensions, and the switch from wage indexation to a mixed indexation formula comprising wages and prices with equal weights (the Swiss indexation formula). Under these assumptions, the pension fund would shift into deficit in 2015 and would run out of its accumulated assets in 2037 (Figure 6.4). This represents a considerable improvement compared to the current system, but it should be noted that it is still insufficient to restore long-run equilibrium.[73] Note also that changes in indexation of pensions

---

[73] Taking into account interest income, the fund would shift into deficits only in 2025. However, the deficits would increase rapidly at the end of the projection period, because of fast growing interest expenditures.

becomes frequently a politically sensitive topic, but most OECD countries have already abandoned full wage indexation, in efforts to reduce the underlying imbalances of their pension systems. Recent examples within the EU include France and Italy, which have adopted price indexation, and Finland, which has adopted a mixed indexation formula.[74]

While the overall direction for pension reform is clear, many important questions remain unanswered, in particular regarding the computation of benefits. In the projections produced to date, the combination of changes proposed, including (i) lengthening the service requirement for old-age pensions from 25 to 30 years; (ii) lengthening the period included in the wage base from the best five of the last 10 years to lifetime career earnings; (iii) changing the pension earnings base to a point system; (iv) reducing the maximum income included in the base, are assumed to result in an average entry replacement rate that is identical to the current system (around 60 percent of net average wages). This result is not self-evident, however, and there will be pressures to increase replacement rates. Further, current plans would increase the number of credited non-employment years for caring for children at home from three to five years of age for each child. With continued very favorable early retirement ages, the incentives for childbearing would be out of step with current European practice. Ultimately, the actuarial model used by Government to evaluate reform proposals must be able to incorporate all proposed changes into the modeling process. This will involve further immediate model development to meet the targets Government proposes.

Figure 6.5
Projected Balance of the Pension System with Partial Reforms,
Reduced Contribution Rates and Increase in the Retirement Age (percent of GDP)

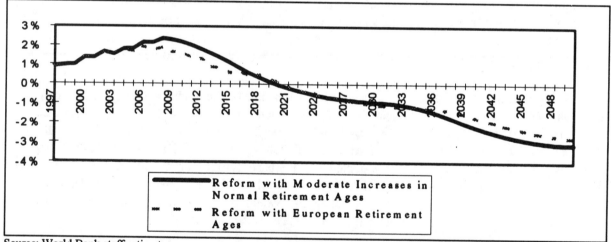

Source: World Bank staff estimates.

One of the most important decisions Government must reach is how and when to raise the retirement age. Raising the retirement age to 63 for men and 60 for women would restore long-run equilibrium (defined as a zero asset position at the end of the projection period),[75] and allow for a 3 percent decrease in the contribution rate that could foster a moderate expansion of employment (Figure 6.5). An even better policy would involve an increase in retirement ages in line with those of Western Europe, by gradually raising them to age 65 for both men and women. While life expectancies may be lower than

[74] See European Commission (1996), "Ageing and Pension Expenditure Prospects in the Western World," Reports and Studies, No. 3, Brussels.

[75] This implies the full use of assets accumulated during the initial period.

those of the EU countries now, the Slovak Republic could expect gradual improvements in life expectancies in line with the gradual convergence of its per capita income to EU levels. If retirement ages were raised to EU levels, the fund would achieve long-run equilibrium, and the contribution rate could be set at 21 percent for the long run (Figure 6.5), a reduction of 6.5 percent from current rates that would bring it very close to the European average (Table 6.3), generating more significant effects on the labor market.[76]

To reduce future deficits and maintain a minimum levels of assets relative to the fund's obligations, the authorities would have either to implement more moderate reductions in contribution rates, or make efforts to reduce further expenditures. This could be achieved by a full move to price indexation. The second alternative would generate stronger benefits in the labor market, and could also open room for a faster expansion of the voluntary private pension system. Since the tax incidence of payroll contributions usually falls on the employee, the decrease in contribution rates would probably lead to an increase in net wages. In such a circumstance, both employers and employees would become more interested in expanding the private pension system. If the complementary system were to become sufficiently widespread on a voluntary basis, Parliament might decide to expand private pensions to all employees.

The key requirement of the pension system for EU accession is to harmonize social security schemes in order to facilitate coordination and ensure portability across countries. This coordination requires the development of an up-to-date system to track social insurance entitlements for all contributors. An additional administrative consideration, not directly linked to EU accession, but important for the long-run finances of the system, is the improvement of collection and compliance procedures. While social insurance assessments suggest that 95 percent of all contributions are collected, calculations based on labor force figures and average earnings suggest that the compliance rate may be somewhat under 80 percent. As the number of small employers multiplies and companies change ownership or go out of business, better auditing and targeting procedures will be needed to ensure a high rate of compliance. As mentioned before, efforts to reduce the contribution rate would also greatly enhance incentives to comply.

The Current Status of Short-term Benefits

Short-term social insurance benefits associated with employment are financed by a 4.8 percent payroll contribution, 1 percent of which is levied on the employee. Short-term benefits include sickness benefits, family leave, maternity leave, payments made to women who switch to lower paying jobs during pregnancy, funeral leave and childbirth benefits.

---

[76] Taking into account interest income, the fund would shift into deficits around 2038. The deficits would increase rapidly after that date, due to growing interest expenditures.

As the bulk of these benefits are payments to workers in support of lost wages, they appropriately fall under the rubric of social insurance. The sick-leave benefit formula is generous, with payments made at a rate of 70 percent of the individual's net daily wage for the first three days of illness, and 90 percent thereafter (although benefits are limited to Sk300 per day). Duration is based on medical certification. Maternity benefits are set at 90 percent of the daily net wage for a period of 28 weeks with the same Sk300 limit. These benefits are relatively expensive, amounting to around 1.1 percent of GDP in 1995 (Table 6.6).

Table 6.6
Expenditures of the Sickness Fund, 1995

	Recipients (thousands)	Expenditures (percent of GDP)	Percent of total
Total	n.a.	1.1	100
Sickness Benefits	2,630	0.9	76
Maternity Leave	357	0.2	15
Family Leave	456	0.0	5
Child Birth	49	0.0	3
Funeral	50	0.0	1
Wage Equalization	8	0.0	0

n.a.: not available
Source: Ministry of Social Affairs and Family.

The primary focus of short-term benefit reform must be on the provision of sick leave, which increased during transition in concert with the rise in unemployment. In 1989, 4.4 percent of the insured workforce was out on sick leave, whereas in 1995 that percentage had risen to 5 percent (although it has tended to decline from the 5.2 percent peak reached in 1993). The use of sick leave as safety valve against unemployment does not even require the collusion of certifying physicians, as employers encourage workers to apply for sick leave in borderline cases of illness. For workers making less than the average wage, taking sick leave results in little income loss, and clearly provides higher benefits than unemployment insurance. By contrast, unemployment benefits are initially 60 percent of the net wage, and 50 percent thereafter. Consequently, the expanded use of sick leave can lower expenses for employers, reduce the need for layoffs, and/or lengthen the period of paid unemployment for workers.

One reform under consideration would transfer the initial responsibility for sick leave from social insurance to the employer. This measure would certainly reduce abuse, but the duration of employer-financed sick leave should be limited, to maintain incentives for enterprises to comply with the law and continue to make sick leave contributions. Further, the medical conditions under which sick leave can be granted should be reviewed to determine whether they need to be more stringent. A product of this analysis could be the identification of patterns of abuse. The statistical monitoring of sick leave should be continued to ensure that these benefits are not substituted for, or used to extend, insured unemployment.

Throughout Europe, maternity leave is provided through social insurance. Like retirement, it represents a life cycle event rather than a true insurable risk, since insurable risks are generally beyond the control of the insured and free of moral hazard. At this juncture, maternity is likely to present a greater risk to the employer than the employee. Government might wish to reconsider its current policy of six months of paid maternity as small private sector employers may become reluctant to hire women of childbearing ages in jobs in which significant on-the-job training is required. The fixed costs of hiring and retraining replacement employees are relatively higher for small employers. Consequently, the Government may consider reducing the period of maternity leave for small enterprises.

Family Support and Social Assistance

The Current Situation

Two types of non-employment related benefits are provided in the Slovak Republic: (i) support for families through state-funded cash-benefit programs; and (ii) social assistance and services for needy families and individuals (funded through the budget and managed at the local level).[77] Family support currently includes means-tested child allowances, parental allowances for non-working parents, expenditures for health and recreational facilities, and allowances for the families of soldiers. Family support expenditures have amounted to 2.5 percent of GDP, with child allowances accounting for the majority of the spending (Table 6.7). Social assistance provides cash benefit to needy families on a one-time or ongoing basis and in-kind goods and services, including institutional care. Social assistance expenditures have amounted to around 1.1 percent of GDP, with almost half of the funds also directed towards families with children (Table 6.7).

Table 6.7
Expenditures on Social Programs, 1995

	Recipients (thousands)	Expenditures (percent of GDP)
Family Support	n.a.	2.5
Child Allowances	673	1.9
Non-working Parent	154	0.4
Health and Recreational Facility (spas)	92	0.1
Soldier's Rent	0.2	0.1
Military Family Sustenance	9	0.0
Social Assistance	n.a.	1.1
Families with Children	179	0.5
Individuals with Special Needs	167	0.3
Elderly	n.a.	0.1
Severely Disabled	132	0.1
Subsistence Contribution	130	0.1
Socially Non-adaptive Individuals	4	0.0

n.a.: not available.
Source: Ministry of Social Affairs and Family.

Child allowances have been means-tested since 1994, with the cut-off related to the official minimum living standard. Specifically, child allowances are received by families with children whose incomes are less than 1.5 times the minimum living standard and families with children whose income is between 1.5 and 2 times the minimum. Despite means-testing, these benefits account for 75 percent of the social support payments provided by the State. Overall, 48 percent of all families are in the first group, and 30 percent are in the second group, showing that the means-testing mechanism is generous, only excluding the upper quartile of the income distribution. The per-child allowance granted families in the first group is one-half the minimum living standard; the allowance for the second group is one-third the minimum. Allowances are graduated according to the age of the child, with a higher amount granted to older children. With no scale factor built-in, families with many children automatically receive benefits higher than the minimum wage.

Recommendations for Further Improvements

Government is in the process of developing new legislation to substantially reform both family support and social assistance programs. Since the bulk of payments are directed towards families with children, the focus of reform should rest in this area. Government's framework for reform stresses redistribution between families with children and other families; and between higher and lower income groups. It also indicates the need for families to provide for themselves. Cost-effective guidelines for

---

[77] While a complex of social services are provided, this section focuses primarily on cash benefits which make up the bulk of social assistance expenditures.

reform which are consistent with the principals cited above would include expenditure control, improved targeting of the poverty population, and the minimization of work disincentives.

The most obvious way to exercise expenditure control would be to reduce the number of families eligible to receive child allowances. The current system is too generous, as most families not only receive a child allowance, but may also receive a Sk750 per child tax exemption under the income tax. If child allowances were targeted to the lowest quartile of the income distribution, expenditures would be reduced and a floor of protection provided. The narrowing of eligibility may also require the reconstruction of the minimum living standard, which is under current consideration. Any new standards should be designed according to international norms and should scale consumption requirements by family size, so that benefit eligibility is not unduly biased towards large families. Allowances for non-working parents should also be means-tested, as there is no need to subsidize one-earner families who can care for their children on their own. Allowances should be designed to supplement other sources of income to ensure that poor families reach a minimum consumption standard. Consolidation of parent and child allowances into one unified system of payment would be the most efficient form of targeting.

One concept under current discussion is the expansion of benefits to include a housing allowance for families who would be unable to afford low-cost housing under free market conditions. This draft legislation will be considered in conjunction with government housing policies to free the rental market. A housing allowance could help overcome some of the constraints that a thin housing market places on population mobility, but it should be limited and closely coordinated with other cash benefit programs, to avoid manipulation of the system by beneficiaries.

Family support programs should also be closely coordinated with social assistance to ensure that all sources of income are included in the determination of each allowance or grant. Benefit coordination could be achieved in a number of ways. For example, regional differences in living costs for families eligible for child allowances could be addressed through supplementary social assistance payments. One policy currently under consideration is to have district social assistance offices pay out all allowances and grants. This would be strengthened by the development of a central data base to track benefit recipiency and help control fraud and abuse. Currently, beneficiaries are required to report on their income only once a year. Substantial changes in economic status are likely to take place among recipients, particularly among the unemployed. Consequently, a consistent strategy to identify and track recipients most likely to experience an unreported change in income would be important for expenditure control and policy development.

Survey data on income recipiency could be used to analyze work disincentives inherent in cash benefit programs. Monthly payments per recipient family average roughly half the minimum wage for child allowances and social assistance. Thus, there appears to be little incentive for recipients to select one benefit rather than another or to prefer social assistance to work. However, beneficiary families can receive more than one benefit. For example, allowances for non-working parents also average half the minimum wage and benefits for families with many children quickly exceed the minimum wage. Multiple benefit recipiency may create incentives to avoid job search and remain out of the labor market. The receipt of social assistance by the unemployed may create work disincentives under current program conditions. Further, sick leave benefits may also be used by employers to avoid paying wages, or by employees to avoid registering for unemployment. Work disincentives and/or false reporting may be particularly compelling due to the relatively narrow distribution of wages and the sharp reduction in family allowance payments when an income-eligibility threshold is crossed. Consequently, in addition to targeting benefits to the poor, social policies should be explicitly designed to make work more attractive than benefit recipiency.

Several social programs appear anomalous in a market economy. Support to military families would be better placed within the military budget and not as state social support, even if benefits are ultimately distributed at the social assistance offices. Further, expenditures on health and recreation facilities should be operated on a fee basis and privatized as recreational facilities. To the extent that these facilities serve as sanitariums, they should be included in health insurance expenditures. Lastly, several special provisions could be eliminated, including additional benefits for additional children.

Many proposals under current consideration by Government have positive features. For example, measures to encourage school attendance that are coordinated with family assistance would have important national benefits if they encourage poor families to invest in education. The shift away from institutionalization to foster care represents an initiative that is finding favor in many countries, because it is both cost-effective and generally ensures that children receive better care. Incentives to provide home care for the elderly and disabled often have similar beneficial effects. The overall thrust of Government policies, to grant district offices greater autonomy in the provision of services and encourage private delivery of services can potentially improve efficiency and quality. At the same time, Government will need to monitor the budget allocated to social assistance programs closely, as district offices will have incentives to increase the size of their programs, while assisting groups with special needs, such as the elderly and disabled. Further, the allocation of funds across districts should be done using objective criteria, as such funding could be subject to the whims of the political process.

Summary of Recommendations

Labor Law and Labor Market:
- Exempt small employers from specific restrictive provisions on hiring and firing
- Increase the scope for decentralized enterprise-level bargaining
- Grant extensions of collective bargaining agreements with caution
- Reduce contribution rates to the Employment Fund

Unemployment Benefits:
- Coordinate unemployment insurance and social assistance to reduce work disincentives
- Enforce job search and availability-to-work tests more strictly
- Active Labor Market Programs
- Target programs to groups most likely to benefit
- Institute program evaluation on an ongoing basis
- Remove mandatory reporting of job vacancies to employment office

Pensions:
- Remove social benefits; limit disability pensions
- Restructure benefit formula, providing a floor of protection
- Avoid increasing average replacement rate
- Institute Swiss indexation formula
- Raise retirement age gradually to Western European standards
- Develop system to track pension entitlements on an ongoing basis
- Reduce contribution rates
- Monitor performance of private pensions; consider mandatory coverage

Short-term Benefits:
- Shift initial days of sick leave to the employer
- Reduce period of maternity leave required for small firms

Social Support and Social Assistance:
- Redesign minimum living standard according to international norms
- Develop coordinated means-tested programs that reduce notches and work disincentives
- Develop a coordinated data base to analyze programs and monitor recipients

CHAPTER VII: THE CHALLENGE OF EU ACCESSION FOR THE ENVIRONMENT

Introduction

As most other CEE countries, the Slovak Republic (then part of Czechoslovakia) also suffered from 40 years of environmental negligence under the former central planning system. After the political changes at the end of the 1980s, the significant damage inflicted on water, air, and soil over the last 40 years became evident. Those damages were mostly concentrated in the heavy industrialized regions of the country. Over the past seven years, considerable environmental improvements were achieved through new environmental policies, but also through the decline of heavy industries, which remain the major cause of Slovak environmental problems.

This chapter aims at contributing to the Government's efforts, by reviewing the progress already achieved in improving the environment and identifying the policies that should be put in place to ensure continuing progress in this area. The chapter is structured as follows. The second section reviews briefly the current situation in the environmental area. The third section examines the implications of EU accession for environmental policy, examines the progress already achieved in the area of legal approximation and compliance, and presents preliminary estimates of the investments required for compliance with EU requirements in the environmental area. Finally, the last section provides an evaluation of the revolving environmental fund--the scheme which is being envisaged to finance environment expenditures.

The Quality of the Environment in the Slovak Republic

Air Quality

The amount of pollutants emitted into the air has been substantially reduced since the late 1980s. As shown in Figure 7.1, particulate matter (PM) emissions were reduced by more than 70 percent from 1987 to 1995, and Sulfur Oxide (SO_2) emissions by more than 60 percent during the same period. Nitrogen Oxide (NO_x) and Carbon Dioxide (CO_2) emissions have also been reduced considerably, although the reduction has not been so dramatic as the reduction in PM and SO_2 emissions.

The improvement in air quality since the late 1980s has been due both to the initial contraction of economic activity and to emission reduction measures. The collapse of economic activity was the major reason for the reduction in air emissions in the first stages of the transition (1990-1993). The 20 percent drop of real GDP between 1990 and 1993 resulted in a 14 percent reduction in energy consumption that constituted the dominant factor behind the reduction in air emissions. During this period, average emissions per unit of output may have actually increased in some areas, suggesting that emission reduction measures were still not having a powerful effect.

The rapid recovery of GDP and industrial output since 1993 has not translated into an immediate deterioration of air quality, suggesting that emission reduction measures became the dominant factor of the improvement in air quality after 1993. However, the improvement in air quality has been very modest since that year (Figure 7.1), revealing the difficulties of achieving additional progress in the environment in the context of a growing economy. In fact, the main challenge facing the environmental authorities in the Slovak

Republic is to ensure additional improvements in environmental quality in a scenario of continued economic recovery.[78]

Figure 7.1
Emissions of Major Pollutants, 1987-95

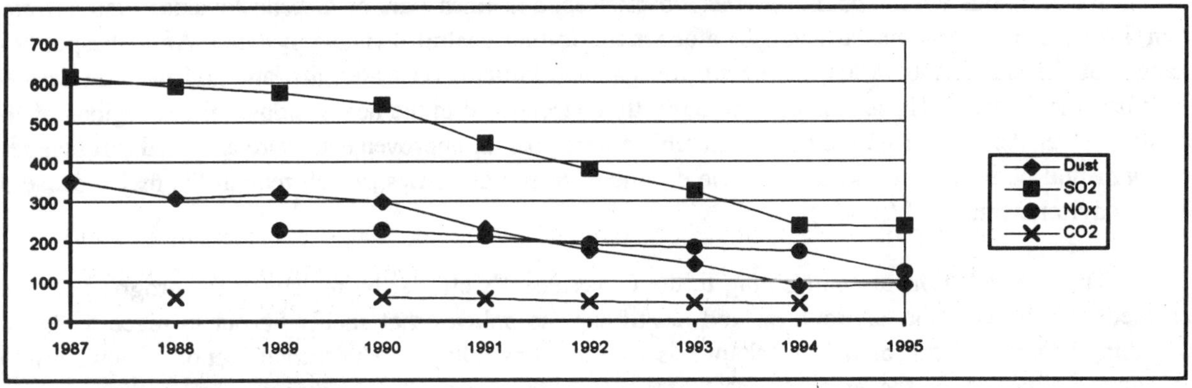

Source: Ministry of Environment

Ambient air quality has also improved in the Slovak Republic since the start of the transition. According to the monitoring system (32 stationary measuring installments), annual average SO_2 concentrations in the different stations range from 17.9 ug/m^3 to 51 ug/m^3 for the urban regions of Bratislava, Banka Bistrica and Kosice, whereas NO_x (as NO_2) concentrations range from 31.5 ug/m^3 to 137.4 ug/m^3. Today, most Slovak municipalities comply with EU air quality standards for annual mean concentrations. Annual average concentrations of surface ozone range from 11 ug/m^3 to almost 70 ug/m^3 depending, among other factors, on the altitude. The critical level of 50 micro g/m^3 (UN ECE), calculated as an average of daily hours in vegetation period, is exceeded each year. However, it must be noted that high surface ozone concentrations also remain an unsolved problem in most EU member states.

Water Quality

In 1995, the total amount of waste water collected in public sewage systems was 558 million m^3, 86 percent of which was discharged to treatment plants, and the remaining 14 percent disposed off without any treatment. Approximately 87 percent of treatment plants have biological treatment (compared to 84 percent in 1990). The average reduction of the Biological Oxygen Demand (BOD) within the treatment plants is about 75 percent, but some waste water entering the plants bypasses the biological treatment stage.

In 1995, about 52 percent of households were linked to sewer systems, compared to 50 percent in 1990 (Table 7.1). About 86 percent of household waste water is treated at least with primary treatment, and more than 80 percent of the treatment plants for municipal waste water have also a secondary (biological) stage. The total amount of waste water resulting from industry, agriculture, construction, and other activities is 441,769 million m^3 per year, out of which 85 percent is treated and 15 percent emitted without treatment.

---

[78] Emissions in the Slovak Republic are highly concentrated in a selected number of emitters: Eighty-one plants with a capacity of more than 50 MegaWatthours thermal (MWth) are in operation in the country and account for 70 percent of the total annual SO_2 emissions. Four main polluting plants are responsible for about 44 percent of total SO_2 emissions.

Table 7.1
Connections to Sewer Systems, 1975-95

	1975	1980	1985	1990	1993	1995
Inhabitants	4,743	4,985	5,160	5,303	5,318	5,347
Connected to Sewer with Treatment (percent)	18.6	27.3	36.4	43.0	47.0	48.2
Connected to Sewer without Treatment (percent)	15.3	13.3	9.6	7.7	4.6	4.0
Total Connection to Sewer System (percent)	33.9	40.6	46.0	50.7	51.6	52.2

Source: Ministry of Environment.

Waste

The yearly amount of waste produced decreased from 34 million tons in 1992 to 25.7 million tons in 1995. Hazardous waste decreased from 3.3 to 2.5 million tons during the same period, whereas municipal waste remained constant at 1.6 million tons per year (i.e., about 300 kg per inhabitant). The number of registered landfill sites fell from 8,372 in 1993 to 5,530 in 1995, but only 102 of these conform with the Slovak technical regulations. There is a great need to reduce the number of landfills further and to upgrade those which will be kept in operation. Approximately 78 waste incinerators are in operation in the country, 39 of which are being used for incineration of clinical waste. Two main incinerators (one in Bratislava and the other in Kosice) are incinerating municipal waste, and the Bratislava incinerator is being restructured. Thirty seven incinerators are also burning hazardous waste. The Slovak authorities are planning to construct additional incinerators.

New Challenges in the Environment

The Slovak Republic and the other transforming countries of Central Europe are now facing the problem of shifting pollution types. Heavy industry, which used to be the major cause of pollution problems, is retrenching, and is being overtaken by smaller and more dispersed pollution sources, such as traffic or chemical waste from the growing number of private sector enterprises, which are far more difficult to control. In addition, while in the past only a limited number of large polluters had to be supervised, now a much larger number of smaller and medium-sized enterprises has to be controlled, imposing a major challenge for the national and regional environmental administrations.

The Implications of EU Accession in the Environmental Field

Complying with EU environmental legislation is a formidable task for all CEE countries, and the Slovak Republic is no exception. Compliance involves not only legal harmonization issues, but also developing a strategy that will enable the Slovak Republic to meet these membership requirements as rapidly and as cost-effectively as feasible. Compliance is absolutely necessary for the efficient and fair working of the EU internal market, since national legislation should not compromise product standards or trade fairness if aspiring members are to confront both the rights and the responsibilities of full EU membership. Moreover, while transitional periods will be required to comply with EU legislation, if only because of the time needed to develop the necessary infrastructure, substantial benefits can be expected. This section describes the status of legal approximation and compliance with EU environmental legislation, and provides preliminary estimates of the required investments for complying with this legislation.

A General Assessment of Legal Approximation

A detailed study on legal issues commissioned by the Ministry of Environment (MoE)[79] concludes that the process of approximation with EU environmental law is proceeding relatively successfully, and has become more systematic since the release of the White Paper. The task of legal approximation has been performed by a special division for legal approximation of the legal department of the MoE, and the work has been facilitated by the access to the EU legal regulations through the Phare program. Some obstacles to more rapid progress include the divided responsibility between ministries in some fields of environmental protection (for example, chemicals and noise reduction), the demands of legal harmonization (which imposes a strain on human resources, especially lawyers), and the absence of financial resources for translation of all EU regulations into Slovak.

As a general conclusion, it may be said that there has been significant progress in harmonizing Slovak environmental law with EU law. However, there are some areas where Slovak legislation still faces major challenges. One particular area to mention here is the Integrated Pollution Prevention and Control (IPPC) directive, which has not yet been incorporated into Slovak law.

EU environmental directives usually require member states to pass and implement legislation designed to address particular environment problems. In general, the legislation requires that national authorities ensure that all activities which could generate any significant amount of pollution be subject to a specific permit, specifying limits on discharges of pollutants and other wastes, modes of operations, and other relevant parameters. In the Slovak Republic, as in many other European countries, the legislation under which such permits are issued relates to discharges to specific media, such as air, water, or soil. However, the recent EU directive on Integrated Pollution Prevention and Control lays out a new framework for the authorization of industrial activities, which may be seen as a broader change in the philosophy underpinning EU environmental policies.

The directive applies strictly to six categories of industry, namely energy, metal production and processing, minerals, chemicals, waste management, and "others" (including paper and pulp production, textile treatment, tanning, food processing, and intensive livestock operations). The directive sets the standards for all activities for which permits may be required. The coverage of permits is expected to be much broader than in the past, since they are expected to deal with the arrangements for discharges to any medium, as well as issues of waste minimization, energy efficiency, resource utilization, the avoidance of accidents, and the restoration of sites after the industrial activity has ceased. Permits are to be reconsidered and updated at periodic intervals, especially when excessive pollution occurs, or when technical or other developments allow a significant reduction in emissions at reasonable cost.

One critical aspect of the directive is the shift from a focus on emissions, which has tended to promote a reliance upon end-of-pipe controls, to one on waste minimization, for which clean technologies and good management are usually critical. This is embodied in the concept of Best Available Techniques (BAT), which replaces the previous concept of Best Available Technology Not Entailing Excessive Costs (BATNEEC) used in many previous directives. The use and definition of the term "techniques" is clearly intended to emphasize the role of management and operating practices, as well as technology. In sum, there will be a greater focus on operational standards rather than just on the installation of controls. As far as

---

[79] Bozena Gasparikova et. al., (1996), in "Approximation of European Union Environmental Legislation: Case Studies of Bulgaria, Czech Republic, Estonia, Hungary, Latvia, Lithuania, Poland, Romania, Slovak Republic and Slovenia," Regional Environmental Center for Central and Eastern Europe, Budapest.

possible, plants will be expected to meet "good practice" levels of environmental performance within the context of their industry. Since good housekeeping and maintenance have been notorious weaknesses in the environmental performance of all firms in Central and Eastern Europe, this will involve major adjustments in management attitudes and behavior.

It would be reasonable to assume that the environmental quality standards should be based on an assessment of costs and benefits, at least in the short- and medium term. Thus, violations of environmental quality standards are most likely to arise when there are significant emissions from sources which are not covered by permits. This leads to the conclusion that systems of tradable discharge permits or other offset arrangements would be within the spirit of the directive, even though it does not cover such possibilities explicitly. The alternative would be policies that would encourage the dispersal of plants which may individually comply with BAT requirements but whose concentrated impact leads to excessive ambient concentrations of some pollutants.

Overall, the IPPC directive and other trends in EU legislation provide an opportunity for the Slovak Republic and the other CEE countries to develop a system of industrial pollution control and environmental management which combines economic and environmental assessments in setting quality standards, emission limits, and permit requirements. This is fully consistent with the country's existing reliance on pollution charges as a major instrument of environmental policy. However, it will also mean that regional and/or local environmental agencies will need to be considerably restructured and strengthened, if they are to play an effective role within a decentralized system of environmental management that focuses on pollution prevention and environmental quality, rather than pollution control and uniform emission standards.

Assessment of Approximation and Compliance in Specific Areas

Air pollution. The Slovak Republic, as some of the other CEE countries, faces two separate challenges in meeting the requirements of EU legislation on air pollution and air quality. Despite the significant reductions in industrial emissions of particulates and other air pollutants since 1989, a small number of urban areas violate current EU limit values for annual exposure to particulates, while many more have average levels of particulates above the EU's target values. The limit values are being reviewed and are likely to be substantially lowered within the next 2-3 years. In almost all areas where air quality standards are violated, the problem is linked to emission of particulates from the burning of coal for household heating or in small boilers. If the draft directive on ambient air quality is enacted, the Slovak Republic will be expected to implement measures to ensure that the limit values agreed by the EU are attained either by the time that the country joins the EU or by the end of some relatively short transitional period.

At the same time, the EU directive dealing with emissions from large combustion plants together with the Second Sulfur Protocol imply that the Slovak Republic has to reduce total emissions of sulfur dioxide to meet agreed targets for 2000, 2005, and 2010, and to ensure that power plants and other major sources of sulfur dioxide emissions meet specific emission standards. In practice, there is some scope for exempting existing plants where compliance with the emission standards would involve excessive costs[80]. Even so, it will be necessary to invest in fitting flue gas desulphurization units (FGDs) to new or rehabilitated power plants as well as to reduce emissions of sulfur dioxide outside the power sector. Slovak

---

[80] This provision is explicit in the Second Sulfur Protocol and is implied by the decisions of the EU Council of Ministers in allowing Spain exemptions from some of the provisions of the large combustion plants directive.

Republic, in contrast in particular with the Czech Republic and some other CEE countries, did not undertake major investments to reduce SO_2 in the last five years, and will have to make greater efforts in this direction in the future.

Unfortunately, there is only a small overlap between the measures necessary to comply with these different elements of EU legislation on air pollution. A substantial amount of total sulfur dioxide emissions are generated outside the power sector, but there are few urban areas where the EU's limit or target values for sulfur dioxide are exceeded. Policies designed to reduce emissions of particulates will contribute in a small way to meeting the sulfur dioxide reduction targets, but otherwise it may be necessary to make difficult choices between options which contribute to meeting different air pollution targets.

Water pollution and management. The quality of Slovak rivers has improved since 1989 as a result of the reduction in emissions from industrial sources. However, the country's basic water infrastructure falls short of what would be required by EU directives. The quality of drinking water delivered to customers often does not meet EU standards. This is not a matter of microbiological contamination which might pose a serious threat to health. Rather, the problem is linked to the presence of minerals and pollutants, either because of the quality of the water source used for the elaboration of drinking water, or because of the contamination that arises during distribution as a result of neglected infrastructure maintenance. EU quality standards for water sources used for the abstraction of drinking water supplies and for drinking water itself are already strict, and will probably become even stricter in the future. Thus, investments will be required to improve raw water quality, upgrade treatment facilities, and replace parts of the water distribution system. There is also need to improve the quality of water supplies for the rural households which currently rely upon shallow wells and similar sources, which may contain high levels of nitrates and/or other chemicals.

The 1991 directive on urban waste water treatment will require sewer systems with at least secondary treatment of sewage for most villages, towns, and cities with a population equivalent of 2,000 or more. Stricter standards apply to "sensitive areas", which discharge into water bodies that are under threat of eutrophication or that are used for the abstraction of drinking water and contain high levels of nitrates. In this case, it is necessary to remove of 70-80 percent of the total nitrogen and phosphorus in the waste water. While the majority of large and medium urban areas (with more than 20,000 people) have sewer systems covering 90 percent or more of their population, the proportion of sewage that is currently subject to biological treatment is less than 50 percent. In small towns and rural communities the picture is much worse, with low levels of sewer coverage and limited treatment of the sewage that is collected. As shown in Table 7.1, less than 50 percent of the population are connected to a sewer system with treatment.

Meeting the EU water quality legislation is likely to be the most important issue with regard to EU accession. Transitional periods might be necessary to develop and implement a cost-effective strategy for approximation with EU requirements. Such a strategy would need to identify: (i) the investments required to upgrade or extend existing infrastructure; and (ii) the mechanisms by which any investments would be financed, both in terms of sources of funds and the generation of the revenues required to repay loans. This strategy will have to address important issues about the fiscal relationship between different levels of government and the role of private financing.

Waste. There are a variety of other issues related to compliance with EU environmental legislation. Perhaps the most important is the management and disposal of municipal and hazardous wastes. These issues could be dealt with by the private sector, provided that an appropriate legal and institutional framework is established, together with the necessary financial incentives. If local authorities attempt to retain their traditional dominant role in this area, however, the problem of waste management will be more difficult to solve as they are likely to face tight constraints on their ability to finance the consolidation, improvement, and operation of waste disposal sites which meet the new standards.

Some additional key elements of EU environmental legislation in this area can be grouped into different categories: (i) the management of dangerous chemicals; (ii) waste management issues, including packaging materials; and (iii) the composition and distribution of fuels, especially for motor vehicles. Approximation and compliance in these three areas are examined below.

Disposal of dangerous chemicals. The EU has developed an extensive legislation dealing with dangerous chemicals which covers administrative procedures, risk assessments and classifications of existing and new chemicals, labeling and packaging, notification of new substances, and provisions concerning their import and export. Various elements of the EU legislation overlap with the recommendations or requirements of a number of international organizations and conventions, including FAO and OECD guidelines or codes of conduct, and the Basle Convention.

Slovak legislation covers the management of dangerous chemicals in general terms, and is supplemented by specific acts or regulations, similar to German regulations, covering particular chemicals or groups of chemicals. The major step required would seem to be the establishment of a single regulatory body, either within the Ministry of Environment or as an independent agency, which would act as the national "Competent Authority" to ensure that existing regulations, procedures and standards are aligned with the requirements of EU legislation. The costs of compliance need not be large and should, in any case, fall on the producers and users of controlled chemicals through a system of registration and licensing fees, rather than on the Government. The chemical industry and others affected are likely to support a clear policy of moving to the adoption and implementation of EU regulations, since it will ease their access to the EU market.

Waste management topics. The EU has been gradually developing its policies on waste management. Much of the relevant legislation focuses on specific products (e.g., waste oils, PCBs and PCTs, sewage sludge, batteries, packaging materials, incineration of hazardous waste, and landfills), but there are also separate framework directives on wastes and hazardous wastes. The overall thrust of the EU's waste policies is to promote clean technologies and waste minimization, while ensuring that waste streams are properly monitored and managed. Despite the overriding principle of unrestricted trade within the internal market, there is a strong preference for disposal at sites relatively close to the origin of waste streams, provided that these "guarantee a high level of protection for the environment and public health". Thus, member states are expected to develop a network of disposal facilities meeting high standards rather than relying upon the transport of wastes to distant disposal sites, whether within a country or in some other country. This poses some problems in considering how best to manage wastes which are generated in small quantities but require specialized treatment facilities, perhaps with significant economies of scale.

The main framework directive was promulgated in 1975 and amended in 1991, and lays down the basic requirements for national systems of waste management. Countries are expected to: (i) establish and/or designate the competent authority for implementing the directive; (ii) adhere to a common categorization of wastes according to the degree of risk; (iii) follow the polluter-pays-principle in financing waste management and disposal; (iv) establish a network of disposal installations with appropriate technologies on the basis of the BATNEEC principle; (v) ensure that separate waste streams are not mixed (in particular, hazardous and non-hazardous wastes are to be managed separately); (vi) require that disposal and recycling facilities operate in compliance with permits, maintain appropriate records, and are subject to regular monitoring; and (vii) produce national and local plans for waste management. The specific directives effectively fill out the details of such requirements for particular products or categories of waste. In addition, the directive on batteries and accumulators bans the sale of most batteries containing more than 0.025 percent of mercury.

To comply with this legislation, the Slovak Republic will have to update much of its legislation covering wastes in order to bring national definitions in line with EU requirements, and to establish an appropriate regulatory framework. The current system of managing wastes contains few specific requirements for permits and record-keeping that would, for example, enable hazardous wastes to be tracked from their point of origin to their final disposal. Thus, a substantial legislative and administrative effort will be required in order to bring the country's waste management policies and procedures in line with EU legislation within the next 5-8 years and, as above, the costs should ultimately be borne by those responsible for generating wastes, either directly or via fees for waste management and disposal.

Fuel standards. EU directives cover the lead and benzene content of gasoline and the sulfur content of diesel fuel and gas oil used in vehicles. The Slovak Republic has already adopted and implemented regulations which comply with the directive on gasoline, and is the first CEE country which has phased out leaded gasoline.

Industrial pollution. The restructuring of the Slovak industry has already contributed to an improvement in environmental quality, though largely as a consequence of the decline in production at old, inefficient, heavy industrial plants. As the economy continues to recover, a balance needs to be found between improvements in the environmental performance of industrial enterprises (including compliance with EU legislation) and sustaining the rapid economic growth required to narrow the gap between income per capita in the Slovak Republic and in the European Union. The key to achieving this balance lies in better management and in the adoption of production methods and technologies which both increase efficiency and (perhaps at a modest cost) reduce pollution.

An Investment Strategy for Approximation

Reduction of air pollution: To comply with European Union Directives, the Slovak Republic must implement a series of investment projects designed to contain pollution from five emission sources: (i) large combustion plants (i.e., power plants with a minimum installed thermal capacity of 50 MWth); (ii) medium and small sources of emissions; (iii) waste incinerators; (iv) emission sources of ozone-depleting substances; and (v) industrial air pollution. Preliminary estimates of the investments required to contain air pollution are provided in Table 7.2. Note that industrial air pollution sources often overlap with the other four categories. Therefore, reductions from these sources are not explicitly included in the estimates presented below.

Table 7.2
Preliminary Estimates of Investments Required to Reduce Air Pollution

Air Source Categories	Methodology, Sources of Data	Cost Estimates World Bank (US$ million)
Large Combustion Plants	Documentation of 81 large sources, unit prices for Flue Gas Desulphurization and other measures	900
Small and Medium Sources/Improvement of Ambient Air Quality	Gas-network extension (district heating network, others), comparable regions in CEEC, rough estimation	900
Waste Incineration	Individual project documentation	40
Ozone Layer Substances	Slovak publication	100
Industrial Air Pollution (additional pollutants)	EU-Industrial Pollution Prevention Directive (Sept. 1996)	not calculated
Total	compare with: NEAP (incomplete): US$1,404 million IIASA (incomplete): US$2,040 million	2,000–2,400

Source: World Bank staff estimates.

Water and water management. The estimates of investments required in the area of water and water management (Table 7.3) are based on the EU Directive 91/271, which deals with urban waste water. The demand for *sewage systems* is estimated on the basis of US$2,000 per household and about 800,000 households to be linked, resulting in investments of US$1,600 million for sewage systems. With regard to *water treatment* and in particular the introduction of *biological treatment stages,* some US$400-800 million are needed. This estimate is based on the assumption that average costs for machinery employed in the biological stage are US$50--70 (Sk1,500--Sk2,000) per inhabitant equivalent in the Slovak Republic. Since these costs account for 30--50 percent of total costs, it follows that total biological stage costs would amount to about US$150--300 per inhabitant equivalent. Additional upgrading of existing treatment plants is estimated at US$200--300 million.

Table 7.3
Preliminary Estimates of Investments Required to Improve Water Quality

Water Sub-Categories	Methodology, Sources	Cost Estimates (US$ million)
Municipal Waste Water, Biological Stage	Current linkage of households to sewage systems: 52 percent (year 1995); unit prices based on Slovakian and Polish cost estimates	400–800
Municipal Waste Water, Sewage Systems	Unit prices, US$2,000 per household	1,600
Municipal Waste Water, Upgrading, Maintenance	Estimate based on figures for other CEE countries	200–300
Water Supply	Estimate based on figures for other CEE countries	400–800
Total Water	(compare: NEAP: US$ 680 million until 2010: US$420 million 1996 to 1998)	2,600–3,500

Source: World Bank staff estimates.

Waste management. The cost estimate for necessary investments for waste management is based on the Slovak National Environmental Action Plan and the waste management program of 1994. According to these sources, the required investments amount to US$800--US$1,000 million.

Summary of total investments. The Slovak Republic needs to undertake a series of investments to comply with EU legislation. Preliminary estimates suggest that total investments would amount to around US$5-6 billion, including approximately US$2.6 billion of investments in water, US$2 billion of investments in air, and US$0.8 billion of investments in waste management. This would imply annual investments of around US$300 million distributed over a period of 20 years. In such a case, annual investments would amount to approximately 1.5 percent of GDP, an amount which is typical for EU countries. It must be emphasized, however, that these estimates are very preliminary and subject to considerable uncertainty.[81]

Detailed least cost planning may reduce these figures. In addition, these investments should be considered not only as requirements for EU accession, but also in relation to the direct benefits and the positive externalities that they are likely to generate. In fact, since many of these benefits are likely to extend beyond Slovak soil due to the potential flow of pollution across borders, its positive externalities are increased even further. Also, compliance with EU requirements is a necessary condition to materialize the full benefits of a functioning internal market.

The transboundary flow of air and water pollution could be an important guide for the phasing of investments and the potential of attracting financial support from bilateral and international donors, although only to a limited degree. Most of the water pollution originating in the Slovak Republic flows out of the country (with the exception of the Danube, which is a border river). The Slovak Republic's contribution to the pollution of the Danube ranks high in the priority list of the Danube Program. With respect to air pollution, the Slovak Republic receives considerable amounts from the Czech Republic and Poland; the Slovak Republic's amounts of transboundary flow of air pollution are much smaller. The extent of the Slovak border with European Union countries is, compared to the Czech Republic, Poland and Hungary, rather limited. Therefore, the Slovak Republic may have limited access to the funds under the European Union's Cross Border Program, an important source of grant funding for environmental protection. That increases even more the need for the design of an environment strategy and least cost planning.

The Financing of Environmental Expenditures

Over the past few years, the Slovak Republic has spent between US$33 million (1996) and US$60 million (1992) in environmental projects. This implies the need to increase expenditures significantly to implement all the investments needed to meet the EU accession targets. The Ministry of Environment has indicated that the State Environmental Fund (SEF) and the envisaged Revolving Environmental Fund (REF) would be possible instruments to reach this goal. This section reviews the status and concept of both Funds, and provides a number of recommendations regarding: (i) policy issues; (ii) operational issues; and (ii) institutional aspects, based on the Draft Law for the Funds and other available information.

---

[81] At the same time, these estimates do not include investments required in other areas, such as management of hazardous chemicals, nuclear safety, and noise. Obligations for the Slovak Republic under international treaties like the greenhouse gas reduction agreements and biodiversity were also excluded. It should also be stressed that the costs of complying with the various directives on environment will depend heavily on the way the process is managed. In the water management area, for example, costs will be especially high if municipalities act independently to improve or construct water treatment and distribution systems. Investment planning on the basis of water basins would significantly reduce costs.

Policy Issues

Financing environmental projects through Environmental Funds (EFs) is only effective if the environmental problems are simultaneously tackled at the policy level and strong efforts are undertaken to strengthen environmental regulations and enforcement. Although the Slovak Republic has undertaken considerable efforts to set environmental priorities, more work seems to be needed in this area. Indeed, the National Environmental Action Plan lists a large number of supposedly high priority investments in the environmental field, but this seems to be more a listing of possible projects than a prioritized inventory of investments. It is crucial to select the projects which would guarantee the highest environmental benefits and/or are important to help reach the goals of the Slovak EU pre-accession strategy in the environmental field.

The proposed Revolving Environmental Fund (REF) still does not have a clear set of priorities. Although the priorities set by state environmental policy should guide the resource allocation of the REF, other funds in Central and Eastern Europe have found those objectives too broad and general in their day-to-day operations. More specific project selection criteria would be needed. Focusing on a well defined set of priority areas or issues could ensure better results and also make the operation of REF more transparent. In particular, the objectives and mechanisms for "subsidies of investment activities" (under "Use of Fund Resources") should be more clearly defined to ensure that REF will not simply substitute for commercial financing.

A sunset clause and requirements for periodic reviews of the role of REF would be desirable. These reviews should be integrated into the programming and monitoring cycle, which consists of annual programming, project specific appraisal, and ex-post evaluation. For annual programming, the Fund's council (in its role as advisory body with representatives of main interest groups and Ministries) should be involved. The priorities of the Ministry of Environment regarding the country's environmental policy would have to be incorporated. The project appraisal should be undertaken in close co-operation with the Fund with experts of the Ministry of Environment (regarding the technical evaluation) and of commercial banks (regarding the financial appraisal). The ex-post evaluation would again be undertaken by the council.

Operational Issues

Setting a maximum interest rate for loans to be financed from the REF by legislation is not advisable, since the real interest rate may be easily eroded by inflation. It may be better to define a range for the interest rate in relation to the National Bank of Slovakia's base interest rate.

The draft law does not define the distribution of risks and responsibilities in project evaluation and selection between the REF and the selected financial intermediary to carry out financial transactions. This may create a situation in which the bank is responsible for evaluating the commercial and financial viability of project proponents and projects, but the REF is carrying all the risks. This is an inherent problem with EFs that distribute public funds for commercial or quasi-commercial purposes. Risk sharing with the commercial bank may be a solution to this problem. In any case, accountability has to be clearly defined. Commercial banks should provide guarantees for the loans made through the Fund. This would result in a more comprehensive project appraisal by the banks, and representatives of commercial banks have confirmed their willingness to consider this procedure.

There is no mechanism for the evaluation of fund operation and provision of feedback from experience. Focusing on the investment side and neglecting the achievement and maintenance of results are general weaknesses of EFs in CEE countries. Imposing legal requirements for evaluation would be desirable.

Institutional Aspects

Environmental Funds do not mix easily. For this reason, it would be preferable to separate the two funds institutionally to a larger extent than it is envisaged in the draft. On the other hand, the SEF's considerable experience in project processing should benefit the REF.

The Minister of Environment has very significant control over the fund's operation that may lead to strong political influence on spending. The Minister appoints (and can remove) the Fund's director and all Fund council members and must approve the Fund Statute elaborating the organization and activities of the Fund. This renders the fund open to political manipulation because of the appointment process. In addition, unless the Minister enjoys the confidence of the Government, the Fund is at risk, because of the important role of budgetary contributions to the Fund's working capital. A semi-independent structure within the Ministry of Environment may be a solution to this problem.

It is not clear whether the Fund Council provides a forum for consultation among various interests, such as other ministries, industry groups, and municipalities. According to the draft, Council members would be appointed by the Minister. However, it is still necessary to ensure high level representation in decision making and supervision of various interests.

The transparency of project application and selection is still not ensured. This, together with the strong control by the Ministry of Environment of the fund, could lead to serious mismanagement problems. Procedures for publicly open advertising, application, bidding and selection processes, such as those designed by the EU Phare program, could be helpful. Finally, it has to be stated that even a functioning environmental fund will not be in a position to cover all expenses that are necessary to bring the country in line with EU requirements in the environmental field. It will also be necessary to enforce strategies like the "polluter-pays-principle" more strongly than in the past and to strengthen regional environmental authorities.

CHAPTER VIII: STRATEGY FOR SUSTAINABLE GROWTH AND EU ACCESSION

Introduction

There are many reasons behind the successful macroeconomic performance experienced by the Slovak Republic since the dissolution of the former Czechoslovakia. Worth highlighting is the remarkable fiscal restraint of the past which, to a large extent, should be credited for the high output growth and increased price stability of recent years, by creating an environment for financial discipline and opening room for the growth of the private sector. In addition, much has been done to transform the country from a centrally planned system to a market-based society, and the prospect of EU accession is only likely to consolidate these achievements. The accession process will also serve to strengthen many other features typical of democratic societies which, in turn, are also likely to improve the living standards of the Slovak Republic's diverse population.

Recent economic developments have, however, also exposed the limitations and weaknesses of the Slovak Republic's growth performance. The very high investment ratios, in good part responsible for this performance, have been accompanied by excessive current account deficits, financed in a disproportionate amount by increased indebtedness. While a transition economy should be expected to register current account deficits as its capital stock is modernized and past repressed consumption loosens, these deficits should remain at sustainable levels.

The Slovak Republic faces the challenge of adopting a new growth strategy, one that is conducive to high growth without the emergence of large imbalances in the external accounts. The country faces this challenge with advantageous initial conditions when compared to those faced by other transition economies. In particular, a sustainable growth strategy for the Slovak Republic does not require a major effort to increase domestic investment and savings ratios--a major challenge faced by many other transforming countries. Instead, it requires an increased emphasis in efficiency gains. If these gains are achieved, then significant headroom exists to reduce investment levels, therefore reducing the large external imbalances of 1996 and 1997 without compromising economic growth.

This chapter summarizes the recommendations of this report in the context of a proposed framework for sustained growth. The chapter is structured as follows. The next section identifies the main macroeconomic components of such a strategy and reviews the major measures required to increase microeconomic efficiency. Section three assesses the Slovak Republic's potential growth rate under different scenarios, based on an econometric analysis of long-run growth over a large cross-section of countries, and examines the medium-run macroeconomic sustainability of these scenarios. Finally, section four provides some concluding remarks.

The Components of a Sustainable Growth Strategy

The Importance of Sustained Growth for Early Convergence to EU Income Levels

Meeting the dual challenges of sustainable growth and integration with the EU is possibly the main task faced by the Slovak Republic and other CEE countries. As mentioned in Chapter I, these objectives are closely intertwined, as the efficiency-improving measures required to sustain high growth rates would, to a good extent, coincide with the set of requirements for EU accession.

The number of years it will take to converge to EU income levels will prove very sensitive to the policy framework and its impact on growth rates. Slovak Republic's GDP per capita (and that of other Visegrad countries) is currently equivalent to 38 percent of the weighted EU average level (both defined on a PPP basis). If the Slovak Republic experiences a growth rate of per capita income only 2 percentage points higher than that of the EU (a growth rate of real GDP of around 4 percent p.a.), then it will take approximately 50 years to reach the EU's average per capita income. However, if the growth rate differential is increased to 4 percentage points (a growth rate of real GDP of around 6 percent p.a.), then the period of convergence would be reduced by half (Table 8.1). Similarly, with a growth differential of 2 and 4 percentage points, it takes 34 and 17 years, respectively, to reach 75 percent of the EU's average per capita income.[82]

Table 8.1
Years for Convergence - The Implications of Differences in GDP per Capita Growth Rates

Difference between the EU's and Slovak Republic's Annual Growth Rates in Per Capita Incomes (percentage points)	Years Required to Reach 75 percent of the EU Average Per Capita Income	Years Required to Reach the EU Average Per Capita Income
1	69	98
2	34	49
3	23	33
4	17	25
5	14	20

Source: World Bank staff estimates.

Macroeconomic Framework Supportive of Sustained Growth

The capacity to bridge the income gap depends not only on growing at higher rates than the EU at the time of accession, but also on the ability to sustain this growth differential over long periods of time. Countries that approach the accession period with high growth rates, but at the cost of large external imbalances, may fall short of proving their capacity to converge to the EU's average per capita income, as the external imbalance would have to be dealt with sooner or later, possibly at the cost of more severe disruptions to the growth process.

A credible growth scenario for the Slovak Republic would involve a decline in the ratio of fixed investment to GDP from its 1996 peak of over 36 percent to around 30 percent. This scenario would imply a return of the ratio to "historic" levels (the investment ratio in the second half of the 1980s and the first half of the 1990s averaged 30 percent--Appendix Table 2.3), and offsetting the growth impact of such a reduction by an increase in efficiency.[83] As shown below, this would allow the country to sustain grow rates of 5-6 percent p.a., and to concurrently stabilize the current account deficit at a level not higher than 4 percent of GDP. This long-run growth scenario also relies on success in attracting larger non-debt flows. An increase in the flows of FDI and portfolio investment, above the very low levels recorded after independence, would reduce the required flows of debt finance and contribute to the improvement in efficiency that underlies the envisaged scenario of high growth. If approximately half of the current

---

[82] Although the threshold of 75 percent of the average EU per capita income is somewhat arbitrary, it is worth highlighting that an important share of the development funds transferred from the EU budget to its member countries are directed to regions with incomes per capita below such a threshold.

[83] Investment and savings are endogenously determined by the structural underpinnings of an economy, themselves affected by policy and non-policy factors. While it is difficult to assess the consequences of all these factors on the Slovak economy, it can be argued that the investment ratios registered during the first few years of the 1990s reflected an equilibrium of the Slovak Republic's underlying structural and policy factors.

account deficit is financed by non-debt flows, and the GDP annual growth rate of 5-6 percent materializes, the ratios of external debt to GDP and to exports would be stabilized or even decline gradually, after moderate increases in the next few years.

This long-run scenario is well within the reach of Slovak policy-makers. As mentioned before, the completion of some very large infrastructure projects (the Mochovce nuclear power plant and the modernization and expansion in the steel and petrochemical sectors), will naturally result in some reduction of the level of investment relative to GDP. To ensure further convergence to a sustainable investment ratio, NBS should keep adhering to the tighter monetary targets pursued since end-1996 (avoiding the excessive expansion of money and credit that was partly responsible for the sharp increase in investment and the deterioration in external accounts), and the Government should return to the same fiscal discipline that was adopted in the period that followed independence. Although fiscal policy was not a major cause of the current account shift in 1996, the government has followed in 1997 an expansive fiscal policy which, if not reversed, will hinder the adjustment that is needed in domestic spending and external accounts.

Fiscal policy design should involve, *inter alia*, a smoother implementation of the public investment program over time (particularly the extra-budgetary projects), containing the growth of real wages in the public sector, avoiding ad-hoc and excessive increases in pension benefits, and strengthening tax compliance, so as to stabilize the General Government deficit at levels around 1 percent of GDP. In the medium-run, Slovak policy-makers should make additional efforts in the fiscal policy area, in order to allow some reduction in the Slovak Republic's high tax rates, particularly the high payroll tax rate. That could be accomplished, *inter alia*, through reforms to the pension system, such as an increase in the retirement age, and the adoption of a Swiss indexation formula, involving a combination of wages and prices.

In addition to a return to fiscal discipline, the Government should also avoid the policies that could have led to artificially high levels of investment or consumption, or to excessive foreign borrowings by enterprises. These would include abstaining from making excessively generous concessions in future privatizations (such as the cancellation of payments in exchange for additional investment), abstaining from extending special temporary tariff concessions in the purchase of small cars or any other investment/consumption item, and ensuring that foreign creditors are not extending credits to enterprises on the expectation of guarantees by the National Property Fund or the Government.

Microeconomic Reforms and Efficiency Gains

As mentioned in the previous chapters of this report, the persistence of enterprise losses (not only in industry, but also in agriculture and in services), the lingering portfolio problems and other inefficiencies of the State banks, the lack of liquidity, transparency and depth of capital market, and the lack of labor mobility across sectors and regions, are all indications of a significant misallocation of scarce resources, and suggest that the Slovak economy may still be growing well below its potential, for any given ratio of fixed investment to GDP. Efficiency gains are obtained essentially by the relocation of capital and labor to the enterprises and sectors with the greatest potential, to be achieved, *inter alia*, by reducing loss-making activities in the various sectors of the economy, improving the access of the most dynamic enterprises to financial resources and services, both in the banking system and in the capital markets, and improving labor mobility across sectors and regions.

The previous chapters of this report provide a number of recommendations and suggestions as to how these efficiency gains could be achieved. These recommendations (summarized in Table 8.2) would include strengthening the financial sector, through introduction of the tax treatment of provisions and privatization of the major banks through strategic investors, and the reform of the bankruptcy and liquidation framework. This set of reforms would enhance the capacity of banks and other creditors to deal with loss-makers, allow viable enterprises to grow at their full potential and liquidate enterprises which have no credible prospects for recovery and growth. This desirable outcome would have more possibilities of being achieved if the process is not subject to undue political interference. In this regard, the report recommends that the role of ministries in the revitalization program be minimized, and that the number of enterprises participating in this plan be restricted, as a large revitalization program subject to political criteria could lead to a waste of fiscal resources, result in a contamination of banks' portfolios, and the survival of non-viable enterprises for longer periods of time.

The report also suggests a number of additional measures that would contribute to better enterprise governance and further restructuring. Foreign investors have been virtually excluded from the transformation of Slovak economy, and could contribute to a faster absorption of modern technology and greater access to Western markets. In addition, corporate governance could be further enhanced through greater protection of minority shareholders, as that would decrease the risk of profit transfers, or other operations that are not conducive to the full development of enterprises. Protecting minority shareholders' interests would also contribute to the development of Slovak capital markets and greater access of enterprises to a potentially important source of investment finance.

To reduce the losses still generated by segments of the agriculture sector (especially cooperatives) and foster further increases in productivity, the report recommends, *inter alia*, measures that would help reduce the fragmentation of land ownership, allowing viable producers to exploit economies of scale more effectively and to facilitate their access to credits. Improving mortgage law and finance would also be essential to improve the flow of financial resources to agriculture. The recommendations for strengthening the banks and improving the bankruptcy framework would also contribute to a reduction of losses in agriculture.

The report has also emphasized the need to develop more efficient and flexible labor markets, in order to allow enterprises to adjust more effectively to a more competitive environment. This is particularly pressing, since the Slovak Republic suffers, as many other transition economies, from large unemployment disparities between regions. Rather than developing programs that aim at maintaining the existing sources of employment, such as the recently enacted Revitalization Act, the Slovak Republic would benefit more from developing the mechanisms to increase labor mobility between skills and across regions. The recommendations include greater decentralization in wage-setting, exempting small enterprises from some of the restrictions on hiring and firing and other provisions in the labor code, and reducing contribution rates through reforms to the pension system and the sickness insurance.

Finally, the report recommends a number of improvements in the institutional and regulatory framework, governing the operations of enterprises, banks and capital market institutions. These changes would result in the greater harmonization of the Slovak regulatory framework to EU legislation, and also contribute to the development of a more competitive environment in the enterprise and financial sectors. The transfer of regulatory and supervisory functions of all financial sector-related activities from the MoF to independent and professional agencies is one of the recommended measures.

Table 8.2
Summary of Key Policy Recommendations

Trade Policies	Stick to the current low tariffs in the pre-accession period. Consider further reducing tariffs in the cases where they are above the EU's, as permitted by situation in external accounts. Extending liberalization of services on an MFN basis. Deal with pressures for protection by replacing emphasis on anti-dumping mechanisms by safeguard mechanisms.
Enterprise Reform	Complete the privatization of enterprises still in State ownership. Refrain from restricting joint ventures or transfers of ownership of privatized enterprises to new investors, both domestic and foreign. Improve minority shareholder protection by introducing, *inter alia*, functioning take-over rules, accounting rules which inhibit manipulation of financial records and that provide information on the situation of holdings, mechanisms to facilitate transparency, such as credit rating agencies. Improve the bankruptcy framework by, *inter alia*, establishing priority for secured creditors, applying the Bankruptcy Act to all enterprises, facilitating filing by creditors, and ensuring adequate protection to creditors during procedures, particularly by linking the voting rights of creditors to the size of their claims. Restrict the application of the revitalization act to few enterprises, and allow banks and other creditors to engage in workouts without political interference.
Financial Reform	Complete the privatization of VUB and IRB through share sales and capital increase involving the participation of strategic investors, and restrict new lending during the privatization stage. Change tax law to allow tax deduction of provisions. Improve further banking supervision by, inter alia, clarifying the legal independence and powers of NBS, developing the accounting and auditing professions, and developing skills based on risk assessment and analysis. Allow de-listing of companies to enhance liquidity and transparency. Improve regulatory and institutional framework by, *inter alia*, improving minority shareholder protection, integrating the BSE and RMS markets, removing regulatory barriers, and introducing tax neutrality. Transfer supervisory tasks in capital market and insurance from MoF to new independent and professional agencies. Proceed with further approximation of legislation in banking sector, capital markets and insurance to EU legislation.
Agriculture	Reduce fragmentation of land ownership in cooperatives by, *inter alia*, providing active members more options to buy out land owners, and redesign subsidies to support ownership consolidation. Reduce minimum prices from the current level of 90 percent of estimated production costs, de-link from costs and reflect carrying charges. Modify income support from a per hectare basis to targeted support programs. Improve collateral law, including land mortgage law.
Social Policies	As the stabilization is consolidated, allow for more decentralization in wage setting, to enable more adjustment of real wages to sectoral productivity and local labor market conditions, and enhance labor mobility. Exempt small firms from some of the restrictions on hiring and firing contained in the labor code. Introduce reforms to the pension system by, *inter alia*, gradually increasing retirement age and moving towards Swiss indexation, to restore long-run financial viability while allowing some reduction in contribution rates. Encourage private pensions through tax deductibility of contributions, up to a reasonable ceiling. Increase moderately the initial responsibility of sick leave to employer Coordinate unemployment insurance and social assistance to reduce work disincentives.

Evolution of the Macroeconomic Framework Under Alternative Growth Strategies

Simulating Long-run Growth Under Alternative Reform Scenarios

Investigating econometrically the growth performance of a large number of countries over the last three decades, allows the assessment of any country's long-run growth potential, under key assumptions about its levels of physical and human capital, and its policy environment.[84] It also enables the comparison of the Slovak Republic's future growth rates relative to the EU's, under different assumptions about Slovak Republic's policy framework.[85] To this end, two different scenarios were constructed, hereafter referred to as the reform and the non-reform scenarios. Both scenarios assume, for simplicity, that Slovak levels of human capital and rates of growth of the labor force are the same as the EU's. This is roughly consistent with Slovak educational standards and population projections (the differences in population growth rates amount to less than 0.3 percent a year). Therefore, these growth determinants are assumed to have no impact on the growth rate differentials between the Slovak Republic and the EU.

By contrast, the scenarios allow for differences in investment ratios and in efficiency. The first scenario assumes that the Slovak Republic's share of fixed investment remains at 30 percent of GDP, while the average EU country maintains an investment level equal to 22 percent of GDP. This assumption is in line with Slovak investment ratios in the second half of the 1980s and the first half of the 1990s, and with the EU's average investment ratio (weighted by GDP) in the 1980-1994 period, and implies that the Slovak Republic should grow more quickly, controlling for all the other factors. This scenario also assumes that the Slovak Republic implements structural reforms in line with the recommendations of previous chapters, resulting in an increase in efficiency to levels that match those of the average EU country (see Annex 8.1 for a discussion of this index and of the economic analysis underlying the simulations).[86]

The second scenario assumes that the Slovak Republic makes no further progress in the implementation of reforms. As a result, the Slovak Republic maintains the present levels of efficiency, currently below the EU average levels of efficiency. Moreover, because of the lack of reforms, Slovak firms would be missing many business opportunities, ultimately resulting in somewhat lower export and investment ratios. It is assumed that the investment ratio in steady-state would drop to 27.5 percent of GDP, while those of the EU would still remain at 22 percent.

If the Slovak Republic proceeds with economic reforms and is able to increase efficiency to levels consistent with those of the EU, its per capita income would grow during the next three decades at an average of 2.4 percentage points above the EU's growth rates (Table 8.3). Since the EU is expected to grow on average at 2 percent p.a., Slovak per capita income growth rates would average 4.4 percent p.a.,

---

[84] Barbone, L., and J. Zalduendo (1997), "EU Accession of Central and Eastern Europe, Bridging the Income Gap," Policy Research Working Paper No. 1721, The World Bank, Washington DC.

[85] The long-run growth path of an economy is determined by a set of fixed factors, such as resource endowments and geographical location, and a set of variable factors that can be affected by government policy, such as policies for developing human capital and policies that promote private sector development. See, e.g., Barro, R., and X. Sala-i-Martin (1995), *Economic Growth*, McGraw-Hill, and Sachs, J., and A. Warner (1996), "Achieving Rapid Growth in the Transition Economies of Central Europe," Harvard Institute for International Development, Cambridge.

[86] In both scenarios, efficiency is measured by an index (see Johnson, B. and Sheehy, T. (1996). 1996 - Index of Economic Freedom. Washington, DC, The Heritage Foundation) composed of ten different indicators. These indicators reflect the extent to which the legal, regulatory, and policy framework of a country strengthen the business environment.

and its GDP growth would average 4.7 percent p.a. (adding 0.3 percent p.a. of population growth). Slovak Republic's growth rates could start at levels between 5 and 6 percent p.a. and gradually decrease to rates of about 4 percent p.a., the decline over time resulting from diminishing returns to capital accumulation.[87] In this context, Slovak Republic's per capita income would increase 2.5 times and equal 75 percent of the average EU per capita income by the mid-2020s (Table 8.3).

Table 8.3
GDP per Capita Growth with Different Efficiency and Investment Levels

	GDP per Capita in 1996 (PPP US$)	Fixed Investment as percent of GDP	Efficiency Level (IEF)	Average Difference in Growth Rates (percent per annum)	Increase in Slovak Republic's GDP x Capita by 2025	Slovak Republic's GDP x Capita as a Share of the EU Average in 2025
EU Average	19051	22.0	3.8	–	–	–
Slovak Republic:						
• Reform Scenario	7323	30.0	3.8	2.34	2.52 times	75 percent
• No Reform Scenario High Investment Level	7323	30.0	2.9	1.66	2.09 times	62 percent
• No Reform Scenario, Low Investment Level	7323	27.5	2.9	1.51	2.00 times	59 percent

Source: World Bank staff projections.

If the Slovak Republic does not proceed with structural reforms, its growth performance would be negatively affected for two reasons. First, the non-reform scenario implies that Slovak efficiency levels will be lower than those of the EU. Second, Slovak firms would be missing many business opportunities, ultimately resulting in lower investment ratios. Assuming investment ratios decline slightly to 27.5 of GDP and Slovak efficiency remains at its current level, then the per capita growth differential with the EU would decline to levels of about 1.5 percent per year. This implies an average GDP growth rate in the Slovak Republic of about 3.8 percent p.a. after including population growth and the EU's own growth rate. Although the less than 1 percent p.a. difference between growth rates in the two scenarios may look moderate, the implications for the standards of living of the Slovak Republic's population in the long-run should not be underestimated. Indeed, by 2025 Slovak per capita income would be about 20 percent lower than in the reform scenario, and correspond to 60 percent of the EU average per capita income. Such a difference would also imply that the Slovak Republic will require 45 years rather than 29 to reach 75 percent of the GDP per capita income of the EU. It is worth highlighting that this deterioration is mostly driven by the negative impact of maintaining the current low levels of efficiency. In fact, even if investment remained at 30 percent of GDP, it would still take about 41 years to converge to the same threshold (Table 8.3).

Evolution of the Macroeconomic Framework in a Reform Scenario

GDP growth in the transition to the new steady-state. Real GDP growth is expected to decline from about 7 percent in 1996 to about 5.5 percent in 1997, due primarily to the restrictive monetary policy

[87] The exercise assigns to the Slovak Republic and the EU average country their initial GDP per capita levels as of 1996. Since the Slovak Republic's initial per capita income is lower than the EU's, this implies that the country should experience a higher growth rate, *ceteris paribus*. This is consistent with the concept of diminishing returns to capital accumulation--the first units of capital per capita have a larger return than the following units--and is also referred to in the literature as the catch-up effect.

followed by the NBS (Table 8.4).[88] GDP growth is expected to slow further in 1998, as a result of the continuation of tight credit conditions and the fiscal adjustment--the fiscal deficit would be reduced from 4.5 percent of GDP in 1997 to 2 percent of GDP in 1998. The tight monetary and fiscal policies are expected to affect GDP primarily through a slowdown in investment (part of the investment slowdown is directly related to the postponement of some public investment projects). The fiscal adjustment would allow some easing of credit policy and a much better policy mix overall, allowing growth to pick up again in future years, in line with the recovery of exports, investment and consumption. However, the recovery of exports is expected to proceed at much lower rates than after independence, and the recovery of investment would not nearly approach the peak rates of 1996. During the next few years, efficiency gains are expected to materialize, allowing GDP growth to stabilize at about 5.5 percent p.a. for an investment ratio of around 30 percent. For simplicity, the simulations do not take into account the gradual decline in long-run growth rates that would result from diminishing returns on capital accumulation.

Table 8.4:
Reform Scenario - Main Economic Variables, 1996-2006
(percent, unless otherwise indicated)

	1996	1997	1998	1999	2000	2001	2002	2003	2004	2005	2006
Real GDP Growth	6.9	5.5	4.0	4.5	5.0	5.5	5.5	5.5	5.5	5.5	5.5
Real GDP per Capita Growth	6.6	5.3	3.8	4.3	4.8	5.3	5.3	5.3	5.3	5.3	5.3
Real Private Consumption Growth	4.6	5.5	2.3	4.3	4.9	5.5	5.8	5.5	5.5	5.5	5.7
Real Fixed Investment Growth	32.5	-0.4	-3.6	1.2	1.6	5.5	5.5	5.5	5.5	5.5	5.5
Real Exports GNFS Growth	-5.0	5.8	8.4	6.9	5.9	5.9	5.8	5.9	5.9	5.9	5.9
GDP Inflation (average)	5.6	5.5	4.5	3.0	3.0	3.0	3.0	3.0	3.0	3.0	3.0
Consumption/GDP	72.9	71.7	68.9	68.1	67.8	68.2	68.3	68.3	68.1	68.2	68.3
Private Consumption/GDP	49.0	48.7	47.4	47.0	46.6	46.5	46.6	46.5	46.5	46.4	46.4
Government Consumption/GDP	23.9	23.0	21.5	21.1	21.2	21.6	21.7	21.8	21.6	21.8	21.9
Fixed Investment/GDP	36.6	34.5	32.0	31.0	30.0	30.0	30.0	30.0	30.0	30.0	30.0
ICOR GDFI (5 year average)		7.9	5.9	6.0	6.3	6.6	6.3	5.8	5.5	5.4	5.4
Gross National Savings/GDP	27.1	27.5	28.0	28.3	28.5	28.1	28.0	28.0	28.0	28.0	28.0
Exports/GDP	57.5	57.5	59.8	61.1	61.5	61.7	61.9	62.1	62.4	62.6	62.7
Imports/GDP	68.5	64.2	61.7	62.0	61.8	61.9	62.2	62.4	62.4	62.8	63.1
Current Account/GDP	-11.1	-7.5	-5.0	-4.5	-4.0	-4.0	-4.0	-4.0	-4.0	-4.0	-4.0
Direct Investment/GDP (FDI & Portfolio)	1.2	0.8	1.7	2.5	2.5	2.5	2.5	2.5	2.5	2.5	2.5
Gross External Debt (US$ bill.)	7.8	10.7	12.4	13.6	14.6	15.6	16.8	18.1	19.6	20.9	22.3
Gross External Debt/GDP	41.2	55.8	59.1	60.4	60.1	59.2	59.0	58.8	58.6	57.8	57.1
Total Reserves (months of Imports GNFS)	6.5	7.2	7.2	7.3	7.2	7.1	7.1	7.1	7.0	6.9	6.8
NBS Reserves (months of Imports GNFS)	3.5	3.2	3.5	3.8	3.9	3.9	4.0	4.1	4.2	4.2	4.2
General Government Balance/GDP (- = deficit)	-1.4	-4.5	-2.0	-1.5	-1.0	-1.0	-1.0	-1.0	-1.0	-1.0	-1.0
General Government Revenues/GDP	46.9	41.5	41.7	41.0	41.6	41.5	41.6	41.5	41.3	41.3	41.3
General Government Expenditures/GDP	48.4	46.0	43.7	42.6	42.7	42.6	42.6	42.5	42.3	42.3	42.3
Government Debt/GDP	22.8	25.4	25.3	25.0	24.2	23.3	22.2	21.4	20.8	20.2	19.6

Source: World Bank staff projections.

---

[88] For a discussion of the model used for the simulations, see Annex III of The World Bank (1995), *Hungary: Structural Reforms for Sustainable Growth*, Country Economic Memorandum, The World Bank, Washington DC.

Investment and savings. Most of the projected adjustment in investment would take place in 1998 (Table 8.4). As mentioned before, this would be due to the continuation of tight credit conditions and the postponement of some public investment projects. In addition, the investment ratio should gradually decline due to the near completion of some large projects (e.g. steel restructuring). As major investment programs are completed, the Government is expected to allow public investment to follow a declining trend relative to GDP, from a high of 6.2 percent of GDP in 1997 to a level that stabilizes at around 5 percent of GDP. Finally, elimination of some of the privatization rules allowing cancellation of payments in exchange for investment, and the expected improvements in corporate governance due to a working bankruptcy framework, will likely force more financial discipline at the micro level and lead to the reduction of sub-optimal investment projects. The savings ratio is expected to decline in 1997, as a result of the larger fiscal deficit, but to increase in 1998 and in future years, primarily due to the adjustment in public finances.

Current account. In 1997, the current account is expected to improve to a deficit of around 7.5 percent of GDP from a deficit of over 11 percent of GDP in 1996. This improvement has occurred despite an expansionary fiscal policy in 1997. However, the improved external balances are overly dependent on the temporary import surcharge (which will be phased out before the fourth quarter of 1998) and a very restrictive monetary policy. Under the reform scenario, further improvements in the external balances would be achieved primarily through a process of fiscal adjustment beginning in 1998. Together with the continued implementation of the strict credit policy, this policy mix is expected to contribute to further slow down in the growth of domestic demand, and lead to a decline in the current account deficit to 5 percent of GDP in 1998 (Table 8.4). The current account deficit would be further reduced in 1999 and 2000, mirroring the additional fiscal adjustment in the same period. These deficits would be sustainable, because under a reform scenario conducive to EU accession, the Slovak Republic should attract substantially larger non-debt inflows. Foreign direct investment and portfolio investment are expected to increase from a combined low level of 1 percent of GDP a year in 1996 and 1997, to levels closer to 2.5 percent a year. These levels are in line with those of other CEE countries. The moderate borrowing volumes combined with a good growth performance would lead the ratio of gross external debt to GDP to stabilize at around 57 percent in the medium-run.

Exports and imports. Exports to Western European countries are expected to remain strong in 1997 and future years (although growing at lower rates than after independence), mainly because of the pick-up in economic activity in Slovak Republic's major trading partners, the relaxation of installed capacity constraints that had negatively affected some key exporting industries, and gains in competitiveness resulting from further enterprise restructuring. The share of trade with the Czech Republic in total trade is expected to continue a process of decline, however, since these developments have structural roots. The ratio of total exports to GDP is assumed to gradually approach 63 percent--the levels prevailing after independence.

Financing requirements. Under the reform scenario, the Slovak Republic's credit rating would remain good and its access to international capital markets would remain open. The bulk of foreign borrowings would be conducted by the private sector, through private commercial bank credits and bond issues of longer-term maturities than in 1996. The lengthening of the average debt maturity would be feasible under a reform scenario, as Slovak Republic's credit rating would probably improve further.

An Alternative Scenario

An alternative scenario was elaborated on the assumption that the Slovak Republic adopts the macroeconomic measures necessary to reduce the current account deficit to the same levels as in the previous scenario-- close to 4 percent of GDP--but does not make further progress at structural reform. As previously discussed, under this scenario further efficiency gains do not materialize, and the fixed investment level decreases slightly to about 27.5 percent of GDP, mainly because of a more pessimistic evaluation of the business environment and a deterioration in EU accession prospects.   The main implication of these developments is a decrease in initial growth rates to about 4.5 percent a year (Table 8.5). As in the reform scenario, we assume for simplicity that the simulations do not take into account the gradual decline in long-run growth rates that would result from diminishing returns to capital accumulation, and which over three decades would imply average growth rates of slightly less than 4 percent (Table 8.5).

Table 8.5
No Reform Scenario - Main Economic Variables, 1997-2005
(percent, unless otherwise indicated)

	1996	1997	1998	1999-00	2001-02	2003-04	2005-06
Real GDP Growth	6.9	5.5	4.0	4.5	4.5	4.5	4.5
Real Private Consumption Growth	4.6	5.5	2.3	4.9	5.0	5.0	5.0
GDP Inflation (average)	5.6	5.5	4.5	3.0	3.0	3.0	3.0
Consumption/GDP	72.9	71.7	69.3	68.9	70.2	70.2	70.1
Fixed Investment/GDP	36.6	34.5	31.5	29.5	27.8	27.5	27.5
ICORs (5 year average)		7.9	5.9	6.2	6.9	6.3	6.1
Gross National Savings/GDP	27.1	27.5	27.6	27.4	25.8	25.5	25.6
Current Account/GDP	-11.1	-7.5	-5.0	-4.3	-4.0	-4.0	-4.0
Direct Investment/GDP (FDI and Portfolio)	1.2	0.8	1.0	1.0	1.0	1.0	1.0
Gross External Debt/GDP	41.2	55.8	59.7	63.1	65.4	68.2	69.8
Total Reserves (Months of Imports GNFS)	6.5	7.2	7.2	7.2	7.1	7.1	6.9
General Government Balance/GDP (- = deficit)	-1.4	-4.5	-2.5	-1.8	-1.2	-1.0	-1.0
General Government Revenues/GDP	46.9	41.5	41.6	41.4	42.5	42.3	41.8
General Government Expenditures/GDP	48.4	46.0	44.2	43.2	43.8	43.4	42.8

Source: World Bank staff projections.

This alternative scenario focuses on the impact of lingering inefficiencies on growth performance, but assumes that there would be no major immediate external financing problems, due the reduction in the current account deficit. However, the absence of further reforms would imply lower levels of FDI and result in higher levels of indebtedness in the long-run, relative to the previous scenario. If FDI remains as low as in the years that followed independence, the ratio of external debt to GDP would reach 70 percent of GDP by the year 2006, compared to 57 percent for the reform scenario. The larger indebtedness and the lower GDP growth rates make this scenario much less attractive than the reform scenario.

More pessimistic scenarios could also be envisaged, where policy-makers do not adequately address the large external imbalances. One variant would involve the continuation of the current adverse policy mix, comprising a tight monetary policy and an expansionary fiscal policy. Interest rates would remain excessively high in real terms, leading to further pressures on enterprises and banks, and the growth process would be more disrupted. Another variant would involve again an expansionary fiscal policy and some relaxation of monetary policy due to political pressures to reduce interest rates. This variant would imply even larger current account deficits, increasing the risk of financing problems.   If access to international capital were curtailed, the Slovak Republic would face a more abrupt adjustment process, with disruptive consequences for the growth process.

Concluding Remarks

The Slovak Republic has registered an impressive macroeconomic performance after its independence in 1993. Inflation has declined significantly and is currently one of the lowest among CEE countries, whereas GDP growth rates have been among the highest. Slovak ratios of savings and investment to GDP are also among the highest in the region, raising the possibility of rapid capital accumulation and growth. However, the Slovak Republic's recent investment expansion has been accompanied by very large external imbalances. The Slovak Republic faces the challenge of sustaining its impressive growth performance while eliminating the large external imbalances.

This report argued that the Slovak Republic has the conditions to meet this challenge successfully. Implementing the policies that would lead to a reduction in the investment ratio to the average in the first half of the 1990s would eliminate the external imbalances and still leave the Slovak Republic with the highest investment ratio among CEE countries. Completing the process of economic transformation initiated in the early 1990s would tend to improve economic efficiency and allow the Slovak Republic to maintain its impressive growth performance. The report also argued that the dual challenges of sustained growth and EU accession are intertwined to a large extent. Implementing the reforms that would allow the Slovak Republic to increase the efficiency of its economy would also increase the possibilities of a successful integration with the EU.

Annex: Growth Simulations and Economic Efficiency in the Context of EU Accession

The growth literature suggests that countries which have similar growth determinants (e.g., similar government policies and resource endowments) converge to equivalent incomes per capita, and the opposite is the case when these determinants differ. For the simulations in Chapter 8, a growth equation is estimated for a large cross-section of countries (Barbone, L., and J. Zalduendo, op. cit.). The estimation period is 1965-89. The reduced form growth equation is given by

$$\text{Annual Growth Rate} = 0.0879 - 0.0190 \ln y(0) + 0.0170 \ln (I/GDP) + 0.0098 \ln h + 0.0250 \ln Z - 0.0267 \ln LFDT$$

T-Statistic:	(4.72)	(-6.39)	(3.98)	(2.48)	(2.99)
Adjusted R Squared[89]:		0.491			
Standard Error of Regression:		0.014			
F-Statistic:		21.34			

where $y(0)$ is the initial income per capita of a country, I/GDP is the average level of fixed investment as a share of GDP during the period of estimation, h is a measure of educational attainment, Z is a policy index that intends to reflect the existing policy, regulatory, and legal framework of the economy, and $LFDT$ is an adjusted labor force growth rate.[90] In the equation's reduced form, the coefficient of the last regressor is the negative of the sum of the coefficients for investment and human capital.

An obvious difficulty in estimating the above equation is how to define the policy index Z. It should include, among other variables, indicators of monetary policy, fiscal policy, trade liberalization, and other factors that strengthen the enabling business environment of an economy. The Index of Economic Freedom is used as a proxy for this policy index (see Johnson, B. and Sheehy, T., op. cit.), modified to incorporate a broader definition of trade liberalization. This index is based on ten different indicators, namely: (i) the degree to which tariffs and quotas hinder the free flow of commerce; (ii) the extent to which taxes burden economic activities; (iii) the share of government consumption in output; (iv) the rate of inflation as a proxy for monetary policy; (v) the degree to which a country is receptive to FDI; (vi) the extent of government involvement and level of distortions in the financial sector; (vii) the importance of market forces in determining prices and wages; (viii) the degree to which property rights and rule of law are perceived to be supportive of an enabling business environment; (ix) the role that government regulations might play in hindering private sector development; and (x) an estimate of the size and importance of the underground economy.

Some of these indicators are measurable and some are not measurable. In the latter case, Johnson and Sheehy assign values according to scales based on non-quantifiable criteria. To assign values to the Slovak Republic under a non-reform scenario the rules defined by the authors for each of the described indicators were followed, except for trade policy indicators where an alternative methodology is proposed and used in the estimation. By contrast, the reform scenario assumes that the Slovak Republic adopts the EU average efficiency level, the latter weighted by the GDP of current EU members.[91]

---

[89] The exclusion of Guyana and Zambia from the sample result in an improvement of the R squared to levels above 0.6 without altering in any meaningful way the coefficients and their statistical significance.

[90] Barro, R. and Lee, J. (1993). "International Comparisons of Educational Attainment," Journal of Monetary Economics, vol. 32-3.

[91] For simplicity, the reform scenario assumes that the Slovak Republic adopts from the outset the EU average efficiency level. Alternatively, different scenarios could be posited as to the speed with which reforms are introduced and how these compare with those observed among EU members.

List of Statistical Tables

131

Table A1.1
Social Indicators

	1986	1987	1988	1989	1990	1991	1992	1993	1994	1995
Population and vital statistics										
Total population end-year (thousands)	5208.7	5237.0	5264.2	5287.7	5310.7	5295.9	5314.2	5336.5	5356.2	5367.8
Total population growth (percent)		0.5	0.5	0.4	0.4	-0.3	0.3	0.4	0.4	0.2
Total population mid-year (thousands)	5192.8	5223.6	5251.1	5276.2	5297.8	5283.4	5306.5	5324.6	5347.4	5363.6
Total population growth (percent)		0.6	0.5	0.5	0.4	-0.3	0.4	0.3	0.4	0.3
Life expectancy at birth (years)										
Male	67.1	67.2	67.1	66.9	66.6	66.8	67.6	68.3	68.3	68.4
Female	75.0	75.1	75.5	75.4	75.4	75.2	76.2	76.7	76.5	76.3
Population age structure (percent)										
0-14	26.4	26.2	25.9	25.5	25.0	24.6	24.1	23.5	22.9	22.3
15-64	63.9	63.9	64.0	64.2	64.6	65.0	65.4	65.8	66.3	66.8
65 and above	9.7	9.9	10.1	10.3	10.4	10.4	10.5	10.7	10.8	10.9
Crude birth rate (per thousand)	16.8	16.1	15.9	15.2	15.1	14.9	14.1	13.8	12.4	11.4
Crude death rate (per thousand)	10.2	10.0	10.0	10.2	10.3	10.3	10.1	9.9	9.6	9.8
Infant mortality rate (per thousand)	15.0	14.2	13.3	13.5	12.0	13.2	12.6	10.6	11.2	11.0
Food, health, and nutrition										
Per capita supply of										
Calories (per day)	3030.0	3084.0	3185.0	3234.0	3333.0	..	..	..	..	..
Proteins (grams per day)	97.6	99.1	101.0	104.1	105.0	98.9	92.2	92.1	91.9	..
Population per physician	279.0	277.0	272.0	273.0	264.0	272.0	281.0	279.0	290.0	371.0
Hospital beds per 100 population	11.1	11.2	11.9	11.9	11.9	12.3	12.3	12.5	11.7	11.4
Labor force 1/										
Total labor force (thousands)	2532.0	2554.0	2568.0	2555.0	2511.4	2548.5	2502.1	2534.4	2543.1	2567.7
Female (percent)	48.4	48.5	48.5	48.6	49.1	47.6	45.7	46.3	46.5	46.7
Education										
Enrollment rates (percent of school age children) 2/										
Primary: Total	99.0	98.3	97.9	97.7	98.1	99.6	99.6	99.5	99.5	99.5
Secondary: Total	95.9	95.6	95.6	95.8	96.3	96.6	96.6	95.9	94.5	93.8
Colleges, specialized schools and universities	24.0	23.8	24.3	24.8	26.1	26.9	29.5	29.1	30.8	32.1
Pupil-teacher ratio										
Primary	26.5	26.1	25.7	25.0	23.9	23.2	22.1	22.4	22.0	21.1
Secondary	16.9	16.9	16.8	16.7	16.3	16.0	14.7	14.7	14.4	14.0
Other										
Telephones (per thousand)	201.0	209.0	217.0	227.0	236.0	247.0	256.0	268.0	284.0	301.0
Private cars (per thousand) 3/	141.0	147.0	151.0	158.0	165.0	171.0	179.0	186.0	186.0	189.0

.. = not available.
1/ End of year. Excludes the armed forces and double employment. Includes women on maternity leave.
2/ All children between the ages of 6 and 15 are subject to compulsory school attendance.
3/ Personal cars.
Source: Slovak Statistical Office.

Table A1.2
Employment by Sector
(As of December 31, thousands)

	1991	1992	1993	1994	1995	1996 1/
Total employment	2151.6	2174.6	2117.9	2096.3	2146.8	2164.0
1. Agriculture, hunting, forestry and fishing	271.8	256.5	199.0	214.2	201.2	189.0
As a percent of total	12.6	11.8	9.4	10.2	9.4	8.7
2. Mining and quarrying	36.6	31.8	26.2	25.7	25.0	26.0
As a percent of total	1.7	1.5	1.2	1.2	1.2	1.2
3. Electricity, gas and water supply	45.2	47.1	52.4	50.8	52.6	53.0
As a percent of total	2.1	2.2	2.5	2.4	2.4	2.4
4. Manufacturing	625.1	578.5	548.9	537.7	551.1	545.0
As a percent of total	29.1	26.6	25.9	25.7	25.7	25.2
5. Construction	241.2	197.8	173.7	159.4	154.9	151.0
As a percent of total	11.2	9.1	8.2	7.6	7.2	7.0
6. Wholesale and retail trade	186.3	227.3	297.6	292.1	316.8	331.0
As a percent of total	8.7	10.5	14.1	13.9	14.8	15.3
7. Restaurants and hotels	21.5	28.3	37.8	36.3	38.0	38.0
As a percent of total	1.0	1.3	1.8	1.7	1.8	1.8
8. Transport, storage and communication	169.3	161.3	166.7	158.2	159.5	159.0
As a percent of total	7.9	7.4	7.9	7.5	7.4	7.3
9. Financial intermediation	15.1	19.0	23.3	30.0	34.3	38.0
As a percent of total	0.7	0.9	1.1	1.4	1.6	1.8
10. Real estate, renting and business services	109.3	150.8	146.4	141.3	142.5	149.0
As a percent of total	5.1	6.9	6.9	6.7	6.6	6.9
11. Public administration, and defense; compulsory social security	56.5	83.7	72.7	72.8	81.5	85.0
As a percent of total	2.6	3.8	3.4	3.5	3.8	3.9
12. Education	159.4	203.2	179.4	180.8	183.0	184.0
As a percent of total	7.4	9.3	8.5	8.6	8.5	8.5
13. Health and social work	128.7	127.9	128.8	129.4	128.2	129.0
As a percent of total	6.0	5.9	6.1	6.2	6.0	6.0
14. Other community, social and personal service activities	85.5	61.4	64.6	67.6	78.2	87.0
As a percent of total	4.0	2.8	3.0	3.2	3.6	4.0

Note: Excluding women on regular and additional maternity leave, and including employees with a second job.
1/ Data are preliminary.
Source: Statistical Office of the Slovak Republic.

133

Table A1.3
Employment by Industry
(Annual averages, thousands)

	1991	1992	1993	1994	1995	1996
Industry in total with 25 and more employees	675.5	595.1	539.8	513.5	517.0	512.1
Mining and quarrying	34.1	29.8	24.3	21.3	21.2	21.0
Mining and quarrying of energy producing material	20.1	18.3	14.1	13.1	13.0	12.8
Mining and quarrying except energy producing material	14.0	11.5	10.2	8.2	8.2	8.2
Manufacturing	641.3	565.3	515.5	492.2	495.8	491.1
Manufacture of food products	57.7	53.9	51.4	51.0	50.1	51.0
Manufacture of textiles	66.4	60.2	55.4	55.7	55.3	53.3
Manufacture of leather	26.9	24.9	23.0	20.5	22.2	21.7
Manufacture of wood and wood products	20.3	18.5	14.5	14.9	15.0	14.7
Manufacture of pulp, paper and paper products	22.8	21.1	23.1	22.5	22.7	22.2
Manufacture of coke, refined, petroleum products	8.5	8.0	7.5	6.5	6.1	5.8
Manufacture of chemicals	38.3	33.3	29.3	27.5	27.0	26.9
Manufacture of rubber and plastic products	15.0	13.7	13.4	14.0	15.1	15.3
Manufacture of other non-metallic mineral products	37.9	33.1	29.2	27.2	26.1	25.2
Manufacture of basic metals and fabricated metals	58.0	52.4	54.3	54.3	57.0	58.9
Manufacture of machinery and equipment N.E.C.	123.2	100.8	80.6	72.6	71.9	69.3
Manufacture of electrical and optical equipment	61.3	49.2	40.2	35.6	37.5	37.3
Manufacture of transport equipment	40.2	33.8	28.7	26.5	28.8	28.3
Manufacture N.E.C.	25.5	23.6	21.0	18.7	17.3	17.0
Electricity, gas and water supply	39.2	38.8	43.9	44.7	43.7	44.2

Source: Slovak Statistical Office.

Table A1.4
Employment by Training
(percent)

	1983	1989	1991	1994	1995	1996
Employment by Training 1/						
University	8.3	10.0	10.8	13.0	12.6	12.7
Secondary school	24.7	27.8	30.7	39.7	39.7	41.0
School for apprentices	31.7	34.3	37.5	35.5	36.4	35.7
Primary school	35.3	27.9	20.3	11.8	11.3	10.6

1/ Civil employment excluding the private sector. 1983 data are as of end October; 1989 data are as of end September; 1991 data are from the 1991 Census. 1994 and 1995 data are from the Labour Force Survey (LFS). Data from LFS includes employment in the private sector. Women on childcare leave are excluded from the LFS data.
Source: Slovak Statistical Office.

Table A1.5
Employment by Ownership Forms
(thousands)

	1990	1991	1992	1993	1994	1995	1996
Total 1/	2477.6	2008.0	2013.4	2012.3	1976.9	2019.8	2036.4
State organizations	1829.4	1444.2	1301.9	948.9	902.2	815.5	750.6
Economic organizations	1265.2	747.1	623.0	564.3	537.2	438.7	378.7
Budgetary organizations	343.0	273.2	278.3	256.3	218.0	220.5	218.8
Organizations based on contributions	43.8	114.6	122.6	128.3	147.0	141.7	135.7
Other	177.4	309.3	278.0	..	..	14.6	17.4
Local organizations	..	12.7	14.6	20.6	47.9	54.6	56.5
Cooperatives	390.1	302.4	242.0	187.2	168.1	153.7	142.0
Agriculture	256.6	199.1	160.6	131.6	114.7	86.3	78.6
Private enterprises and organizations 2/	121.5	204.3	365.0	420.9	623.7	858.8	966.1
Social organizations	22.5	16.8	17.0	11.8	16.0	16.9	17.4
International organizations	..	5.6	10.2	23.5	40.4	56.6	63.1
Other	114.1	22.0	62.7	399.4	178.6	63.7	40.7
Share of employment							
State organizations	73.8	71.9	64.7	47.2	45.6	40.4	36.9
Local organizations	..	0.6	0.7	1.0	2.4	2.7	2.8
Cooperatives	15.7	15.1	12.0	9.3	8.5	7.6	7.0
Private enterprises and organizations	4.9	10.2	18.1	20.9	31.5	42.5	47.4
Social organizations	0.9	0.8	0.8	0.6	0.8	0.8	0.9
International organizations	..	0.3	0.5	1.2	2.0	2.8	3.1
Other	4.6	1.1	3.1	19.8	9.0	3.2	2.0

.. = not available.
1/ Average. Data exclude women on maternity leave, apprentices, and armed forces.
2/ Including foreign organizations.
Source: Slovak Statistical Office.

Table A1.6
Unemployment by Regional Districts

	End 1992 Number of Unemployed	Percent	End 1993 Number of Unemployed	Percent	End 1994 Number of Unemployed	Percent	End 1995 Number of Unemployed	Percent	End 1996 Number of Unemployed	Percent
Total	260274	10.4	368095	14.4	371481	14.8	333291	13.1	329749	12.8
Banska Bystrica	7191	7.6	10539	11.1	10236	9.7	9437	10.6	9161	10.2
Bardejov	5345	15.7	7480	20.8	7593	22.3	6928	18.2	6982	17.8
Bratislava	10883	3.8	13510	4.5	11594	3.9	10780	4.7	9731	4.1
Bratislava-vidiek	5104	9.6	6620	13.3	5630	11.3	5128	7.4	4781	6.3
Cadca	7042	16.2	9931	21.0	9670	22.0	7900	13.8	7589	12.8
Dolny Kubin	6932	12.9	9635	17.9	9109	17.6	7962	14.2	7890	14.3
Dunajska Streda	7231	16.3	10025	20.4	10465	20.9	9573	16.6	9052	15.2
Galanta	8292	14.9	11824	19.9	12145	21.1	10324	15.5	10133	15.1
Humenne	5464	10.5	7623	14.8	8309	16.7	7152	13.3	8097	15.5
Komarno	6028	12.7	10361	21.7	10618	20.6	9446	18	9423	18.2
Kosice-mesto	9661	6.8	14278	10.0	14534	9.3	13227	11.3	11855	10.5
Kosice-vidiek	4883	16.5	7007	22.6	7379	25.4	7384	16.6	7643	16.4
Levice	7175	11.8	10439	16.6	10995	18.2	10387	17.9	10919	18.5
Liptovsky Mikulas	4147	6.5	7065	11.1	6790	11.4	6011	9.1	6577	10.1
Lucenec	6558	14.3	9143	20.3	9371	22.5	8866	19.2	8688	19.2
Martin	4348	7.6	5999	10.7	5978	11.7	5031	8.7	5560	9.8
Michalovce	8600	16.4	11796	22.5	11176	22.0	10894	20.9	10411	20.5
Nitra	11763	12.6	14405	14.7	16658	16.9	14426	14.2	12473	11.9
Nove Zamky	7405	11.3	12276	17.8	12819	19.0	11776	16.5	11757	16.4
Porad	7845	10.6	11957	15.7	13678	18.8	12352	17	14436	19.3
Povazska Bystrica	7213	9.3	10884	13.6	9803	12.6	7949	9.4	7117	8.5
Presov	9406	10.4	15031	16.4	15193	17.9	15488	16.5	15132	15.6
Prievidza	5847	8.9	8929	13.6	8974	14.3	7440	11	7169	10.5
Rimavska Sobota	7348	16.6	11703	26.4	12685	29.4	11536	26.4	10952	23.8
Roznava	6969	17.0	9285	22.3	10296	24.7	9494	22	9224	22.5
Senica	5661	8.9	8570	13.4	8051	12.2	7028	9.6	7285	10.3
Spisska Nova Ves	9226	14.8	14407	23.3	14703	25.3	13025	19.3	13278	19.1
Stara Lubovna	1848	9.9	2660	14.3	2942	16.2	2835	13.5	2984	14.5
Svidnik	3051	13.7	4275	19.4	4499	22.2	3626	18.3	3674	18.6
Topolcany	8517	11.8	11215	15.9	11417	16.6	9390	12.4	9540	12.7
Trebisov	9459	19.3	10249	19.6	11960	24.1	9803	19	11747	22.4
Trencin	6903	8.2	6844	8.1	6121	7.6	5414	6.6	5218	6.3
Trnava	11697	10.2	15485	13.6	13472	12.9	12822	11.4	10837	9.2
Velky Krtis	3012	13.8	4349	21.7	4321	20.0	4213	20.9	4421	22
Vranov nad Toplou	4599	16.0	6524	22.6	7396	27.4	6608	19	6891	21
Zvolen	5740	9.0	7770	12.7	7554	12.7	7003	11.5	7045	11.3
Ziar nad Hronom	3573	7.9	5319	12.2	5915	13.8	5179	12.5	5626	13.4
Zilina	8308	9.0	12683	13.2	11432	12.3	9454	10.4	8451	9.4

Note: According to the territorial and administrative order of the Slovak Republic valid until July 24, 1996.
Source: Slovak Statistical Office.

Table A2.1
Nominal Gross Domestic Product
(billions of koruny)

	1985	1986	1987	1988	1989	1990	1991	1992	1993	1994	1995	1996
GDP (current prices)	232.0	241.7	247.7	256.9	267.3	277.9	319.7	332.3	369.1	440.5	515.1	581.3
By sector												
Agriculture	15.0	17.3	17.2	17.2	25.0	20.5	18.2	17.7	17.3	29.3	29.0	30.1
Industry	120.5	125.8	127.2	130.4	131.8	138.7	168.4	106.2	113.1	126.6	147.2	152.8
Construction	22.3	22.1	23.2	24.1	24.4	25.6	23.7	19.9	17.5	20.1	23.8	27.5
Services	74.2	76.5	80.1	85.2	86.1	93.1	109.4	140.7	177.3	244.3	274.6	318.8
Other	0.0	0.0	0.0	0.0	0.0	0.0	0.0	47.8	43.9	20.2	40.5	52.1
By expenditure												
Total consumption	161.2	169.3	176.1	181.2	191.1	210.8	229.4	249.6	288.6	315.8	356.6	424.9
Total private consumption	115.7	119.6	123.6	127.2	133.3	149.9	163.6	164.6	196.2	221.9	252.6	286.1
Total government consumption	45.5	49.7	52.5	54.0	57.8	60.9	65.8	85.0	92.4	93.9	104.0	138.8
Gross investment	73.4	76.1	80.8	80.4	85.1	92.3	99.9	93.3	100.9	101.8	146.8	221.8
Fixed investment	68.2	69.9	67.8	69.7	73.6	86.9	90.4	109.3	120.7	129.4	150.6	212.7
Changes in stocks	5.2	6.2	13.0	10.7	11.5	5.4	9.5	-16.0	-19.8	-27.6	-3.8	9.1
Domestic demand	234.7	245.5	256.9	261.6	276.1	303.1	329.2	342.9	389.5	417.6	503.4	646.7
Resource balance	-2.6	-3.8	-9.2	-4.8	-8.8	-25.0	-9.5	-13.1	-20.4	23.0	9.4	-64.3
Exports of GNFS			80.1	82.6	77.1	73.8	148.1	233.7	227.8	286.7	325.8	334.0
Imports of GNFS	2.6	3.8	89.3	87.4	85.9	98.8	157.6	246.8	248.2	263.7	316.4	398.3
Statistical discrepancy	-0.1	0.0	0.0	0.1	0.0	-0.2	0.0	2.5	0.0	-0.1	2.3	-1.1

Source: Slovak Statistical Office.

138

Table A2.2
Gross Domestic Product
(billions of koruny, 1993 prices)

	1995	1986	1987	1988	1989	1990	1991	1992	1993	1994	1995	1996
GDP	448.8	467.4	479.0	488.3	493.2	481.0	410.9	384.1	369.1	387.4	414.5	443.3
By sector												
Agriculture	27.4	30.1	29.4	31.0	32.2	28.9	28.0	20.5	17.3	26.7	24.4	25.2
Industry	220.7	232.5	239.5	246.7	252.1	243.6	187.6	122.8	113.1	117.2	126.8	127.1
Construction	44.4	44.0	46.4	47.5	45.6	46.1	32.3	23.0	17.5	18.2	19.2	19.2
Services	156.3	160.8	163.7	163.1	163.3	162.4	163.0	162.7	177.3	214.2	219.5	241.2
Other	0.0	0.0	0.0	0.0	0.0	0.0	0.0	55.1	43.9	11.1	24.6	30.6
By expenditure												
Total consumption	328.8	342.4	357.9	369.6	387.9	401.4	298.6	293.4	288.6	275.8	286.6	321.4
Total private consumption	246.3	252.9	264.1	274.2	284.2	296.9	212.7	199.0	196.2	195.3	202.7	217.2
Total government consumption	82.5	89.5	93.8	95.4	103.7	104.5	85.9	94.4	92.4	80.5	83.9	104.2
Gross investment	154.3	160.3	155.2	154.3	159.6	162.9	127.5	108.9	100.9	92.4	117.7	168.1
Fixed investment	142.7	146.9	147.7	151.8	158.0	176.3	131.9	125.9	120.7	114.1	121.2	161.6
Changes in stocks	11.6	13.4	7.5	2.5	1.6	-13.4	-4.4	-17.0	-19.8	-21.7	-3.5	6.5
Domestic demand	483.1	502.7	513.1	523.9	547.5	564.3	426.1	402.3	389.5	368.2	404.3	489.5
Resource balance	-34.3	-35.3	-34.1	-35.6	-54.3	-83.3	-15.2	-21.8	-20.4	19.2	6.8	-45.9
Exports of GNFS			144.6	147.2	134.5	116.0	154.8	228.2	227.8	259.0	269.2	265.0
Imports of GNFS	34.3	35.3	178.7	182.8	188.8	199.3	170.0	250.0	248.2	239.8	262.4	310.9
Statistical discrepancy								3.6	0.0	0.0	3.4	-0.3

Source: Slovak Statistical Office.

Table A2.3
Percentage Distribution of Gross Domestic Product

	1985	1986	1987	1988	1989	1990	1991	1992	1993	1994	1995	1996
By sector												
Agriculture	6.5	7.2	6.9	6.7	9.4	7.4	5.7	5.3	4.7	6.7	5.6	5.2
Industry	51.9	52.0	51.4	50.8	49.3	49.9	52.7	32.0	30.6	28.7	28.6	26.3
Construction	9.6	9.1	9.4	9.4	9.1	9.2	7.4	6.0	4.7	4.6	4.6	4.7
Services	32.0	31.7	32.3	33.2	32.2	33.5	34.2	42.3	48.0	55.5	53.3	54.8
Other	0.0	0.0	0.0	0.0	0.0	0.0	0.0	14.4	11.9	4.6	7.9	9.0
By expenditure												
Total consumption	69.5	70.0	71.1	70.5	71.5	75.9	71.8	75.1	78.2	71.7	69.2	73.1
Total private consumption	49.9	49.5	49.9	49.5	49.9	53.9	51.2	49.5	53.2	50.4	49.0	49.2
Total government consumption	19.6	20.6	21.2	21.0	21.6	21.9	20.6	25.6	25.0	21.3	20.2	23.9
Gross investment	31.6	31.5	32.6	31.3	31.8	33.2	31.2	28.1	27.3	23.1	28.5	38.2
Fixed investment	29.4	28.9	27.4	27.1	27.5	31.3	28.3	32.9	32.7	29.4	29.2	36.6
Changes in stocks	2.2	2.6	5.2	4.2	4.3	1.9	3.0	-4.8	-5.4	-6.3	-0.7	1.6
Domestic demand	101.2	101.6	103.7	101.8	103.3	109.1	103.0	103.2	105.5	94.8	97.7	111.3
Resource balance	-1.1	-1.6	-3.7	-1.9	-3.3	-9.0	-3.0	-3.9	-5.5	5.2	1.8	-11.1
Exports of GNFS	..	..	32.3	32.2	28.8	26.6	46.3	70.3	61.7	65.1	63.2	57.5
Imports of GNFS	1.1	1.6	36.1	34.0	32.1	35.6	49.3	74.3	67.2	59.9	61.4	68.5

Note: Shares of nominal GDP.
Source: Slovak Statistical Office.

Table A2.4
Nominal Quarterly Gross Domestic Product
(billions of koruny)

| | 1993 | | | | | 1994 | | | | |
	I	II	III	IV	Year	I	II	III	IV	Year
GDP (current prices)	87.0	92.5	95.4	95.0	369.9	102.1	111.7	114.1	113.4	441.3
By sector										
Agriculture	4.6	5.9	10.8	3.1	24.3	5.1	6.3	11.4	6.5	29.3
Industry	24.7	24.0	28.3	31.0	108.0	31.2	31.8	31.6	32.0	126.6
Construction	3.3	7.0	7.0	7.4	24.6	4.0	5.3	5.6	5.2	20.1
Services	47.3	55.2	54.4	44.5	201.4	56.9	69.6	63.9	53.9	244.3
Other	7.1	0.3	-5.0	9.0	11.5	4.9	-1.3	1.5	15.8	21.0
By expenditure										
Total consumption	63.8	72.8	73.4	78.3	288.3	77.7	76.9	80.4	84.0	319.0
Total private consumption	43.1	49.6	51.2	52.1	196.0	53.9	53.5	57.5	57.7	222.6
Total government consumption	20.7	23.2	22.2	26.2	92.3	23.8	23.4	22.9	26.3	96.4
Gross investment	17.6	22.7	25.9	34.8	101.0	23.9	22.3	30.7	25.7	102.6
Fixed investment	18.2	25.1	33.8	43.6	120.7	26.6	27.1	33.4	42.9	130.0
Changes in stocks	-0.6	-2.4	-7.9	-8.8	-19.7	-2.7	-4.8	-2.7	-17.2	-27.4
Domestic demand	81.4	95.5	99.3	113.1	389.3	101.6	99.2	111.1	109.7	421.6
Resource balance	2.1	-5.7	-1.0	-15.8	-20.4	-1.2	8.0	8.7	8.9	24.4
Exports of GNFS	48.5	55.7	59.6	64.0	227.8	58.8	72.3	74.2	82.5	287.8
Imports of GNFS	46.4	61.4	60.6	79.8	248.2	60.0	64.3	65.5	73.6	263.4
Statistical discrepancy	3.5	2.7	-2.9	-2.3	1.0	1.7	4.5	-5.7	-5.2	-4.7

| | 1995 | | | | | 1996 | | | | |
	I	II	III	IV	Year	I	II	III	IV	Year
GDP (current prices)	117.6	129.2	134.8	133.5	515.1	133.5	145.7	152.1	150.0	581.3
By sector										
Agriculture	5.8	6.5	11.1	5.6	29.0	5.8	6.1	10.7	7.5	30.1
Industry	35.6	38.6	37.4	35.5	147.2	38.0	36.6	38.5	39.5	152.8
Construction	5.2	5.9	6.4	6.3	23.8	5.7	6.9	7.9	7.0	27.5
Services	62.9	75.2	70.5	65.9	274.6	75.9	83.1	84.6	75.2	318.8
Other	8.1	2.9	9.4	20.2	40.6	8.0	13.0	10.3	20.8	52.0
By expenditure										
Total consumption	83.1	89.0	89.0	95.5	356.6	102.5	103.6	106.1	112.7	424.9
Total private consumption	59.1	63.2	63.9	66.4	252.6	67.3	72.5	72.5	73,.8	286.1
Total government consumption	24.0	25.8	25.1	29.1	104.0	35.2	31.1	33.6	38.9	138.8
Gross investment	30.3	37.6	37.0	41.9	146.8	43.0	51.8	57.8	69.2	221.8
Fixed investment	26.3	33.1	34.2	57.0	150.6	36.0	45.5	50.2	81.0	212.7
Changes in stocks	4.0	4.5	2.8	-15.1	-3.8	7.0	6.3	7.6	-11.8	9.1
Domestic demand	113.4	126.6	126.0	137.4	503.4	145.5	155.4	163.9	181.9	646.7
Resource balance	4.3	5.2	6.1	-6.2	9.4	-13.8	-11.4	-9.6	-29.5	-64.3
Exports of GNFS	76.5	85.3	82.8	81.2	325.8	75.1	80.6	87.1	91.2	334.0
Imports of GNFS	72.2	80.1	76.7	87.4	316.4	88.9	92.0	96.7	120.7	398.3
Statistical discrepancy	-0.1	-2.6	2.7	2.3	2.3	1.8	1.7	-2.2	-2.4	-1.1

Note: Possible differences between the yearly data and sum of quarters are caused by rounding off from Mill. SKK to Bill. SKK, and by recent updating of past annual data and not the quarterly data.
Source: Slovak Statistical Office.

Table A2.5
Gross Fixed Investment
(billions of koruny, current prices)

	1992	1993	1994	1995	1996 1/
Agriculture, hunting, forestry and fishing	5.5	4.9	6.2	6.4	10.5
Mining and quarrying	3.0	2.1	2.4	5.2	3.6
Manufacturing	34.3	37.8	28.0	34.7	40.3
Electricity, gas and water supply	16.7	17.1	26.7	30.7	26.0
Construction	3.6	4.0	5.0	5.1	6.3
Trade 2/	3.3	4.6	6.3	8.7	33.3
Hotels and restaurants	1.9	1.1	0.9	1.5	2.5
Transport, storage and communication	9.5	11.8	15.6	20.2	28.3
Financial intermediation	5.8	10.0	13.4	13.7	24.7
Real estate, renting and business activities	10.8	14.1	13.5	14.7	36.8
Public administration 3/	2.7	5.6	6.4	6.8	13.0
Education	3.0	2.2	2.3	4.1	3.6
Health and social work	2.8	3.4	3.5	5.0	5.6
Other 4/	4.8	7.4	5.5	6.0	7.8
Total	107.6	126.1	135.7	162.8	242.3
Memorandum items					
Tangible investment	105.3	123.7	132.4	159.2	234.3
Construction works	51.5	59.9	58.3	74.1	108.6
Machines and equipment	51.5	61.0	61.9	79.6	117.0
Other	2.3	2.8	12.2	5.5	8.7
Non-tangible investment	2.3	2.4	3.3	3.6	8.0

Note: NACE: Nomenclature des activites de Communaute Europeenne.
1/ 1996 data is preliminary.
2/ Wholesale and retail trade; repair of motor vehicles.
3/ Includes defense and compulsory social security.
4/ Community, social and personal service activities.
Source: Slovak Statistical Office.

Table A2.6
Production and Yields of Selected Agricultural Crops and Livestock Products
(thousands of tons)

	1990	1991	1992	1993	1994	1995
Production						
Cereals in total	3617	4004	3552	3152	3700	3490
Thick drill	3247	3293	2876	2478	3179	2883
Wheat	2083	2124	1697	1529	2145	1938
Rye	178	131	76	69	96	89
Barley	914	960	1038	823	874	794
Oats	47	44	41	36	35	42
Grain maize	370	711	676	674	521	597
Legume in total	96	117	158	123	160	108
Edible	78	101	145	114	141	99
Peas	74	96	138	110	136	96
Lentils	1	2	3	1	1	1
Beans	3	3	4	3	3	2
Feeding	18	16	13	9	19	9
Potatoes	779	669	658	857	399	442
Early potatoes	66	56	71	58	50	48
Sugar beets	1581	1501	1338	1128	1112	1176
Oil plants in total	141	214	133	126	155	236
Rape	76	97	48	58	94	149
Sunflower	56	101	79	64	55	81
Soya	4	11	4	1	1	1
Poppy seeds	3	3	2	1	3	3
Flax	12	2	3	3	3	3
Tobacco	5	5	3	2	2	2
Market vegetables	497	552	459	535	483	498
Fruits in total	164	165	140	175	123	92
Hops	1	1	1	1	1	1
Feeding root-crops	393	395	262	299	257	270
Fodder on arable land (in terms of hay)	2758	2908	2554	2104	1911	1812
Annual	1226	1346	1215	998	750	812
Unripe and ensilage maize	1005	1115	993	849	626	681
Lasting more years	1532	1562	1339	1106	1161	1000
Lucerne	955	1049	886	768	787	651
Red double-cut clover	267	235	206	137	136	109
Permanent growths of grass (in terms of hay)	1915	1852	1338	1149	1394	1385
Yields (Tons per hectare)						
Cereals in total	4.7	5.0	4.4	3.8	4.3	4.1
Thick drill	4.8	4.9	4.4	3.6	4.3	4.0
Wheat	5.0	5.2	4.8	3.8	4.8	4.4
Rye	3.9	3.4	3.2	3.0	3.1	2.9
Barley	4.8	4.6	4.1	3.3	3.7	3.4
Oats	3.5	3.2	2.8	2.5	2.5	2.7
Grain maize	3.6	5.4	4.5	4.6	4.1	4.9
Legume in total	2.2	2.3	2.4	1.9	2.9	2.2
Edible	2.4	2.4	2.5	1.9	2.9	2.2
Peas	2.6	2.6	2.7	1.9	3.0	2.3
Lentils	0.6	1.1	1.0	1.0	0.9	0.7
Beans	1.1	1.1	1.2	1.3	1.7	1.6
Feeding	1.6	1.5	1.7	1.8	3.2	2.0
Potatoes	14.1	12.3	12.9	18.2	9.7	11.1
Early potatoes	11.4	10.1	11.5	10.2	9.5	9.8
Sugar beets	30.8	31.1	29.4	34.3	34.5	34.3
Oil plants in total	1.9	2.2	1.9	1.7	1.8	1.9
Rape	2.4	2.6	1.8	1.6	2.1	2.2
Sunflower	1.9	2.3	2.2	2.0	1.6	1.7

Table A2.6
Production and Yields of Selected Agricultural Crops and Livestock Products
(thousands of tons)

	1990	1991	1992	1993	1994	1995
(continued)						
Yields (Tons per hectare)						
Soya	0.8	1.4	0.9	1.2	1.4	1.4
Poppy seeds	0.9	0.7	0.6	0.5	0.6	0.6
Flax	2.7	1.1	2.2	2.4	2.2	3.0
Tobacco	1.5	1.6	1.2	1.3	1.5	1.6
Feeding root-crops	42.9	47.2	38.3	45.7	38.6	41.3
Fodder on arable land (in terms of hay)						
Annual	4.4	5.9	5.1	4.7	3.7	4.4
Unripe and ensilage maize	4.4	6.3	5.4	5.1	3.9	4.7
Lasting more years	8.1	8.6	6.8	6.1	6.7	6.2
Lucerne	8.4	9.4	8.2	7.6	8.3	7.5
Red double-cut clover	8.2	8.0	6.5	5.2	5.9	5.7
Hop-gardens	0.9	1.0	0.9	0.8	1.2	0.9
Permanent growths of grass (in terms of hay)	2.5	2.4	1.7	1.4	1.7	1.7
Livestock Production						
Meat (thousand tons, live yield)	599.1	545.2	493.0	477.6	422.3	403.2
Beef (thousand tons)	211.0	207.2	172.0	170.4	122.1	108.3
Veal (thousand tons)	2.0	0.7	0.7	6.2	5.1	3.3
Pork (thousand tons)	376.0	328.4	313.2	294.2	290.4	287.2
Sheep and goat	10.1	8.9	7.1	6.8	4.7	4.4
Slaughtered poultry	116.4	98.7	88.4	70.0	76.7	85.8
Eggs (million pieces)	1983.0	1824.0	1720.8	1526.8	1606.4	1608.5
Milk (millions of liters)	1920.0	1526.0	1330.6	1214.4	1154.7	1151.4
Fish (thousand tons)	1.2	0.6	0.5	0.4	0.8	0.9
Wool (thousand tons)	3.0	1.3	1.2	1.2	1.1	1.1
Sheep cheese (thousand tons)	3.5	2.4	1.9	1.9	2.0	2.1
Yields						
Average live weight (kg)						
Slaughtered cattle	483.0	479.0	471.5	426.0	425.0	434.0
Veal	65.0	56.0	56.0	92.0	94.0	88.0
Slaughtered pigs	129.0	133.3	136.1	119.0	113.0	114.0
Average annual milk yield/cow (liters)	3573.0	2887.0	2887.7	2952.8	3175.2	3292.0
Average annual egg-laying per hen (pieces)	249.0	241.0	240.0	226.5	228.1	227.9
Number of calves born per 100 cows (pieces)	101.8	92.0	90.6	93.5	96.2	97.0
Number of piglets born per sow (pieces)	17.5	16.7	15.7	15.2	15.5	15.9
Number of lambs per ewe (pieces)	99.5	87.6	74.0	71.8	79.7	80.0

Source: Slovak Statistical Office; and staff estimates.

Table A2.7
Money Incomes and Expenditures - Household Sector
(billions of current koruny)

	1992	1993	1994	1995
Income of employees	145.5	178.3	205.4	232.8
Gross salaries and wages	105.5	130.4	150.1	178.0
Gross operational surplus	30.2	53.4	61.7	72.6
Income from ownership and business	10.3	14.2	15.8	19.5
Insured accident transactions	3.9	4.3	4.5	4.0
Current transfers - income	58.7	76.5	70.3	77.3
Social benefits	53.5	68.5	65.9	71.9
Total current revenues	248.6	326.7	357.7	406.3
Income from ownership and business	1.0	5.6	2.6	4.8
Insured accident transactions	3.4	4.3	4.6	5.0
Current transfers - expenditure	58.3	73.7	87.3	97.6
Taxes from income of natural persons	..	..	11.2	15.8
Total current expenditure	62.7	83.6	94.5	107.4
Gross disposable income	185.9	243.1	263.1	298.9
Final consumption of households	164.6	196.2	221.9	252.6
Gross savings of households	21.3	46.8	41.2	46.3

.. = not available.
Source: Statistical Office of the Slovak Republic.

Table A2.8
Indices of Industrial Production

	1991	1992	1993	1994	1995	1996
Industry in total (industrial enterprises with 25 and more employees)	131.4	111.0	100.0	102.7	113.3	113.9
Mining and quarrying	149.9	125.2	100.0	96.7	95.2	101.3
Mining and quarrying of energy producing material	197.0	158.6	100.0	92.9	96.4	99.7
Mining and quarrying except energy producing material	121.5	105.0	100.0	98.9	94.5	102.3
Manufacturing	135.6	113.6	100.0	101.5	110.4	113.6
Manufacture of food products	143.8	115.0	100.0	92.3	90.3	95.4
Manufacture of textiles	137.1	123.2	100.0	98.1	87.2	84.5
Manufacture of leather	164.6	133.1	100.0	90.8	104.2	105.0
Manufacture of wood and wood products	188.5	152.7	100.0	105.0	119.5	116.2
Manufacture of pulp, paper and paper products	106.3	102.4	100.0	113.8	120.4	126.3
Manufacture of coke, refined, petroleum products	117.8	101.0	100.0	123.4	131.0	125.9
Manufacture of chemicals	113.1	112.6	100.0	105.8	117.2	120.9
Manufacture of rubber and plastic products	114.1	108.8	100.0	111.9	131.2	135.6
Manufacture of other non-metallic mineral products	118.6	110.1	100.0	94.1	92.7	92.6
Manufacture of basic metals and fabricated metals	106.9	100.5	100.0	105.1	114.7	105.0
Manufacture of machinery and equipment N.E.C.	212.8	137.7	100.0	88.5	101.7	109.1
Manufacture of electrical and optical equipment	149.7	113.7	100.0	99.4	108.5	124.1
Manufacture of transport equipment	176.3	125.1	100.0	107.3	174.2	212.7
Manufacture N.E.C.	124.1	117.6	100.0	92.7	101.7	112.9
Electricity, gas and water supply	85.6	82.6	100.0	115.9	113.0	118.7

Notes: NACE: Nomenclature des activites de Communaute Europeenne. Data for enterprises with 25 and more employees.
Source: Slovak Statistical Office.

Table A2.9
Annual Growth Rates of Industrial Production

	1992	1993	1994	1995	1996
Industry in total (industrial enterprises with 25 and more employees)	-15.5	-9.9	2.7	10.3	0.5
Mining and quarrying	-16.5	-20.1	-3.3	-1.6	6.4
Mining and quarrying of energy producing material	-19.5	-36.9	-7.1	3.8	3.4
Mining and quarrying except energy producing material	-13.6	-4.8	-1.1	-4.4	8.3
Manufacturing	-16.2	-12.0	1.5	8.8	2.9
Manufacture of food products	-20.0	-13.0	-7.7	-2.2	5.6
Manufacture of textiles	-10.1	-18.8	-1.9	-11.1	-3.1
Manufacture of leather	-19.1	-24.9	-9.2	14.8	0.8
Manufacture of wood and wood products	-19.0	-34.5	5.0	13.8	-2.8
Manufacture of pulp, paper and paper products	-3.7	-2.3	13.8	5.8	4.9
Manufacture of coke, refined, petroleum products	-14.3	-1.0	23.4	6.2	-3.9
Manufacture of chemicals	-0.4	-11.2	5.8	10.8	3.2
Manufacture of rubber and plastic products	-4.6	-8.1	11.9	17.2	3.4
Manufacture of other non-metallic mineral products	-7.2	-9.2	-5.9	-1.5	-0.1
Manufacture of basic metals and fabricated metals	-6.0	-0.5	5.1	9.1	-8.5
Manufacture of machinery and equipment N.E.C.	-35.3	-27.4	-11.5	14.9	7.3
Manufacture of electrical and optical equipment	-24.0	-12.0	-0.6	9.2	14.4
Manufacture of transport equipment	-29.0	-20.1	7.3	62.3	22.1
Manufacture N.E.C.	-5.2	-15.0	-7.3	9.7	11.0
Electricity, gas and water supply	-3.5	21.1	15.9	-2.5	5.0

Source: Slovak Statistical Office and staff estimates.

Table A2.10
Profits and Losses of Enterprises, 1993-96
(billions of koruny)

	1993			1994			1995			1996		
	Profits	Losses	Net	Profits	Losses	Net	Profits	Losses	Net	Profits	Losses	Net
Total	82.2	46.3	35.9	85.5	38.2	47.3	87.4	50.4	37.0	110.7	65.2	45.5
Agriculture	4.5	11.2	-6.7	1.3	5.5	-4.2	1.5	4.1	-2.6	5.0	7.5	-2.5
Industry	45.0	18.6	26.4	42.0	16.6	25.4	48.0	15.0	33.0	48.0	27.9	20.1
Mining	1.2	0.4	0.8	0.9	0.1	0.8	1.2	0.1	1.1	1.2	0.4	0.8
Manufacturing	16.8	17.4	-0.6	17.7	16.4	1.3	22.9	14.9	8.0	26.2	26.5	-0.3
Electricity	27.0	0.8	26.2	23.4	0.1	23.3	23.9	0.0	23.9	20.6	1.0	19.6
Construction	2.4	2.2	0.2	1.8	1.6	0.2	2.3	1.3	1.0	5.3	2.9	2.4
Services	30.3	14.3	16.0	40.4	14.5	25.9	35.6	30.0	5.6	52.4	26.9	25.5
Trade and repairs	3.3	5.4	-2.1	4.2	3.2	1.0	7.6	2.9	4.7	10.4	4.3	6.1
Hotels and restaurants	0.2	0.6	-0.4	0.2	0.4	-0.2	0.4	0.4	0.0	0.7	0.5	0.2
Transport and communication	8.4	2.1	6.3	7.8	1.1	6.7	5.6	1.2	4.4	7.6	3.9	3.7
Financial services 1/	13.9	3.8	10.1	23.7	6.3	17.4	15.5	21.3	-5.8	25.5	13.6	11.9
Real estate	3.3	1.9	1.4	3.2	0.7	2.5	5.0	1.4	3.6	6.7	2.7	4.0
Other	1.2	0.5	0.7	1.3	2.8	-1.5	1.5	2.8	-1.3	1.5	1.9	-0.4

Note: Enterprises with 25 or more employees including subsidized public organizations.
1/ Data for financial intermediaries refer to all enterprises, rather than only to enterprises with 25 or more employees.
Source: Statistical Office of the Slovak Republic.

Table A3.1
Balance of Payments
(millions of current US dollars)

	1992	1993	1994	1995	1996
Trade balance	-714.0	-931.9	58.5	-227.5	-2292.5
Exports, f.o.b.	6515.0	5447.4	6691.0	8579.0	8831.0
Imports, f.o.b. 1/	7229.0	6379.3	6632.5	8806.5	11123.5
Services balance	-54.0	230.7	537.1	526.6	-8.3
Receipts NFS	1535.0	1950.4	2256.1	2376.2	2068.1
Shipment and other	414.0	459.6	538.3	615.3	643.5
Transit of gas	343.0	382.8	395.9	404.7	385.6
Other	71.0	76.8	142.4	210.6	257.9
Travel	200.0	390.2	666.2	622.3	672.8
Other	921.0	1100.6	1051.6	1138.6	751.8
Factor income	170.0	189.5	155.2	249.0	222.1
Interest		83.4	79.8	212.6	190.4
Investment		26.5	26.7	10.6	15.0
Employee compensation		79.6	48.7	25.8	16.7
Expenditures NFS	1554.0	1681.7	1599.5	1835.8	2031.8
Shipment and other	263.0	292.3	161.5	306.1	395.1
Travel	165.0	216.3	318.0	320.4	482.8
Other	1126.0	1173.1	1120.0	1209.3	1153.9
Factor payments	205.0	227.5	274.7	262.8	266.7
Interest		183.9	235.7	242.7	238.4
Investment		42.1	33.1	17.5	19.4
Employee compensation		1.5	5.9	2.6	8.9
Unrequited transfers	814.0	100.0	69.2	92.2	202.8
Private	70.0	96.1	62.9	75.5	193.0
Official	744.0	3.9	6.3	16.7	9.8
Current account	46.0	-601.2	664.8	391.3	-2098.0
Current account/GDP (percent) 2/	0.4	-5.0	4.8	2.3	-11.1
Net medium- and long-term capital	351.0	181.9	908.4	974.9	1458.0
Foreign investment, net	100.0	-372.5	249.7	380.1	224.6
Direct foreign investment	100.0	134.0	169.5	134.0	129.0
Portfolio investment		-506.5	80.2	246.1	95.6
MLT credits received	196.0	305.7	476.8	526.0	1097.0
Disbursements	266.0	795.2	949.7	1570.3	1642.0
Repayments	-70.0	-489.5	-472.9	-1044.3	545.0
MLT credits extended	55.0	248.7	181.9	68.8	136.4
Disbursements		-22.1	-21.0	-80.8	-211.8
Repayments		270.8	202.9	149.6	348.2
Net short-term capital	-436.0	42.4	-198.1	73.6	871.2
Capital transfers	0.0	529.4	87.0	45.7	-94.2
Clearing account balance (surplus,-)		189.4	-623.0	-951.0	0.0
Clearing account settlement (payment,-)	0.0	0.0	275.3	1034.0	0.0
Total capital account	-85.0	943.1	449.6	1177.2	2235.0
Errors and omissions, nei	-500.0	14.0	495.7	193.8	225.1
Overall balance	-539.0	355.9	1610.1	1762.3	362.1
Change in reserves (-= increase)	539.0	-355.9	-1610.1	-1762.3	-362.1
Use of IMF credit, net	94.0	90.1	50.7	-200.9	-124.9
Purchases		90.1	140.1	0.0	0.0
Repurchases		0.0	-89.4	-200.9	-124.9
Change in gross reserves (-= increase)	-95.0	-520.6	-1687.7	-1770.5	-237.1
State bank	5.0	-58.6	-1289.9	-1579.0	-237.1
Commercial banks	-100.0	-462.0	-397.8	-191.5	..
Short-term liabilities	540.0	74.6	26.9	209.1	..
State bank		0.0	3.4	0.0	..
Commercial banks		74.6	23.5	209.1	..

.. = not available.
1/ Total imports include private imports for convertible currency.
2/ Calculated using the period average exchange rates for Czechoslovakia for 1992.
Source: National Bank of Slovakia.

Table A3.2
External Reserves
(millions of US dollars)

	1989	1990	1991	1992	1993	1994	1995	1996
Total external reserves	369.7	151.2	772.6	899.9	1401.3	2973.0	4913.7	5840.9
External reserves: IMF definition	369.7	151.2	535.1	409.2	449.5	1623.5	3298.3	3428.0
Official reserves	369.7	151.2	535.1	409.2	449.5	1623.5	3298.3	3428.0
Gold 1/	51.0	33.3	30.7	53.1	54.5	54.5	54.5	54.5
Foreign exchange held by state bank	318.7	117.9	504.4	343.3	415.3	1605.2	3305.9	3402.7
Foreign currency from gold swaps	..	..	..	..	20.6	122.2	120.1	45.4
SDR holding	0.0	0.0	0.0	12.8	0.3	86.0	58.0	16.2
Foreign exchange held by other banks	0.0	0.0	237.5	490.7	951.8	1349.5	1615.5	2412.95

Note: For 1980-91, data were derived by applying 2:1 ratio to Czechoslovakia's assets.

1/ Gold in accounting value = US$ 42.22 per ounce.

Source: National Bank of Slovakia; and staff estimates.

Table A3.3
External Trade by SITC
(millions of current koruny, F.O.B)

	1991	1992	1993	1994	1995	1996
By SITC classification						
Exports to nonsocialist countries						
Food and live animals	4182	3791	2711	2329	3101	2571
Beverages and tobacco	24	65	37	46	125	81
Inedible crude materials, nonfuel	3185	4062	3428	4198	5366	5202
Minerals, fuels	806	405	1698	2174	2140	3053
Animal and vegetable oils and fats	90	55	57	69	59	56
Chemicals	6627	7462	6491	9893	12714	12928
Manufactures by material	19241	31155	29415	44143	51746	50859
Machinery and equipment	8055	10836	9333	17085	22377	36782
Manufactures: miscellaneous	9296	12018	10879	15188	17764	19048
Others	32	0	1	0	11	162
I + II 1/	4	0	0	5	0	0
Not specified	0	0	12	15	0	0
Total	51543	69848	64061	95146	115403	130742
Exports to socialist countries						
Food and live animals	2618	4168	6508	7388	9725	7579
Beverages and tobacco	702	476	1443	1965	2104	1867
Inedible crude materials, nonfuel	1218	1719	4869	6776	7635	6854
Minerals, fuels	315	446	6557	7770	8608	10249
Animal and vegetable oils and fats	5	49	115	149	215	314
Chemicals	5326	4339	13740	17732	20949	20685
Manufactures by material	16052	12975	35623	40241	51406	52714
Machinery and equipment	14253	7800	23236	23649	25637	25955
Manufactures: miscellaneous	6139	4157	11677	13445	13322	13598
Others	0	0	3	15	55	60
I + II 1/	0	12	54	21	0	0
Not specified	0	0	76	76	3	0
Total	46627	36142	103901	119227	139659	139876
Total exports						
Food and live animals	6800	7959	9219	9717	12826	10150
Beverages and tobacco	726	541	1480	2011	2229	1948
Inedible crude materials, nonfuel	4403	5780	8297	10974	13001	12057
Minerals, fuels	1121	851	8255	9944	10748	13301
Animal and vegetable oils and fats	95	104	172	218	274	369
Chemicals	11953	11801	20231	27625	33663	33613
Manufactures by material	35293	44130	65037	84384	103152	103574
Machinery and equipment	22308	18636	32569	40734	48014	62737
Manufactures: miscellaneous	15435	16175	22556	28633	31086	32646
Others	32	0	4	15	65	222
I + II 1/	4	12	54	26	0	0
Not specified	0	0	88	91	3	0
Total	98170	105990	167962	214373	255062	270618
Not specified	6	175	152	2	34	11
Total export	98176	106165	168114	214375	255096	270628

Table A3.3
External Trade by SITC (continued)
(millions of current koruny, C.I.F.)

	1991	1992	1993	1994	1995	1996
Imports from nonsocialist Countries						
Food and live animals	3978	4011	7526	9138	11248	12593
Beverages and tobacco	762	562	779	804	762	833
Inedible crude materials, nonfuel	5209	3385	2299	3401	6038	7487
Minerals, fuels	4353	684	941	724	1192	2536
Animal and vegetable oils and fats	96	41	126	193	272	323
Chemicals	7117	7555	10195	14379	19192	21968
Manufactures by material	4322	6330	8764	12951	16459	20663
Machinery and equipment	22861	33279	34063	40325	52896	82689
Manufactures: miscellaneous	4904	7895	9305	10946	13130	16042
Others	4	2	5	55	231	276
I + II 1/	0	0	13	2	0	0
Not specified	0	23	117	133	1	0
Total	53607	63765	74134	93052	121420	165411
Imports from socialist countries						
Food and live animals	1323	1094	7390	5902	7214	8071
Beverages and tobacco	343	272	2186	1967	2141	2846
Inedible crude materials, nonfuel	8992	4946	8200	7936	9723	9216
Minerals, fuels	34767	29895	41668	40591	45359	54871
Animal and vegetable oils and fats	10	13	376	421	252	295
Chemicals	3198	3357	12941	13706	16281	16656
Manufactures by material	5122	3329	22004	23033	30268	31105
Machinery and equipment	5195	3562	25464	18653	23669	36122
Manufactures: miscellaneous	2345	1590	9039	8436	8202	14006
Others	0	0	86	21	19	89
I + II 1/	0	0	4	0	0	0
Not specified	0	0	127	157	1	0
Total	61295	48058	129485	120822	143129	173277
Total Imports						
Food and live animals	5301	5105	14915	15040	18462	20664
Beverages and tobacco	1106	833	2966	2770	2903	3679
Inedible crude materials, nonfuel	14201	8332	10499	11337	15761	16703
Minerals, fuels	39120	30579	42608	41315	46551	57408
Animal and vegetable oils and fats	106	53	502	614	524	618
Chemicals	10315	10911	23136	28086	35473	38624
Manufactures by material	9444	9659	30768	35984	46726	51768
Machinery and equipment	28057	36841	59527	58977	76565	118811
Manufactures: miscellaneous	7249	9485	18344	19382	21332	30048
Others	4	2	91	76	250	365
I + II 1/	0	0	17	3	0	0
Not specified	0	23	244	290	2	0
Total	114902	111823	203618	213874	264548	338688
Not specified	36	27	231	195	400	495
Total import	114938	111850	203849	214069	264948	339183

Note: 1991-1995 data are definitive;1996 are preliminary; data prior to 1993 excludes trade with the Czech Republic.
1) I - Gold, coinage; II - Gold coins and current coins.
Source: Statistical Office of the Slovak Republic.

Table A3.4
Geographical Composition of Trade
(Millions of SKK C.I.F./F.O.B.)

Country	Indicator	1990	1991	1992	1993	1994	1995	1996
Total foreign trade of the Slovak Republic	Export	52,032	98,176	106,165	168,114	214,375	255,096	270,628
	Import	61,258	114,938	111,850	203,849	214,069	264,948	339,183
	Balance	-9,226	-16,763	-5,685	-35,735	306	-9,852	-68,555
Czech Republic	Export	-	-	-	71,158	80,154	89,920	83,907
	Import	-	-	-	73,201	63,596	74,323	84,078
	Balance	-	-	-	-2,042	16,558	15,597	-172
Bulgaria	Export	497	719	634	513	373	539	603
	Import	707	565	243	338	334	336	301
	Balance	-209	153	391	176	39	203	301
Croatia	Export	-	-	1,026	1,482	1,943	2,151	2,248
	Import	-	-	184	440	559	607	656
	Balance	-	-	843	1,042	1,384	1,544	1,592
Hungary	Export	2,801	6,700	7,326	7,624	11,718	11,623	12,361
	Import	2,742	3,424	2,874	2,721	3,564	5,776	6,686
	Balance	59	3,277	4,451	4,904	8,154	5,847	5,675
Poland	Export	3,401	7,852	4,348	4,902	6,065	11,240	13,083
	Import	5,458	4,312	3,503	3,964	5,100	7,276	8,288
	Balance	-2,057	3,540	845	939	965	3,965	4,795
Romania	Export	481	1,192	1,286	743	855	1,267	1,752
	Import	606	434	299	230	247	319	464
	Balance	-125	758	986	513	608	948	1,288
Russian Federation	Export	-	-	7,305	7,896	8,893	9,836	9,433
	Import	-	-	8,162	39,799	38,166	43,397	59,391
	Balance	-	-	-857	-31,903	-29,273	-33,561	-49,957
Ukraine	Export	-	1	5,336	4,307	3,739	5,672	7,239
	Import	-	0	4,555	4,898	3,809	3,657	5,307
	Balance	-	0	781	-591	-70	2,015	1,932
EU countries 1/	Export	16,753	33,746	44,282	40,510	61,730	95,395	111,679
	Import	19,073	27,593	38,561	41,957	56,174	92,058	124,688
	Balance	-2,320	6,153	5,720	-1,447	5,557	3,337	-13,009
Austria	Export	3,769	5,839	7,879	8,362	11,258	12,664	16,363
	Import	8,278	9,791	11,401	12,694	12,268	13,372	15,668
	Balance	-4,509	-3,951	-3,522	-4,332	-1,010	-709	695
France	Export	2,106	2,378	4,019	2,707	3,630	5,095	5,722
	Import	1,007	2,325	2,644	3,073	4,797	6,439	10,785
	Balance	1,099	53	1,376	-366	-1,167	-1,344	-5,062
Italy	Export	1,895	5,001	5,802	4,603	9,238	12,292	13,200
	Import	1,631	3,255	6,292	6,104	9,400	12,276	20,169
	Balance	264	1,746	-489	-1,501	-163	16	-6,969
Germany	Export	7,180	19,440	25,888	25,569	36,650	47,948	57,343
	Import	8,835	16,469	23,238	23,279	28,761	37,902	49,058
	Balance	-1,655	2,971	2,650	2,289	7,889	10,046	8,285
United Kingdom	Export	1,233	1,075	1,967	1,717	2,743	3,343	4,148
	Import	1,674	1,153	1,272	2,564	3,409	4,469	6,284
	Balance	-441	-78	694	-847	-666	-1,126	-2,136

Notes: Data prior to 1993 excludes trade with the Czech Republic. Statistical data are published under the economic conditions and methodology of investigation of current year. Data are definitive on customs basis in 1993-1995. Date of the year 1996 are preliminary on customs basis of January 1997.
1/ EU includes Austria, Finland and Sweden from 1995 on.
Source: Slovak Statistical Office.

153

Table A3.5
Monthly Exchange Rates

	SK/US$	SK/DM	Basket
Jan-93	28.90	17.89	22.29
Feb-93	28.56	17.78	22.09
Mar-93	29.03	17.72	22.24
Apr-93	29.03	18.00	22.41
May-93	28.60	17.94	22.20
Jun-93	28.78	17.71	22.14
Jul-93	29.59	18.72	23.07
Aug-93	32.09	19.37	24.46
Sep-93	32.58	19.78	24.90
Oct-93	32.01	19.74	24.65
Nov-93	32.68	19.36	24.69
Dec-93	33.04	19.28	24.79
Jan-94	33.20	19.16	24.78
Feb-94	33.31	19.18	24.83
Mar-94	33.09	19.36	24.85
Apr-94	32.64	19.33	24.65
May-94	32.62	19.56	24.78
Jun-94	32.30	19.70	24.74
Jul-94	31.58	20.08	24.68
Aug-94	31.53	20.09	24.66
Sep-94	31.62	20.14	24.73
Oct-94	31.22	20.29	24.66
Nov-94	30.58	20.20	24.35
Dec-94	31.37	20.00	24.55
Jan-95	31.28	20.20	24.63
Feb-95	30.74	20.36	24.51
Mar-95	30.06	20.88	24.55
Apr-95	29.00	21.06	24.23
May-95	28.96	20.96	24.16
Jun-95	29.27	21.00	24.31
Jul-95	29.35	21.05	24.37
Aug-95	29.19	20.75	24.13
Sep-95	30.33	20.60	24.49
Oct-95	29.54	20.84	24.32
Nov-95	29.44	20.80	24.25
Dec-95	29.71	20.62	24.26
Jan-96	29.90	20.50	24.26
Feb-96	30.00	20.44	24.26
Mar-96	30.01	20.37	24.23
Apr-96	30.40	20.23	24.30
May-96	30.91	20.17	24.46
Jun-96	31.03	20.31	24.60
Jul-96	30.74	20.41	24.54
Aug-96	30.37	20.50	24.45
Sep-96	30.71	20.43	24.54
Oct-96	31.18	20.40	24.71
Nov-96	30.95	20.50	24.68
Dec-96	31.58	20.37	24.85
Jan-97	32.24	20.13	24.98
Feb-97	32.76	19.62	24.87
Mar-97	33.23	19.58	25.04
Apr-97	33.26	19.48	24.99
May-97	33.26	19.53	25.02

Note: Period average exchange rates. Basket weights: DM = 0.6 and US$ = 0.4.
Source: National Bank of Slovakia; and staff estimates.

Table A4.1
Gross External Debt by Creditors and Debtors
(millions of current US dollars)

	1992	1993	1994	1995	1996
Debt with the rest of the world					
By creditors					
Convertible debt	2828.8	3483.6	4659.9	5678.1	7669.4
Medium and long-term	2261.7	2820.6	3423.8	3964.4	4723.8
Multilateral	248.4	288.4	375.9	447.4	427.4
Governments	127.2	130.2	136.2	135.2	132.6
Suppliers credits 1/	437.5	542.5	885.0	383.8	238.1
Government bank credits	695.3	640.3	571.3	364.8	225.8
NBS Bonds	74.2	347.9	541.7	569.2	556.7
IMF	480.0	569.8	638.8	456.0	320.0
Other creditors	199.1	301.4	275.0	1608.1	2823.2
Short-term	567.1	663.0	1236.1	1713.7	2945.7
Nonconvertible debt	152.5	133.8	140.2	148.5	139.7
Medium and long-term	152.5	133.8	140.2	148.5	139.7
Short-term	0.0	0.0	0.0	0.0	0.0
Total	2981.3	3617.4	4800.1	5826.6	7809.2
Medium and long-term	2414.3	2954.4	3564.0	4113.0	4863.5
Short-term	567.1	663.0	1236.1	1713.7	2945.7
By debt holders					
Medium and Long-term	2261.7	2820.6	3423.8	3964.4	4723.8
National bank	554.2	917.7	1180.5	1025.1	877.1
Government	1071.0	1058.9	1083.4	947.4	779.2
Corporations	437.5	630.1	884.9	1399.1	2231.9
Commercial banks	199.1	213.8	275.0	528.9	778.5
Municipalities				63.9	57.2

1/ Suppliers credit includes financing sources of municipalities and private bond issues.
Source: Staff estimates and National Bank of Slovakia.

Table A4.2
Debt Service in Convertible Currencies
(millions of current US dollars)

	1990	1991	1992	1993	1994	1995	1996
Principal repayments							
Convertible debt with ROW							
Medium and long-term	171.0	246.9	377.4	422.1	543.1	813.3	858.1
Multilateral	2.6	2.6	0.0	0.0	0.0	0.0	0.0
IBRD	0.0	0.0	0.0	0.0	0.0	..	..
Bilateral	19.0	17.4	11.9	0.0	0.0	0.0	0.0
Suppliers credits 1/	93.2	153.5	111.2	179.0	190.2	267.6	34.9
Banks	56.2	73.4	201.9	243.1	200.6	344.6	682.4
Bonds	0.0	0.0	36.0	0.0	63.0	0.0	0.0
IMF	0.0	0.0	16.4	0.0	89.4	201.1	124.9
Interest payments							
Convertible debt with ROW							
Medium and long-term	83.9	122.0	160.9	134.3	188.4	269.0	301.1
Multilateral 2/	8.8	6.8	22.5	22.0	15.1	27.5	25.2
IBRD	0.0	0.0	5.0	9.1	11.3	..	..
Bilateral	3.3	2.3	4.2	10.0	10.0	17.1	7.0
Suppliers credits	16.9	26.7	32.1	39.4	51.3	79.6	125.9
Banks	52.6	52.5	45.0	17.9	39.3	24.8	47.6
Bonds	2.3	17.6	25.2	11.7	50.3	52.7	57.6
IMF	0.0	16.0	32.0	33.3	22.4	31.1	17.8
Short-term	63.0	32.7	44.0	46.4	86.5	120.0	206.2
Total interest payments	146.9	154.7	205.0	180.7	274.9	389.0	507.3
Total debt service	320.9	429.7	582.4	602.8	818.0	1202.3	1365.4

1/ Part of suppliers debt service was shifted to Foreign Banks debt service in 1996.
2/ Including IBRD in 1995-96.
Source: Staff estimates and National Bank of Slovakia.

Table A5.1
Central Government Budget
(billions of koruny)

	1992	1993	1994	1995	1996 (Preliminary)
Total revenue	139.5	142.7	135.9	158.4	159.4
Current revenue	139.5	142.7	135.9	158.4	159.4
Tax revenue	125.5	127.3	114.6	136.5	140.1
Indirect tax	40.3	47.0	58.3	72.3	70.3
VAT	0.0	27.5	37.1	52.3	48.7
Excises	0.0	15.4	21.1	20.0	21.6
Turnover	40.3	4.1	0.0	0.0	0.0
Customs duties and import surcharge	5.3	4.5	7.2	8.8	9.9
Direct tax	49.0	30.8	44.5	53.4	59.0
Profit taxes	31.0	22.0	30.3	33.7	33.6
Income tax	18.0	8.9	14.2	19.7	25.5
Wages	16.1	5.1	7.8	12.2	15.7
Entrepreneurial activity 1/	1.9	3.2	3.5	3.6	4.7
Dividends/interest		0.6	3.0	3.9	5.1
Other tax revenue	0.8	2.1	0.6	2.1	0.9
Social security contributions	30.1	42.9	4.0	0.0	0.0
Nontax revenue	14.0	15.4	21.4	21.9	19.3
Revenue from budget organizations	4.0	4.1	6.5	10.4	1.278
Interest	0.2	0.6	0.8	0.9	0.9
Fees and fine	1.6	1.7	2.2	2.5	5.7
Repayments of government loans	3.8	4.2	3.8	3.7	2.5
NBS profits transferred		4.0	6.7	1.4	2.4
Other	4.4	0.8	1.4	3.0	6.6
Capital revenue	0.0	0.0	0.0	0.0	0.0

Table A5.1
Central Government Budget
(billions of koruny)

	1992	1993	1994	1995	1996 (Preliminary)
(continued)					
Total expenditure	170.4	167.6	140.6	160.7	169.0
Current expenditure	154.3	153.1	104.1	116.6	121.1
Budget organizations	79.6	67.9	53.2	66.3	71.1
Wages	15.4	15.9	16.7	18.8	21.3
Health care, excluding wages	15.3	15.8	0.6	0.6	0.5
Education, excluding wages	8.0	8.0	7.6	7.7	13.9
Other	40.9	28.3	28.3	39.2	35.4
Social expenditure 2/	49.5	54.3	15.3	20.9	21.2
Pensions	28.0	32.7	1.4	1.9	1.7
Employment policies	5.5	3.0	0.0	0.0	0.0
Sickness benefits	4.9	5.2	0.0	0.0	0.0
Social assistance	2.2	3.1	5.2	5.5	5.5
Other	8.9	10.3	8.7	13.5	14.0
Subsidies	13.3	14.3	13.9	14.3	13.7
Agriculture	8.5	8.7	7.6	7.4	6.0
Economy	1.2	0.6	0.3	0.4	0.3
Transportation	1.6	2.6	2.8	3.0	2.9
Heating	2.0	2.5	3.0	3.5	4.3
Other; unclassified	0.0	0.0	0.2	0.1	0.2
State equalization allowance	7.2	4.3	2.5	0.0	0.0
Debt service	4.7	12.3	19.2	15.0	15.0
Interest	3.6	11.2	16.7	12.0	12.1
Lending and Guarantees	1.1	1.1	2.5	3.0	2.9
Capital expenditure	12.1	11.3	10.4	14.4	19.2
Investment projects	10.0	7.8	8.1	12.0	16.1
Transfers to enterprises	2.1	3.5	2.3	2.4	3.1
Intragovernmental transfers	4.0	3.1	26.1	29.8	28.7
Transfers to local government	2.4	1.5	1.1	1.2	1.3
Transfers to social security sector 3/	0.0	0.0	22.5	25.3	23.4
Transfers to state funds	1.6	1.6	2.5	3.3	4.1
Balance (before intragovernmental transfers)	-26.9	-21.7	21.5	27.4	19.1
Balance (after intragovernmental transfers)	-30.9	-24.8	-4.6	-2.4	-9.6
(Balance excluding NBS profits)	-30.9	-28.8	-11.4	-3.8	-12.0
(Surplus/deficit)/GDP (percent)	-9.3	-6.7	-1.1	-0.5	-1.6

1/ 1996 budget figure includes dividends/interest.
2/ Includes social assistance and social benefits.
3/ Includes social security contributions paid by the state as an employer and on behalf of so-called "dependent" persons.
Source: Ministry of Finance, Slovak Republic; and IMF.

Table A5.2
Social Security Funds
(millions of Sks)

	1994	1995	1996	1994	1995	1996
				(Percentage of GDP)		(Projected)
Health funds						
Revenue	20806.0	28010.0	37755.9	4.7	5.4	6.5
SS contributions	17713.0	26002.0	34192.0	4.0	5.0	5.9
Other	3093.0	2008.0	1752.1	0.7	0.4	0.3
Expenditure	22316.0	26808.0	36215.5	5.1	5.2	6.2
Balance	-1510.0	1203.0	1540.4	-0.3	0.2	0.3
Sickness fund						
Revenue	8429.0	7942.0	10313.6	1.9	1.5	1.8
SS contributions	7034.0	7693.0	7309.6	1.6	1.5	1.3
Other	1395.0	249.0	189.3	0.3	0.0	0.0
Expenditure	5103.0	6148.0	7388.4	1.2	1.2	1.3
Balance	3326.0	1794.0	2925.2	0.8	0.3	0.5
Pension fund						
Revenue	38372.0	44852.0	52740.0	8.7	8.7	9.1
SS contributions	36977.0	44603.0	50932.2	8.4	8.7	8.8
Other	1395.0	249.0	556.5	0.3	0.0	0.1
Expenditure	38010.0	44738.0	46088.6	8.6	8.7	7.9
Balance	362.0	115.0	6651.4	0.1	0.0	1.1
Employment fund						
Revenue	5140.0	7225.0	9241.1	1.2	1.4	1.6
SS contributions	4663.0	6183.0	7158.8	1.1	1.2	1.2
Other	477.0	1042.0	1062.4	0.1	0.2	0.2
Expenditure	4459.0	6203.0	7695.1	1.0	1.2	1.3
SS contributions 1/	0.0	580.0	1125.7	0.0	0.1	0.2
Balance	681.0	1022.0	1546.0	0.2	0.2	0.3
Total						
Revenue	72747.0	87451.0	105999.0	16.5	17.0	18.2
SS contributions	66387.0	83902.0	101686.0	15.1	16.3	17.5
Other	6360.0	3549.0	4313.0	1.4	0.7	0.7
Expenditure	69222.0	83317.0	97614.0	15.7	16.2	16.8
Balance	2859.0	4134.0	8385.0	0.6	0.8	1.4
Memorandum item:						
Nominal GDP (millions of Sk)	440500.0	515100.0	581300.0			

Note: Social security funds includes 12 health insurance companies, the sickness fund, pension funds and employment funds.
1/ Contributions made by the employment fund to the health, sickness and pension funds on behalf of unemployed persons.
Source: Public Expenditure Department at the Slovak Ministry of Finance and IMF.

Table A5.3
Extrabudgetary Funds
(millions of koruny)

	Own revenue	Tranfers from budge	Total revenue	Current expenditure	Capital expenditure	Total expenditure	Balance
1993 outcome							
Environment fund	618.0	360.0	978.1	269.4	811.6	1081.0	-102.9
Fund for culture "Pro Slovakia"	8.0	210.0	218.0	95.7	95.7	191.4	26.7
Fund for physical culture	..	..	..	..	..	..	..
Health fund	..	..	..	..	..	..	..
Fund for market regulation in agriculture	1263.5	884.9	2148.4	1806.2	0.0	1806.2	342.2
Road fund	..	..	..	..	..	..	..
Forestry fund	7.7	53.4	61.0	5.4	57.5	62.8	-1.8
Fund for agricultural land protection	168.9	53.4	222.3	0.0	243.3	243.3	-21.0
Fund for water management	0.1	20.0	20.1	0.0	0.0	0.0	20.1
Financial support fund for agriculture	..	..	..	..	..	..	..
Nuclear waste fund	..	..	..	..	..	..	..
Funds for housing development	11.7	760.0	771.7	5.5	349.1	354.6	417.2
State funds, total	2077.9	2341.7	4419.6	2182.2	1557.2	3739.3	680.5
1994 outcome							
Environment fund	707.7	270.0	977.7	110.4	896.6	1006.9	-29.1
Fund for culture "Pro Slovakia"	4.7	80.0	84.7	130.4	0.0	130.4	-45.7
Fund for physical culture	111.0	17.0	128.0	122.4	0.0	122.4	5.6
Health fund	47.0	0.0	47.0	31.6	0.0	31.6	15.5
Fund for market regulation in agriculture	535.5	650.0	1185.5	1933.0	0.0	1933.0	-747.5
Road fund	953.8	1000.0	1953.8	1069.8	996.6	2066.4	-112.6
Forestry fund	31.8	177.4	209.2	196.0	187.2	383.2	-174.0
Fund for agricultural land protection	147.8	25.0	172.8	127.2	55.6	182.8	-10.0
Fund for water management	2.3	0.0	2.3	0.0	26.1	26.1	-23.8
Financial support fund for agriculture	506.7	300.0	806.7	46.7	0.0	46.7	760.0
Nuclear waste fund	..	..	..	..	..	..	..
Funds for housing development	..	..	..	..	..	..	..
State funds, total	3048.3	2519.4	5567.7	3767.5	2162.1	5929.5	-361.6
1995 outcome							
Environment fund	808.4	250.0	1058.4	154.7	868.3	1023.0	35.4
Fund for culture "Pro Slovakia"	8.1	377.6	385.7	377.1	0.0	377.1	8.6
Fund for physical culture	126.1	18.0	144.1	108.6	28.8	137.4	6.7
Health fund	114.0	0.0	114.1	14.5	18.4	32.9	81.2
Fund for market regulation in agriculture	1889.0	650.0	2539.0	2092.9	0.0	2092.9	446.1
Road fund	1112.8	1000.0	2112.8	1379.7	2201.6	3581.2	-1468.5
Forestry fund	58.6	513.2	571.8	555.9	0.0	555.9	15.8
Fund for agricultural land protection	261.0	25.0	286.0	112.9	42.8	155.8	130.2
Fund for water management	24.4	0.0	24.4	0.0	0.0	0.0	24.4
Financial support fund for agriculture	736.8	100.0	836.8	16.3	810.2	826.5	10.4
Nuclear waste fund	803.8	348.6	1152.4	15.0	208.4	223.4	929.0
Funds for housing development	..	..	..	..	..	..	..
State funds, total	5943.0	3282.4	9225.5	4827.6	4178.5	9006.1	219.3
1996 outcome							
Environment fund	1013.2	297.0	1310.1	58.8	1194.3	1253.1	57.1
Fund for culture "Pro Slovakia"	62.8	116.7	179.5	153.9	0.0	153.9	25.6
Fund for physical culture	475.1	18.3	493.4	311.6	0.0	311.6	181.7
Health fund	595.8	0.6	596.4	62.9	441.2	504.1	92.3
Fund for market regulation in agriculture	4757.6	653.5	5411.0	5307.8	0.0	5307.8	103.2
Road fund	3957.0	1174.0	5131.0	1830.8	2959.4	4790.2	340.8
Forestry fund	179.7	571.1	750.8	647.9	0.2	648.1	102.8
Fund for agricultural land protection	829.0	25.2	854.2	297.5	130.1	427.6	426.6
Fund for water management	91.8	200.2	292.0	139.2	87.5	226.7	65.3
Financial support fund for agriculture	1918.8	135.3	2054.1	1861.3	0.0	1861.3	192.8
Nuclear waste fund	2447.6	139.3	2586.9	0.7	656.1	656.9	1930.1
Funds for housing development	11.7	760.0	771.7	5.5	349.1	354.6	417.2
State funds, total	16340.0	4091.1	20431.1	10678.0	5817.7	16495.7	3935.4

.. = not available.
Source: Slovak Ministry of Finance and IMF.

Table A5.4
General Government Budget
(billions of current koruny)

	1992	1993	1994	1995	1996 (Projected)
Total revenue	153.1	163.5	204.6	242.5	272.9
Current revenue	153.1	163.5	204.6	242.5	272.9
Tax revenue	130.9	134.6	170.9	205.3	227.9
Indirect tax	40.3	47.0	58.3	72.3	70.3
VAT	0.0	27.5	37.1	52.3	48.7
Excises (including also unspecified)	0.0	15.4	21.1	20.0	21.6
Oil products	0.0	8.6	13.0	11.8	
Spirits	0.0	1.8	3.1	3.6	
Wine	0.0	0.4	0.4	0.4	
Beer	0.0	0.8	1.2	1.3	
Tobacco	0.0	1.6	2.6	2.9	
Turnover	40.3	4.1	0.0	0.0	
Customs duties	5.3	4.5	7.2	8.8	9.9
Direct tax	54.4	36.5	50.1	58.5	64.9
Profits taxes	31.2	22.0	31.9	35.2	34.8
Income tax	23.2	14.5	18.1	23.2	30.1
Wages	21.3	10.7	11.7	15.7	20.3
Entrepreneurial activity	1.9	3.2	3.5	3.6	4.7
Dividends/interest	0.0	0.6	3.0	3.9	5.1
Other tax revenues	0.8	3.7	4.0	5.7	6.2
Road tax	0.0	1.6	1.4	1.5	1.4
Other taxes	0.8	2.1	2.6	4.2	4.8
Social security contributions	30.1	42.9	51.4	60.1	76.6
Nontax revenue	22.2	29.0	33.7	37.2	45.0
Fees and fines	6.5	3.8	2.2	3.9	7.2
Budgetary organizations	5.3	6.3	6.5	11.9	1.3
Interest	0.3	0.6	0.8	0.9	1.2
Repayments of loans	3.8	4.2	3.8	3.7	2.6
NBS profits	0.0	4.0	6.7	1.4	2.4
Other	6.3	10.1	13.7	15.3	30.4

Table A5.4
General Government Budget
(billions of current koruny)

	1992	1993	1994	1995	1996 (Projected)
(continued)					
Total expenditure 1/	192.6	189.5	210.4	241.4	280.6
Current expenditure	167.8	168.3	190.5	216.6	243.1
Subsidies to enterprises	16.2	17.2	18.5	19.0	20.4
Agriculture	8.5	8.7	7.6	7.4	6.0
Industry	1.2	0.6	0.3	0.4	0.3
Transport	1.6	2.6	2.8	3.0	2.9
Heating	2.0	2.5	3.0	3.5	4.3
Other (including state funds)	2.9	2.9	4.8	4.8	6.9
Social expenditures	49.5	54.3	62.8	77.4	84.1
Pensions	28.0	32.7	39.3	46.6	48.5
Labor policies	5.5	3.0	3.6	5.5	7.7
Unemployment benefits	1.7	1.9	1.7	1.6	3.2
Active employment policies and administration	3.8	1.1	1.9	3.9	4.5
Social assistance	2.2	3.1	5.2	5.5	5.5
Sickness benefits	4.9	5.2	5.2	6.1	8.2
Other	8.9	10.3	9.5	13.6	14.2
State equalization allowance	7.2	4.3	2.5	0.0	0.0
Consumption	90.2	79.4	86.5	104.4	121.1
Wages	15.4	15.9	16.7	18.8	21.3
Health care	15.3	15.8	22.9	27.5	33.7
Education	8.0	8.0	7.6	7.7	13.9
Other	51.5	39.7	39.3	50.4	52.1
Debt service	4.7	13.2	20.2	15.8	17.5
Own interest	3.6	11.6	17.2	12.4	12.7
Guarantees	1.1	1.5	3.0	3.4	4.9
Total capital expenditure	24.8	21.2	19.9	24.8	37.5
Investment expenditure ROs 2/ 3/	21.8	14.3	16.0	20.0	32.4
Road fund expenditure	0.0	1.8	0.0	2.2	3.0
Other	21.8	12.5	16.0	17.8	29.4
Transfer to enterprises	3.0	6.9	3.9	4.8	5.2
Intragovernmental transfers paid	4.0	3.1	26.1	29.8	28.7
Local authorities	2.4	1.5	1.1	1.2	1.3
Social security sector	0.0	0.0	22.5	25.3	23.4
Other extrabudgetary sectors	1.6	1.6	2.5	3.3	4.1
Total expenditure (including transfers)	196.6	192.6	236.5	271.2	309.3
Contingency reserve	0.0	0.0	0.0	0.0	0.0
Surplus/deficit (before transfers)	-35.5	-22.9	20.4	30.9	21.0
Surplus/deficit (after transfers)	-39.5	-26.0	-5.8	1.1	-7.7
Balance excluding NBS profits	-39.5	-30.0	-12.5	-0.3	-10.1
(Surplus/deficit (before transfers))/GDP (percent)	-10.7	-6.2	4.6	6.0	3.6
(Surplus/deficit (after transfers))/GDP (percent)	-11.9	-7.0	-1.3	0.2	-1.3
(Balance excluding NBS profits)/GDP (percent)	-11.9	-8.1	-2.8	-0.1	-1.7
Financing	35.5	22.9	-20.4	-30.9	-21.0
External borrowing net	5.8	-0.3	1.2	-5.6	-2.7
Net monetary system	46.7	25.9	-3.9	-3.3	-1.0
Net other domestic borrowing	-17.0	-2.7	-17.7	-22.0	-17.3

Note: Includes central government, local government and social funds.
1/ Excluding military imports of US$ 170 million in 1993 in exchange for a write-down of claims on Russia.
2/ ROs: Budgetary organizations.
3/ Excluding transfers to enterprises.
Source: Ministry of Finance, Slovak Republic; and IMF.

Table A5.5
State Financial Assets & Liabilities
(millions of koruny)

	1992 c/ End-Dec	1993 End-Dec	1994 End-Dec	1995 End-Dec	1996 End-Dec	1993 Annual	1994 Annual	1995 Annual	1996 Annual
Assets									
Bank accounts of reserve character	474.0	474.0	474.0	474.0	474.0	0.0	0.0	0.0	0.0
Counterpart deposits on foreign loans	10830.0	4056.0	6493.0	8341.0	8341.0	-6773.0	2437.0	1848.0	0.0
SAL from the IBRD	3107.0	793.0	793.0	793.0	793.0	-2313.0	0.0	0.0	0.0
Borrowing from the G-24	3263.0	3263.0	3263.0	3263.0	3263.0	0.0	0.0	0.0	0.0
SAL from the IBRD	0.0	0.0	2437.0	2532.0	2532.0	0.0	2437.0	95.0	0.0
Borrowing from JEXIM BANK	0.0	0.0	0.0	1753.0	1753.0	0.0	0.0	1753.0	0.0
Borrowing from EU	4460.0	0.0	0.0	0.0	0.0	-4460.0	0.0	0.0	0.0
Other bank accounts	633.0	644.0	557.0	534.0	535.0	11.0	-88.0	-22.0	1.0
Claims on foreign countries; other than CSO	52097.0	58982.0	59011.0	52254.0	49151.0	6886.0	30.0	-6757.0	-3103.0
Civil; nonconvertible	23882.0	28393.0	24683.0	23321.0	18995.0	4512.0	-3710.0	-1362.0	-4326.0
Civil; convertible	8603.0	10134.0	9307.0	8772.0	9341.0	1531.0	-826.0	-535.0	569.0
Special; nonconvertible	108.0	112.0	119.0	118.0	121.0	4.0	7.0	-1.0	3.0
Special; convertible	15975.0	18508.0	17654.0	18339.0	20326.0	2533.0	-854.0	685.0	1967.0
Claims on FSU; VIA	3529.0	1835.0	1381.0	480.0	0.0	-1694.0	-454.0	-901.0	-460.0
Clearing account: Czech Republic	0.0	0.0	5867.0	1224.0	368.0	0.0	5867.0	-4643.0	-856.0
Claims on foreign countries; CSOB 2/	31813.0	34134.0	29775.0	28557.0	28584.0	2322.0	-4359.0	-1218.0	27.0
Nonconvertible	30517.0	32601.0	28805.0	27556.0	27535.0	2085.0	-3796.0	-1249.0	-21.0
Convertible	1296.0	1533.0	970.0	1001.0	1049.0	237.0	-563.0	31.0	48.0
Participations in international banks	1646.0	2803.0	2892.0	2172.0	2308.0	1157.0	89.0	-720.0	136.0
IBEC	300.0	883.0	832.0	324.0	343.0	583.0	-51.0	-508.0	19.0
IIB	363.0	765.0	720.0	392.0	415.0	402.0	-45.0	-328.0	23.0
EBRD	173.0	290.0	335.0	468.0	511.0	117.0	45.0	133.0	43.0
World Bank institutions	810.0	865.0	1005.0	988.0	1039.0	55.0	140.0	-17.0	51.0
Deposits from domestic companies	163.0	221.0	792.0	919.0	925.0	58.0	571.0	127.0	6.0
Receivables from returnable assistance	523.0	1029.0	643.0	1389.0	3456.0	506.0	-386.0	746.0	2067.0
Receivables from state guarantees	1094.0	1584.0	1683.0	2742.0	3487.0	491.0	99.0	1059.0	725.0
Securities held by state	0.0	0.0	0.0	0.0	0.0	0.0	0.0	0.0	0.0
Other receivables	60.0	240.0	240.0	240.0	240.0	180.0	0.0	0.0	0.0
(see note) 3/	0.0	0.0	0.0	5700.0	1422.0	0.0	0.0	5700.0	-4258.0
Claims against Mochovce project	0.0	0.0	0.0	0.0	783.0	0.0	0.0	0.0	783.0
Total assets	99333.0	104167.0	102560.0	103322.0	99706.0	4838.0	-1607.0	763.0	-3616.0
(percentage of GDP)	29.9	28.2	23.3	20.1	17.2	1.5	-0.4	0.2	-0.7

Table A5.5
State Financial Assets and Liabilities
(millions of koruny)

	1992 1/ End-Dec	1993 End-Dec	1994 End-Dec	1995 End-Dec	1996 End-Dec	1993 Annual change	1994 Annual change	1995 Annual change	1996 Annual change
(continued)									
Liabilities									
Credit from NBS	39382.0	54461.0	46475.0	31442.0	30067.0	15079.0	-7986.0	-15026.0	-1375.0
Due to lending abroad	13053.0	13053.0	13053.0	13053.0	13053.0	0.0	0.0	0.0	0
Due to exchange rate changes	8663.0	8663.0	8663.0	8663.0	8663.0	0.0	0.0	0.0	0
Direct credit	17666.0	32745.0	24759.0	9726.0	8351.0	15079.0	-7986.0	-15026.0	-1375.0
Slovak budget deficit of 1991	7400.0	7400.0	7400.0	7393.0	6018.0	0.0	0.0	0.0	0.0
Federal budget deficit of 1992	2333.0	2333.0	2333.0	2333.0	2333.0	0.0	0.0	0.0	0.0
Slovak budget deficit of 1992	7933.0	0.0	0.0	0.0	0.0	-7933.0	0.0	0.0	0.0
Treasury bills issued in 1992	4920.0	0.0	0.0	0.0	0.0	-4920.0	0.0	0.0	0.0
Direct credit in 1992	3013.0	0.0	0.0	0.0	0.0	-3013.0	0.0	0.0	0.0
Budget deficit of 1993	0.0	23012.0	15026.0	0.0	0.0	23012.0	-7986.0	-15026.0	-1375.0
Treasury bills issued in 1993	0.0	7892.0	0.0	0.0	0.0	7892.0	-7892.0	0.0	0
1.3.4.2. Direct credit in 1993	0.0	15120.0	15026.0	0.0	0.0	15120.0	-94.0	-15026.0	-1375
Budget deficit of 1994	0.0	0.0	0.0	0.0	0.0	0.0	0.0	0.0	0.0
Treasury bills issued in 1994	0.0	0.0	0.0	0.0	0.0	0.0	0.0	0.0	0.0
Direct credit in 1994	0.0	0.0	0.0	0.0	0.0	0.0	0.0	0.0	0.0
Credit from commercial banks	8833.0	6451.0	4846.0	3464.0	2168.0	-2381.0	-1605.0	-1381.0	-1469.0
Related to CSOB	5219.0	3198.0	1955.0	934.0	0.0	-2020.0	-1244.0	-1020.0	-1108
Investment bank/KTUK Dolsinka	3614.0	3253.0	2891.0	2530.0	2168.0	-361.0	-361.0	-361.0	-361
Balance of payments support loans	10845.0	13601.0	15664.0	16486.0	17473.0	2756.0	2063.0	821.0	987.0
SAL/IBRD	3138.0	4877.0	4692.0	4458.0	4784.0	1739.0	-185.0	-234.0	327
EU	4364.0	4652.0	4704.0	4758.0	4946.0	288.0	51.0	54.0	188
G-24	3343.0	4072.0	3834.0	3424.0	3674.0	729.0	-237.0	-411.0	251
ERL/IBRD	0.0	0.0	2434.0	2377.0	2552.0	0.0	2434.0	-57.0	174
JEXIM BANK	0.0	0.0	0.0	1469.0	1517.0	0.0	0.0	1469.0	47
Clearing account debt: Czech Republic	0.0	5801.0	0.0	0.0	0.0	5801.0	-5801.0	0.0	0
Liabilities related to CSOB	24794.0	25743.0	22874.0	14339.0	11532.0	948.0	-2868.0	-8535.0	-2807.0
Convertible currencies	20122.0	21260.0	18387.0	9921.0	7113.0	1137.0	-2872.0	-8466.0	-2807
Nonconvertible currencies	4672.0	4483.0	4487.0	4418.0	4419.0	-189.0	4.0	-69.0	0
Issued state bonds	7278.0	9231.0	17692.0	54326.0	53895.0	1953.0	8461.0	36634.0	-431.0
KBV	4200.0	4852.0	5206.0	4200.0	4200.0	652.0	354.0	-1006.0	0
Rehabilitation bonds	298.0	431.0	520.0	0.0	0.0	133.0	89.0	-520.0	0
Budget deficit of 1991	600.0	600.0	600.0	600.0	0.0	0.0	0.0	0.0	-600
Bills of exchange; IBRD participation	230.0	230.0	230.0	230.0	230.0	0.0	0.0	0.0	0
Gabcikovo, Turcek, Malinec	1950.0	3118.0	3150.0	3150.0	0.0	1168.0	32.0	0.0	-3150
Bonds to refinance 1993 deficit	0.0	0.0	7986.0	23080.0	15100.0	0.0	7986.0	15094.0	-7980
Bonds to refinance the 1994 deficit	0.0	0.0	0.0	23066.0	23066.0	0.0	0.0	23066.0	0
Bonds to Motorway	0.0	0.0	0.0	0.0	3000.0	0.0	0.0	0.0	3000
Bonds to refinance the 1995 deficit	0.0	0.0	0.0	0.0	8299.0	0.0	0.0	0.0	8299
Treasury bills outside NBS	0.0	0.0	22892.0	14830.0	27000.0	0.0	22892.0	-8062.0	12170
Government loan from the Russian Federation	0.0	0.0	0.0	0.0	802.0	0.0	0.0	0.0	802
Total liabilities 4/	91132.0	115288.0	130443.0	134887.0	142937.0	24156.0	15156.0	4451.0	7877.0
(Percentage of GDP)	27.4	31.2	29.6	26.2	24.6	7.3	4.1	1.0	1.5
Net assets 5/	8201.0	-11121.0	-27883.0	-31565.0	-43231.0	-19318.0	-16763.0	-3688.0	-11493.0
(Percentage of GDP)	2.5	-3.0	-6.3	-6.1	-7.4	-5.8	-4.5	-0.8	-2.2
Nominal GDP (Million Sk)	332300.0	369100.0	440500.0	515100.0	581300.0				

1/ Including liabilities taken over from the federation.
2/ CSOB - Ceskoslovenska Obchodni Banka.
3/ Temporary means for the liquidity in respect from the issue of treasury bills.
4/ Excluding Sk 4,920 million of treasury bills at the end of 1992 and Sk 7.891 million of treasury bills at the end of 1993, which had been included
twice in the original source.
5/ Change in net assets includes valuation changes, for example, due to the exchange rate devaluation in July 1993 and differs from the flow deficit.
Source: Slovak Ministry of Finance, and IMF.

Table A6.1
Monetary Survey (current exchange rates)
(billions of korunys)

	1/01/1993	1/31/1993	2/28/1993	3/31/1993	4/30/1993	5/31/1993	6/30/1993	7/31/1993	8/31/1993	9/30/1993	10/31/1993	11/30/1993	12/31/1993
Net foreign assets	-28.4	-34.7	-33.7	-31.1	-30.4	-29.1	-31.1	-28.4	-32.0	-30.5	-32.1	-33.3	-34.8
Foreign assets	26.0	19.3	21.4	24.7	23.8	26.9	25.5	36.8	34.5	42.1	43.4	43.8	47.2
Foreign liabilities	54.4	54.0	55.1	55.8	54.2	56.0	56.6	65.2	66.5	72.6	75.5	77.1	82.0
Net domestic assets	242.0	239.0	236.6	238.1	242.0	245.5	246.8	251.0	254.4	254.5	258.2	264.9	288.0
Domestic credit	294.9	298.4	299.0	308.2	309.4	313.3	327.5	327.9	334.1	335.4	340.2	346.3	363.9
- Net credit to government	57.7	60.8	60.0	68.5	66.4	66.8	76.5	73.6	78.3	79.7	80.2	84.1	94.5
- Net credit to property funds	-1.6	-0.9	-1.0	-1.0	-1.0	-0.8	-0.8	-1.5	-1.6	-0.7	-0.3	-0.2	4.9
- Total credit households and enterprises	238.8	238.5	240.0	240.7	244.0	247.3	251.8	255.8	257.4	256.4	260.3	262.4	264.5
- Credit to SKK	235.1	234.2	235.6	235.1	238.2	241.0	245.5	248.1	248.7	249.1	252.0	253.9	256.4
- Credit to enterprises	215.3	214.5	216.1	215.8	219.0	222.0	226.7	229.4	230.2	230.7	233.8	235.9	237.8
- Credit to households	19.8	19.7	19.5	19.3	19.2	19.0	18.8	18.7	18.5	18.4	18.2	18.0	18.6
- Credit in foreign currency	3.7	4.3	4.4	5.6	5.8	6.3	6.3	7.7	8.7	7.3	8.3	8.5	8.1
Liquid liabilities [M2]	213.6	204.3	202.9	207.0	211.6	216.4	215.7	222.6	222.4	224.0	226.1	231.6	253.2
Money [M1]	108.2	96.6	94.4	92.3	95.9	98.7	98.0	102.3	101.2	101.2	100.8	104.3	116.3
Quasi money	105.4	107.7	108.5	114.7	115.7	117.7	117.7	120.3	121.2	122.8	125.3	127.3	136.9
Other items net	52.9	59.4	62.4	70.1	67.4	67.8	80.7	76.9	79.7	80.9	82.0	81.4	75.9

	1/01/1994	1/31/1994	2/28/1994	3/31/1994	4/30/1994	5/31/1994	6/30/1994	7/30/1994	8/31/1994	9/30/1994	10/31/1994	11/30/1994	12/31/1994
Net foreign assets	-34.7	-37.4	-37.0	-31.2	-25.6	-20.3	-12.3	-9.1	-5.6	5.1	8.5	10.9	15.5
Foreign assets	46.6	44.4	46.1	48.6	52.0	55.6	62.2	77.0	81.2	89.6	94.9	98.9	101.9
Foreign liabilities	81.3	81.8	83.1	79.8	77.6	75.9	74.5	86.1	86.8	84.5	86.4	88.0	86.4
Net domestic assets	287.9	285.4	283.9	272.5	273.2	269.9	265.3	268.3	268.3	261.0	263.9	264.5	284.8
Domestic credit	361.0	360.4	361.9	359.4	355.7	354.2	356.2	352.5	354.1	357.3	358.5	361.0	368.7
- Net credit to government	94.4	95.4	95.3	94.5	89.7	89.2	93.3	89.7	89.1	92.3	91.4	92.9	101.0
- Net credit to property funds	4.9	5.0	5.0	5.3	5.2	4.9	4.6	4.2	4.9	4.8	4.3	3.1	1.0
- Total credit households and enterprises	261.7	260.0	261.6	259.6	260.8	260.1	258.3	258.6	260.1	260.2	262.8	265.0	266.7
- Credit to SKK	253.6	251.0	251.9	249.3	250.0	249.5	247.6	247.1	247.7	247.7	249.9	251.6	252.3
- Credit to enterprises	235.0	232.7	233.9	231.6	232.6	232.3	230.7	230.4	231.2	231.5	233.8	235.7	235.8
- Credit to households	18.6	18.3	18.0	17.7	17.4	17.2	16.9	16.7	16.5	16.2	16.1	15.9	16.5
- Credit in foreign currency	8.1	9.0	9.7	10.3	10.8	10.6	10.7	11.5	12.4	12.5	12.9	13.4	14.4
Liquid liabilities [M2]	253.2	248.0	246.9	241.3	247.6	249.6	253.0	259.2	262.7	266.1	272.4	275.4	300.3
Money [M1]	116.3	108.4	106.2	100.3	104.4	103.3	105.9	110.8	112.5	115.2	116.5	119.5	128.9
Quasi money	136.9	139.6	140.7	141.0	143.2	146.3	147.1	148.4	150.2	150.9	155.9	155.9	171.4
Other items net	73.1	75.0	78.0	86.9	82.5	84.3	90.9	84.2	85.8	96.3	94.6	96.5	83.9

Table A6.1

Monetary Survey (current exchange rates)

(billions of korunys)

(continued)

	1/01/1995	1/31/1995	2/28/1995	3/31/1995	4/28/1995	5/31/1995	6/30/1995	7/31/1995	8/31/1995	9/30/1995	10/31/1995	11/30/1995	12/31/1995
Net foreign assets	15.6	18.0	18.2	22.2	23.5	27.2	36.7	43.1	49.6	52.4	54.3	57.9	63.9
Foreign assets	101.8	103.8	106.6	112.8	116.1	122.7	130.8	130.3	135.2	136.1	135.4	142.7	150.1
Foreign liabilities	86.2	85.8	88.4	90.6	92.6	95.5	94.1	87.2	85.6	83.7	81.1	84.8	86.2
Net domestic assets	279.1	270.3	273.9	269.8	273.2	271.5	266.6	265.0	265.6	265.7	265.4	268.1	293.3
Domestic credit	367.5	361.1	366.3	373.1	371.6	374.4	375.8	376.5	377.5	379.8	379.7	387.0	395.2
- Net credit to government	99.3	93.7	96.2	94.1	90.3	91.0	89.7	87.1	85.9	85.2	81.7	88.1	91.0
- Net credit to property funds	1.0	0.9	0.9	0.8	0.4	1.8	2.0	1.6	1.0	1.3	0.4	0.3	-2.3
- Total credit households and	267.2	266.5	269.2	278.2	280.9	281.6	284.1	287.8	290.6	293.3	297.6	298.6	306.5
enterprises													
- Credit to SKK	252.8	252.6	253.2	260.9	264.2	264.8	267.5	269.7	271.8	273.4	276.8	277.2	283.8
- Credit to enterprises	236.4	236.4	237.3	245.2	248.7	249.5	252.3	254.7	256.9	258.6	262.1	262.7	268.5
- Credit to households	16.4	16.2	15.9	15.7	15.5	15.3	15.2	15.0	14.9	14.8	14.7	14.5	15.3
- Credit in foreign currency	14.4	13.9	16.0	17.3	16.7	16.8	16.6	18.1	18.8	19.9	20.8	21.4	22.7
Liquid liabilities [M2]	294.7	288.3	292.1	292.0	296.7	296.7	303.3	308.1	315.2	318.1	319.7	326.0	357.2
Money [M1]	123.2	114.7	116.8	114.6	119.2	119.6	121.2	123.9	126.8	130.7	130.0	134.1	148.4
Quasi money	171.5	173.6	175.3	177.4	177.5	179.1	182.1	184.2	188.4	187.4	189.7	191.9	208.8
Other items net	88.4	90.8	92.4	103.3	98.4	102.9	109.2	111.5	111.9	114.1	114.3	118.9	101.9

	1/01/1996	1/31/1996	2/29/1996	3/31/1996	4/30/1996	5/30/1996	6/30/1996	7/31/1996	8/31/1996	9/30/1996	10/31/1996	11/30/1996	12/31/1996
Net foreign assets	64.1	63.9	65.9	64.4	62.2	62.2	57.7	58.0	61.0	59.6	57.1	56.2	65.0
Foreign assets	153.5	149.7	150.5	150.6	149.2	149.2	145.5	146.3	153.2	151.6	146.9	149.4	187.8
Foreign liabilities	89.4	85.8	84.6	86.2	87.0	87.0	87.8	88.3	92.2	92.0	89.8	93.2	122.8
Net domestic assets	293.3	285.9	290.9	297.2	295.6	302.8	310.2	314.0	316.0	316.9	319.9	331.7	351.9
Domestic credit	395.3	392.2	400.2	407.8	409.5	409.9	420.3	421.0	429.5	431.9	437.1	443.8	455.2
- Net credit to government	91.1	83.2	87.8	86.4	84.9	80.5	82.9	80.0	82.2	83.9	83.6	84.2	96.2
- Net credit to property funds	-2.3	-1.7	-2.4	-1.9	-2.1	-1.0	-1.4	-2.5	-2.3	-2.8	-3.1	-3.3	-3.2
- Total credit households and	306.5	310.7	314.8	323.3	326.7	330.4	338.8	343.5	349.6	350.8	356.6	362.9	362.2
enterprises													
- Credit to SKK	283.8	283.8	288.3	293.4	294.9	297.6	303.8	307.0	311.1	311.7	317.5	324.0	331.4
- Credit to enterprises	268.5	268.6	273.3	278.5	280.1	282.7	288.8	291.9	295.8	296.1	301.5	307.4	313.6
- Credit to households	15.3	15.2	15.0	14.9	14.8	14.9	15.0	15.1	15.3	15.6	16.0	16.6	17.8
- Credit in foreign currency	22.7	26.9	26.5	29.9	31.8	32.8	35.0	36.5	38.5	39.1	39.1	38.9	30.8
Liquid liabilities [M2]	357.4	349.8	356.8	361.6	357.8	365.0	367.9	372.0	377.0	376.5	377.0	387.9	416.9
Money [M1]	148.4	137.4	140.5	143.8	140.6	143.2	147.2	147.8	150.2	153.7	149.5	156.1	173.9
Quasi money	209.0	212.4	216.3	217.8	217.2	221.8	220.7	224.2	226.8	222.8	227.5	231.8	243.0
Other items net	102.0	106.3	109.3	110.6	113.9	107.1	110.1	107.0	113.5	115.0	117.2	112.1	103.3

Table A6.1
Monetary Survey (current exchange rates)
(billions of korunys)

	1/01/1997	1/31/1997	2/28/1997	3/31/1997
(continued)				
Net foreign assets	65.0	61.6	67.0	64.6
Foreign assets	187.8	189.8	202.0	201.8
Foreign liabilities	122.8	128.2	135.0	137.2
Net domestic assets	351.9	342.8	338.4	342.2
Domestic credit	455.2	447.2	449.8	458.2
- Net credit to government	96.2	90.9	93.6	97.8
- Net credit to property funds	-3.2	-2.8	-2.2	-2.1
- Total credit households and enterprises	362.2	359.1	358.4	362.5
- Credit to SKK	331.4	327.8	328.1	331.9
- Credit to enterprises	313.6	309.8	310.1	313.7
- Credit to households	17.8	18.0	18.0	18.2
- Credit in foreign currency	30.8	31.3	30.3	30.6
Liquid liabilities [M2]	416.9	404.3	405.4	406.8
Money [M1]	173.9	153.8	154.8	156.2
Quasi money	243.0	250.5	250.6	250.6
Other items net	103.3	104.4	111.4	116.0

Source: National Bank of Slovakia.

167

Table A6.2
Monthly Interest Rates (1993-1996)

	Short-term deposit rates	Medium-term deposit rates	Long-term deposit rates	Short-term lending rates	Medium-term lending rates	Long-term lending rates
Jan-93	10.2	12.8	18.5	17.0	15.2	9.8
Feb-93	10.3	12.8	18.5	17.3	15.2	9.9
Mar-93	10.5	12.8	18.5	18.3	16.0	10.2
Apr-93	10.5	12.9	18.5	18.3	16.1	10.3
May-93	10.6	12.9	18.5	18.4	16.0	10.4
Jun-93	10.7	12.9	18.3	18.2	15.8	9.8
Jul-93	10.8	13.1	18.3	18.1	15.9	9.9
Aug-93	10.9	13.1	18.3	17.8	15.7	10.1
Sep-93	12.5	13.3	17.8	17.6	16.4	10.2
Oct-93	12.4	13.3	17.7	16.2	16.4	9.9
Nov-93	13.6	14.8	15.6	16.1	16.6	10.4
Dec-93	13.6	14.7	16.5	16.3	16.6	11.1
Jan-94	13.6	14.7	16.7	17.0	17.0	11.4
Feb-94	13.7	14.7	16.5	16.1	17.0	11.4
Mar-94	13.7	14.7	16.4	16.7	17.1	11.2
Apr-94	13.9	14.8	16.3	16.5	17.3	11.3
May-94	13.8	14.7	16.1	17.4	17.8	11.4
Jun-94	13.7	14.7	16.1	17.3	17.8	11.5
Jul-94	13.8	14.8	15.8	16.9	17.8	11.5
Aug-94	13.5	14.6	15.0	16.8	17.8	11.5
Sep-94	13.6	14.7	15.6	16.8	17.9	11.6
Oct-94	13.5	14.7	15.5	16.6	17.7	11.7
Nov-94	13.4	14.6	15.2	16.4	17.8	11.7
Dec-94	13.4	14.5	14.5	16.5	17.6	11.3
Jan-95	13.3	14.4	14.6	15.6	17.4	11.6
Feb-95	13.1	15.4	10.0	15.7	17.2	11.5
Mar-95	13.2	15.4	9.9	15.0	17.1	11.7
Apr-95	11.5	14.6	9.8	14.8	17.1	11.5
May-95	11.1	14.6	9.5	14.7	17.0	11.5
Jun-95	11.0	14.6	9.4	14.4	16.7	11.1
Jul-95	10.9	14.6	9.3	14.1	16.6	10.6
Aug-95	10.7	14.6	9.1	14.2	16.5	10.7
Sep-95	10.7	14.6	8.8	14.0	16.5	11.1
Oct-95	10.2	13.3	8.8	13.3	16.3	10.6
Nov-95	9.6	12.3	8.5	12.9	16.0	10.4
Dec-95	10.1	12.9	7.7	13.7	16.3	10.3
Jan-96	9.9	12.7	5.5	13.9	16.2	10.6
Feb-96	9.6	12.0	5.8	13.4	15.5	10.5
Mar-96	8.4	10.8	5.8	12.8	15.3	10.5
Apr-96	8.4	10.5	5.7	12.8	15.1	10.7
May-96	8.3	10.4	5.6	12.0	14.8	10.5
Jun-96	8.5	9.9	5.5	11.9	14.3	10.3
Jul-96	8.6	10.6	5.5	11.8	14.2	10.1
Aug-96	8.8	10.7	5.3	12.1	14.0	10.0
Sep-96	8.9	10.6	5.3	12.0	13.9	9.9
Oct-96	8.8	10.6	5.2	12.2	13.6	9.9
Nov-96	8.9	10.7	5.1	12.4	13.6	9.8
Dec-96	8.9	10.6	4.9	12.0	13.0	9.3

Source: National Bank of Slovakia.

Table A6.3
Money Supply
(Billions of korunys)

	01/01/1993	31/1/93	28/2/93	31/3/93	30/4/93	31/5/93	30/6/93	31/7/93	31/8/93	30/9/93	31/10/93	30/11/93	12/31/1993
Liquid liabilities [M2]	213.6	204.3	202.9	207.0	211.6	216.4	215.7	222.6	222.4	224.0	226.1	231.6	253.2
Money [M1]	108.2	96.6	94.4	92.3	95.9	98.7	98.0	102.3	101.2	101.2	100.8	104.3	116.3
Currency outside Banks	30.9	18.1	17.8	20.3	22.4	23.4	24.7	25.3	25.9	25.7	22.5	24.0	25.1
Demand deposits	77.3	78.5	76.6	72.0	73.5	75.3	73.3	77.0	75.3	75.5	78.3	80.3	91.2
- households	26.5	33.7	33.6	32.4	31.5	31.6	30.3	29.9	29.0	28.4	31.3	31.0	31.3
- enterprises	50.0	44.1	41.2	37.5	40.3	42.5	42.0	46.2	45.3	46.5	46.5	49.0	58.9
- insurance company	0.8	0.7	1.8	2.1	1.7	1.2	1.0	0.9	1.0	0.6	0.5	0.3	1.0
Quasi money	105.4	107.7	108.5	114.7	115.7	117.7	117.7	120.3	121.2	122.8	125.3	127.3	136.9
Time and savings deposits	92.8	94.0	94.6	98.1	97.9	99.5	98.7	98.3	97.9	98.1	99.7	100.4	108.4
- households	72.9	75.3	75.2	74.7	74.3	74.2	74.2	73.8	72.9	72.6	73.5	73.9	82.2
- enterprises	5.0	5.1	5.5	9.4	9.9	10.9	10.1	10.3	10.8	10.8	11.6	12.1	11.8
- insurance company	14.9	13.6	13.9	14.0	13.7	14.4	14.4	14.2	14.2	14.7	14.6	14.4	14.4
Foreign currency deposits	12.6	13.7	13.9	16.6	17.8	18.2	19.0	22.0	23.3	24.7	25.6	26.9	28.5
- households	10.7	11.0	11.4	12.4	12.9	14.0	13.8	17.4	19.0	20.4	21.3	22.5	24.1
- enterprises	1.9	2.7	2.5	4.2	4.9	4.2	5.2	4.6	4.3	4.3	4.3	4.4	4.4

	01/01/1994	01/31/1994	02/28/1994	03/31/1994	04/30/1994	05/31/1994	06/30/1994	07/30/1994	08/31/1994	09/30/1994	10/31/1994	11/30/1994	12/31/1994
Liquid liabilities [M2]	253.2	248.0	246.9	241.3	247.6	249.6	253.0	259.2	262.7	266.1	272.4	275.4	300.3
Money [M1]	116.3	108.4	106.2	100.3	104.4	103.3	105.9	110.8	112.5	115.2	116.5	119.5	128.9
Currency outside banks	25.1	26.3	27.7	27.6	28.6	28.8	29.8	31.0	31.8	32.3	32.7	33.2	34.1
Demand deposits	91.2	82.1	78.5	72.7	75.8	74.5	76.1	79.8	80.7	82.9	83.8	86.3	94.8
- households	31.3	31.1	30.8	30.1	30.1	30.0	30.0	30.2	30.2	30.0	29.8	30.1	31.5
- enterprises	58.9	50.8	46.3	41.2	44.8	43.6	45.3	48.0	49.1	51.7	53.0	55.2	61.7
- insurance company	1.0	0.2	1.4	1.4	0.9	0.9	0.8	1.6	1.4	1.2	1.0	1.0	1.6
Quasi money	136.9	139.6	140.7	141.0	143.2	146.3	147.1	148.4	150.2	150.9	155.9	155.9	171.4
Time and savings deposits	108.4	109.6	110.0	109.6	110.6	112.6	113.0	113.4	114.3	115.3	118.6	118.8	133.0
- households	82.2	82.0	82.1	82.0	82.3	82.6	83.2	83.6	84.3	84.7	85.6	86.6	98.0
- enterprises	11.8	12.6	12.8	12.6	13.3	14.9	14.8	15.2	15.3	16.0	18.3	17.4	20.2
- insurance company	14.4	15.0	15.1	15.0	15.0	15.1	15.0	14.6	14.7	14.6	14.7	14.8	14.8
Foreign currency deposits	28.5	30.0	30.7	31.4	32.6	33.7	34.1	35.0	35.9	35.6	37.3	37.1	38.4
- households	24.1	25.6	26.3	27.0	27.7	28.5	29.2	29.8	30.8	30.6	30.9	31.2	32.3
- enterprises	4.4	4.4	4.4	4.4	4.9	5.2	4.9	5.2	5.1	5.0	6.4	5.9	6.1

Table A6.3
Money Supply
(billions of korunys)

(continued)

	01/01/1995	01/31/1995	02/28/1995	03/31/1995	04/28/1995	05/31/1995	06/30/1995	07/31/1995	08/31/1995	09/30/1995	10/31/1995	11/30/1995	12/31/1995
Liquid liabilities [M2]	294.7	288.3	292.1	292.0	296.7	298.7	303.3	308.1	315.2	318.1	319.7	326.0	357.2
Money [M1]	123.2	114.7	116.8	114.6	119.2	119.6	121.2	123.9	126.8	130.7	130.0	134.1	148.4
Currency outside banks	28.1	28.2	28.6	28.2	29.5	29.4	30.3	30.4	31.2	32.0	31.8	32.7	34.5
Demand deposits	95.1	86.5	88.2	86.4	89.7	90.2	90.9	93.5	95.6	98.7	98.2	101.4	113.9
- households	31.5	32.0	32.3	32.1	32.8	33.2	33.6	34.2	34.3	34.8	34.9	35.5	37.4
- enterprises	62.0	53.0	53.9	51.8	54.1	54.8	55.5	57.8	59.7	62.1	62.0	64.6	75.0
- insurance company	1.6	1.5	2.0	2.5	2.8	2.2	1.8	1.5	1.6	1.8	1.3	1.3	1.5
Quasi money	171.5	173.6	175.3	177.4	177.5	179.1	182.1	184.2	188.4	187.4	189.7	191.9	208.8
Time and savings deposits	133.1	135.2	137.2	138.3	138.4	139.9	142.5	144.4	148.6	147.1	150.1	152.4	169.1
- households	98.0	99.4	100.7	101.8	102.7	103.9	105.4	106.5	107.7	108.6	110.6	112.6	125.7
- enterprises	20.3	21.0	21.7	21.7	21.0	20.3	21.6	22.0	25.0	22.7	23.4	23.8	27.7
- insurance company	14.8	14.8	14.8	14.8	14.7	15.7	15.5	15.9	15.9	15.8	16.1	16.0	15.7
Foreign currency deposits	38.4	38.4	38.1	39.1	39.1	39.2	39.6	39.8	39.8	40.3	39.6	39.5	39.7
- households	32.3	33.0	33.4	33.8	34.1	34.3	34.7	35.0	34.9	35.3	35.1	35.0	35.4
- enterprises	6.1	5.4	4.7	5.3	5.0	4.9	4.9	4.8	4.9	5.0	4.5	4.5	4.3

	01/01/1996	01/31/1996	02/29/1996	03/31/1996	04/30/1996	05/30/1996	06/30/1996	07/31/1996	08/31/1996	09/30/1996	10/31/1996	11/30/1996	12/31/1996
Liquid liabilities [M2]	357.4	349.8	356.8	361.6	357.8	365.0	367.9	372.0	377.0	376.5	377.0	387.9	416.9
Money [M1]	148.4	137.4	140.5	143.8	140.6	143.2	147.2	147.8	150.2	153.7	149.5	156.1	173.9
Currency outside banks	34.5	34.3	35.9	36.3	36.9	37.4	39.0	39.1	40.6	41.6	41.6	42.8	43.5
Demand deposits	113.9	103.1	104.6	107.5	103.7	105.8	108.2	108.7	109.6	112.1	107.9	113.3	130.4
- households	37.4	38.7	39.4	39.7	40.6	41.1	42.3	43.0	43.8	43.7	43.6	44.5	46.2
- enterprises	75.0	62.8	63.0	65.8	61.5	63.0	64.1	64.5	64.6	67.0	63.2	67.7	82.5
- insurance company	1.5	1.6	2.2	2.0	1.6	1.7	1.8	1.2	1.2	1.4	1.1	1.1	1.7
Quasi money	209.0	212.4	216.3	217.8	217.2	221.8	220.7	224.2	226.8	222.8	227.5	231.8	243.0
Time and savings deposits	169.0	172.4	176.1	177.9	177.7	182.8	182.3	185.7	187.3	184.1	187.8	191.9	201.2
- households	125.7	128.4	129.9	130.6	131.0	132.3	133.5	134.2	134.9	135.1	135.9	136.9	148.4
- enterprises	27.6	28.1	29.8	29.9	29.9	33.2	31.2	34.0	34.5	31.4	34.4	37.6	35.0
- insurance company	15.7	15.9	16.4	17.4	16.8	17.3	17.6	17.5	17.9	17.6	17.5	17.4	17.8
Foreign currency deposit	40.0	40.0	40.2	39.9	39.5	39.0	38.4	38.5	39.5	38.7	39.7	39.9	41.8
- households	35.5	35.2	34.9	34.3	34.0	33.9	33.8	33.5	34.0	34.0	34.6	34.7	35.9
- enterprises	4.5	4.8	5.3	5.6	5.5	5.1	4.6	5.0	5.5	4.7	5.1	5.2	5.9

Table A6.3
Money Supply
(billions of korunys)

	01/01/1997	01/31/1997	02/28/1997	03/31/1997
(continued)				
Liquid liabilities [M2]	416.9	404.3	405.4	406.8
Money [M1]	173.9	153.8	154.8	156.2
Currency outside banks	43.5	43.4	43.9	44.7
Demand deposits	130.4	110.4	110.9	111.5
- households	46.2	48.0	48.7	48.6
- enterprises	82.5	61.1	60.0	61.3
- insurance company	1.7	1.3	2.2	1.6
Quasi money	243.0	250.5	250.6	250.6
Time and savings deposits	201.2	209.2	209.6	209.5
- households	148.4	149.6	150.2	150.6
- enterprises	35.0	41.6	41.4	40.4
- insurance company	17.8	18.0	18.0	18.5
Foreign currency deposits	41.8	41.3	41.0	41.1
- households	35.9	35.9	36.4	36.2
- enterprises	5.9	5.4	4.6	4.9

Source: National Bank of Slovakia.

Table A6.4
Monetary Base
(billions of korunys)

	Jan-94	Feb-94	Mar-94	Apr-94	May-94	Jun-94	Jul-94	Aug-94	Sep-94	Oct-94	Nov-94	Dec-94
Monetary base	42.99	43.45	41.53	40.73	42.34	44.61	46.02	48.24	50.75	50.24	51.46	53.07
Uses of monetary base	42.99	43.45	41.53	40.73	42.34	44.61	46.02	48.24	50.75	50.24	51.46	53.07
Currency in circulation	29.49	30.07	30.90	31.47	32.10	32.84	34.20	34.86	35.84	36.35	36.87	37.21
Reserves	13.51	13.37	10.63	9.25	10.24	11.77	11.82	13.38	14.92	13.89	14.59	15.86
Required reserves	12.79	13.55	13.99	13.31	13.11	13.07	12.91	13.10	13.42	13.54	13.72	14.08
Excess reserves	0.72	-0.18	-3.36	-4.06	-2.81	-1.30	-1.09	0.29	1.50	0.34	0.87	1.79
Bills of NBS outside NBS	0.00	0.00	0.00	0.00	0.00	0.00	0.00	0.00	0.00	0.00	0.00	0.00
Resources of monetary base	42.99	43.45	41.53	40.73	42.34	44.61	46.02	48.24	50.75	50.24	51.46	53.07
Net foreign assets	-15.85	-17.32	-15.02	-12.65	-9.63	-7.65	-5.21	-1.92	3.82	8.63	12.05	15.02
Reserves	13.55	12.14	14.00	15.94	18.69	19.74	23.29	37.27	41.48	44.85	49.14	49.04
Net foreign liabilities	29.40	29.46	29.02	28.59	28.32	27.40	28.51	39.20	37.67	36.22	37.08	34.02
Net credit to government	46.11	49.18	51.24	50.10	49.76	47.62	48.41	48.32	44.61	41.42	38.36	38.59
Net credit without treasury bills	45.62	48.58	50.68	49.67	49.45	47.44	48.18	47.84	43.41	41.33	38.17	38.23
Holding of treasury bills	0.49	0.60	0.56	0.43	0.30	0.18	0.22	0.48	1.20	0.10	0.19	0.36
Credits to banks (without redistributed credit)	8.00	7.34	1.75	3.01	3.22	3.98	3.34	1.66	1.34	1.64	1.97	1.96
Refinancing	3.88	3.71	0.35	1.18	0.11	1.75	2.21	0.70	0.09	0.00	0.00	
Bills of exchange	2.85	2.37	1.23	0.42	0.21	0.27	0.47	0.87	1.25	1.64	1.97	1.96
Lombard credit	0.09	0.38	0.16	1.05	1.92	1.83	0.66	0.09		0.00	0.00	
SWAP's	1.18	0.88	0.01	0.36	0.98	0.13				0.00	0.00	
Other	4.73	4.25	3.56	0.27	-1.01	0.65	-0.53	0.17	0.98	-1.47	-0.93	-2.50
Net domestic assets	58.85	60.77	56.55	53.38	51.97	52.26	51.22	50.15	46.92	41.59	39.39	38.05

	Jan-95	Feb-95	Mar-95	Apr-95	May-95	Jun-95	Jul-95	Aug-95	Sep-95	Oct-95	Nov-95	Dec-95
Monetary base	47.47	50.23	49.32	49.14	50.15	50.53	51.11	54.87	58.95	64.57	64.90	71.81
Uses of monetary base	47.47	50.23	49.32	49.11	50.15	50.53	51.11	54.87	58.95	64.57	64.90	71.81
Currency in circulation	32.86	32.31	32.67	33.30	33.97	34.81	35.40	35.37	36.64	37.37	37.63	40.00
Reserves	14.61	16.89	16.65	15.50	15.46	15.72	15.71	16.50	16.49	17.02	17.20	17.85
Required reserves	14.53	15.35	15.07	15.26	15.37	15.65	15.73	15.95	16.36	16.89	17.07	17.28
Excess reserves	0.09	1.54	1.58	0.24	0.08	0.07	-0.01	0.55	0.13	0.13	0.13	0.58
Bills of NBS outside NBS	0.00	0.00	0.00	0.00	0.00	0.00	0.00	0.00	0.00	0.00	0.00	0.00
Resources of monetary base	47.47	50.23	49.32	49.14	50.15	50.53	51.11	54.87	58.95	64.57	64.90	71.81
Net foreign assets	17.28	18.18	20.15	21.42	24.91	34.78	41.20	46.49	48.42	51.96	57.88	64.25
Reserves	53.45	53.54	56.79	60.31	63.85	73.87	78.23	82.29	80.98	83.52	89.18	95.20
Net foreign liabilities	36.17	35.36	36.64	38.89	38.95	39.09	37.03	35.80	32.55	31.57	31.30	30.94
Net credit to government	36.60	37.20	33.86	32.28	30.97	21.65	18.27	16.41	12.22	21.13	17.98	17.74
Net credit without treasury bills	36.12	36.98	33.76	31.40	30.05	18.38	15.96	16.16	11.91	21.08	17.60	17.73
Holding of treasury bills	0.48	0.23	0.11	0.88	0.92	3.28	2.31	0.26	0.31	0.05	0.38	0.02
Credits to banks (without redistributed credit)	1.73	1.42	1.03	0.61	0.37	0.33	0.35	0.39	0.52	0.76	1.05	1.28
Refinancing	0.00	0.00	0.00	0.00	0.00	0.00	0.00	0.00	0.00	0.00	0.00	0.00
Bills of exchange	1.73	1.42	1.03	0.61	0.37	0.33	0.35	0.39	0.52	0.76	1.05	1.28
Lombard credit	0.00	0.00	0.00	0.00	0.00	0.00	0.00	0.00	0.00	0.00	0.00	0.00
SWAP's	0.00	0.00	0.00	0.00	0.00	0.00	0.00	0.00	0.00	0.00	0.00	0.00
Other	-8.15	-6.57	-5.72	-5.20	-6.11	-6.22	-8.71	-8.43	-2.22	-9.90	-12.04	-11.53
Net domestic assets	30.18	32.05	29.17	27.69	25.24	15.76	9.91	8.37	10.52	11.99	6.99	7.49

Table A6.4
Monetary Base
(billions of korunys)

(continued)

	Jan-96	Feb-96	Mar-96	Apr-96	May-96	Jun-96	Jul-96	Aug-96	Sep-96	Oct-96	Nov-96	Dec-96
Monetary base	74.90	77.56	79.01	77.94	81.38	79.52	79.37	87.49	87.85	87.04	87.39	88.41
Uses of monetary base	74.90	77.56	79.01	77.94	81.38	79.52	79.37	87.49	87.85	87.04	87.39	88.41
Currency in circulation	40.43	40.86	41.99	42.92	44.11	44.95	46.23	46.99	48.06	48.95	49.38	52.43
Reserves	17.81	18.93	18.48	19.01	19.20	19.27	19.42	32.61	33.26	33.38	33.65	34.52
Required reserves	17.68	18.81	18.29	18.90	19.07	19.01	19.27	32.49	33.08	33.33	33.52	33.62
Excess reserves	0.13	0.12	0.19	0.11	0.13	0.26	0.15	0.12	0.18	0.05	0.13	0.90
Bills of NBS outside NBS	16.66	16.66	16.66	16.66	16.66	16.66	16.66	16.66	16.66	16.66	16.66	16.66
Resources of monetary base	74.90	77.56	79.01	77.94	81.38	79.52	79.37	87.49	87.85	87.04	87.39	88.41
Net foreign assets	70.70	71.70	74.42	75.83	74.69	74.48	76.53	83.34	84.13	83.80	81.30	82.85
Reserves	100.20	100.79	103.34	104.26	103.84	103.00	104.88	111.36	112.15	111.78	109.14	111.22
Net foreign liabilities	29.50	29.10	28.92	28.43	29.15	28.52	28.35	28.02	28.02	27.97	27.84	28.37
Net credit to government	14.88	15.17	14.84	13.13	17.51	17.82	17.22	18.22	17.18	17.60	20.04	21.56
Net credit without treasury bills	14.88	14.90	14.84	12.51	14.92	15.46	14.99	12.62	12.58	14.55	14.67	15.89
Holding of treasury bills	0.00	0.27	0.00	0.62	2.60	2.36	2.23	5.60	4.60	3.06	5.37	5.67
Credits to banks (without redistributed credit)	1.27	1.09	0.84	0.67	0.45	0.35	0.39	0.45	0.70	1.06	1.42	1.58
Refinancing	0.00	0.00	0.00	0.00	0.00	0.00	0.00	0.00	0.00	0.00	0.00	0.00
Bills of exchange	1.27	1.09	0.84	0.67	0.45	0.35	0.39	0.45	0.70	1.06	1.42	1.58
Lombard credit												
SWAP's												
Other	-11.96	-10.40	-11.08	-11.83	-11.41	-13.36	-14.93	-14.96	-14.58	-15.75	-15.85	-17.60
Net domestic assets	4.20	5.86	4.59	1.97	6.55	4.82	2.68	3.71	3.31	2.91	5.61	5.54

	Jan-97	Feb-97	Mar-97	Apr-97
Monetary base	86.23	88.41	90.30	90.38
Uses of monetary base	86.23	88.41	90.30	90.38
Currency in circulation	52.14	51.10	51.77	51.88
Reserves	34.10	37.05	36.37	36.60
Required reserves	34.23	36.08	36.16	36.33
Excess reserves	-0.13	0.98	0.22	0.28
Bills of NBS outside NBS	0.00	0.00	0.00	0.00
Resources of monetary base	86.23	88.41	90.30	90.38
Net foreign assets	80.24	85.68	86.51	86.75
Reserves	108.09	112.92	114.53	114.91
Net foreign liabilities	27.85	27.24	28.04	28.16
Net credit to government	22.34	16.66	17.72	16.81
Net credit without treasury bills	13.83	13.00	13.88	13.86
Holding of treasury bills	8.51	3.66	3.84	2.95
Credits to banks (without redistributed credit)	1.54	1.49	1.56	1.56
Refinancing	0.00	0.00	0.00	0.00
Bills of exchange	1.54	1.49	1.56	1.56
Lombard credit				
SWAP's				
Other	-17.88	-16.42	-15.53	-14.75
Net domestic assets	6.00	1.73	3.75	3.62

Source: National Bank of Slovakia.

Table A6.5
Credit (millions of Sk)

SHORT-TERM

	Total	Nonfinancial organization			Money organization			Insurance company			Government sector			Nonprofit organization			Small enterprises	Households
		Total	Public	Private	Total	Public	Private	Total	Public	Private	Total	Republic extrabudgetary funds	Local extrabudgetary funds	Total	Public	Private		
1/1/93	82927.5	81348.0	61502.3	19382.8	0.3	..	0.3	..	..	..	272.9	68.4	204.5	37.2	..	34.2	963.6	29.6
Jan-93	83179.3	80820.7	58110.8	21762.5	0.6	..	0.6	..	..	..	235.6	127.0	108.6	37.2	..	33.1	805.9	19.5
Feb-93	84729.7	82694.8	58252.1	23447.2	0.7	..	0.7	..	..	..	211.3	106.7	101.7	40.5	..	14.5	882.9	24.2
Mar-93	86208.5	84266.8	58702.3	24571.4	0.9	..	0.9	..	..	..	237.6	138.3	96.4	46.3	..	19.1	628.5	30.4
Apr-93	87429.6	85764.1	58751.1	25901.0	..	..	..	..	..	..	79.7	..	76.6	44.7	..	23.4	697.2	27.0
May-93	89597.3	87096.6	59535.1	26373.7	..	..	..	..	..	..	74.5	..	74.5	42.1	..	34.9	1379.1	27.3
Jun-93	92780.0	90810.3	60831.9	27994.1	..	..	..	..	..	..	79.3	..	79.3	39.1	..	33.9	1343.8	31.2
Jul-93	94057.3	92130.3	60654.9	28959.2	92.0	..	92.0	..	..	..	84.9	..	84.9	43.3	..	36.0	1480.9	27.7
Aug-93	94660.5	92475.6	61191.1	28687.1	86.0	..	86.0	..	..	..	78.0	..	78.0	34.9	..	31.1	1703.7	40.6
Sep-93	97080.0	94957.0	62604.4	29618.3	90.7	..	90.7	..	..	..	63.8	..	63.8	36.2	..	32.3	1594.0	48.6
Oct-93	97951.0	95821.0	62080.9	30950.2	92.0	..	11.0	92.7		1.4	47.6	..	47.6	30.2	..	9.9	1525.9	45.1
Nov-93	100507.8	97740.3	64225.7	30403.2	92.5	..	92.5	15.6		15.6	73.2	0.8	72.4	9.5	..	3.6	1866.3	49.5
Dec-93	90671.0	87005.4	53845.8	30088.2	220.7	..	124.1	886.5		30.5	257.8	200.0	57.8	142.3	..	40.6	1900.4	57.4
Jan-94	99242.0	96372.8	61280.0	31813.3	237.6	..	104.0	33.3		33.3	274.0	200.0	74.0	140.8	..	18.4	1888.0	112.5
Feb-94	98278.3	95654.3	61432.2	30993.8	186.8	..	53.2	33.3		33.3	244.9	200.0	44.9	146.2	..	20.7	1789.5	37.6
Mar-94	85845.6	82944.8	50096.3	29828.0	154.9	..	50.0	0.0		0.0	319.0	200.0	119.0	31.4	..	21.1	2187.3	29.7
Apr-94	86985.6	84207.9	49836.0	31272.8	321.7	..	153.8	0.0		0.0	111.7	0.0	111.7	30.0	..	14.9	2067.5	48.9
May-94	86616.5	84090.6	49567.2	31570.0	372.8	..	204.3	0.0		0.0	157.9	0.0	157.9	28.2	..	14.5	1789.0	56.6
Jul-94	87477.9	84666.1	48055.3	33610.8	293.4	..	184.4	0.0		0.0	218.0	0.0	218.0	35.3	..	15.0	2080.7	66.6
Aug-94	88360.1	85688.0	48628.9	33725.7	372.9	..	196.2	0.0		0.0	188.3	0.0	188.3	34.0	..	15.1	1890.7	67.2
Sep-94	89295.1	86611.5	48620.5	34803.3	364.5	..	228.5	0.0		0.0	198.0	0.0	198.0	46.1	..	19.0	1874.0	67.7
Sep-94	90175.7	87336.2	48143.7	35771.4	421.9	..	344.3	23.2		0.0	280.9	173.8	107.1	54.5	..	20.9	1878.2	75.4
Oct-94	91559.3	88489.5	49681.0	35193.6	547.0	..	434.4	0.0		0.0	523.4	396.3	127.1	51.1	..	17.1	1770.4	80.2
Nov-94	94235.9	89871.2	49510.0	36514.1	780.1	..	666.4	0.0		0.0	768.2	547.0	221.2	237.7	..	11.3	2074.4	88.1
Dec-94	95920.8	90956.1	48819.9	38230.5	718.9	..	586.1	549.2		0.0	1074.5	898.4	176.1	35.5	..	8.3	2457.7	82.1
Jan-95	96278.7	91740.9	48298.6	39398.9	1244.1	0.0	1096.7	213.8	213.8	0.0	924.7	798.5	126.2	40.5	27.4	13.1	1708.7	80.1
Feb-95	96596.6	92454.5	48010.6	40396.6	1245.8	1.3	1131.0	0.0	0.0	0.0	820.2	698.4	121.8	37.9	26.6	11.3	1693.6	92.6
Mar-95	104097.9	95613.4	44399.6	47311.3	1466.6	90.5	1262.6	0.0	0.0	0.0	656.6	523.7	132.9	80.6	67.8	12.8	1757.8	92.3
Apr-95	105922.6	97614.5	43450.4	49976.6	1370.5	172.3	1198.2	1.8	1.8	0.0	352.3	215.4	136.9	41.7	27.0	14.7	1826.2	73.4
May-95	106114.0	97532.1	41569.4	51620.5	1508.8	174.4	1334.4	0.0	0.0	0.0	383.7	249.2	134.5	32.5	16.2	15.2	1742.7	87.6
Jun-95	108770.7	100632.2	41152.6	54792.3	1248.5	18.2	1230.3	3.7	3.7	0.0	240.7	98.6	128.8	27.6	11.2	16.4	1476.9	89.3
Jul-95	111154.8	102185.4	41072.2	56002.4	1470.0	17.7	1452.3	0.0	0.0	0.0	536.0	383.7	139.0	27.3	11.5	15.8	1585.9	80.2
Aug-95	111944.6	101970.6	37861.5	59541.5	1462.6	17.7	1439.9	0.6	0.6	0.0	1008.4	876.4	118.7	26.3	10.3	16.0	1816.1	86.3
Sep-95	112504.2	102477.6	36651.3	61353.0	1439.8	17.2	1422.6	0.0	0.0	0.0	1224.8	1070.8	120.0	23.1	9.5	13.6	1624.3	110.4
Oct-95	113849.7	103478.0	35587.1	63565.9	1242.6	16.4	1226.2	9.8	9.8	0.0	1164.5	1024.0	106.5	25.3	10.5	14.8	1662.0	131.5
Nov-95	112685.6	102348.2	32667.2	64883.1	1064.7	15.0	1049.7	0.0	0.0	0.0	988.6	874.0	114.6	35.1	10.7	24.4	1750.1	113.3
Dec-95	105754.1	101244.2	29554.6	66185.6	960.4	0.0	860.4	3.5	3.5	0.0	1095.5	964.7	130.8	33.5	9.8	23.7	1710.2	89.4
Jan-96	103794.5	99446.6	27671.0	66229.7	935.9	0.0	835.9	90.0	0.0	90.0	877.7	766.1	111.6	38.2	13.8	24.4	1647.4	129.4
Feb-96	106492.7	102339.5	28548.1	67712.9	775.4	0.0	624.0	90.0	0.0	90.0	901.3	764.8	136.5	15.8	8.0	7.8	1598.3	152.0
Mar-96	110761.5	106476.2	30073.4	69824.0	818.2	5.0	713.0	90.0	0.0	90.0	960.9	764.8	138.9	14.9	6.8	8.1	1639.1	137.5
Apr-96	110340.4	106417.9	29784.0	70609.0	973.0	5.0	841.0	90.5	0.5	90.0	516.0	365.4	115.6	14.6	6.2	8.4	1588.0	134.1
May-96	111567.1	107651.9	29369.9	71708.3	835.4	5.0	827.3	0.0	0.0	0.0	719.5	564.8	154.7	14.4	6.0	8.4	1578.1	145.0
Jun-96	117500.4	113567.1	30513.1	76470.0	646.5	5.0	632.6	0.0	0.0	0.0	845.3	664.8	180.5	14.2	5.7	8.5	1685.1	153.6
Jul-96	116128.2	112060.4	28984.4	76167.5	687.4	0.0	665.6	0.0	0.0	0.0	832.6	670.0	162.6	17.7	5.9	9.9	1582.4	149.5
Aug-96	120430.9	113499.8	29045.4	78577.6	3465.9	2938.1	523.6	0.0	0.0	0.0	950.9	806.2	144.7	38.5	7.4	29.2	1524.4	152.1
Sep-96	123098.8	114153.7	29448.9	78426.7	4965.0	3556.8	1404.2	0.0	0.0	0.0	1172.2	928.4	243.8	17.5	7.6	7.9	1871.0	165.2

(continued)

Table A6.5
Credit (millions of Sk)

MEDIUM-TERM

	Total	Nonfinancial organization			Money organization			Insurance company			Government sector			Nonprofit organization			Small enterprises	Households
		Total	Public	Private	Total	Public	Private	Total	Public	Private	Total	Republic extrabudgetary funds	Local extrabudgetary funds	Total	Public	Private		
Jan-93	50589.7	42703.2	22740.6	19858.3	10.1	:	:	:	:	:	483.1	9.3	473.8	98.5	:	97.3	4002.3	2887.9
Jan-93	50648.6	42192.5	21379.9	20696.6	10.1	:	:	:	:	:	481.3	18.3	463.0	31.0	:	21.0	4653.5	2855.8
Feb-93	50492.6	41643.1	20760.2	20645.0	10.1	:	:	:	:	:	488.2	19.3	468.9	28.3	:	10.3	5140.8	2712.3
Mar-93	49712.3	42105.5	19756.1	22022.4	10.1	:	:	:	:	:	466.5	15.6	450.9	40.5	:	12.9	4064.9	2657.8
Apr-93	49804.7	42229.6	19585.8	22440.1	10.1	:	10.1	:	:	:	508.6	:	508.6	25.5	:	11.7	4051.0	2632.0
May-93	49740.7	40910.5	19510.2	21186.3	10.1	:	10.1	:	:	:	565.1	:	565.1	27.0	:	10.1	5231.7	2584.0
Jun-93	48874.7	40014.4	18668.7	21130.9	15.1	:	10.1	:	:	:	591.4	:	591.4	32.8	:	9.5	5184.7	2527.3
Jul-93	49585.4	40768.3	19477.4	21053.0	20.1	:	10.1	:	:	:	587.9	:	587.9	29.9	:	12.0	5083.2	2515.4
Aug-93	49911.8	40874.1	19227.5	21352.1	47.2	:	10.1	:	:	:	601.3	:	601.3	31.4	:	28.1	5209.0	2499.4
Sep-93	48565.7	39470.8	17712.9	21560.7	49.4	:	9.9	:	:	:	574.3	:	574.3	38.2	:	35.0	5305.9	2494.1
Oct-93	49167.1	40611.4	17427.0	22963.1	46.3	:	9.9	:	:	:	584.4	:	584.4	27.9	:	13.7	4833.7	2435.7
Nov-93	50757.6	40723.9	17488.6	22638.8	138.7	:	102.2	:	:	:	613.9	:	613.9	26.7	:	13.7	6068.0	2379.6
Dec-93	53468.9	39908.1	17662.7	21631.1	125.7	:	93.6	:	:	:	3894.1	3284.5	609.6	25.8	:	12.0	6145.9	2659.3
Jan-94	52616.5	39594.4	17354.4	21658.5	118.4	:	89.1	0.0	:	0.0	3381.4	2774.2	607.2	31.1	:	0.8	6320.2	2466.8
Feb-94	53751.3	40830.5	18241.1	22047.3	140.9	:	114.6	0.0	:	0.0	3406.3	2774.2	632.1	29.6	:	0.7	6178.3	2449.2
Mar-94	53188.4	40153.4	17207.5	22401.4	135.4	:	112.1	0.0	:	0.0	3891.8	3263.0	628.8	26.8	:	0.5	5986.3	2350.0
Apr-94	51698.2	39356.6	16879.0	21941.3	136.0	:	117.2	0.0	:	0.0	3650.9	3039.8	611.1	27.3	:	0.5	5591.6	2255.3
May-94	52063.5	39527.8	16607.4	22320.7	130.2	:	111.4	0.0	:	0.0	4269.2	3039.8	1229.4	30.9	:	0.5	5798.2	2172.1
Jun-94	49963.3	37928.6	15657.0	22477.1	519.4	:	501.1	0.0	:	0.0	3710.0	2529.6	1180.4	31.7	:	0.3	5573.5	2091.2
Jul-94	49553.3	37472.1	15428.1	21247.9	518.5	:	501.8	0.0	:	0.0	3766.1	2529.6	1236.5	40.1	:	0.3	5633.7	2016.9
Aug-94	49298.0	37554.1	15544.7	21213.5	497.6	:	480.9	0.0	:	0.0	3665.4	2529.6	1335.8	33.3	:	0.3	5294.7	1957.3
Sep-94	48790.8	37173.6	15115.2	21259.7	478.3	:	461.6	0.0	:	0.0	3922.5	2529.6	1392.9	32.3	:	0.3	5153.1	1950.1
Oct-94	48607.3	36848.3	14736.2	21293.5	469.8	:	454.8	0.0	:	0.0	4027.9	2529.6	1498.3	31.9	:	0.0	5235.6	1919.0
Nov-94	47669.0	36083.2	13755.5	21502.2	316.4	:	301.4	5.6	:	5.6	3979.0	2529.6	1449.4	26.9	:	1.6	5252.7	1914.9
Dec-94	46912.0	35442.3	12904.1	21559.3	408.5	:	373.5	25.6	:	25.6	3976.9	2529.6	1447.3	30.3	:	1.4	4791.0	2163.1
Jan-95	46431.3	34189.1	12209.9	21068.4	883.2	0.0	864.7	21.5	0.0	21.5	3537.8	2019.4	1497.7	57.5	53.6	3.9	4983.9	2087.5
Feb-95	46507.3	34507.5	12003.1	21610.1	816.6	0.0	799.6	28.8	0.0	28.8	3432.9	1911.5	1499.7	57.0	53.4	3.6	5080.9	2035.6
Mar-95	46232.7	33780.9	11394.3	21428.6	1269.8	0.0	1254.3	43.1	0.0	43.1	3420.0	1911.5	1485.5	56.0	50.3	5.7	5009.3	1998.1
Apr-95	46817.7	34213.3	11145.7	22243.1	1376.8	0.0	1249.4	52.0	0.0	52.0	3454.1	1911.5	1515.8	57.2	49.3	7.9	5008.5	1983.6
May-95	47127.9	34243.3	10965.5	22411.3	1378.6	0.0	1254.8	151.4	0.0	151.4	3541.3	1911.5	1552.7	53.8	48.5	5.3	5098.6	1979.4
Jun-95	47235.4	34816.8	11105.8	22772.8	1450.5	0.0	1331.7	163.7	0.0	163.7	3078.8	1401.3	1599.6	51.5	44.4	7.1	5001.8	1982.5
Jul-95	47336.7	34725.8	10723.1	23259.6	1509.0	0.0	1387.0	203.3	0.0	203.3	3126.2	1401.3	1646.5	51.5	44.5	7.0	5026.9	1967.2
Aug-95	48876.6	36225.1	10419.6	24418.7	1461.3	0.0	1344.4	209.3	0.0	209.3	3142.5	1401.3	1696.2	51.9	44.9	7.0	5108.6	1954.3
Sep-95	48633.1	36232.8	10180.4	24721.3	1099.7	0.0	1038.1	208.7	0.0	208.7	3122.7	1401.3	1676.4	54.2	42.5	6.7	5214.0	1953.5
Oct-95	50364.0	37852.3	10338.8	25750.5	1183.9	0.0	1065.9	215.3	0.0	215.3	3181.1	1401.3	1734.8	53.4	43.8	4.6	5155.2	1965.2
Nov-95	51266.9	38793.9	10477.5	26561.2	955.2	0.0	841.2	216.1	0.0	216.1	3213.5	1401.3	1767.2	87.7	76.2	6.5	5250.4	1984.4
Dec-95	57437.1	43902.3	12700.3	29436.2	1079.2	0.0	967.6	204.1	0.0	204.1	2991.2	1235.9	1708.8	91.2	64.8	21.9	6083.3	2202.9
Jan-96	57636.1	44850.5	13021.4	30082.7	1069.6	0.0	958.7	114.1	0.0	114.1	2372.1	673.0	1652.0	97.1	40.9	56.2	6089.2	2198.2
Feb-96	60350.8	46951.7	13053.0	32156.7	991.6	0.0	882.8	116.5	0.0	116.5	2285.3	673.0	1564.6	124.8	69.9	54.9	6864.5	2137.3
Mar-96	59823.5	47346.3	11920.1	33616.4	1138.1	0.0	1029.4	112.2	0.0	112.2	2140.5	673.0	1467.5	82.5	45.5	37.0	5935.7	2177.7
Apr-96	61060.4	48709.3	12122.6	34770.6	919.9	0.0	811.3	101.8	0.0	101.8	2074.8	673.0	1401.8	78.8	30.2	48.6	6056.2	2228.4
May-96	62734.7	50080.0	12374.3	35679.4	841.8	0.0	733.2	99.3	0.0	99.3	2260.2	844.0	1381.2	139.6	30.3	109.3	6049.6	2356.2
Jun-96	60742.6	48459.7	9455.5	38969.1	803.2	0.0	694.5	125.0	0.0	125.0	1628.9	276.8	1320.9	139.7	32.1	107.6	6087.7	2572.3
Jul-96	64704.1	52096.3	9991.9	40147.5	772.5	0.0	689.8	124.5	0.0	124.5	1522.3	222.3	1267.0	134.9	32.1	103.6	6278.0	2854.3
Aug-96	65108.5	52049.1	9671.8	40431.6	780.2	0.0	697.5	124.5	0.0	124.5	1533.6	222.3	1280.1	130.1	31.3	99.2	6399.2	3155.0
Sep-96	65469.8	52315.2	9204.0	41159.9	703.3	0.0	634.5	120.3	0.0	120.3	1394.3	114.0	1247.8	122.9	27.8	95.1	6383.4	3484.4

(continued)

Table A6.5
Credit (millions of Sk)

LONG-TERM

		Nonfinancial organization			Money organization			Insurance company			Government sector			Nonprofit organization			Small enterprises	Households
	Total	Total	Public	Private	Total	Public	Private	Total	Public	Private	Total	Republic extrabudgetary funds	Local extrabudgetary funds	Total	Public	Private		
1/1/93	102482.6	80139.0	47107.3	32560.6	..	..	..	..	..	..	157.0	6.1	149.8	13.5	..	13.5	2393.7	16912.7
Jan-93	101138.4	78760.3	45506.4	32779.9	..	..	..	..	..	..	161.2	5.1	155.0	13.5	..	13.5	2204.6	16832.0
Feb-93	101200.0	79742.5	46223.6	33055.4	..	..	..	..	..	..	177.9	5.1	171.7	25.9	..	25.9	3190.8	16743.5
Mar-93	100051.0	78551.9	45137.4	32905.8	..	..	..	..	..	..	173.0	15.8	156.1	15.5	..	15.5	3412.7	16606.1
Apr-93	101689.7	79796.5	46087.3	33173.1	..	..	..	..	..	..	186.8	0.5	185.2	15.5	..	15.5	3405.7	16508.9
May-93	102535.5	80325.5	46189.2	33600.1	..	..	..	..	..	..	193.8		193.8	20.9	..	20.9	3836.6	16380.4
Jun-93	104760.6	82932.2	48621.4	33372.3	..	..	..	..	..	..	193.2		193.2	28.1	..	28.1	3687.3	16257.9
Jul-93	105307.3	85168.7	48816.5	36289.9	..	..	..	..	..	..	202.7		202.7	30.2	..	30.2	3739.5	16133.3
Aug-93	105112.1	85028.5	48352.3	36650.9	62.0	..	..	..	..	..	210.1		210.1	38.2	..	38.2	3731.9	16006.7
Sep-93	104282.8	84595.9	47273.7	37289.8	40.0	..	..	..	..	..	217.0		217.0	46.6	..	46.6	3496.1	15855.5
Oct-93	105713.7	86422.8	47904.2	38478.8	83.0	..	..	..	..	..	229.1		229.1	49.2	..	49.2	3186.3	15710.1
Nov-93	103523.3	84244.5	45336.0	38869.1	123.0	..	..	..	..	..	223.8		223.8	57.3	..	57.3	3245.6	15556.8
Dec-93	116672.3	90356.5	50831.1	39488.4	6521.1	..	6521.1	0.0	0.0	0.0	224.2	2883.4	228.0	59.6	0.0	59.6	3580.9	15698.1
Jan-94	105931.8	83485.6	44594.3	38854.6	0.0	..	0.0	0.0	0.0	0.0	230.6	0.0	230.6	61.0	0.0	61.0	3540.8	15702.0
Feb-94	103704.5	84290.3	44648.1	39607.1	6521.1	..	6521.1	0.0	0.0	0.0	239.8	0.0	239.8	59.8	0.0	59.8	3575.0	15513.9
Mar-94	114745.0	88996.7	48011.4	40950.7	6521.1	..	6521.1	0.0	0.0	0.0	244.0	0.0	244.0	58.4	0.0	58.4	3579.4	15314.7
Apr-94	115331.0	89782.9	48664.6	41074.9	6521.1	..	6521.1	0.0	0.0	0.0	242.0	0.0	242.0	58.1	0.0	58.1	3560.1	15130.0
May-94	115750.3	90273.6	48824.6	41332.6	6521.1	..	6521.1	0.0	0.0	0.0	246.6	0.0	246.6	57.3	0.0	57.3	3670.6	14947.4
Jun-94	114377.0	89134.3	48010.7	40998.0	5916.3	..	5916.3	0.0	0.0	0.0	240.3	0.0	240.3	56.3	0.0	56.3	3609.0	14772.0
Jul-94	113406.6	89308.7	47801.1	41385.6	5916.3	..	5916.3	0.0	0.0	0.0	246.8	0.0	246.8	57.2	0.0	57.2	3243.5	14602.5
Aug-94	113421.3	89367.8	47812.0	41431.6	6244.9	6237.9	7.0	0.0	0.0	0.0	291.0	0.0	291.0	64.5	0.0	64.5	3363.7	14430.0
Sep-94	113241.1	89052.4	47414.2	41512.2	6260.9	6237.9	23.0	0.0	0.0	0.0	177.0	0.0	177.0	66.7	0.0	66.7	3341.5	14212.3
Oct-94	114460.4	90413.5	47809.2	42469.9	6277.9	6237.9	40.0	0.0	0.0	0.0	270.9	0.0	270.9	65.5	0.0	65.5	3427.5	14080.4
Nov-94	114709.0	90500.4	46829.2	43536.2	6524.2	6484.2	40.0	0.0	0.0	0.0	263.9	0.0	263.9	65.0	0.0	65.0	3654.9	13904.0
Dec-94	114806.8	90136.2	46593.6	43383.9	6524.2	6484.2	40.0	0.0	0.0	0.0	267.3	0.0	267.3	64.4	0.0	64.4	3539.5	14231.8
Jan-95	114625.9	89651.6	46225.6	43238.4	6344.0	6304.0	40.0	0.0	0.0	0.0	266.6	0.0	266.6	91.4	91.4	0.0	3921.9	14046.8
Feb-95	114565.7	89941.6	46216.3	43559.3	6344.0	6304.0	40.0	0.0	0.0	0.0	246.6	0.0	246.6	87.9	87.9	0.0	3802.9	13776.1
Mar-95	114898.3	90637.4	45899.4	44554.1	6344.0	6304.0	40.0	0.0	0.0	0.0	241.9	0.0	241.9	86.8	85.6	1.2	3822.8	13596.0
Apr-95	115479.2	91264.8	46444.4	44618.3	6248.4	6208.4	40.0	0.0	0.0	0.0	242.5	0.0	242.5	84.2	83.0	1.2	3911.6	13432.5
May-95	115803.7	92091.7	46173.0	45693.6	6248.4	6208.4	40.0	0.0	0.0	0.0	237.6	0.0	237.6	81.8	80.7	1.1	3570.4	13273.2
Jun-95	115043.7	91755.5	45742.3	45777.3	6248.4	6208.4	40.0	0.0	0.0	0.0	237.5	0.0	237.5	81.2	80.1	1.1	3396.5	13125.7
Jul-95	115170.6	91889.6	44895.8	46769.5	6248.4	6208.4	40.0	0.0	0.0	0.0	238.0	0.0	238.0	78.3	77.2	1.1	3534.1	12984.8
Aug-95	115392.3	92363.8	42425.6	49789.8	6248.4	6208.4	40.0	0.0	0.0	0.0	242.0	0.0	242.0	50.9	49.9	1.0	3445.9	12854.0
Sep-95	116822.7	93406.9	42553.0	50630.7	6643.4	6208.4	435.0	0.0	0.0	0.0	274.0	0.0	274.0	50.4	49.4	1.0	3577.7	12711.1
Oct-95	117224.3	93316.5	41732.1	51365.9	6778.2	6208.4	569.8	0.0	0.0	0.0	258.1	0.0	258.1	48.2	47.2	1.0	3621.7	12572.1
Nov-95	117686.8	93512.8	40786.3	52056.1	6992.2	6208.4	783.8	0.0	0.0	0.0	272.2	0.0	272.2	121.1	70.2	50.9	4183.1	12427.5
Dec-95	124950.0	97636.3	42399.5	54491.7	9119.1	8285.1	834.0	40.5	0.0	40.5	313.0	0.0	313.0	120.3	69.4	50.9	4547.0	13011.1
Jan-96	125902.3	97336.7	41695.7	54914.9	10494.8	9652.8	842.0	40.5	0.0	40.5	381.9	0.0	381.9	118.2	67.3	50.9	4501.9	12883.7
Feb-96	125019.0	96425.9	41399.1	54301.6	10480.8	9651.4	829.4	100.0	0.0	100.0	501.2	0.0	501.2	93.4	42.6	50.8	4604.9	12725.1
Mar-96	126384.8	98192.0	41667.0	55696.3	10620.7	9793.3	827.4	110.0	10.0	100.0	542.4	0.0	542.4	87.8	37.0	50.8	4072.7	12598.3
Apr-96	126679.4	98545.5	41430.3	56320.3	10627.8	9793.6	834.2	110.8	10.8	100.0	587.5	0.0	587.5	97.3	18.2	79.1	4084.6	12478.5
May-96	126862.2	98830.8	41004.0	57026.4	10625.6	9795.7	829.9	110.8	10.8	100.0	863.7	0.0	863.7	45.4	16.3	29.1	4101.5	12353.1
Jun-96	128886.9	100617.6	42268.7	57531.0	10600.7	9776.2	824.5	110.8	10.8	100.0	1040.2	0.0	1040.2	36.7	6.6	30.1	4181.5	12246.8
Jul-96	129553.1	102015.9	43301.2	57910.7	10079.4	9789.8	289.6	112.7	12.7	100.0	1173.3	0.0	1173.3	36.4	6.3	30.1	3954.0	12092.5
Aug-96	129294.8	102766.7	43077.2	58882.1	9082.6	8797.5	285.1	115.0	15.0	100.0	1363.2	0.0	1363.2	23.0	6.0	17.0	3884.8	12026.3
Sep-96	127046.7	100621.3	41899.7	57915.4	8799.9	8520.3	279.6	116.0	16.0	100.0	..	0.0	..	23.3	5.7	17.6	3972.1	11928.5

.. = not available.
Source: National Bank of Slovakia.

Table A7.1
Monthly Price Indices (1993-1996)

	CPI index Jan 1994 = 1	Monthly CPI inflation	Annual CPI inflation	PPI index Jan 1994 = 1	Monthly PPI inflation	Annual PPI inflation
Jan-93	0.86	8.96	17.72	0.93	7.11	15.87
Feb-93	0.87	1.62	19.31	0.94	1.49	15.63
Mar-93	0.88	1.01	20.39	0.95	0.69	16.74
Apr-93	0.89	1.19	21.70	0.95	-0.15	16.70
May-93	0.90	0.52	22.02	0.95	0.29	16.16
Jun-93	0.90	0.42	23.49	0.95	-0.29	15.14
Jul-93	0.91	1.12	23.91	0.95	0.54	15.20
Aug-93	0.93	2.40	26.04	0.97	2.09	18.05
Sep-93	0.96	2.44	27.02	0.98	1.09	19.46
Oct-93	0.97	1.45	26.25	1.00	1.36	19.56
Nov-93	0.98	1.09	25.51	1.00	0.56	18.85
Dec-93	0.99	0.64	25.09	1.00	-0.05	15.54
Jan-94	1.00	1.32	16.32	1.00	-0.23	7.62
Feb-94	1.01	0.76	15.34	1.02	2.18	8.35
Mar-94	1.01	0.46	14.71	1.03	0.45	8.09
Apr-94	1.02	0.42	13.83	1.02	-0.54	7.67
May-94	1.02	0.58	13.90	1.03	0.54	7.94
Jun-94	1.03	0.49	13.98	1.03	0.09	8.35
Jul-94	1.03	0.74	13.55	1.04	1.22	9.08
Aug-94	1.05	1.34	12.37	1.14	9.93	17.46
Sep-94	1.07	2.37	12.30	1.16	1.50	17.93
Oct-94	1.09	1.30	12.12	1.08	-6.66	8.59
Nov-94	1.10	0.70	11.69	1.09	0.86	8.91
Dec-94	1.10	0.62	11.66	1.10	0.42	9.42
Jan-95	1.12	1.41	11.76	1.12	2.11	11.99
Feb-95	1.12	0.49	11.46	1.14	1.45	11.19
Mar-95	1.13	0.30	11.28	1.14	0.37	11.10
Apr-95	1.13	0.41	11.28	1.15	0.69	12.47
May-95	1.13	0.34	11.01	1.15	0.44	12.36
Jun-95	1.14	0.07	10.54	1.16	0.28	12.57
Jul-95	1.15	1.00	10.83	1.16	0.32	11.58
Aug-95	1.15	0.44	9.84	1.17	0.60	2.11
Sep-95	1.17	1.35	8.75	1.17	0.63	1.24
Oct-95	1.17	0.51	7.90	1.18	0.43	8.94
Nov-95	1.18	0.36	7.54	1.18	-0.39	7.59
Dec-95	1.18	0.25	7.15	1.17	-0.08	7.05
Jan-96	1.19	0.71	6.41	1.17	-0.24	4.59
Feb-96	1.19	0.25	6.15	1.19	1.46	4.60
Mar-96	1.20	0.25	6.10	1.19	0.43	4.67
Apr-96	1.20	0.28	5.96	1.19	-0.08	3.87
May-96	1.20	0.49	6.13	1.20	1.01	4.46
Jun-96	1.21	0.17	6.23	1.20	-0.27	3.88
Jul-96	1.21	0.31	5.51	1.20	-0.12	3.43
Aug-96	1.22	0.52	5.60	1.21	0.66	3.49
Sep-96	1.23	0.94	5.16	1.21	0.54	3.39
Oct-96	1.24	0.70	5.36	1.23	0.97	3.94
Nov-96	1.24	0.40	5.41	1.23	0.19	4.55
Dec-96	1.25	0.29	5.44	1.23	0.10	4.74
Jan-97	1.26	1.14	5.89	1.24	1.15	6.19
Feb-97	1.26	0.38	6.02	1.25	0.57	5.26

Source: National Bank of Slovakia.

Table A7.2
Average Monthly Earnings by Sector, 1991-96
(koruny)

	1991	1992	1993	1994	1995	1996
Total economy 1/	3770	4543	5379	6294	7195	8154
Enterprises with 25 or more employees 2/	3776	4483	5275	6160	7144	8221
Agriculture	3771	4149	4556	5191	5835	6579
Industry	3836	4535	5496	6464	7477	8508
Mining and quarrying	4445	5458	6482	7383	8621	9382
Manufacturing	3757	4370	5234	6193	7194	8230
Electricity	4480	6006	7767	8766	9905	10902
Construction	3845	4617	5533	6502	7489	8722
Services						
Financial services and insurance	5260	7667	10386	11770	13529	15328
Real estate	3733	4516	5559	6642	7883	9648
Trade and repairs	3386	4049	4848	5748	6848	8600
Hotels and restaurants	3169	3843	4474	5192	5746	6958
Transport and communications	3840	4427	5467	6634	7742	8810
State administration						
Administration	4189	5110	6179	7350	8350	9818
Education	3547	4448	4706	5157	6205	7005
Health	3942	4605	4813	5443	6247	6947
Other social services	3683	4342	4933	5626	5805	6337
Enterprises with 1 to 24 employees	2844	5118	6675	9039	9074	9722
Employees of private entrepreneurs	4000	4950	5850	5900	6300	6773
Memorandum item						
Minimum wage	2000	2200	2450	2450	2450	2700

Notes: Includes wages, bonuses and other payments. Data based on NACE branch classification of economic activity.
 1991 data are reported in 1992 organizational form; and 1992-94 data are in current organizational form.
1/ 1992-94 data including estimates for earnings in small scale private sector firms.
2/ Includes budgetary organizations and subsidized organizations.
Source: Statistical Office of the Slovak Republic.

Table A7.3
Indices of Monthly Earnings by Sector, 1991-96
(1993 = 100)

	1991	1992	1993	1994	1995	1996
Total economy	70	84	100	117	134	152
Enterprises with 25 or more employees	72	85	100	117	135	156
Agriculture	83	91	100	114	128	144
Industry	70	83	100	118	136	155
Mining and quarrying	69	84	100	114	133	145
Manufacturing	72	83	100	118	137	157
Electricity	58	77	100	113	128	140
Construction	69	83	100	118	135	158
Services						
Financial services and insurance	51	74	100	113	130	148
Real estate	67	81	100	119	142	174
Trade and repairs	70	84	100	119	141	177
Hotels and restaurants	71	86	100	116	128	156
Transport and communications	70	81	100	121	142	161
State administration						
Administration	68	83	100	119	135	159
Education	75	95	100	110	132	149
Health	82	96	100	113	130	144
Other social services	75	88	100	114	118	128
Enterprises with 1 to 24 employees	43	77	100	135	136	146
Employees of private entrepreneurs	68	85	100	101	108	116
Memorandum item						
Minimum wage	82	90	100	100	100	110

Source: Slovak Statistical Office.

Table A8.1
Industrial Production by Ownership

	1991		1992		1993		1994		1995		1996	
	Million Kcs	Percent	Million Kcs	Percent	Million Kcs	Percent	Million Kcs	Percent	Million Kcs	Percent	Million Kcs	Percent
Total	403051.0	100.0	345628.0	100.0	362592.0	100.0	413326.0	100.0	497239.0	100.0	531798	100
Public 1/	353941.0	87.8	293267.0	84.9	253568.0	69.9	175536.0	42.5	175883.0	35.4	169002	31.8
Private 2/	28459.0	7.1	52361.0	15.1	109024.0	30.1	237793.0	57.5	321356.0	64.6	p	68.2

1/ State and municipal ownership.
2/ Includes cooperatives, international, foreign and unidentified enterprises. 1994 data for private sector includes domestic private ownership, cooperatives, associate, ownership of political parties and churches, foreign and international private enterprises.
Source: Slovak Statistical Office; and staff estimates.

Table A8.2
Share of Private Sector in Production

	1991	1992	1993	1994 1/	1995	1996
Share of private sector in:						
GDP	26.6	32.4	39.0	58.2	62.6	76.8
Production of: 2/						
Industry	8.6	15.2	30.1	57.5	64.6	68.2
Construction 3/	33.0	44.4	53.2	74.2	81.8	83.2
Commerce and repair services	49.1	73.2	80.9	88.5	91.7	94.6
Selected market services	.	63.7	74.6	73.2	87.9	86.5
Road freight transport 4/	25.4	36.6	49.8	56.3	62.1	82.1
Receipts for sales of agricultural products	..	..	..	..	81.8	86.1

.. = not available.
Note: Private sector includes ownership domestic private, cooperative, associate, ownership of political parties
   and churches, foreign and international with prevailing private sector.
1/ 1994 data includes enterprises with 25 or more employees.
2/ In terms of production of physical units.
3/ Construction production carried out by own workers.
4/ From the transportation of goods in material units.
Source: Slovak Statistical Office.

Table A9.1
International Comparisons--Main Economic Indicators

	1990	1991	1992	1993	1994	1995	1996
GDP (US$ million)							
Czech Republic	31599	24308	28395	31238	36043	47177	52091
Hungary	33055	33429	37255	38596	41669	43712	43400
Poland	58976	76427	84326	85853	92580	117978	134925
Slovak Republic	15479	10845	11757	11996	13746	17336	18963
Slovenia	17357	12679	12523	12672	14330	18579	18464
Real GDP growth rates (percent change over previous year)							
Czech Republic	-1.2	-14.2	-6.6	-0.7	2.6	5.1	4.4
Hungary	-3.5	-11.9	-3.1	-0.6	3.0	1.5	0.2
Poland	-11.6	-7.0	2.6	3.8	5.2	7.1	6.0
Slovak Republic	-2.5	-14.6	-6.5	-3.9	5.0	7.0	6.9
Slovenia	-4.7	-8.1	-5.4	2.8	5.3	3.9	3.0
Gross domestic investment/GDP (percent)							
Czech Republic	28.6	29.9	24.0	18.4	20.4	27.8	30.9
Hungary	25.4	20.5	16.1	20.0	22.2	22.8	23.3
Poland	25.6	19.9	15.2	15.6	15.9	18.3	19.8
Slovak Republic	33.2	31.2	28.1	27.3	23.1	28.5	38.2
Slovenia	16.8	15.2	17.3	20.0	20.3	22.3	23.1
Fixed investment/GDP (percent)							
Czech Republic	26.3	23.1	24.7	26.6	27.1	31.0	32.6
Hungary	17.8	20.9	19.9	18.9	20.2	19.3	20.8
Poland	21.0	19.5	16.8	15.9	16.2	17.1	18.2
Slovak Republic	31.3	28.3	32.9	32.7	29.4	29.2	36.6
Slovenia	18.2	19.0	18.4	18.7	19.6	21.1	21.7
Consumption/GDP (consumption = government consumption + private consumption)							
Czech Republic	70.1	63.3	74.7	79.8	79.9	76.7	77.1
Hungary	72.0	80.5	84.2	88.3	84.3	81.3	77.5
Poland	67.2	82.0	83.3	83.5	83.1	81.5	82.3
Slovak Republic	75.9	71.8	75.1	78.2	71.7	69.2	73.1
Slovenia	66.3	70.5	73.4	79.4	77.4	78.9	78.5
Current account balance (US$ million)							
Czech Republic			-487	684	-50	-1362	-4476
Hungary	333	396	296	-3458	-3911	-2500	-1679
Poland	642	-778	-270	-2287	-944	5455	-1392
Slovak Republic			46	-601	665	391	-2098
Slovenia	527	190	926	192	540	-36	46
Current account/GDP (percent)							
Czech Republic			-1.7	2.2	-0.1	-2.9	-8.6
Hungary	1.0	1.2	0.8	-9.0	-9.4	-5.7	-3.9
Poland	1.1	-1.0	-0.3	-2.7	-1.0	4.6	-1.0
Slovak Republic			0.4	-5.0	4.8	2.3	-11.1
Slovenia	3.0	1.5	7.4	1.5	3.8	-0.2	0.2
Industrial productivity (1990 = 100)							
Czech Republic	100.0	81.1	81.1	80.5	87.6	107.8	120.0
Hungary	100.0	84.6	86.9	102.5	121.4	133.8	145.8
Poland	100.0	100.0	112.6	128.2	144.9	156.2	169.0
Slovak Republic	100.0	93.0	90.5	91.6	97.3	104.0	108.1
Slovenia	100.0	95.0	86.8	86.7	95.4	97.6	95.5
Real wages (1990 = 100) using CPI							
Czech Republic	100.0	74.4	81.0	82.3	87.4	94.9	102.6
Hungary	100.0	98.8	99.9	99.4	102.6	97.0	94.0
Poland	100.0	96.3	95.1	94.2	98.7	100.6	107.0
Slovak Republic	100.0	72.3	79.2	75.3	77.2	81.7	87.9
Slovenia	100.0	84.0	82.8	95.1	101.7	107.2	109.2
Real unit cost of labor (1990 = 100)							
Czech Republic	100.0	91.8	99.9	102.1	99.8	88.1	85.5
Hungary	100.0	116.8	115.0	97.0	84.5	72.5	64.5
Poland	100.0	96.4	84.5	73.5	68.1	64.4	63.3
Slovak Republic	100.0	77.8	87.6	82.3	79.4	78.6	81.3
Slovenia	100.0	88.5	95.5	109.6	106.7	109.9	114.3

Table A9.1
International Comparisons--Main Economic Indicators

	1990	1991	1992	1993	1994	1995	1996
(continued)							
Gross external debt (US$ million)							
Czech Republic	6383	8032	7762	9605	12210	17190	20748
Hungary	21270	22658	21438	24560	28521	31655	27646
Poland	48500	48400	47000	47300	42174	42999	40423
Slovak Republic			2981	3617	4800	5827	7809
Slovenia			1741	1873	2258	2970	4010
Gross external debt/GDP (percent)							
Czech Republic	20.2	33.0	27.3	30.7	33.9	36.4	39.8
Hungary	64.3	67.8	57.5	63.6	68.4	72.4	63.7
Poland	82.2	63.3	55.7	55.1	45.6	36.4	30.0
Slovak Republic			25.4	30.2	34.9	33.6	41.2
Slovenia			13.9	14.8	15.8	16.0	21.7
Net external debt (US$ million)							
Czech Republic	5327	5422	4176	3170	3210	37	3972
Hungary	15938	14555	13276	17824	21752	19687	17896
Poland	43826	44600	42713	43019	36145	28036	22161
Slovak Republic			2081	2216	1827	913	1968
Slovenia			841	471	-835	-2064	-686
Net external debt/GDP (percent)							
Czech Republic	16.9	22.3	14.7	10.1	8.9	0.1	7.6
Hungary	48.2	43.5	35.6	46.2	52.2	45.0	41.2
Poland	74.3	58.4	50.7	50.1	39.0	23.8	16.4
Slovak Republic			17.7	18.5	13.3	5.3	10.4
Slovenia			6.7	3.7	-5.8	-11.1	-3.7
Gross enterprise losses/GDP (percent)							
Czech Republic			7.4	10.9	5.7	3.5	4.3
Hungary	2.6	8.4	14.2	10.1	7.2	3.1	
Poland			8.6	6.2	3.9	3.5	3.8
Slovak Republic			6.5	11.5	7.2	5.6	8.8
Slovenia	7.5	9.0	16.7	8.1	6.4	6.2	
Net enterprise losses/GDP (percent)							
Czech Republic			-12.9	-5.5	-7.9	-8.3	-4.6
Hungary	-13.3	-4.1	6.1	3.4	-0.1	-2.2	
Poland			-3.0	-4.1	-6.1	-6.7	-5.3
Slovak Republic			-1.1	-7.0	-6.8	-8.3	-5.7
Slovenia	6.1	6.4	14.2	4.2	1.9	0.0	

NOTE: + equals loss, - equals profit. All data is for non-financial enterprises.

	1990	1991	1992	1993	1994	1995	1996
Government deficit/GDP (percent) (- = deficit)							
Czech Republic			-1.0	1.4	0.5	0.6	-0.1
Hungary	0.4	-2.1	-5.3	-6.6	-7.5	-3.9	-1.1
Poland	3.7	-6.7	-4.9	-2.3	-2.2	-1.9	-2.8
Slovak Republic			-10.7	-6.2	4.6	6.0	3.6
Slovenia		2.6	0.3	0.3	-0.2	0.0	0.0
Government deficit/GDP excluding private revenues (percent) (- = deficit)							
Czech Republic			-1.0	1.4	0.5	0.6	-0.1
Hungary	0.4	-2.1	-6.1	-7.0	-8.3	-6.7	-3.3
Poland	3.4	-6.9	-5.3	-3.1	-3.3	-3.1	-4.0
Slovak Republic			-10.7	-6.2	4.6	6.0	3.6
Slovenia		2.6	0.3	0.3	-0.2	0.0	0.0
CPI inflation (average)							
Czech Republic	9.6	56.6	11.1	20.8	10.0	9.1	8.8
Hungary	28.2	35.0	23.0	22.5	18.8	28.2	23.6
Poland	585.8	70.3	43.0	35.3	32.2	27.8	19.9
Slovak Republic	10.6	61.2	10.0	23.2	13.4	9.9	5.8
Slovenia	549.7	117.7	201.3	32.3	19.8	12.6	9.7

Noe: 1996 data are for first half only.
Source: IMF-IFS and National Sources.

Table A9.2
International Comparisons of Tax Rates

	PIT	CIT	VAT	Total pension to total labor cost 1/	Total payroll tax for SS to total labor cost 1/
Slovak Republic	42.0	40.0	23.0	19.6	34.1
Czech Republic	40.0	39.0	22.0	20.1	35.9
Hungary	48.0	20.5	25.0	20.5	40.6
Poland	45.0	40.0	22.0	30.4	32.4
Slovenia	50.0	25.0		25.2	37.2
OECD average	43.9	40.6	8.2	12.9	24.9
EU 15 average	43.9	39.5	18.1	15.3	32.5

1/ OECD and EU averages do not include Denmark.

Sources: Individual Taxes-A Worldwide Summary. Price Waterhouse, 1996.
Corporate Taxes-A Worldwide Summary. Price Waterhouse, 1996.
IMF. The VAT rates are standard rates applied to goods and services not covered by other especially high or low rates.

Distributors of World Bank Publications

Prices and credit terms vary from country to country. Consult your local distributor before placing an order.

ARGENTINA
Oficina del Libro Internacional
Av. Cordoba 1877
1120 Buenos Aires
Tel: (54 1) 815-8354
Fax: (54 1) 815-8156
E-mail: olilbro@satlink.com

AUSTRALIA, FIJI, PAPUA NEW GUINEA, SOLOMON ISLANDS, VANUATU, AND WESTERN SAMOA
D.A. Information Services
648 Whitehorse Road
Mitcham 3132
Victoria
Tel: (61) 3 9210 7777
Fax: (61) 3 9210 7788
E-mail: service@dadirect.com.au
URL: http://www.dadirect.com.au

AUSTRIA
Gerold and Co.
Weihburggasse 26
A-1011 Wien
Tel: (43 1) 512-47-31-0
Fax: (43 1) 512-47-31-29

BANGLADESH
Micro Industries Development Assistance Society (MIDAS)
House 5, Road 16
Dhanmondi R/Area
Dhaka 1209
Tel: (880 2) 326427
Fax: (880 2) 811188

BELGIUM
Jean De Lannoy
Av. du Roi 202
1060 Brussels
Tel: (32 2) 538-5169
Fax: (32 2) 538-0841

BRAZIL
Publicacões Tecnicas Internacionais Ltda.
Rua Peixoto Gomide, 209
01409 Sao Paulo, SP
Tel: (55 11) 259-6644
Fax: (55 11) 258-6990
E-mail: postmaster@pti.uol.br
URL: http://www.uol.br

CANADA
Renouf Publishing Co. Ltd.
5369 Canotek Road
Ottawa, Ontario K1J 9J3
Tel: (613) 745-2665
Fax: (613) 745-7660
E-mail: order.dept@renoufbooks.com
URL: http://www.renoufbooks.com

CHINA
China Financial & Economic Publishing House
8, Da Fo Si Dong Jie
Beijing
Tel: (86 10) 6333-8257
Fax: (86 10) 6401-7365

China Book Import Centre
P.O. Box 2825
Beijing

COLOMBIA
Infoenlace Ltda.
Carrera 6 No. 51-21
Apartado Aereo 34270
Santafé de Bogota, D.C.
Tel: (57 1) 285-2798
Fax: (57 1) 285-2798

COTE D'IVOIRE
Center d'Edition et de Diffusion Africaines (CEDA)
04 B.P. 541
Abidjan 04
Tel: (225) 24 6510/24 6511
Fax: (225) 25 0567

CYPRUS
Center for Applied Research
Cyprus College
6, Diogenes Street, Engomi
P.O. Box 2006
Nicosia
Tel: (357 2) 44-1730
Fax: (357 2) 46-2051

CZECH REPUBLIC
National Information Center
prodejna, Konviktská 5
CS – 113 57 Prague 1
Tel: (42 2) 2422-9433
Fax: (42 2) 2422-1484
URL: http://www.nis.cz/

DENMARK
SamfundsLitteratur
Rosenoerns Allé 11
DK-1970 Frederiksberg C
Tel: (45 31) 351942
Fax: (45 31) 357822

ECUADOR
Libri Mundi
Libreria Internacional
P.O. Box 17-01-3029
Juan Leon Mera 851
Quito
Tel: (593 2) 521-606; (593 2) 544-185
Fax: (593 2) 504-209
E-mail: librimu1@librimundi.com.ec
E-mail: librimu2@librimundi.com.ec

EGYPT, ARAB REPUBLIC OF
Al Ahram Distribution Agency
Al Galaa Street
Cairo
Tel: (20 2) 578-6083
Fax: (20 2) 578-6833

The Middle East Observer
41, Sherif Street
Cairo
Tel: (20 2) 393-9732
Fax: (20 2) 393-9732

FINLAND
Akateeminen Kirjakauppa
P.O. Box 128
FIN-00101 Helsinki
Tel: (358 0) 121 4418
Fax: (358 0) 121 4435
E-mail: akatilaus@stockmann.fi
URL: http://www.akateeminen.com/

FRANCE
World Bank Publications
66, avenue d'Iéna
75116 Paris
Tel: (33 1) 40-69-30-56/57
Fax: (33 1) 40-69-30-68

GERMANY
UNO-Verlag
Poppelsdorfer Allee 55
53115 Bonn
Tel: (49 228) 949020
Fax: (49 228) 217492
URL: http://www.uno-verlag.de
E-mail: unoverlag@aol.com

GHANA
Epp Books Services
P.O. Box 44
TUC
Accra

GREECE
Papasotiriou S.A.
35, Stournara Str.
106 82 Athens
Tel: (30 1) 364-1826
Fax: (30 1) 364-8254

HAITI
Culture Diffusion
5, Rue Capois
C.P. 257
Port-au-Prince
Tel: (509) 23 9260
Fax: (509) 23 4858

HONG KONG, MACAO
Asia 2000 Ltd.
Sales & Circulation Department
Seabird House, unit 1101-02
22-28 Wyndham Street, Central
Hong Kong
Tel: (852) 2530-1409
Fax: (852) 2526-1107
E-mail: sales@asia2000.com.hk
URL: http://www.asia2000.com.hk

HUNGARY
Euro Info Service
Margitszgeti Europa Haz
H-1138 Budapest
Tel: (36 1) 350 80 24, 350 80 25
Fax: (36 1) 350 90 32
E-mail: euroinfo@mail.matav.hu

INDIA
Allied Publishers Ltd.
751 Mount Road
Madras - 600 002
Tel: (91 44) 852-3938
Fax: (91 44) 852-0649

INDONESIA
Pt. Indira Limited
Jalan Borobudur 20
P.O. Box 181
Jakarta 10320
Tel: (62 21) 390-4290
Fax: (62 21) 390-4289

IRAN
Ketab Sara Co. Publishers
Khaled Eslamboli Ave., 6th Street
Delafrooz Alley No. 8
P.O. Box 15745-733
Tehran 15117
Tel: (98 21) 8717819; 8716104
Fax: (98 21) 8712479
E-mail: ketab-sara@neda.net.ir

KowKab Publishers
P.O. Box 19575-511
Tehran
Tel: (98 21) 258-3723
Fax: (98 21) 258-3723

IRELAND
Government Supplies Agency
Oifig an tSoláthair
4-5 Harcourt Road
Dublin 2
Tel: (353 1) 661-3111
Fax: (353 1) 475-2670

ISRAEL
Yozmot Literature Ltd.
P.O. Box 56055
3 Yohanan Hasandlar Street
Tel Aviv 61560
Tel: (972 3) 5285-397
Fax: (972 3) 5285-397

R.O.Y. International
PO Box 13056
Tel Aviv 61130
Tel: (972 3) 5461423
Fax: (972 3) 5461442
E-mail: royil@netvision.net.il

Palestinian Authority/Middle East
Index Information Services
P.O.B. 19502 Jerusalem
Tel: (972 2) 6271219
Fax: (972 2) 6271634

ITALY
Licosa Commissionaria Sansoni SPA
Via Duca Di Calabria, 1/1
Casella Postale 552
50125 Firenze
Tel: (55) 645-415
Fax: (55) 641-257
E-mail: licosa@ftbcc.it
URL: http://www.ftbcc.it/licosa

JAMAICA
Ian Randle Publishers Ltd.
206 Old Hope Road, Kingston 6
Tel: 876-927-2085
Fax: 876-977-0243
E-mail: irpl@colis.com

JAPAN
Eastern Book Service
3-13 Hongo 3-chome, Bunkyo-ku
Tokyo 113
Tel: (81 3) 3818-0861
Fax: (81 3) 3818-0864
E-mail: orders@svt-ebs.co.jp
URL: http://www.bekkoame.or.jp/~svt-ebs

KENYA
Africa Book Service (E.A.) Ltd.
Quaran House, Mfangano Street
P.O. Box 45245
Nairobi
Tel: (254 2) 223 641
Fax: (254 2) 330 272

KOREA, REPUBLIC OF
Daejon Trading Co. Ltd.
P.O. Box 34, Youida, 706 Seoun Bldg
44-6 Youido-Dong, Yeongchengpo-ku
Seoul
Tel: (82 2) 785-1631/4
Fax: (82 2) 784-0315

MALAYSIA
University of Malaya Cooperative Bookshop, Limited
P.O. Box 1127
Jalan Pantai Baru
59700 Kuala Lumpur
Tel: (60 3) 756-5000
Fax: (60 3) 755-4424
E-mail: umkoop@tm.net.my

MEXICO
INFOTEC
Av. San Fernando No. 37
Col. Toriello Guerra
14050 Mexico, D.F.
Tel: (52 5) 624-2800
Fax: (52 5) 624-2822
E-mail: infotec@rtn.net.mx
URL: http://rtn.net.mx

Mundi-Prensa Mexico S.A. de C.V.
c/Rio Panuco, 141-Colonia Cuauhtemoc
06500 Mexico, D.F.
Tel: (52 5) 533-5658
Fax: (52 5) 514-6799

NEPAL
Everest Media International Services (P) Ltd.
GPO Box 5443
Kathmandu
Tel: (977 1) 472 152
Fax: (977 1) 224 431

NETHERLANDS
De Lindeboom/InOr-Publikaties
P.O. Box 202, 7480 AE Haaksbergen
Tel: (31 53) 574-0004
Fax: (31 53) 572-9296
E-mail: lindeboo@worldonline.nl
URL: http://www.worldonline.nl/~lindeboo

NEW ZEALAND
EBSCO NZ Ltd.
Private Mail Bag 99914
New Market
Auckland
Tel: (64 9) 524-8119
Fax: (64 9) 524-8067

NIGERIA
University Press Limited
Three Crowns Building Jericho
Private Mail Bag 5095
Ibadan
Tel: (234 22) 41-1356
Fax: (234 22) 41-2056

NORWAY
NIC Info A/S
Book Department, Postboks 6512 Etterstad
N-0606 Oslo
Tel: (47 22) 97-4500
Fax: (47 22) 97-4545

PAKISTAN
Mirza Book Agency
65, Shahrah-e-Quaid-e-Azam
Lahore 54000
Tel: (92 42) 735 3601
Fax: (92 42) 576 3714

Oxford University Press
5 Bangalore Town
Sharae Faisal
PO Box 13033
Karachi-75350
Tel: (92 21) 446307
Fax: (92 21) 4547640
E-mail: ouppak@TheOffice.net

Pak Book Corporation
Aziz Chambers 21, Queen's Road
Lahore
Tel: (92 42) 636 3222; 636 0885
Fax: (92 42) 636 2328
E-mail: pbc@brain.net.pk

PERU
Editorial Desarrollo SA
Apartado 3824, Lima 1
Tel: (51 14) 285380
Fax: (51 14) 286628

PHILIPPINES
International Booksource Center Inc.
1127-A Antipolo St, Barangay, Venezuela
Makati City
Tel: (63 2) 896 6501; 6505; 6507
Fax: (63 2) 896 1741

POLAND
International Publishing Service
Ul. Piekna 31/37
00-677 Warzawa
Tel: (48 2) 628-6089
Fax: (48 2) 621-7255
E-mail: books%ips@ikp.atm.com.pl
URL: http://www.ipscg.waw.pl/ips/export/

PORTUGAL
Livraria Portugal
Apartado 2681, Rua Do Carmo 70-74
1200 Lisbon
Tel: (1) 347-4982
Fax: (1) 347-0264

ROMANIA
Compani De Librarii Bucuresti S.A.
Str. Lipscani no. 26, sector 3
Bucharest
Tel: (40 1) 613 9645
Fax: (40 1) 312 4000

RUSSIAN FEDERATION
Isdatelstvo <Ves Mir>
9a, Kolpachniy Pereulok
Moscow 101831
Tel: (7 095) 917 87 49
Fax: (7 095) 917 92 59

SINGAPORE, TAIWAN, MYANMAR, BRUNEI
Ashgate Publishing Asia Pacific Pte. Ltd.
41 Kallang Pudding Road #04-03
Golden Wheel Building
Singapore 349316
Tel: (65) 741-5166
Fax: (65) 742-9356
E-mail: ashgate@asianconnect.com

SLOVENIA
Gospodarski Vestnik Publishing Group
Dunajska cesta 5
1000 Ljubljana
Tel: (386 61) 133 83 47; 132 12 30
Fax: (386 61) 133 80 30
E-mail: repansekj@gvestnik.si

SOUTH AFRICA, BOTSWANA
For single titles:
Oxford University Press Southern Africa
Vasco Boulevard, Goodwood
P.O. Box 12119, N1 City 7463
Cape Town
Tel: (27 21) 595 4400
Fax: (27 21) 595 4430
E-mail: oxford@oup.co.za

For subscription orders:
International Subscription Service
P.O. Box 41095
Craighall
Johannesburg 2024
Tel: (27 11) 880-1448
Fax: (27 11) 880-6248
E-mail: iss@is.co.za

SPAIN
Mundi-Prensa Libros, S.A.
Castello 37
28001 Madrid
Tel: (34 1) 575-3998
Fax: (34 1) 575-3998
E-mail: libreria@mundiprensa.es
URL: http://www.mundiprensa.es/

Mundi-Prensa Barcelona
Consell de Cent, 391
08009 Barcelona
Tel: (34 3) 488-3492
Fax: (34 3) 487-7659
E-mail: barcelona@mundiprensa.es

SRI LANKA, THE MALDIVES
Lake House Bookshop
100, Sir Chittampalam Gardiner Mawatha
Colombo 2
Tel: (94 1) 32105
Fax: (94 1) 432104
E-mail: LHL@sri.lanka.net

SWEDEN
Wennergren-Williams AB
P.O. Box 1305
S-171 25 Solna
Tel: (46 8) 705-97-50
Fax: (46 8) 27-00-71
E-mail: mail@wwi.se

SWITZERLAND
Librairie Payot Service Institutionnel
Côtes-de-Montbenon 30
1002 Lausanne
Tel: (41 21) 341-3229
Fax: (41 21) 341-3235

ADECO Van Diemen Editions Techniques
Ch. de Lacuez 41
CH1807 Blonay
Tel: (41 21) 943 2673
Fax: (41 21) 943 3605

THAILAND
Central Books Distribution
306 Silom Road
Bangkok 10500
Tel: (66 2) 235-5400
Fax: (66 2) 237-8321

TRINIDAD & TOBAGO AND THE CARRIBBEAN
Systematics Studies Ltd.
St. Augustine Shopping Center
Eastern Main Road, St. Augustine
Trinidad & Tobago, West Indies
Tel: (868) 645-8466
Fax: (868) 645-8467
E-mail: tobe@trinidad.net

UGANDA
Gustro Ltd.
PO Box 9997, Madhvani Building
Plot 16/4 Jinja Rd.
Kampala
Tel: (256 41) 251 467
Fax: (256 41) 251 468
E-mail: gus@swiftuganda.com

UNITED KINGDOM
Microinfo Ltd.
P.O. Box 3, Alton, Hampshire GU34 2PG
England
Tel: (44 1420) 86848
Fax: (44 1420) 89889
E-mail: wbank@ukminfo.demon.co.uk
URL: http://www.microinfo.co.uk

VENEZUELA
Tecni-Ciencia Libros, S.A.
Centro Cuidad Comercial Tamanco
Nivel C2, Caracas
Tel: (58 2) 959 5547; 5035; 0016
Fax: (58 2) 959 5636

ZAMBIA
University Bookshop, University of Zambia
Great East Road Campus
P.O. Box 32379
Lusaka
Tel: (260 1) 252 576
Fax: (260 1) 253 952

1/798